Iran

the Bradt Travel Guide

**Patricia Baker & Hilary Smith
with Maria Oleynik**

edition
4

www.bradtguides.com

Bradt Tra
The Globe

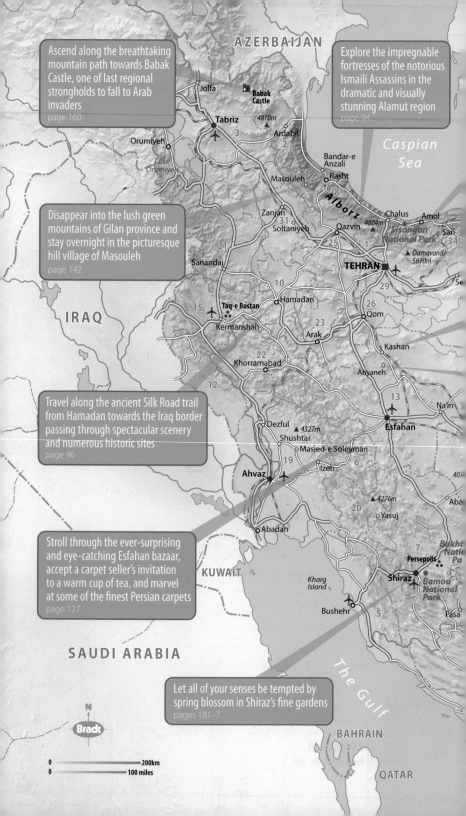

Ascend along the breathtaking mountain path towards Babak Castle, one of last regional strongholds to fall to Arab invaders
page 160

Explore the impregnable fortresses of the notorious Ismaili Assassins in the dramatic and visually stunning Alamut region
page 91

Disappear into the lush green mountains of Gilan province and stay overnight in the picturesque hill village of Masouleh
page 142

Travel along the ancient Silk Road trail from Hamadan towards the Iraq border passing through spectacular scenery and numerous historic sites
page 96

Stroll through the ever-surprising and eye-catching Esfahan bazaar, accept a carpet seller's invitation to a warm cup of tea, and marvel at some of the finest Persian carpets
page 127

Let all of your senses be tempted by spring blossom in Shiraz's fine gardens
pages 181–7

AZERBAIJAN

Caspian Sea

IRAQ

KUWAIT

SAUDI ARABIA

BAHRAIN

QATAR

The Gulf

Jolfa
Babak Castle
Tabriz
4810m
Ardabil
Orumiyeh
Lake Orumiyeh
Bandar-e Anzali
Rasht
Masouleh
Zanjan
Soltaniyeh
Qazvin
Chalus
Amol
4804m
Sisangan National Park
Sari
Sanandaj
Hamadan
TEHRAN
Damavand 5610m
Taq-e Bostan
Qom
Kermanshah
Arak
Kashan
Khorramabad
Ahyaneh
Na'in
Dezful
4327m
Shushtar
Masjed-e Soleyman
Esfahan
Ahvaz
Izeh
4276m
Abadan
Yasuj
Kharg Island
Persepolis
Shiraz
Bakht Natie Pa
Bamou National Park
Bushehr
Fasa
Aba

Alborz

N

Bradt

0   200km
0   100 miles

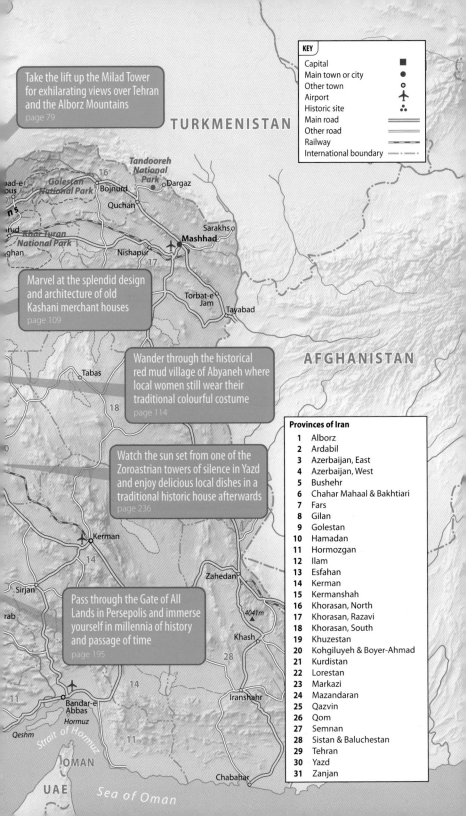

Take the lift up the Milad Tower for exhilarating views over Tehran and the Alborz Mountains
page 79

Marvel at the splendid design and architecture of old Kashani merchant houses
page 109

Wander through the historical red mud village of Abyaneh where local women still wear their traditional colourful costume
page 114

Watch the sun set from one of the Zoroastrian towers of silence in Yazd and enjoy delicious local dishes in a traditional historic house afterwards
page 236

Pass through the Gate of All Lands in Persepolis and immerse yourself in millennia of history and passage of time
page 195

KEY

Capital	■
Main town or city	●
Other town	○
Airport	✈
Historic site	⬦
Main road	
Other road	
Railway	
International boundary	

TURKMENISTAN

AFGHANISTAN

Tandooreh National Park
Golestan National Park
Bojnurd
Dargaz
Quchan
Sarakhs
Mashhad
Khar Turan National Park
Nishapur
Torbat-e Jam
Tayabad
Tabas
Kerman
Sirjan
Zahedan
4041m
Khash
Iranshahr
Bandar-e Abbas
Hormuz
Qeshm
Strait of Hormuz
OMAN
UAE
Chabahar
Sea of Oman

16
17
18
14
28
14
11
11

Provinces of Iran

1	Alborz
2	Ardabil
3	Azerbaijan, East
4	Azerbaijan, West
5	Bushehr
6	Chahar Mahaal & Bakhtiari
7	Fars
8	Gilan
9	Golestan
10	Hamadan
11	Hormozgan
12	Ilam
13	Esfahan
14	Kerman
15	Kermanshah
16	Khorasan, North
17	Khorasan, Razavi
18	Khorasan, South
19	Khuzestan
20	Kohgiluyeh & Boyer-Ahmad
21	Kurdistan
22	Lorestan
23	Markazi
24	Mazandaran
25	Qazvin
26	Qom
27	Semnan
28	Sistan & Baluchestan
29	Tehran
30	Yazd
31	Zanjan

Iran
Don't
miss...

Kandovan
The troglodyte village of
Kandovan boasts a unique
rock hotel, the only one of
its kind in Iran
(S/MR) page 165

Tehran
The Azadi monument, clad
in white marble, has been
a symbol of Tehran since
its completion in 1971
(S/WC) pages 78–9

Shiraz

The mausoleum of 13th-century poet, Saadi, whose powerful verses were quoted by President Obama during his 2009 address to Iran

(S/AT) pages 182–3

Persepolis

The zenith of the Achaemenid Empire, Persepolis is simply magnificent both in scale and beauty

(S/S) pages 195–200

Esfahan

Masjed-e Sheikh Lotfallah is a marvellous example of Shah Abbas's ambitious design for his new capital – Esfahan

(SS) pages 119–36

Iran in colour

top This painted ceiling in Shiraz, decorated with traditional motifs, probably dates from the Qajar dynasty (AB) pages 13–14

above left An evening stroll along Chahar Bagh Street in Esfahan takes you past the delicately decorated arched porticos of Madrasa Chahar Bagh (MO) page 129

above right The interior of the Arg-e Karim Khan Zand in Shiraz shows architectural functionality and decorative beauty (AB) pages 183–4

below Ferdowsi's Mausoleum in Tus is the last resting place of Iran's national poet (MO) pages 262–3

top   Vank Cathedral is one of the few Armenian churches in Iran to include a dome (MO) pages 135–6

above left   Persian garden architectural design, seen here at Bagh-e Fin, incorporated one of the most sophisticated water management systems of the 17th century (S/DO) page 114

above right   This traditional-style cistern, or *ab anbar*, is designed so that cool air is circulated over water held 7m underground (CK)

below   UNESCO-listed Naqsh-e Jahan (Half the World) square in Esfahan stands as a monument to social and cultural life in Persia in the 17th and 18th centuries (S/MR) page 124

top   One of the Towers of Silence rises above the now-deserted Zoroastrian village of Cham, near Yazd (S/A) page 231

above   Splendid interior frescoes of the 17th-century Armenian Vank Cathedral, decorated with scenes from the Old and New testaments (SS) pages 135–6

below   Chasing pigeons in the courtyard of the UNESCO-listed Masjed-e Jame in Esfahan, Iran's oldest preserved structure of its kind (MO) pages 130–3

AUTHORS

Patricia Baker PhD was the author of the first two editions of this guide but died in 2008. Prior to her death she was working with Jennifer Wearden on cataloguing 19th-century Iranian textiles in the Victoria and Albert Museum, London. The resulting book was published in October 2010.

Patricia was an independent lecturer and researcher specialising in Islamic art, who spent a decade teaching the history of ceramics and glass to undergraduates. She first visited Iran in 1971 and subsequently went back numerous times. Her interests were primarily Islamic glass and especially Islamic court dress, on which, along with aspects of Zoroastrian costume, she wrote for various academic journals; her monograph *Islamic Textiles* was published by the British Museum Press in 1995 and *Islam and the Religious Arts* by Continuum, 2004.

Hilary Smith MPhil, who took over the update of the third edition, is an independent lecturer and guide with wide-ranging interests focusing particularly on the cultural history of central Asia and the Indian subcontinent. She first visited Iran in 1976 and has been returning regularly ever since.

Maria Oleynik MLitt, who has updated this fourth edition, is a freelance writer and translator who is fluent in ten languages, including Persian, Arabic and Hebrew. She has studied in Yemen, Lebanon and Egypt, and was hired to translate a biography of a Libyan politician from Arabic, whilst based in Tripoli, Libya. She has also studied Persian at the University of Esfahan and has a profound interest and knowledge of the Middle East.

DEDICATION

To the pessimistic optimist and the optimistic pessimist

'A friend in need is a friend indeed.'

PUBLISHER'S FOREWORD   *Hilary Bradt*

In 1996 I was invited to visit Iran, which was just starting to open up to tourism. I accepted with some hesitation, having been thoroughly brainwashed by the media's portrayal of a dangerous, restrictive and intolerant country. But I loved the place from the moment I stepped off the plane, dressed in my headscarf and long rupush. Far from being restrictive, it left me feeling freer to explore the markets and other places on my own than almost anywhere else I've been. Since I looked just like the Iranian women around me, there were no stares, and no hassle. And the sights! The great ruins of Persepolis and Bishapur, and the cities of Esfahan and Shiraz, all left an indelible impression. Iran has gone through turbulent times and is still at the fringes of the international community, but the integrity and kindness of the people and the variety and beauty of their country remain untouched.

Reprinted September 2016
Fourth edition January 2014
First published 2001

Bradt Travel Guides Ltd,
IDC House, The Vale, Chalfont St Peter, Bucks SL9 9RZ, England
www.bradtguides.com
Print edition published in the USA by The Globe Pequot Press Inc, PO Box 480, Guilford, Connecticut 06437-0480

Text copyright © 2013 Patricia L Baker & Hilary A Smith
Maps copyright © 2013 Bradt Travel Guides Ltd
Tehran metro map © UrbanRail.Net (R Schwandl), 2012
Photographs copyright © 2013 Individual photographers (see below)
Project Manager: Claire Strange
Cover image research: Pepi Bluck

British Library Cataloguing in Publication Data
A catalogue record for this book is available from the British Library
ISBN: 978 1 84162 402 0
e-ISBN: 978 1 84162 708 3 (e-pub)
e-ISBN: 978 1 84162 608 6 (mobi)

Photographers Adam Balogh; FLPA: Egmont Strigl/Imagebroker (ES/I/FLPA), Imagebroker/ Imagebroker (I/I/FLPA); Getty Images: Andrea Thompson Photography (GI/ATP); Chloe Kenward (CK); Maria Oleynik (MO); Shutterstock: Arazu, (S/A), Wojtek Chmielewski (S/WC), M Khebra (S/MK), Doin Oakenhelm (S/DO), M R (S/MR), Steba (S/S), Aleksandar Todorovic (S/AT); SuperStock (SS)
Front cover The ornate Fin Garden in Kashan (GI/ATP)
Back cover Iranian girl in Yazd (SS); an Iranian fresco depicting Persian myths and scenes from the 11th-century poem, *Shahnameh*, by Fedowsi (SS)
Title page Griffins were symbols of divine power in Persian poetry; this one can be found at Persepolis (EG/I/FLPA); Iranian artists make the most of Iran's huge copper reserves to create some of the finest craft pieces (AB); Arg-e Karim Khan Zand, the Citadel of Shiraz, basking in the twilight (SS)

Maps David McCutcheon FBCartS
Colour map: relief map bases by Nick Rowland FRGS

Typeset from the authors' disc by Wakewing
Production managed by Jellyfish Print Solutions and manufactured in India
Digital conversion by the www.dataworks.co.in

Acknowledgements

Patricia Baker PhD was the author of the first two editions of this guide. After her death in 2008, her friend Hilary Smith took over the update of the third edition. This fourth edition has been updated by Maria Oleynik.

It was a fellow postgraduate student, Manijeh Bayani, who in 1971 introduced me not only to Iran but also to the legendary kindness and hospitality of Iranians. We were both students of Professor Geza Fehevari, who managed to instil such a love of and enthusiasm for Islamic art into all his students that even after 30 years and few career openings, most of us have remained 'hooked'. He was also responsible for giving me the opportunity of returning to Iran in the role of guest lecturer on several Swan Hellenic Art Treasure tours during 1975–78. I have never been able to repay the kindness and thoughtfulness of them both, and the hospitality of their families.

In those years one could always identify people with a common interest in Iranian archaeology and architecture by their battered copies of Sylvia Matheson's *Persia: An Archaeological Guide* and although it was last reprinted (excluding pirate copies) in 1976, it still is an invaluable source of information. Even today, Iranian tour guides who were in their infancy during the Islamic Revolution mention her name with great respect and affection although their knowledge of her is purely through this work. I, too, wish to record my debt to her, and also to the authors of two other publications: Lisa Golombek and Donald Wilber (*Timurid Architecture in Iran and Turan*, 1988) and Bernard O'Kane (*Timurid Architecture in Khurasan*, 1987).

These publications were based on research conducted prior to the Islamic Revolution, and of course things have changed. Sylvia Matheson's dirt tracks from one site to another through small villages are no longer there. The 'tracks' are now dual carriageways, the archaeological sites have largely vanished from public view after decades of dust storms or neglect while many villages have either developed into large townships or been abandoned because a vital water source has been diverted.

For the first edition of this guide one particular person, Amir Bayat, was extremely generous with his time and help and few of his colleagues, especially Iraj Zowghi, were able to escape involvement. My heartfelt thanks.

I am also most grateful to Nasser Mouradi of Thunder Tours and Travel, Tehran, for his assistance and evident concern that all the travel arrangements went smoothly, even if it involved him in a hair-raising motorcycle ride. A number of local guides have generously given not only their time but also fascinating information about their cities and regions: Jamshid Zarinfer and Aria Gojerati of Shiraz, Hossein Nasr and Iraj Jahanbakhsh of Esfahan. For the third edition, Mahmoud Karimi of ITC and his colleague, Mahshid, diligently traced information, while Aria in Shiraz, Hossein in Esfahan and Iraj Zowghi in Tehran epitomised that renowned Iranian generosity, despite my endless enquiries. I do most sincerely thank them all, as well as the numerous drivers who have patiently stopped, reversed and skilfully found a way to so many unsignposted places.

Yet again I must record my appreciation to the staff of the School of Oriental and African Studies, University of London, and of the British Library, London, who have uncomplainingly found obscure publications and pamphlets, and reshelved piles of books. I must also thank all my travelling companions, whether they suffered me as a group leader enthusing about textiles, ceramics and glass, or as a fellow visitor tramping across fields in search of a carved boulder or column base; to Barbara Brend for her astute comments in eastern Iran and her translation of certain Saadi couplets used in this text; Alan Forsyth for valuable information and support; John and Val Imber for their witty one-liners in southern Iran and guiding me through certain electronic complexities; to Peter Kelly and another businessman, who wishes to remain anonymous, for their useful and inexhaustible supply of insights into Iranian society, culture and politics; and to Peg and Dick Foster. I also acknowledge the supplementary information on southwestern Iran provided in May 2008 by Graham Greenfield. To Gila Salimi I owe particular thanks for having such confidence in her former teacher writing about her country, the people and the art. The way that Sugra Zaman of Watson, Little Ltd took so much pressure off my shoulders yet gently kept my nose to the grindstone has really been appreciated. And I must express gratitude to Bradt Travel Guides for having faith in this project, and to Bradt readers for their comments.   Patricia Baker

My first assignment with Swan Hellenic Art Treasures tours in 1976 was as tour manager on an archaeological visit to Iran; I subsequently returned many times and was privileged to meet Patricia L Baker as well as her mentors, Manijeh Bayani and Professor Geza Fehevari, who all became friends and encouraged my interests. I am grateful to them and the other lecturers with whom I had the privilege to work before 'graduating' to leadership status myself. I should like to thank Patricia L Baker for inviting me to work with her on the third edition. Regrettably, 'Paddy', as she was known to friends and colleagues, died in 2008. As a result I also wish to acknowledge here the help I have received from various of her colleagues, in particular Graham Greenfield, independent scholar and lecturer whose minutely detailed diaries of recent visits to remote areas of the country have proved invaluable and who has also, with unfailing patience, answered my many questions. I am also immensely indebted to Frances Harrison for contributing the textbox on living in Iran. I have also relied heavily on friends and colleagues in Iran and thank in particular Aria Gojerati in Shiraz and Saeed Alizadeh, national guide and lecturer, and Lida Yasmin Carucci Mahdavi in Tehran. Thanks are also due to Jane Makin and Deirdre Holding.   Hilary Smith

Iran is simply striking. It is easily the most beautiful country in the world and is certainly the safest place to travel in the Middle East. I am grateful to all Iranians that I have had the pleasure to speak to on my travels, for putting up with my Persian language skills, and for sharing their lives and thoughts and encouraging me to learn more. Travel guides mentioned in this edition are some of the most knowledgeable, and their help and impartial advice have been invaluable to my understanding of the practicalities of travel in Iran. And, of course, none of this would have been possible without the staff and teachers of the International Scientific Cooperation Office at the University of Esfahan, as their patience and efforts in teaching me Persian have been instrumental in giving me courage to leap forward and explore, something I would strongly advise anyone coming to visit this country to do.   Maria Oleynik

Contents

LIST OF MAPS

NOTE ABOUT MAPS

Several maps use grid lines to allow easy location of sites. Map grid references are listed in square brackets after listings in the text, with page number followed by grid number, eg: [72 C4]. Accommodation and restaurants and their grid references are listed in key boxes next to maps of towns and cities.

FOLLOW BRADT

For the latest news, special offers and competitions, subscribe to the Bradt newsletter via the website www.bradtguides.com and follow Bradt on:

 www.facebook.com/BradtTravelGuides
 @BradtGuides
 @bradtguides
 pinterest.com/bradtguides

If you would like information about advertising in Bradt Travel Guides please contact us on +44 (0)1753 893444 or email info@bradtguides.com

IMPORTANT CHANGE TO PHONE CODES

Most city phone codes have recently changed in Iran (2015). Below is the list of up-to-date codes in Iran. Please remember to drop the '0' in the code when calling Iran from abroad (eg: 0098 45 33 614011). For more information, see www.bradtupdates.com/iran.

Abadan	0631	
Ahvaz	0611	
Ardabil	045	**NB:** All provincial centre numbers now have 8 digits. Ardabil numbers start with 045 followed by 33. Individual town codes have also changed. Sareyn phone code, for example, starts with 32.
Bam	0344	
Bandar-e Abbas	0761	
Bandar-e Anzali	0181	
Bushehr	0771	
Damgan	023	**NB:** All numbers start with an additional digit – 3.
Dezful	0641	
Esfahan	031	NB: All numbers now have 8 digits and start with an additional digit – 3.
Gorgan	017	NB: All numbers now have 8 digits. Gorgan numbers (after the code) start with 32.
Hamadan	081	
Ilam	0841	
Karaj	026	**NB:** All numbers now have 8 digits and start with an additional digit – 3.
Kerman	0341	
Kermanshah	083	**NB:** All numbers now have 8 digits and start with an additional digit – 3.
Mashhad	051	**NB:** All numbers start with an additional digit – 3.
Masjed-e Soleyman	0681	
Orumiyeh	044	**NB:** All numbers start with an additional digit – 3.
Qazvin	028	**NB:** All numbers start with an additional digit – 3.
Qom	025	**NB:** All numbers now have 8 digits and start with an additional digit – 3.
Rasht	0131	
Sari	011	**NB:** All numbers now have 8 digits.
Semnan	023	**NB:** All numbers that start with '3' have another '3' added; all numbers that start with '4', drop the '4' and start with '33' instead.
Shahrud	023	**NB:** All numbers that start with '2' have digit '3' added (32); all numbers that start with '3', have '2' added (32).
Shiraz	071	**NB:** All numbers in Fars Province now have 8 digits. Landline numbers in Shiraz area have an additional digit – 3; landline numbers in Kazerun, Marvdasht and Abade area have an additional digit – 4; landline numbers in Lar, Fasa and Jahram area have an additional digit – 5.
Shush	0642	
Shushtar	0612	
Tabriz	041	
Tehran	021	
Yazd	035	**NB:** All numbers start with an additional digit – 3.
Zahedan	054	**NB:** All numbers start with an additional digit – 3.
Zanjan	024	

Introduction

Mention to relatives and friends that you are going to Iran, and the chances are that they will stare, swallow and, hesitantly if not incredulously, ask 'Iran? Are you sure?' You may well feel they have a point after your first contact with Iranian consulate staff as it seems that officialdom (but not necessarily any official) is conspiring against your visiting Iran and learning first-hand something about the country, its history and its culture, past and present. Filling in a visa application form seems nothing short of a spy-movie security check. Why do they want to know where and who I am meeting in Iran? Is there really no easier way that will save everyone concerned time, energy and good humour? Just play along and dress accordingly. Ladies are strongly advised to cover their hair and lower torso when entering the embassy grounds, although there's no official instruction to do so. Remember, this is part of the cultural etiquette that you should already be familiar with. Be patient and persevere and the rewards will be worth all the angst.

Iran is one of those countries where issues concerning religion and the modern world confront you at all turns and compel you to consider your own stance. It is impossible to return from even a short visit and not feel that, while seeing magnificent historic architecture and evidence of ancient civilisations, you have also been witnessing history in the making. Make it a point of visiting one of the Iranian coffee shops to observe the ingenuous youth embody all the dilemmas and contrasts of this complex society and rest assured, your dogmas will be shaken.

Yet some people will say that, having travelled and stayed in Iran before the Islamic Revolution, they have no wish to return to see it now. We cannot agree. The experience is invaluable, and one comes back with a better-informed opinion – perhaps changed, perhaps confirmed, but at least based on evidence seen at first hand.

Of course, there have been changes since the early days of the revolution when officialdom frowned on all music save for martial tunes and religious songs. Western instruments such as pianos may now be purchased, and Iranian 'rap' is broadcast on the airwaves. Besides, Iranians appreciate good cinema and national movies openly talk about un-Islamic issues that, living abroad, one thinks could never be possible in the Islamic Republic of Iran.

But not all changes are occasioned by official policy. It is true that women now tend to wear more black *chadors* and black or dark blue *manteaux* on the streets of Tehran, instead of the pastel coats seen earlier, but it is also true that more women are now working for the government (where black is the standard uniform) and that Tehran's increasing pollution was persuading many to wear darker colours to reduce washing and dry-cleaning bills. Besides, you will be amazed to find out how many girls are attending universities (where the *chador* is next to mandatory). When in Esfahan, and with some free time on your hands, drop in to the extensive

University of Esfahan campus and be smitten by the friendly chatty *chador*-clad aspiring scholars.

And while the appalling, senseless driving of many private car-owners is certainly a problem, foreign visitors to Iran are pleasantly surprised at the general cleanliness of the streets, and the care and upkeep of the central reservations and the roundabouts, resplendent with park benches, tea houses and children's swings, as if they're rewards for risking life and limb against oncoming cars. And thanks to the Iranian obsession with picnics, the country is awash with green roadside or inner-city picnic areas.

As a foreign visitor, you will be struck by the friendliness, warmth and genuine curiosity of the locals throughout Iran. In other countries it is sometimes difficult for individuals within a tour group to talk with anyone other than the guide, the driver, or the hotel and shop staff, and some argue that to experience fully a country and a people, one must be an independent traveller. In Iran this is not the case. Indeed, it could be argued that in Iran, forces conspire against the independent traveller, especially those who don't know the language; the country is just not geared up to this kind of tourism. Everything takes so much longer to sort out, and indeed the visitor is so dependent on Iranians helping that the term 'independent traveller' is almost a misnomer. Group travel in Iran can and does open doors in more senses than one – it cuts down endless queuing and waiting for buses and the like.

No Iranian is deterred by numbers; guides and lecturers are often interrupted in their 'spiel' by a crowd asking if the group is American or German, how long are they staying, will they come for tea, how many children do they have, do they like Iran and have they visited the breathtaking Persepolis or have they tasted a *fesenjan* dish, etc. Yes, Iranians know their country and its history well and will happily share what they can with you.

What else can we say? Of course there are downsides to Iran, as to everywhere, but go now, while it is still authentic and untouched by mass tourism and so special, only yours to discover.

Part One

GENERAL INFORMATION

IRAN AT A GLANCE

Location Asia; borders with Iraq, Caucasian and central Asian republics, Afghanistan and Pakistan.

Area 1,650,000km², three times the size of France

Climate Most regions: long, hot summers; short, sharp winters. Marked contrasts in northwest, east and central desert regions.

Population Over 79 million (2013); more than 70% living in cities and towns.

Government A theocracy with a Supreme Leader, an Assembly of (Theological) Experts, a Council of Guardians and elected Parliament and President

Capital Tehran (population over 12 million)

Other major cities Mashhad (population over two million), Esfahan, Shiraz, Tabriz, Ahvaz (over 1.5 million each) and Hamadan (one million)

Language Farsi (an Indo-Aryan language) alongside dialects of Turkish, Arabic and Kurdish

Alphabet Based on the Arabic script, reading from right to left

Religion Predominantly Shi'a Muslims, with some Sunnis; also Zoroastrians, Christians and Jews.

Currency Rial IRR (10 rials = 1 tuman)

Exchange rate US$1 = IRR27,000; £1 = IRR42,400; €1 = IRR33,000 (Nov 2014)

International telephone code +98

Time GMT +3.5

Weights and measures Metric

Electricity 220 volts, 50Hz

National flag Three horizontal stripes of green, white and red with repeated legend 'Allah Akbar' ('God is great') around the edge and the red emblem of Iran on the white stripe

National anthems 'Sourud-e Jomhuri Islami Iran' (Song of the Islamic Republic of Iran); 'Sourud-e Iran' (Song of Iran).

Public holidays Fixed holidays: 11 February, 20 March and the week following (Nou Rouz), 1 April, 4 and 5 June. Also numerous Muslim holidays dated to the lunar calendar, which means these fall approximately 11 days earlier each Gregorian year.

1

Background Information

GEOGRAPHY AND CLIMATE

It is difficult to convey the reality of a land mass of 1,650,000km², but Iran, with its 31 provinces, is three times the size of France, or the size of the United Kingdom, France, Spain, Italy and Switzerland combined. The Zagros Mountains in the west form a natural barrier with Iraq, and to the north are the Caucasian republics and those of central Asia, all of which were once within the territory of the former Soviet Union. To the east are Afghanistan and Pakistan, while the Gulf and the Sea of Oman mark Iran's southern limits. It is a land of great contrasts, physically and climatically, as mountain ranges push up the mostly desert plateau of the centre. Apart from the green Zagros chain in the west, there are the snowy crags of the Alborz range in the north, the Makran Mountains in the south and the westernmost extension of the Hindu Kush, which force up the landscape of Iran's eastern provinces.

This geological 'upturned bowl' effect means that towns on the same latitude but on either side of the same mountain range receive very different amounts of rainfall: Dezful (western Zagros, 143m altitude) gets approximately 358mm a year whereas Esfahan (eastern Zagros, 1,570m altitude) receives a mere 108mm. Much less rain falls in the Great Desert basin, where some areas are pretty much unable to support any life at all. Generally speaking, regions south of latitude 34°N get rain mainly during January, while those north of this receive most rainfall during the spring, especially April. An exception is the Caspian region, where the heaviest month for rain is October.

Few in the West are likely to associate snow with their mental image of Iran, yet about two-thirds of the Islamic Republic's land mass usually endures heavy winter snowfalls (January–February) because of the average high altitude throughout the country. Tabriz (1,349m) in the northwest has about 30 days of snow a year, about ten days more than Arak (1,753m) to the east, whereas Esfahan, at a higher altitude, gets about seven days and Yazd (1,230m) about half this. Of course, areas of very high altitude such as Mount Damavand (the so-called roof of Iran 5,610m high) and especially its northeast face, Takht-e Soleyman in the Alborz range, and Sabalan (4,500m) in Iranian Azerbaijan have perennial snow as well as glaciers. Indeed, many Tehranis escape the smog and pressure of life within the overcrowded capital by flocking to the ski runs that drape the mountains, within a few hours' drive of the city.

There are three if not four distinct climates in Iran: most regions have the continental climate of long, hot summers and short, sharp winters. In the northwest, the Iranian province of Azerbaijan shares a similar climate to that of Switzerland, and further east, along the south shore of the Caspian, it is as humid as the south, but without those gruesome higher temperatures. In the central desert region it is dry and insanely hot (indeed, NASA's infrared satellites measured the Dasht-e Lut desert cindering at 70.7°C during the summer of 2005).

NATURAL HISTORY AND CONSERVATION

FAUNA Despite the enormous area of the country, only around 5% of the landscape is officially protected by designation as national parks or preserves, and there is little supervision of hunting even amongst these regions; sadly, the government ministry concerned is massively underfunded and understaffed. Most of the 19 national parks and more than 100 reserves are strewn with rubbish and under constant encroachment from illegal construction and resource extraction nibbling at their borders.

Ironically, it was at Ramsar on the Caspian coast in 1971 that the Ramsar Convention was signed by many of the planet's nations, formalising the protection of wetlands worldwide for the survival of both indigenous and migrating **birds**. Although little in practice has been done in recent years to keep up Iranian obligations to the treaty they helped organise, nearly 500 species of bird have been recorded within the borders of the country, and many species are easily observed from the road when driving across Iran. Serious birders should consider packing a copy of *Birds of the Middle East* by Christenson, Porter and Schiermacker-Hansen. The desert regions south and southeast of Tehran are home to bustards, coursers, sandgrouse and ground jays, while in the steppes the long-legged buzzard, Eurasian kestrel, various species of roller and bee-eaters can be seen. As one would expect, birds preferring colder temperatures such as the golden eagle, bearded vulture, alpine swift, wallcreeper and snow finch frequent the mountain ranges, while in the forests and woodlands of Iranian Azerbaijan there are wood pigeons, green woodpeckers, shrikes, nightingales and thrushes. Lake Orumiyeh in this region was made a bird reserve in 1967 and a breeding colony of over 20,000 pairs of wintering greater flamingos has been recorded in the past, but with the shrinking of the lake in recent years the population has plummeted. A little further south, the seasonal marsh of Talab-e Aqgul, some 90km south of Hamadan and 20km south of Malayer, is a favourite migration stage for Siberian and Scandinavian wetland birds for some four or five months. The lush wetlands of the southern Caspian shore are wintering grounds for pelicans, Siberian cranes, herons, gulls, spoonbills and cormorants. Caspian seals and otters may very rarely be seen there, but even this tiny vestigial population is under threat from urban development, overfishing and industrial pollution related to oil and gas extraction further north and out in the Caspian. As temperatures drop, so the herons and pelicans, along with plovers, ospreys and oystercatchers, make their way south towards the Gulf, where the mangroves and palm forests are home to oriental Afro-tropical birds such as the palm dove and Indian roller.

As for **mammals**, the mountains and forests of the north have many types of deer, such as red, roe and fallow deer, as well as the Mesopotamian deer, and predators like wolves and foxes, but hunting (totally unlicensed) has taken a very heavy toll. The Red Caspian deer, which inhabits the lush forests of Northern Iran, is now a protected species. It used to fall prey to shah's hunting endeavours while now the Persian leopard is its only threat. Wild boar in northern Iran is on the increase, partially due to the cultural Islamic tradition of avoiding these animals and also because there are fewer threats for them, than before. There are also a few dozen Persian brown bears remaining in the Alborz mountains area, but their numbers are decreasing due to illegal logging. Wild sheep and goats were once common in the northeast Alborz and north of Shiraz, with wild boars further east and Pazan ibexes in the Bisotun area, but few survive. It seems likely that snow leopards, which once inhabited the area east of Mashhad, and certainly the Mazandaran tigers are now extinct, as is the lion, last seen in 1942. There are few details about the cheetah population, officially estimated at fewer than 50 in number in 1991. Despite the official Asian Cheetah Conservation Project, their probable fate seems as desolate as the deserts they recently roamed. The hotter central and southern provinces of Iran are home to jackals and mongooses, who haunt the ruins of both Persepolis, where they are understandably nervy, and the Sassanid site of Firuzabad, where bolder mongooses fed from the hand on the remnants of the author's chicken picnic lunch. Date and palm squirrels, gerbils and jerboas also scurry in these regions. Camels, signifier of any desert worthy of the name, are usually dromedary rather than the shaggy twin-humped Bactrians of eastern central Asia. Several areas are known for bat caves: Shapur's cave near Bishapur for *Rhinolophus euryale* and *Miniopterus schreibersi*; the village of Ahmad Mahmudi, southwest of Shiraz, for *R. hardwickei* and *Rousettus aegyptiacus*; and the northern shores of Lake Parishan (formerly Famur) nearby for *Pipistrellus kuhli*. Perhaps the most curious (and unlikely) animals to be found within the borders of Iran are the small population of 250 to 300 mugger crocodiles (*Crocodylus palustris*) that lurk in the Gando River and surrounding waterways of desert Sistan province, the far southeastern tip of the country. Crocodiles were historically widely spread across Asia and the muggers of Iran are a vestigial population of a subspecies still to be found hunting in the Ganges and Indus. Iranian crocs also carry their full set of teeth and the last fatal attack was in 2003, when a 12-year-old boy was taken and eaten while swimming in the Gando River on a hot afternoon. The government has organised an official protection programme for the species, and despite the very real risk of injury to local communities it seems to have stabilised the population of crocodiles thanks to somewhat surprising local support.

Pollution of the Caspian Sea during the dying years of the Soviet Union and current illegal netting (much of it controlled by mafia groups from Russia and Azerbaijan) has had a severe effect on Iranian **fisheries**, but sturgeon are still breeding – just. Salmon trout, chub and carp are found in mountain streams, while warm-water sea fish abound off the southern coast of Iran.

FLORA The best time to see the natural flora of Iran, some 6,000 recorded species, is around April and early May when the mountains and steppes are once more carpeted with new grass, fruit-tree blossom and masses of wild flowers, now that the high price of imported artificial fertilisers and pesticides has led to a decrease in extensive use. Wild irises and poppies can be seen almost everywhere, but *Iris barnumae* is found only in the Azerbaijan region and *Iris spurgia* in the Caspian wetlands. Of the 80 species of tulip, 12 are recorded in Iran, the most widespread being *Tulipa biflora*. Especially striking is *Tulipa clusiana* with its red and white petals and the yellow *Tulipa urmiensis*, found, as its name suggests, north of Lake Orumiyeh. The saffron crocus (*crocus sativus*), one of the eight Iranian species, is mainly found in eastern Iran and the so-called autumn crocus, although it has six stamens rather than the three of crocuses, is well represented, including the *Colchicum persicum* of central Iran, which flowers from March to April. The city of Shiraz is justly proud of its sweet-smelling roses, which are used in the local production of rose jam, syrup, and rosewater perfume. And of course most people know of the Shiraz grape. Most of Iran's vineyards were ripped up during the early years of the Islamic Revolution but there has been extensive replanting in the last decade, albeit not for wine production.

WATER Water has always been a perennial concern in Iran, especially after 13th-century Mongol conquests destroyed dams and irrigation channels; indeed, parts of Khorasan and Sistan provinces have never recovered their populations. The ingenious engineering of *qanat* (underground water channels), whereby water was tapped from the aquifer level on the mountainsides and guided down to the cultivated fields, has largely fallen into complete disuse now that new irrigation systems are being installed. However, the lines of *qanat* inspection holes, looking like disintegrating termite hills, still mark the landscape, especially in the Yazd region. Features of Iranian towns are the roadside water channels (*jub*), which are permanently or daily flooded with water. These serve to lower the temperature as well as move rubbish, but can also trap unwary car drivers attempting to squeeze into parking spaces.

HISTORY

A note on dates: as in India and China, official circles in the Iranian Republic prefer the designation BCE (before the Common Era) and CE (Common Era) rather than the Western/Christian abbreviations, BC and AD; this will be the system used here. Where the Muslim lunar year – as recorded in a building inscription – falls between two solar years (eg: the Muslim Hijra year 1347 ran from 20 July 1928 to 8 July 1929), only the latter year is noted. Less frequent references to Muslim Hijri Year that start counting from the day of Prophet Mohammed's 'hijra' (migration) to Medina in 622CE, are denoted as 'AH' (anno hegirae).

Archaeological excavations have revealed a Neolithic period in Iran from around 7000BCE, with early cereal and animal domestication occurring in the fertile valleys of the Zagros Mountains. Evidence of copper smelting, pottery making and textile production have been found, along with evidence of the potter's wheel, dating from around 3500BCE. The sites of Tel-e Iblis and Tappeh Yahya, east of Kerman, have provided artefacts and clear signs of settlement dating from the so-called Proto-Elamite period, 3200–2800BCE, and the recently excavated (and sadly looted) site of Jiroft has produced exquisite and extraordinary ceramics, as well as evidence of an indigenous writing system unrelated to either cuneiform or Indus Valley script, dating to the end of the 3rd millennium BCE. A recently published archaeological survey (which was actually conducted in the 1970s) revealed that the region between Susa and Malyan is rich in surface finds from the 4th millennium BCE. Trading contacts with the Sumerians of Mesopotamia (now Iraq) increased as the Elamite centres of Susa and Haft Tappeh were established. It is worth noting, however, that the turmoil following the 1979 Revolution and subsequent Iraq–Iran war (1980–88) made it exceptionally difficult to carry out archaeological digs and research. It would be safe to assume that a lot has yet to be revealed.

For today's visitor, the most important visual evidence of Elamite civilisation is the site of Choga Zanbil, where the remains of a stepped-pyramid temple dominate the landscape, and bear more than a passing resemblance to the great ziggurats of southern Iraq. Political interference by Mesopotamians into Elamite territory and vice versa repeatedly led to armed confrontation, and in c2006BCE an Elamite army captured the last king of Ur, exiling him to Anshan (modern Malyan, southeast of Izeh). Despite stray finds across the central plateau and the stunning material from Jiroft, it is clear that the Elamites never controlled all of Iran.

In the northwest of the country below the Caucasus, archaeological finds from Haftavan and Dinkh Tappeh, near Lake Orumiyeh, reveal that people living here also traded with Mesopotamia, and there was significant technical innovation, with very fine zoomorphic ceramic vessels such as those found in the Hasanlu excavations dating from c1350BCE. Extensive and repeated military campaigns by the martial Assyrian kings throughout the 9th, 8th and 7th centuries BCE spelt the subjugation, if not the end, of most settlements specialising in horse breeding, which were clustered the high, green valleys of the Zagros Mountains, and communities squatting on the eastern flank of the Zagros were repeatedly devastated.

Little is known of eastern Iran during this time, but by the 8th century BCE, two tribal groupings appear in the west of the country from out of the historical murk: the Medes (from the region of Media, in the north of the Zagros) and the Persians (from Pars, the region around Shiraz). We know about them from the tribute lists of vainglorious Assyrian kings. Both groups spoke an Indo-European language, alien to the dwellers of the Mesopotamian plain and Elam alike, and were linked to one another by ties of marriage, culture and a great love of horses and celebratory, drunken feasting. Initially, the Medes were most successful in pushing back against Assyria, and in alliance with Babylon and the southern Persians they successfully scorched the Assyrian capital of Ninevah in bitter house-to-house fighting in 612BCE. The political convulsions emanating from the overthrow of Assyria elevated Media to the rank of ancient superpower. However, rather than accept Median rule, a Persian aristocrat known to Western sources as Cyrus II (the Great), defeated the Median king – who also happened to be his maternal grandfather – at the site of Pasargadae, and pushed the boundaries of his fledgling kingdom to include the rich Elamite cities south of the Zagros, and out on the alluvial plains. This marked the bloody beginnings of the glorious Achaemenid dynasty.

THE ACHAEMENIDS (550–330BCE) From these somewhat ignominious beginnings in the high mountain valleys of southwestern Iran, the Achaemenid Empire stretched west into the Balkans and eastwards perhaps as far as the Tian Shan Mountains (today's Chinese frontier), all controlled from a northern summer capital at Hamadan (former capital of the Medes and the Ecbatana of Alexander the Great); a winter capital at the old Elamite city of Susa, in the south; Pasargadae, the wind-blasted launch site of the Persian imperial mission; and later a grand ceremonial capital at Persepolis ('City of the Persians' in Greek).

Cyrus spectacularly captured Lydian Anatolia and its famed King Croesus during a series of daring military campaigns traditionally dated to 547BCE. (The exact date has however remained a point of contention and is disputed among historians coming up with various interpretations of the events.) Cyrus then took Babylon and Syria in 540/539BCE, earning in the process a particular reputation for both justice and religious tolerance in allowing the Jews to return from Babylonian exile, paying for the construction of a new temple in Jerusalem and returning Babylonian divine images to their traditional shrines. Central Asia was the great conqueror's next goal, but there Cyrus met his end. His death is traditionally dated to c529BCE, and according to Herodotus, at least, was said to be at the hand of a warrior-queen, Tomyris of the Massagatae. Such a setback should have seen the foundations of Cyrus's great imperial venture crumble. With the death of his son Cambyses II four years later, following a successful conquest of Egypt, this was the time when the nascent Achaemenid state – a huge and unprecedented collection of noble ancient cities and kingdoms paying homage to what was effectively a jumped-up mountain bandit king – should have ended as a merely curious footnote in the dusty recess of Near Eastern history. Unfortunately for those subject peoples hoping to wriggle free from beneath the elegantly turned boot of the Persian Great King, an equally brilliant – if surprisingly distant – relative of Cyrus II was proclaimed King: Darius I ('the Great'). His extraordinary triumphs over enemy and birthright alike are recorded at the site of Bisotun (see pages 104–5). Darius inherited both the military genius and ambitions of his distant grandsire, and his own campaigns extended Achaemenid control into Ethiopia from Egypt, Afghanistan and India, and west into Europe along the Danube and into Greece. During Darius's reign he had, in fact, 're-founded' the Achaemenid Empire that could have broken apart during the tumultuous years after the unexpected death of Cyrus's son. Cambyses II succeeded his father to the throne, but his rule was followed by numerous revolts, as recorded on the Bisotun rock relief.

Unlike Cyrus, however, Darius the Great (d486BCE) also clearly understood that the business of empire requires able administrators as much as fierce warriors, and while continuing with the tradition instituted by Cyrus to govern local affairs with a light and deft touch, Darius simultaneously undertook a massive road- and canal-building programme (including the precursor to the Suez Canal) in order to tightly bind together his newly forged, disparate dominion. He also began the construction of a great ceremonial palace complex at Persepolis as a grand showcase for his imperial splendour (see pages 195–200). Darius did not force the numerous peoples subject to him to convert to Zoroastrian beliefs, preserving Cyrus's tradition, and his rule is still associated with unusually farsighted tolerance and economic prosperity. An empire-wide banking system, uniform weights and standard measures were instituted, and a powerful navy was established to repress piracy and encourage trade.

Even under Darius, Persian military momentum occasionally stalled (most famously at Salamis and Platea), and under his successors the famously even-handed administration of Persian satrapies (or provinces) began to ossify into corruption and rebellion. Alexander the Great timed his invasion well, and in a series of incredible campaigns from 334–326BCE subjugated the once-mighty Achaemenid Empire, which at the time stretched across the Asian and European land mass, from Greece to India. Although he survived only seven years after his capture of Persepolis in 330BCE, Alexander has passed into Iranian history with a somewhat mixed image: a great king and warrior, responsible for building a wall (see page 148), protecting truly civilised people (Iranians) from the savage Barbarians of the central Asian steppe, but also the great destroyer of Persian might and power, and the burner of Persepolis, that symbol of supposed eternal Achaemenid and Iranian glory.

Archaeological interest during the 1960s and '70s concentrated on sites associated with Achaemenid history, even more so when the late Shah (see page 15) proclaimed that his reign was a direct extension of 'uninterrupted Iranian rule' established by Cyrus (politely ignoring Alexander and his successors, amongst a panoply of other monarchs). The Shah even introduced a short-lived dating system to embody this idea, for example 21 March 1976 was re-dated as New Year's Day 2535. Massive restoration projects and new excavations were undertaken at Persepolis, Pasargadae, Susa, Naqsh-e Rostam and Bisotun in time for the 2,500th anniversary celebrations of this rule in 1971.

THE SELEUCIDS (323–c240BCE)

Alexander's sudden death stunned his men; he had seemed invincible. His military generals and governors strove to retain control over the conquered territories, with Seleucus Nicator (Seleucus I) grabbing the bulk of Iranian lands in the chaos and civil wars of the Macedonians that followed Alexander's death, and subsequently ruling from Ctesiphon, south of today's Baghdad. Greek cities and temples were established but from around 310BCE an Iranian-speaking people, the Parthians, pushed south from the region of today's Turkmenistan and re-established a Persian-speaking kingdom. The Seleucids withdrew from their eastern provinces in order to defend the rich lands west of the Euphrates, and a series of Greek-speaking breakaway successor states briefly flourished in the mountains of modern-day Afghanistan and Pakistan. With Seleucid abandonment, the conventional frontier between East and West came to be located very definitely west, not east, of the Zagros Mountains. An exhausted Seleucid dynasty finally succumbed to Roman martial prowess after the Battle of Magnesia in 180BCE.

THE PARTHIANS (c238BCE–224CE) The early history of this family (also known as the Arsacids) and its founder Arsaces is shrouded in mystery, but we know that as the Seleucids withdrew the power vacuum was filled by the Parni, a tribe moving down from the central Asian steppes in c238BCE. Preoccupied with defending Syria, the Seleucids failed to challenge Arsaces of Parni, and in 210BCE he was recognised as a powerful vassal ruler in Parthia in the northeast and the southern Caspian regions; the southwest provinces remained largely under the control of the Elymais (c147BCE–c225CE) who paid annual tribute to the Parthian shahs. This regional power group is known from its coinage and a few Aramaic inscriptions, and perhaps represent the last remnants of the earlier non-Indo–European-speaking Elamite people.

The Parthian shah Mithridates I (c171–139BCE) campaigned against the Seleucids, winning control of Media by 148BCE, but in the east Scythian tribes were causing serious problems, a threat implicitly recognised in the location of the first Parthian capital, Nisa (now in Turkmenistan). As internal security was established, so trade along the Silk Road flourished, carrying Chinese silk westwards in payment for glass, jade and the 'blood-sweating' horses of Ferghana, central Asia. By 113BCE Mithridates II (c124–87BCE) had moved into eastern Syria and the Caucasus against Rome, but family squabbles after his death stopped further advances. Rome moved into action, only to have half its forces slain and a further 25% captured. Nevertheless, continuing family feuds prevented the Parthian command from taking advantage. An uneasy truce dramatically ended with the invasion of Mesopotamia by the Roman emperor Trajan in 114CE. His death three years later, as foretold by the oracle at Baalbek, Lebanon, prompted Hadrian to accept the Euphrates as the frontier, but peace was in name only. Major campaigning recommenced in 195, with the Parthians losing most of Mesopotamia but inflicting a massive defeat on the Roman army in 217. However, there was an internal challenger to Parthian domination, the emergent Persian family of Sasan, based at the city of Istakhr, sited near the ruins of Achaemenid Persepolis and within view of the great Achaemenid royal necropolis of Naqsh-e Rostam. In April 224, at the Battle of Golpaygan, Parthian rule was finally brought to an end by the Sassanid dynasty.

The Parthian dynasty lasted 474 years but remarkably little of its civilisation and culture is visible to the visitor in Iran; one has to journey to Hatra in Iraq, Nisa in Turkmenistan or Palmyra in Syria. Apart from the striking bronze Shami statue (see page 81) there are only a few eroded low-reliefs and fragmentary archaeological finds. Later Sassanid occupation of the major Parthian settlements of Damghan, Rayy, Hamadan and Ctesiphon destroyed the architecture, and until recently officialdom had other archaeological priorities. However, the military skill of the Parthians has been recorded throughout Europe and the East, with depictions of the famed Parthian shot, in which the warrior on horseback turns back in the saddle, drawing his bow. Renowned also were the Parthian trousers, dismissed by the Roman military as 'effeminate' garb, but carefully portrayed in all their finery by 2nd- and 3rd-century sculptors of Palmyra (Syria) and Hatra (Iraq). As with the Achaemenids, the Parthians were Zoroastrian (see page 27) and established a firm association between the priesthood and kingship by constructing 'coronation' fire temples and developing the cult or temple fire.

THE SASSANIDS (224–658CE) Persian tradition holds that Sasan, who gave his name to the dynasty, was high priest at the Zoroastrian shrine of Anahita, at Istakhr (see page 202). Claiming family ties to the Achaemenids, one of Sasan's descendants, Ardashir I (d255), then in control of the Shiraz and Kerman regions as a vassal ruler, defeated the last Parthian shah, Artabanus V (see page 192), and established a dynasty that ruled Iran for over 400 years. The main Sassanid sites of Bishapur, Firuzabad and Taq-e Bostan reveal little of the efficient administration, which included town planning, irrigation systems and a system of schools, colleges and hospitals. But Sassanid kings' exploits are recorded in the famous Persian poem, the *Shahnameh* (see box, page 262), an epic combining both magic and part-remembered history, which later inspired many Iranian artists and re-established Persian as a language of culture and art during Islamic rule in the late 10th and early 11th centuries BCE. The Sassanid dynasty instituted an imperial formulation of Zoroastrian scripture, complicated somewhat by Alexander the Great's destruction of the Achaemenid royal archives. However, this new orthodoxy, so at odds with the religious pluralism of Cyrus and Darius, was accompanied by the hearty persecution of existing Buddhist, Jewish, Manichaean and Christian communities in Iran; such intolerance helped to sow the seeds of their own later destruction.

Political and military rivalry with Rome, and later Byzantium, continued throughout the first half of the first millennium CE. Sassanid armies headed west from their capital, Ctesiphon, almost reaching the walls of Constantinople (Istanbul) and regularly occupying the Roman provinces of Syria and Egypt and sacking their wealthy cities. Sassanid victories over Rome were recorded in huge rock carvings (as at Bishapur), but constant military campaigning exhausted both empires, which levied ever-increasing taxes to finance their interminable wars. As they fought their pointless battles and mounted their fruitless sieges, both empires utterly exhausted their wealthiest and most fertile provinces.

ISLAM AND THE ARAB CONQUESTS The Western perception of the spread of Islam is largely based on 19th-century opinion: fanatical Muslims eager to attain paradise by dying in battles against the 'infidel'. However, this fails to explain the staggering speed of the territorial conquests after the death of the Prophet Mohammed in 632 in Arabia: averaging 16–19km a day, Syria was taken in 636, Egypt in 641 and Mesopotamia in 648. One answer is to be found in the centuries of religious intolerance vigorously pursued by both Byzantine and Sassanid empires, a gradual ossifying of social mobility within the Sassanid world, and heavy taxes levied on their subject peoples by both regimes. By contrast, the Muslims offered freedom of religious practice to the 'People of the Book' (ie: Jews and Christians), social equality, in the eyes of God, to those who converted, and lower taxes.

The bulk of the Sassanid army was defeated in 637 in modern-day Iraq, with the last Sassanid shah finally tracked down and killed in 651, but it was some 350 years before cursive Persian Pahlavi script was totally abandoned for the Arabic alphabet. The administration of the Islamic Empire, which in its heyday stretched from Spain/Portugal and north Africa in the west to the Great Wall of China in the east, was run first from Syria, and later from Iraq (Baghdad) under the Abbasid Caliphate (749–1258). Islamic history is tortuously complicated, with territorial boundaries changing in almost every campaign season; today's borders were fixed only during the early part of the 20th century with the demise of the Ottoman Empire. When the opportunity arose, warlords throughout the empire took advantage of weak caliphs, paying only the merest lip service to whoever occupied the throne of Baghdad. This meant that from 800CE various families were in effective control of certain parts of Iran, the most important in this context being the Seljuk dynasty (see below). Despite such fragmentation, this early medieval period (750–1200) was a time of flourishing trade and commerce with Europe and the east, and of great scientific and technological advance in most fields. By contrast, Europe was languishing in the intellectual gloom of the Dark Ages.

THE SELJUKS (1038–c1220) From around 800, numerous Turkic-speaking tribes spread into the Islamic regions from central Asia, mostly to act as mercenaries, or *ghulams*. One of these was the Seljuk clan (also spelt Saljuq), who entered the service of the Khwarizm shah, ruler of the area of modern Turkmenistan, during the 1020s. Quickly tiring of taking orders issued by the Khwarism shah from the comfort of his grand capital at Konya Urgench on the banks of the famed Oxus River, the family turned the tables and by 1043 had seized firm control of Nishapur and the eastern provinces. Seljuk authority spread south and westwards, with governance of the regions shared among the family. The Seljuk sultans gained a reputation for being firm but just rulers of Sunni Islam, and great patrons of the arts and sciences, constructing mosques (see page 109) and tomb towers, colleges and caravanserais. Exciting artistic and technological developments in architecture, ceramics, metalwork and textiles took place, influencing work for centuries after. Trade and commerce also flourished; it looked as if peace, territorial unity and continuity had finally arrived. The invading roughnecks of the 12th century, the Crusaders, were a mere irritation in the Seljuks' western provinces. More problematic were the so-called Assassins (see page 94) of the Ismaili Shi'a, who murdered political and military leaders, and, even more dangerous, the advancing Mongol armies.

THE MONGOLS (c1220–c1340) The first Mongol invasion in 1218 virtually destroyed Seljuk authority. Although modern Mongolian commentators promote Genghis Khan as a statesman and military hero, contemporary 13th-century Persian and Arabic chroniclers portrayed him and his men as an utterly destructive force, perhaps even sent by God as divine retribution for mankind's many crimes. Even if accounts were slightly exaggerated, many historic cities were most definitely razed to the ground and the country's water irrigation system destroyed, with only southern Iran escaping relatively unscathed. To put the Mongol whirlwind of destruction in Iran into a modern context, for the unfortunate inhabitants of cities such as Nishapur and Rayy, it was as if a '9/11' were to have erupted on a monthly basis for three years: their whole world consumed by fire and destruction, great cities entirely depopulated and the countryside emptied of people. The second Mongol invasion of the 1250s under Genghis Khan's grandson, Hulagu, ended Abbasid authority in Baghdad in an equally cataclysmic fashion, with the great libraries of the city (including the famous House of Wisdom) burnt and its population alternately butchered or sold into slavery. Hulagu even managed to eradicate the Ismaili Assassin threat, a feat that was beyond the powers of even the mighty Seljuks, by besieging their mountain-peak castles, which had been thought impregnable. And yet in time even the Mongols – who came to be known as the Ilkhanids within Iran – were seduced by the culture and sophistication of the Persian-speaking world, which they had almost destroyed. They converted to Islam and an exquisite monument survives as evidence of their pious patronage: the Mausoleum of Oljeitu at Soltaniyeh (see pages 172–3). Commerce and trade recovered too, as noted by Marco Polo, although the other Mongol legacy, the Black Death, endured for centuries.

However, Iran experienced political fragmentation: a commander in the Mongol army seized control over central Iran (Esfahan, Yazd and later Kerman and Iraq). His Muzaffarid dynasty was short-lived (1314–93), but a small Sunni madrasa in Esfahan shows artistic quality and craftsmanship (see page 132). In northern Iraq and Azerbaijan, a Mongol tribe, the Jalayrids, took control (1336) but yielded authority to the house of Timur Leng in the closing years of the 14th century.

THE TIMURIDS (1375–c1415 IN WESTERN IRAN; UNTIL c1500 IN EASTERN IRAN)

Today's Republic of Uzbekistan also promotes a tireless warrior with bloodstained hands as its national hero: Amir Temur or Timur Leng (Tamerlane). Claiming direct descent from Genghis Khan, this Turkic chief dreamt of re-establishing the Mongol Empire. Ruling from Samarkand, he led annual campaigns into Syria, Anatolia, India (sacking Delhi in 1399), Russia (up to the gates of Moscow) and even China, before his death in 1405. Family squabbles resulted in territorial fragmentation but by 1420 his son Shah Rukh (d1447) controlled most of the Iranian provinces from his Herat capital, and it is in eastern Iran, around Mashhad, where much Timurid architecture, with its distinctive ceramic-tiled exteriors and 'ribbed' vaulting, still survives.

In western Iran power had passed in the late 14th century to two Shi'a tribal confederations, the Aq Qoyunlu and the Qara Qoyunlu (White and Black sheep, respectively). The heartland of Aq Qoyunlu authority was in today's eastern Turkey, and by 1470 it had taken control of Qara Qoyunlu's Azerbaijan and Iraqi territory. Expansion continued into southern Iran and eastwards, which explains the Aq Qoyunlu buildings in Esfahan. A resounding defeat in 1473, however, against the Ottomans, meant that it was only a matter of time before a new political force, the Safavid family, took centre stage.

THE SAFAVIDS (1501–1736)

Safavid court historians were so successful in manufacturing ancestral links for this dynasty that little is certain about the family's actual origins. The story goes that a famous Sufi sheikh, Safi al-Din (d1334), was a popular Sunni mystic and teacher at Ardabil, on the western Caspian shores, and as the two Qoyunlu confederations battled for supremacy and the Ottomans attacked, people looked to this Turkish-speaking 'guru' for spiritual and political leadership. During the 15th century his followers became known for their commitment to Shi'a Islam (see pages 26–7) and so the lines of future dynastic rivalry were drawn: the Sunni Ottoman sultanate and the emerging Shi'a Safavid dynasty. The Muslim pilgrimage centres of Mecca and Medina passed into Ottoman authority, so in their place the Safavid shahs promoted the Shi'a shrines of Karbala, Mashhad and Ardabil, after proclaiming Ithna 'Ashari Shi'ism as the state religion. Sultan and shah fought constantly for control of the Zagros Mountain regions and their populations, while Uzbek tribes carried out damaging raids in the northeast, and the Afghans attacked from the east.

Despite such turmoil, European traders in Iran marvelled at the magnificence and wealth of the Safavid court in Esfahan. They were seduced – as are so many of today's visitors – by stunning turquoise domes, fine palaces, elegant bridges and lush tree-lined streets, watered by sweet-water fountains, and the soaring tiled portals first seen in Timurid constructions, while fine textiles and carpets attracted hundreds of merchant adventurers vying for trading privileges awarded by the shah.

THE AFSHARIDS (1736–c1750) The Sunni population of Afghanistan increasingly questioned Safavid authority and found a leader in Mir Ways, a former Safavid governor. Attacks began in earnest in 1722, with many Iranian towns falling to the Afghani rebels until Nader Qoli, a Safavid general from eastern Iran, took control. By 1727 Nader Qoli had recaptured territory seized by the Afghans and been rewarded with governorships that amounted to the complete control of all of Iran except Azerbaijan, Esfahan and the southwest. Three years later he forced the Ottoman army out of Hamadan, Azerbaijan and the Caucasus. Tired of installing Safavid puppet rulers, he took the crown and title with the dynastic name of Afshari in 1736, and proclaimed Sunni Islam as the state religion from his Mashhad capital. The campaigning continued even into India, exhausting the Iranian people and an economy already disrupted by Afghan incursions, famine and plague. Nader Shah, as he was now known, was assassinated in 1747, and once again Iran's territorial unity was divided among various regional warlords.

THE ZAND FAMILY (1750–94) Zand rulers, especially the founder, Karim Khan Zand (d1779), never assumed the title 'shah', always claiming that they acted in the capacity of regent (*vakil*) for the Safavids only. An army officer of the last Safavid shah, Karim Khan assumed control of southern Iran in the chaotic years following Nader Shah's assassination and reintroduced Shi'ism. After his death (and tragically for Iran, considering who later seized control during the chaos) the usual family disputes broke out. Despite the reassertion of authority by the able Lotf Ali Khan Zand, this enabled the muscular Qajar family, powerful in the northern provinces, to extend their dominion southwards. Agha Mohammed Qajar captured Lotf Ali Khan in the city of Bam and executed him (and a large number of the unfortunate locals for good measure) in 1794. It was the end of Zand rule, which was noted for its justice and moderation, particularly in Shiraz, the former Zand capital. Ironically, Shiraz retains charming examples of Zand architecture (see pages 175–87).

THE QAJAR DYNASTY (c1757–1924) The Turkoman Qajar family of the Caspian region had fought as vassals and retainers for the Safavid dynasty on the battlefield so, as Safavid authority imploded, the Qajar family seized authority in Azerbaijan, grabbed Esfahan from the Zands and moved into the eastern Iranian provinces, again re-establishing Shi'a Islam. The man in charge was Agha Mohammed, whose renowned brutality was partly attributed to his forced castration by an Afsharid shah. His petty sadism proved too much even for his courtiers, who contrived his murder in 1797. Establishing Tehran as the capital, his nephew and successor Fath (pronounced Fat'h) Ali Shah (d1834) showed considerable political savvy, unusual for his family, and managed to survive the interventionist policies and expansionist ambitions of Napoleonic France, Victorian Britain in India, and Tsarist Russia, while fighting off Ottoman campaigns in the Zagros range and Afghan incursions in the east. It was no easy task: the Treaty of Turkomanchay (1828) alone resulted in Iran losing its Caucasian lands to Russia and paying a massive war indemnity, bankrupting the state.

As with contemporary Ottoman sultans, the Qajars reorganised their army and administration and reckoned a comprehensive modernisation project along European lines as the solution to most of their problems. To the Qajar shahs, such reforms presupposed centralisation of power in royal hands, but many of their disgruntled subjects argued that genuine modernisation should lead to democratic constitutional rule, entirely free from foreign interference. The argument raged throughout the final years of the 19th century, culminating in the 1906 Constitutional Revolution. Shortly before his death in 1907, Shah Muzaffar al-Din was forced (when Shi'a theologians withdrew support) to agree to a constitution on Belgian lines, but his successor was understandably hostile. Nationalist forces seized Esfahan and then Tehran, deposing the new Shah in favour of his son, a minor. The Great Powers were too embroiled in the carnage of World War I and the Bolshevik Revolution in Russia to take any real advantage of the political turmoil in Iran. A brigade commander by the name of Reza Khan quickly cemented his authority over the country, becoming prime minister in 1923. Two years later the National Assembly declared the formal end of Qajar rule. Calls for a republic on the lines of newly established Kemalist Turkey gathered strength and – concerned that this would inevitably mean increased secularism and a decrease in their authority, wealth and influence – Iranian theologians pressed Reza Khan to take the throne and make himself shah.

THE PAHLAVI DYNASTY (1926–79) Reza Shah adopted 'Pahlavi' as the dynastic name, we are told, because it was a popular title for an unbeatable warrior, a champion wrestler (see box, page 120), and recalled the language and cursive script of pre-Islamic Iran. Whatever one's personal views of Reza Shah's rule – his tomb in Rayy was quickly destroyed in the early days of the Islamic Revolution – like Kemal Atatürk in Turkey he successfully managed to save Iran from being totally absorbed by one or other of the Great Powers; other leaders were not so successful. Much of his reform programme was aimed at welding Iran into one nation (compulsory schoolteaching in Farsi, dress reform, etc) while establishing a national system of schools and hospitals, and constructing roads and railways (in the 1910s only two all-weather roads existed in the whole country – a fairly stunning indictment of Qajar governance). When Reza Shah was ousted in 1941 by Britain and the Soviet Union – because of concern for his pro-German leanings – in favour of his son, Mohammed Reza, Iran was a very different nation from when he assumed control. It should be noted that Reza Shah's personal finances had also undergone a great change, mysteriously increasing from one million rials in 1930 to 680 million rials (then £7 million sterling) in 1941.

After World War II British influence at court paled as the USA increasingly exerted its authority, while Soviet military withdrawal from the Tabriz region meant pressure from that quarter lessened, too. An understandable concern over foreign control of Iran occupied the chatter in the middle-class salons, newspaper columns and tea houses of the bazaar alike. The popularly elected (if somewhat mercurial) prime minister Mossadegh nationalised Iran's oil and petroleum industry in the early 1950s, and the young Shah Mohammed Reza was forced into exile. Infamously the CIA instituted a counter-coup, 'Operation Ajax', in 1953, organised chiefly by Kermit Roosevelt, a grandson of the former US president Teddy Roosevelt and a senior CIA operative. This returned the Shah to power and led to the removal of Mossadegh, an action which would haunt American–Iranian relations for many decades. Various reform programmes were introduced by the reinstalled shah, including the so-called White Revolution, primarily designed to reassign land ownership from the clergy and local wealthy landlords to the peasantry. Lauded by many contemporary Western commentators as a savvy political move to counter communist influence, more recent appraisals argue that it was actually disastrous, increasing hardship for farmers and creating a deep resentment among an increasingly hostile clergy, while safeguarding the riches of the wealthy and connected at the imperial court.

Mohammed Reza (crowned in 1967) became increasingly autocratic and remote. Political parties were banned, save for the one which he controlled, and parliament (*majles*) merely rubber-stamped all royal decisions. Leading theologians, including a certain Ayatollah Ruhollah Khomeini (see box, page 18), were deported or jailed, and many Iranians with left-wing or centrist leanings either fled the country or risked imprisonment. Press, radio and television were all heavily censored and even in book publishing, all texts had to be approved or shown to have pre-publication orders for a minimum of 3,000 copies, in an attempt to prevent the dissemination of political tracts. The reputation of Mohammed Reza's secret police, the SAVAK, was fearsome. Meanwhile revenue from oil and petroleum was pouring into the country, only to flow out again to pay for a massive armaments programme. The gap between rich and poor yawned, while middle-class dissatisfaction at soaring inflation and extensive corruption increased. The West, however, being deeply apprehensive of Soviet territorial ambitions, continued with almost unquestioning support of the Shah's rule. Perhaps the ultimate *fin de siècle* follies were the costly celebrations marking the so-called 2,500th anniversary of 'uninterrupted Persian rule' in 1971. By 1976 there was almost no public support for the Shah: soldiers and government employees were bussed into events to provide 'spontaneous' cheering for royal motorcades and celebrations. The following year, government funding for religious institutions and the 'clergy' was substantially cut. As serious unrest grew, those who could do so left Iran, or sent their children abroad. Martial law was imposed in the autumn of 1978 but public demonstrations continued, despite hundreds being killed in hails of bullets. A vicious cycle of funerals, followed by demonstrations, followed by the shooting of demonstrators, engulfed all of Iran's major cities. The most atmospheric telling of this period is perhaps *Shah of Shahs* by Polish journalist and writer Ryzard Kapuściński, who captures the dream-like horror of the time perfectly. Mohammed Reza finally fled the country on 16 January 1979, dying in exile in 1980.

THE ISLAMIC REPUBLIC In the closing years of Mohammed Reza's rule, Muslim theologians throughout Iran had refused to hold the Friday service, as a sign of their disapproval of the regime on religious grounds. Instead, smuggled tape cassettes of the speeches of Ayatollah Khomeini and other banned theologians passed from hand to hand. With the Shah now gone, Khomeini returned from his French exile to ecstatic popular acclaim in February 1979 and quickly set about undermining support for a democratic government, overturning a millennium of Shi'a theological tradition and instead establishing an administration based on Shi'a Islamic law. A referendum was held in 1979, when 98.2% of the population voted for the new Islamic Republic. The first general election in May 1980, following a selective round-up of potential political opponents to the new regime, confirmed Khomeini's new grip on the levers of power. Believing that he had full American support, Saddam Hussein of Iraq invaded four months later, claiming the oil-rich and partly Arabic-speaking region of southwest Iran, and justifying his action on the grounds of 'liberating' the Arabs of Khuzestan from the 'tyranny of the Persian'. Iranian forces quickly regained lost territory (with boys as young as 13 tragically walking into landmines to clear the path for their comrades), but the war continued with grotesque losses on both sides, and hellish rocket attacks on most of western Iran's major cities. Pictures and paintings of the fighters and ordinary men fallen during this war still decorate buildings and streets across Iranian cities, towns and villages. Khomeini utilised the chaos of war to crack down on potential domestic political opponents. As many as 30,000 Iranian leftists, communists, trade unionists, university students, high school pupils, intellectuals and others who disagreed with Khomeini's vision for the country following the revolution were rounded up, imprisoned after short show trials, if any, or tortured and shot. The 'internal security' apparatus of the Shah's feared secret police, the SAVAK, including the infamous Evin prison, was reactivated with a vengeance against the very people who had fought so hard to remove the Shah. A ceasefire was finally agreed between Iraq and Iran in 1988, although an official peace agreement remained unsigned until a Shi'a-dominated government took power in Iraq following the US-led invasion that removed Saddam Hussein from power. By then, however, many young Iranian men had been killed (perhaps as many as one million), martyrdom had become formally enshrined within the Islamic Republic's definition of what it meant to be a good Iranian, and without a fully developed welfare system in place, martyrs' wives and families suffered further distress. Although barely understood in the West, the utter futility of the Iran–Iraq conflict, 1980–88, and its needless extension due to the stubborn pride of Khomeini, who insisted on prolonging the war, had a similar impact on the Iranian culture and psyche as World War I did in the UK or France: no community was left untouched by death, a generation of young men was left crippled and scarred by war wounds, and widows and orphans became commonplace in Iran's streets.

During this difficult time, a full reorganisation of the legal system, administration and taxes was undertaken; Iran was to become a theocracy. Just as the Shah had brooked no opposition in his last years, so the new regime was determined to forestall any restoration of the monarchy. Theologians and officials moved to eradicate every element of *gharbzadegi* ('Westoxification') from Iran (see page 60).

The prolonged detention of American Embassy staff in Tehran from October 1979 for 444 days, and the Western conviction that the Islamic Revolutionary government was deeply involved in the training and funding of certain hard-line politico-military organisations elsewhere, resulted in a total breakdown of diplomatic relations between Iran and the West, exacerbated by the Salman Rushdie (*Satanic Verses*) issue, Iran's backing of Hezbollah, the suicide bombing of a US Marines barracks in Beirut in 1982, and the shooting down of an IranAir passenger jet, killing 250, by the US cruiser, USS *Vincennes*. The official US D'Amato trade embargo (see page 22) and consequent economic sanctions are still in existence, briefly relaxed while the reformist Khatami was president and since hardened again due to fear of Iran's nuclear programme. Diplomatic relations with the United States and the West have increasingly soured since 9/11 despite public demonstrations in the streets of Tehran, Esfahan and Shiraz in support of the victims and official condemnation from Khamenei and Khatami of the Al-Qaeda attacks, and particularly following the second, stolen 'Green' re-election of Iranian president Mahmoud Ahmadinejad in 2009 and the regime's concurrent hardening stance regarding Israel and nuclear research.

Ayatollah Khomeini died in June 1989, and since then there have been changes, some with official blessing, some merely tolerated. For the visitor, perhaps this is most apparent in the changed appearance of Khomeini in paintings. In the first years of the revolution he was shown as a glowering, prophetic figure with black beard, furrowed brow and heavy eyebrows, but increasingly now a benign, avuncular image with soft white beard and a slight smile is portrayed. His tomb is a monstrous carbuncle that grows larger every year, lit up like a Las Vegas casino and for the most part politely ignored by Iranian travellers driving to the new Imam Khomeini International Airport from Tehran.

GOVERNMENT AND POLITICS

THE SUPREME LEADER AND THE PRESIDENT Under the current constitution, Iran is governed by a *faqih* or Supreme (spiritual) Leader in line with Khomeini's theory outlined in his book *Hokumat-e Islami: Velayat-e Faqih* (Islamic Government: Regency of the Jurist), until the re-emergence of the 12th imam, or Mahdi (see page 26). This Supreme Leader is chosen for life by the Assembly of (Theological) Experts, whose members have been elected for a seven-year term once their candidacy has been approved by the Leader and the Council of Guardians of the Constitution. Ayatollah Khomeini, it was widely acknowledged, clearly had been one person able to capably fill this office, and certainly possessed the faculties of a most pious and able theologian, but such unanimity was not immediately accorded to his successor, Ayatollah Ali Khamenei. The important Council of Guardians is headed by the Supreme Leader who selects six voting members, while a similar number is selected by the Supreme Judicial Council and approved by parliament (*majles*). As Iran is a theocracy, all are from the *ulama* ('clergy', theologians-cum-jurists) and, under current legal interpretation, no woman can 'join' the *ulama*. This council undertakes to safeguard and uphold the Islamic state, the constitution, and approve all parliamentary dealings, decisions and resolutions. An Expediency Council of 25 members has been established to 'negotiate' between the *majles* and the Council of Guardians, consisting of the Guardians, the president, the head of the judiciary and the parliamentary speaker.

The president of the republic is directly elected by all resident Iranians over the age of 16 for a four-year term, but stands for office only with the approval of the Council of Guardians. After two successive terms in office he cannot offer himself for a third term.

Mahmoud Ahmadinejad, elected in 2005, was thus eligible to stand again and win the stolen 2009 election. Far from being the overwhelming victory of 62.6% claimed by the regime, however, it soon emerged that the result was highly contested and led to the most serious civic disturbances seen in the country since popular movements overthrew the Shah and established the Islamic Republic in 1979. Demonstrations continued throughout 2009 and many young and vocal opponents of the more oppressive aspects of the Islamic Republic's security apparatus were rounded up, arrested and imprisoned after show trials, or no trial at all. Rumours in Iran have it that Mir Hossein Mousavi, the main opposition candidate who officially received 33.8% of the vote, was notified that he had won immediately after the election. Both Mousavi and Mehdi Karroubi, a former speaker of the parliament and another reformist candidate, are still being held under house arrest in Tehran at the time of going to print. Khamenei was publically forced to back Ahmadinejad's election win by the strength of the protests, and this shredded any pretence or illusion of impartiality on the part of the Supreme Leader. Despite many Shi'a theologians and Iranian politicians having traditionally written off Khamenei as a 'broken reed' or mere compromise candidate amongst bigger political beasts, he has actually shown himself a true master of the political sphere, outmanoeuvring long-standing political rivals such as former president Rafsanjani – even having Rafsanjani's sons and daughter, who publically backed Mousavi, arrested and imprisoned in

1902 Birth of Ruhollah Khomeini. By 1944 he was a Qom madrasa teacher, proposing active 'Muslim' involvement in politics, and supported *velayet-e faqih* (government control by Islamic law), later the cornerstone concept behind the Islamic Revolution.

1962 Khomeini opposed new government ruling revoking requirement of swearing-in on the Quran by any newly elected local and provincial officials, arguing that this would allow Baha'is open participation in politics.

JAN 1963 Joined with other theologians against the Shah's White Revolution, saying it increased the Shah's power and American influence in Iran.

MAR 1963 Paratroopers attacked Khomeini's college in Qom, causing fatalities.

JUN 1963 (Ashura) Khomeini described the Shah's government as 'fundamentally opposed to Iran'. His arrest was followed by demonstrations during which many protestors were killed (the 15th day of Khordad).

AUG 1963 Released; re-arrested and held October 1963–May 1964.

OCT 1964 Khomeini condemned as 'high treason' the new legal status protecting American personnel in Iran. Arrested and exiled first to Turkey, and then to Najaf, Iraq, for 13 years. His lectures, publicly criticising the Shah, were published in 1970.

DEC 1970 Demonstrations were held in Khomeini's name by Tehran University students, and by Qom students in 1975.

OCT 1977 Sudden death of Khomeini's eldest son led to Tehran demonstrations, accusing SAVAK of involvement.

JAN 1978 Mass protest in Qom following scurrilous Tehran press attack on Khomeini; many killed. Forty days later (customary funeral commemoration) a demonstration in Tabriz was held, and 40 days after that there were similar protests in 55 cities across Iran.

8–9 SEP 1978 At least 4,000 protesters killed by the Shah's forces in Tehran: 'Bloody Friday'.

OCT 1978 Khomeini moved to France after the Shah demanded the expulsion of Najaf. Crippling strikes by Iranian oil workers began.

DEC 1978 (Moharram) Iranian theologians and students demonstrated against curfew. On the ninth day, a million demonstrators collected in Shahyad/Azadi Square, near the airport; the next day (Ashura) two million protesters demanded abolition of monarchy.

16 JAN 1979 Shah left Iran.

2012 – and now stands truly supreme in the realm of Iranian domestic politics. Khamenei's/Ahmadinejad's government predictably blamed foreign countries and media for fuelling the protests and, as a result, in 2011 a (presumably) orchestrated attack on the British Embassy in Tehran resulted in both countries withdrawing their ambassadors and closing down direct diplomatic relations.

On 14 June 2013, Iranians elected Hassan Rouhani as the new president of the Islamic Republic. The only cleric in the contest, Rouhani received 50.7 % of the vote, and united support from centrist and reformist politicians, including Rafsanjani and Khatami. Rouhani, Iran's chief nuclear negotiator in 2003, is an open supporter of rapprochement with the West. At his first press conference as president, he called for 'serious and substantive' negotiations on Iran's nuclear programme, while asserting Iran's right to civil nuclear energy. Furthermore, in September 2013, US and Iranian foreign affairs ministers held their first meeting since the 1979 negotiations, as part of the 68th United Nations General Assembly. One of Rouhani's challenges, however, is the conservative-minded Parliament (*majles*), but he is nonetheless voicing some of the concerns of the ordinary Iranians, who feel their views were neglected during the Ahmadinejad's conservative eight years in power. Despite the unrest in the rest of the Middle East and dissatisfaction of Iranians with their own government, the 2013 presidential elections in Iran ran smoothly and without confrontation, albeit not without a little political wrangling (Rafsanjani was disqualified by the Guardian Council from running in the elections).

On taking office, a president may appoint 24 cabinet ministers who have to be confirmed in office by the *majles*; following constitutional amendments during Rafsanjani's presidency, the office of prime minister was abandoned, but new constitutional amendments stripping the office of president of its powers are now under discussion. Perhaps surprisingly, following his contested 2009 victory, Ahmadinejad has proclaimed himself the carrier of a 'popular mandate' and has proven to be the most publically vocal critic of the Supreme Leader; unsurprisingly, many of Ahmadinejad's closest advisors have since been arrested on corruption charges and accusations of 'witchcraft' have even been laid at the door of his chief of staff.

The *majles* currently has 290 directly elected members serving a four-year term, and for the last few parliaments there have been several women MPs. Following the elections in 2012, the Zoroastrian community is represented by two MPs, the Jewish population by three MPs, while Iranian Christians numbering around 100,000 have nine seats in parliament. There are no well-defined, established political parties as in the West, but candidates are known for their individual leanings and factions are the dominant vehicles for political expression and personal ambition. The speaker of the *majles* has an important and influential position. The current speaker is Ali Ardashir Larijani, who was reappointed in 2012.

Immediately prior to the parliamentary elections of March 2012 the Council of Guardians once again disbarred over 5,000 reformist candidates from standing, echoing action taken four years previously. From 2004, the political influence of the Revolutionary Guard has markedly increased in parliament. This has in turn had a definite impact on policy-making, confirming that the new power centre in Iranian politics is an axis of Khamenei, combined with the Revolutionary Guard, whose economic strength and influence has grown to rival its military and political control over the levers of power.

WESTERN PERCEPTIONS OF REVOLUTIONARY IRAN
Anyone visiting Iran for the first time should remember that in the 1970s the Western media was largely

uncritical of the Shah's regime. The praise lavished on the Shah and his immediate family in publications was occasioned more by official stipulation than reasoned investigation. The widespread notion, still found today in the West, that the late Shah had established an active Western-style democracy in Iran before he was ousted, is unfounded; his rule was autocratic.

Many new visitors to Iran presume that all Iranian theologians speak with one voice, but there have been numerous outspoken declarations among the *ulama*, not always finding favour with the authorities. Many senior clerics feel that having established an Islamic state to its satisfaction, the *ulama* should withdraw from active political life and resume its former pastoral responsibilities; presently the official view is that active involvement in politics should continue. The evolving relationship between Islam, Iran and the modern world is avidly discussed and the passion these debates arouse should not be underestimated.

Parliamentary debates are just as highly charged. There are essentially two main positions: the 'conservative' wing which holds that the quickest route to achieve a (spiritual) well-being nationally is by a uniform path; that a woman's role is primarily associated with the family and the home; and that the fortunes of the poor will be improved by spiritual care and government subsidies, with the awarding of franchise allocation in the market. Support for this view is generally found among the rural communities and *bazaaris* (merchants). The 'liberal' wing prefers another vision of society, one relating the spiritual ideal to the individual and the material world, arguing for the individual to progress along the spiritual path at his/her own pace; recognising the importance of investments in major projects to revitalise the economy and to create new jobs for the ever-increasing population; and working towards reintroducing Iran to the international community and creating greater opportunities for women (even within the *ulama*). Such ideas find favour among the increasingly urbanised population and in particular with the voters of Tehran, Shiraz, Esfahan, women and among the young (many having benefited from the educational campaigns of the Islamic Revolution), as seen in the mass demonstrations across the country during 2009, which were met with a swift and brutal reaction from police and militia, and in turn filmed by the outraged population.

Western women may feel an understandable hostility towards the Iranian regime, and in particular to its treatment of women. This is largely based on a (mis)understanding of the situation in pre-revolutionary Iran – and a personal reaction to the official stipulation requiring head coverings for all women in Iran (see pages 67–8). However, while the last Shah of Iran was educated in the West and held Iranian doors open to Western values and foreigners – there were reportedly around 50,000 Americans living in Iran by 1979 – his social reforms at home proved inadequate. Approximately 68% of the population was still illiterate and many of these were women. Fathers from poorer and more conservative backgrounds were afraid to send their daughters to mixed schools. In the post-revolutionary Iran, where classes are segregated and hijab is mandatory, there has been an increase in literacy rates among girls.

Over half of the Iranian population is female, and the government cannot afford to ignore them even if it wishes to do so. In the 1970s, opportunities for Iranian women were virtually confined to the upper socioeconomic classes, and indeed 'grassroots' and 'religious' women's groups played a very important role in bringing about the Islamic Revolution.

Nor can Iranian youth be ignored. Over 65% of the population is under 30 years old; while young they require education and training and later employment to the tune of 800,000 new jobs every year. According to official figures, unemployment is at least 10%, but in reality it is much, much higher, and many in work have to moonlight in order to cope with the continually rising inflation that has worsened markedly since the tightening of economic sanctions. In the late 1970s less than 50% of those aged between six and 24 were literate; today, despite a doubling of the population, Iran has a literacy rate that rivals Western nations at around 98% of the population, and university student numbers have increased tenfold. Places available to study for qualifications in professions such as medicine and law are increasingly dominated by women, and this has recently alarmed the conservative faction within the regime: in 2012 a proposal was put before parliament to restrict the numbers of women studying at the more prestigious institutions. To the disgust of many Iranians, over 30 universities put the restrictions in place for the 2012–13 academic year. At present over 60% of university students are female and it is becoming common for some girls to study for PhDs or apply for another degree in order to avoid being forced into marriage and to maintain some level of independence. The government stance may be explained in part by the fact that many Iranians postpone marriage to later in life and have fewer children, the point Ayatollah Khamenei accentuated in his August 2012 speech.

DIPLOMATIC RELATIONS While certain factions see the need for foreign investment (see opposite), the Council of Guardians, Khamenei, the Revolutionary Guard and other influential bodies do not concur. And headline diplomatic confrontation hasn't helped. Aside from the Salman Rushdie issue, the detention of a German businessman in the late 1990s caused a stand-off in otherwise relatively placid Irano–German relations. The state visits of President Khatami to Europe and the Middle East did raise Iran's national profile, and led to more considered and informed reporting in the foreign media, along with sadly misplaced hopes of an early 'Iranian Spring'. But speeches by the Bush administration leading up to and during the coalition action in Iraq in 2003, describing Iran as part of the 'axis of evil', were less than helpful. On the other hand, the Iranian government's deliberately shifting stance regarding its earlier promises to the UN's atomic watchdog (IAEA) to allow tougher inspection of its nuclear facilities has incurred much criticism, provoking tightened sanctions, rocketing inflation within Iran, and deep suspicion in Western countries and Israel as to the Iranian regime's true nuclear intentions. Irano–Canadian diplomatic relations also suffered after the death in custody of a female Iranian-born Canadian photojournalist arrested for photographing the Tehran Evin jail, and the acquittal of her police interrogator in June 2004.

The contested election of 2009, along with the nuclear programme being pursued by Tehran, hardened international relations to the point where an Israeli/ US-led attack on facilities within Iran has been openly discussed within the Western media. This does not, understandably, reassure the Iranian government, and the almost certain loss of the Islamic Republic's primary ally in the Arab world, Bashar al-Assad's regime in Syria, and the fall-out from the Arab Spring, has left the local international political landscape unfamiliar, dangerous and very volatile. Tehran has close relations with the Shi'a-dominated Iraqi government and Iranian agents and units of the Revolutionary Guard move freely within the country, much to US displeasure. The victory of the moderate cleric Hassan Rouhani at the June 2013 presidential elections, however, has opened a window of opportunity in bi- and multi-lateral relations that Obama's administration seems to appreciate, offering itself as a 'willing partner' in return for Iran's meeting its 'international obligations'.

ECONOMY

For centuries Iran's economy and trade were based on textiles and carpets, in processed or raw yarn, dyes and mordants, but by the end of the 18th century foreign mass-produced fabrics were flooding the home market (watch out for Chinese silk in your Persian carpet). The economy collapsed. In the 19th century under foreign pressure, the Qajar administration sold off trading concessions in tobacco, sugar, railway construction and telegraph installation to non-Iranians; even carpet production was largely foreign owned. By the early 20th century the exploration and exploitation of Iran's oil and petroleum reserves were in foreign hands, prompting nationalisation in the 1950s and a political crisis. The Shah's White Revolution of 1961–63 (reassigning agricultural land rights) resulted in more power passing to the Shah and tens of thousands of peasants barely able to survive. The oil boom and heady prices for petroleum products in the 1970s, especially following the Yom Kippur War in 1973, had nonetheless brought great wealth into the country, but rampant inflation too. The Shah reasserted Iran's position and his leading role in the OPEC (Organization of the Petroleum Exporting Countries)bringing higher returns on oil sales for the country. A lot of money, however, was being spent on the military.

With the establishment of the Islamic Republic all foreign and private industries were nationalised, and work on international projects (like the Tehran metro) was abandoned as foreign consortia withdrew. The new administration faced a brain drain, while heavy losses in the Iran–Iraq war resulted in a further scarcity in skills and expertise. During the war itself, the Khomeini regime was forced to send imprisoned 'shah' pilots to fight the Iraqis. The three-year closure of universities and colleges during Iran's 'Cultural Revolution' in the 1980s meant fewer still were qualified to fill the vacuum. The post-revolutionary government had also set out to spend large amounts of government earnings on the oppressed and disinherited members of the society (*mostazafin*) through the newly set up foundations and institutions. Even today Iran can be described as a welfare state on the basis of the assistance the state provides to the poor.

The economic reforms set in motion by President Rafsanjani in the 1990s and continued subsequently under Khatami have resulted in a siege economy dominated by industrial conglomerates with links to the Revolutionary Guard and Basij militia, senior government figures and powerful members of the clergy. The US trade embargo and other economic sanctions, a drop in world oil prices, production difficulties and a steep decline in tourist numbers (far below the half-million visitors per annum in the mid 1970s) have created additional problems. Fearing yet more assets leaving the country, the government even banned the export of Iranian carpets for some years (see page 59). The two-term Rafsanjani presidency was marked by a massive surge in imports, very lucrative business for the right-wing *bazaari* classes, and little else. Few of Rafsanjani's large-scale projects, which numbered in the tens of thousands, were completed, other than a massive and successful programme of road upgrading and railway construction. Unfortunately, two major projects in the fields of health facilities and sewage provision, supported by Britain and other EU members, were turned down by the World Bank, yielding to American pressure. Khatami's eight years in office saw low oil prices, around US$10 a barrel, so his decisions on the allocation of the national budget were somewhat constrained, though during his presidency, Iran enjoyed a period of delegated authority.

Presently, according to official sources, inflation is running below 24% per annum but is much higher in reality, with shortages of basic foodstuffs occurring in major cities for the first time since the Iran–Iraq war. The sanctions and the isolation of Iran have had a tremendous impact on the Iranian currency, which has lost a substantial chunk of its value, now trading at only 30,100 rials to US$1 (October 2013). It hit the historic low of over 38,000 rials to US$1 in February 2013. Prices soared and in the first six months of 2013 alone car prices tripled, making it almost impossible for an average citizen to buy an Iranian-made Khodro. The corruption and stagnation which so infuriated Iranians during the Shah's sclerotic rule in the 1970s is back with a vengeance and many of the grand houses of northern Tehran seized from figures close to the royal court are now occupied by 'Revolutionary Princes' and their families. Despite the ever-tightening sanctions, Porsche sold 563 models here between March 2011 and 2012, worth nearly US$50 million, with an import tax of 100%.

Some would argue that history is repeating itself with rocketing oil prices of more than US$100 a barrel bringing in an estimated US$50 billion a year and forming 85% of government income. Thirty years ago the Shah spent huge sums importing arms and weapons, which then sat rusting in military stores, and into sending students abroad to further their education. For the past few years money has been poured into the nuclear energy programme; defence and development of religious, architectural, educational and administrative structures. Funds have also been sent abroad to Hezbollah in Lebanon and Syria, and Hamas in Gaza, to the fury of many Iranians. Little has been done to revitalise or restructure the oil industry, partly as a result of sanctions against the Islamic Republic, and because the Iranian government's own economic forecasting unit has predicted that Iran will be a petroleum product importing nation by 2020 due to a lack of refining capacity and skilled personnel.

A number of free trade zones also operate, including the Gulf islands of Kish and Qeshm, and the port of Chabahar, along with a few special economic zones which function in a similar fashion and are primarily dominated by the economic organs of the Revolutionary Guard and the conservative faction. Both types of zone did permit unlimited foreign involvement, including bank operations, a free market exchange, removal of import restrictions and 20 years of tax exemption, but have been effectively closed to Western involvement with the tightening of sanctions. Instead, Chinese and, to a lesser degree, Indian companies are now taking up the economic slack in an attempt to secure Iran's oil at favourable discounts. In 1992 some restrictions concerning foreign shareholding in Iran-based companies were lifted, but a certain official ambivalence remains; rather than amending or revoking laws, it is more usual to turn a blind eye to circumvention. Iranian companies have established offices in Dubai in an attempt to bypass both bureaucratic difficulties and economic sanctions and, in 2012 some 300,000 Iranians were resident in the emirate. According to Dubai's own customs and excise department, trade between the two dropped in 2011 but was still measured at a whopping £9.8 billion.

Agriculture struggles on with a lack of machinery, limited irrigation systems and a poor infrastructure of cold-storage units and refrigerated trucks. Things are slowly improving: the replanting of Iran's famous vines, ripped up in early revolutionary zeal, for instance. Visitors to Esfahan's central *maydan* (square) will now see most of the shops occupied and trading, although poor earnings and high unemployment still affect the bazaars of Yazd and Kerman. The major employer, as in the 1960s and 1970s, continues to be the government, despite a revolutionary pledge to reduce such staffing drastically. An ongoing habit of moving staff every six months or so obviously hampers project continuity and supervision.

It is interesting to note that the Russian-built nuclear plant in the vicinity of Bushehr was finally completed in 2011 and since 2012 has been operating at full capacity, in theory producing electricity for Iran. However, the plant has remained a serious point of contention and all its operations have remained a secret.

PEOPLE

Caught in a Tehran traffic jam, one's thoughts inevitably turn to Iran's population. The 1992 census determined that it totalled just under 60 million, with a density of 35 people per square kilometre. In 2013 United Nations figures suggested the population had risen to more than 79 million. Currently, over 70% live in the major cities: Tehran, the capital, with more than 12 million residents recorded in the 2011 census, Mashhad over two million, Esfahan, Shiraz and Ahvaz over 1.5 million each, Tabriz and Hamadan perhaps slightly less, with more people each year moving from rural areas to find work. During Rafsanjani's presidency (1989–97), 400,000 jobs were created in one year; now 800,000 new jobs are needed each year just to keep pace with the growing population. Iran has also experienced something known as the 'Japanese curse' in recent years: despite semi-apocalyptic predictions of the country's population hitting 110 or 120 million by 2015, Iran has in fact experienced one of the most dramatic declines in birth rate ever recorded. Whereas in the 1970s a typical rural family had five children, now that Iranians are mostly urbanised there are rarely more than two children per family. This is undoubedly a product of improved education for women and increased access to state-run birth control programmes. These are now being slashed, and in July 2012 the government announced financial incentives for women to have more babies, with Khamenei publicly endorsing the changes. Whether they will have the desired effect remains to be seen; economics is perhaps of greater importance. Ask any Iranian why they would not consider having more children, and the answer will be 'it is too expensive'.

Much has been made of Iran's **nomads**. Apart from anthropological studies, most publications could be classed as romantic fiction, extolling the 'freedom' of seasonal wanderings (which are actually finely orchestrated migrations). For decades official concern over epidemics, child education, drug and arms smuggling, national security and taxation led to village-settlement programmes, while the 1960s White Revolution caused serious problems over grazing and water rights for the nomads. It has meant that from making up 25% of the population in 1900, nomad-pastoralist numbers fell to 6% in the 1970s. However, if you happen to be travelling in the Shiraz region during late April or mid/late October, you are still very likely to see one or more extended Qashqai family groups, perhaps numbering as many as 75, accompanied by hundreds of sheep and goats, moving to fresh pastures. Traditional tents are now often fitted with televisions and the traditional horse and donkey replaced by utility vehicle or 4x4, but nomad people are still very much a part of modern Iran's landscape, even if their political and economic influence has waned even further since Freya Stark and Robert Byron penned their elegies during the 1930s.

LANGUAGE

Only about 50% of Iranians speak Farsi (Persian) – the official language of Iran – as their mother tongue, though nearly everyone can understand and read it. In the south and southwest Arabic is spoken, while Azeri (Turkic language of Azerbaijan) is common in the north and northwest. In fact around 16 million Iranians are ethnically Azeri and have family connections in Azerbaijan. Armenian is present in the Caucasian foothills and in an Esfahani enclave; Kurdish-Persian is spoken in the western Zagros, while Bakhtiari and Baluchi dialects are used in the southeast. The recent influx of Afghan refugees has seen an increase in Pushto and Dari. In the 1930s Reza Shah Pahlavi tried to 'purify' Farsi of Turkish and Arabic words along the lines of the Académie Française, but the Islamic Revolution has, of course, led to an increased emphasis on Arabic, the language of the Quran.

In addition to the various ethnic groups originally from Iran, according to the 2011 census a little more than 2% of the total population are foreign nationals. Afghanis make up more than half of the total number of foreigners living in Iran, while Iraqis come second.

Farsi is an Indo-Aryan language so there are some similarities in words (eg: *mader* for mother) and grammar with certain European languages. After the Arab Muslim conquests of the 7th century, the Pahlavi script for Farsi was abandoned and the one now used is based on Arabic (reading from right to left), with additional letter forms for specific Farsi consonants, such as *p*, *g* and *ch*, so the alphabet consists of 32 letter forms not including short vowel markings. Each letter has three written shapes, depending on its location within the word, just as certain European handwritten lower and upper letters (eg: *o*, *e*) have when joined to other letters. Unfortunately, there is no one accepted transliteration system to render Farsi into the Roman (ie: English) alphabet, so the city of Esfahan may be shown as Espahan, Isfahan, Ispahan, etc and Qom as Qomm, Qom or even Ghom (the exact pronunciation of 'q' in Persian is actually 'gh', except for the Quran). Major road signs are usually given both in Farsi and in the Roman alphabet; distances are also shown in both numeral forms, both reading left to right. In this book, the most common or simplest rendering is given, for example Quran rather than Qur'an or Koran, but at times the transliteration found in publications or on maps will also be included. Following usual transliteration convention, the glottal stop in Farsi is indicated by the symbol ' (eg: as in Shi'a). This so-called glottal stop reflects the position of the letter 'eyn', which in Persian, unlike Arabic, is rarely pronounced. 'Hamzeh', which is a letter in the Arabic alphabet, in Persian represents merely a sound and does not have any exact phonetic reference. Generally speaking Persian 'hamzeh' has the same value as Arabic 'eyn' and can both indicate a glottal stop or is not pronounced at all. It is most common in words of Arabic origin.

LINGUISTIC POINTERS

These few linguistic points might help make your journey around Iran easier – *bandar* in Persian means 'port', so any city name that starts with 'bandar' (eg: Bandar-e Anzali) refers to its seaside location; *maydan* means 'square' (eg: Maydan-e Imam); *shahid* stands for 'martyr' (mainly refers to fighters who died in the Iran–Iraq war); *rud* means river and any city name that starts with 'rud' (eg: Rudbar) should in theory be located by a river; *gonbad* means dome, but is essentially used to designate dome-shaped towers (eg: Gonbad-e Qabus); *abad* stands for residence or abode (eg: Najafabad). And most importantly, 'q' in Persian is pronounced as 'gh', which explains occasional double signage (eg: Gandhi Street/Qandhi Street).

Another linguistic curiosity has taken root. Arabs do not have the 'p' and 'v' sounds in their language, but have started giving new sounds to Persian names, such as Gonbad-e Qabus (from Qavus) or Fars (from Pars), etc. This partially explains the myriad alternative spellings of Persian words.

Apart from Arabic (for Quranic studies), the other foreign language taught in schools is English, but some older, educated city dwellers may know French or German. Travelling independently around Iran (with the exception of Tehran) without a modicum of Farsi is an adventure, but made easy thanks to the good nature of Iranians, especially younger people eager to practise English – often the result of expensive private language lessons – means that in the larger urban centres someone nearby will be able to converse with you. However, apart from road signs and the occasional tourist menu, *very* little information is given in any language other than Farsi. (See also *Language*, pages 271–2.)

RELIGION

The state religion of Iran is the Shi'a Ithna 'Ashari branch of Islam, whose members constitute approximately 90% of the more than 98% of Muslims in the country; Sunnis account for only 8% of this total. The remaining 2% of the population consists of non-Muslims, but estimates of numbers vary. Only three small minority religious groups are protected and accorded seats in the parliament: Jews, Christians and Zoroastrians.

Article 13 of the constitution protects the rights of all religious minorities in Iran with the exception of the Baha'is.

ISLAM According to Muslim belief, Allah, the one uncreated God, has revealed the message of salvation three times. The first time, believers mistakenly assumed the revelation was meant only for them, the chosen people (ie: the Jewish community), so it was revealed again through the Prophet Isa (Jesus), but his followers (Christians) erred in believing that Isa was the son of the creator God – an impossibility given that there is but one God. So it was revealed a third and final time as the Quran, through the Prophet Mohammed (d632CE). Thus there are references in the Quran to several biblical episodes, as well as shared beliefs, such as the Day of Judgement, the concept of paradise and hell, free will, the continuing battle between good and evil, and the messianic promise.

There are two main branches of Islam, Sunnism and Shi'ism, the latter being further subdivided. The Shi'a (from *Shi'at Ali* or Party of Ali) do not recognise the three caliphs (from *khalifa*, meaning 'deputy') who assumed control in 632–656 after Mohammed's death, believing that the Prophet had transferred all spiritual and temporal authority to his cousin and son-in-law, Ali, and his descendants through his wife Fatima, Mohammed's daughter. For the Shi'a the prophetic tradition has continued through divinely guided leaders (*imams*) who hold the key to the hidden meaning of the Quran – continued, that is, according to one section of the Shi'a community, until the seventh generation when Imam Ismail went into concealment; in time he will reappear to prepare the community for the Day of Judgement. His followers are known as the Ismailis, with today's temporal leader, the Agha Khan. But other Shi'a (later known as the *Ithna 'Ashari*, which means literally 'Twelvers') believe that another descendant was chosen as the seventh imam and that this line continued for another five generations before the (12th) imam disappeared (or was 'occluded' in theological parlance) in 940, to reappear in due time as the 'Mahdi'. This is the branch of Shi'ism found in Iran. In the 1980s some Iranians wondered if Ayatollah Khomeini was indeed the reappeared 12th imam; the overthrow of the Pahlavi regime and founding of the Islamic state seemed nothing short of miraculous.

The Sunnis, in contrast, believe that the prophetic mission ended with Mohammed's death and so reject the idea that Ali and his family were divinely guided. Accordingly, they accept the validity of the first three caliphs and other rulers who followed, holding that they are acting in accordance with the *sunna* (example) of the Prophet.

ZOROASTRIANISM This faith is often (and erroneously) described as the earliest formulated religious philosophy in the world to have survived to the present day. Recent linguistic analysis of the Avesta scriptures and Gatha hymns indicates that the message preached by 'Zoroaster' (Zarathustra) was promulgated in the Irano-central Asian region in c1400BCE, if not earlier; traditionally it was believed that Zoroaster lived 258 years before Alexander the Great destroyed Persepolis in 330BCE. His message, pre-dating Judaism, Christianity and Islam, centred on the uncreated God, Ahura Mazda, creator of all things, as well as concepts of paradise and hell, on a messianic promise, the struggle between good and evil in which good would ultimately triumph, and, most revolutionary of all in the ancient world, free will for all mankind. To assist in the battle against evil, Ahura Mazda created evocations of Himself as divine manifestations, such as Mithra, the Lord of Contract or Justice (see page 106). The Achaemenids were the first imperial rulers of Iran to establish Zoroastrianism as a regally patronised cult, if not a formal state religion (see page 199), and it remained dominant following reorganisation under the Sassanid dynasty until the spread of Islam in the mid 7th century CE. The status of the Zoroastrian community in Islamic law was not as clearly defined as it was for Jews and Christians, and in the 9th and again in the late 17th/early18th centuries official state persecution caused many Zoroastrian families to flee to northern India, where they became known as the Parsi (from Fars province, Persia).

In 19th-century Qajar Iran their situation improved due to British and Indian diplomatic involvement, and they were great supporters of the official freedom to practise under the Pahlavis. In 1979 the community suddenly announced its support for the Islamic Revolution. Today there are just over 25,000 Zoroastrians living in Iran (2011 census), with constitutionally enshrined parliamentary representation, and the community is concentrated in Tehran and Yazd. There are thriving Iranian Zoroastrian populations in England, the USA, Canada and Australia as well as India (particularly Mumbai).

JUDAISM The religious tolerance shown by Cyrus the Great, the Achaemenid ruler (d529BCE), to the Jewish people is remembered on two counts: first, after conquering Babylon he permitted the Jews to return to Jerusalem from Mesopotamian exile, and second he actively assisted and paid for the rebuilding of the temple there. There were at least two Jewish consorts of Iranian kings. The first of these is the biblical Esther, wife of Ahasuerus, as the name is given in the Book of Esther. Esther may be equated with Xerxes, and her story is depicted in the 3rd-century CE synagogue murals from Dura Europos in the National Museum in Damascus. She is said to be buried in Hamadan. Alternatively, the tomb found there could be that of the second Jewish consort, of the Sassanid shah Yazdegerd I (d420CE). Later Sassanid rule saw persecution of both Jews and Christians, but generally speaking the Jewish community was protected in early Islam because of its Quranic legal status and international trading connections. Life became much harder later, especially under the Safavid and Qajar regimes, although there was some respite under Nader Shah Afshar. Pogroms, especially in Mashhad in 1839, led the community to ask for British protection and many fled to Herat (Afghanistan), only to be forcibly repatriated in 1856. When opportunities arose, many travelled northwards into central Asia and west into Ottoman lands.

The 2011 census suggests that there are fewer than 9,000 Jews still residing in Iran, mainly in Tehran and Esfahan, and the numbers are decreasing. In Hamadan, for example, at present there are only five Jewish families left, numbering 15 people. The BBC has reported ten Jewish families present in Yazd, most of whom are related. It is assumed by the conservative faction within the Iranian government that many have strong Zionist sympathies, and there have been arrests under suspicion or charges of espionage. In the last few years foreign visitors have been occasionally advised by their own governments not to visit Jewish sites, cemeteries or synagogues, but you are unlikely to encounter any problems from the local people. The only difficulty might be gaining access to some sites and finding the man with the key (eg: the Jewish cemetery in Pir-e Bakram in Esfahan). Many Iranians would generally be eager to inform you that whatever the official policy to Israel may be, it should not reflect upon the extraordinary hospitality you will experience from ordinary Iranians.

CHRISTIANITY A certain John of Persis attended the 325CE Council of Nicaea when numerous Christian communities in Mesopotamia, the Caucasus and elsewhere were under Sassanid authority. The reign of Shapur II (d397CE) brought severe persecution during which perhaps 35,000 Christians were killed, but in 424 the Iranian Church was still recognised as largely independent. The official break from Byzantium and the Orthodox Church came in 431, when Patriarch Nestor, a Persian by birth, was accused of denying the concept of Christ born Incarnate, thereby rejecting the title of Theotokos ('Mother of God') for Mary. His followers, later known as the Nestorian Church (now the Assyrian Church), fled for safety into Sassanid lands, only to find that unrest in the Caucasus had provoked Shah Yazdegerd II (439–457) to order the forced conversion of Armenian Christians (Gregorian Church) to Zoroastrianism. Despite such persecution few Christians assisted the Byzantine war effort against the Sassanid regime because Byzantium rejected the theological validity of the Eastern churches, forbidding their rituals and liturgies. When Muslim Arabs entered Iran in the late 7th century and offered religious freedom and lower taxes, they were welcomed and indeed those promises were kept for many years. However, later waves of persecution, particularly under Timurid rule, dramatically reduced the Christian community. Matters improved again under the Safavid regime (1502–1735) as the shahs were mindful of both European trade and Armenian Christian and Jewish expertise in silk trading, along with their international mercantile links. The great influence wielded by the French, British and Russian ambassadors at the 19th-century Qajar court also ensured a measure of protection for the Christians of Iran, and in 1898 a large number of Nestorians in the Orumiyeh region were received into the Russian Orthodox Church.

Today there are around 117,000 Christians in Iran, mainly of the Armenian Church, recognising the Yerevan Patriarch and generally living in Tehran, Esfahan and Shiraz. As a legacy of 19th-century foreign missionary work, there are Presbyterian, Anglican, Lutheran and Catholic congregations, especially in the capital. Immediately following the Islamic Revolution, the then Iranian Anglican bishop and his wife (but not their son) survived assassination, though Anglican schools and hospitals were closed. Later the Persian Bible Society in Tehran was closed and all files confiscated. Other than in Esfahan and Eastern Azerbaijan (with exception of Orumiyeh) – where churches are usually open to visitors – and Tehran, it can sometimes be difficult to get access to churches without prior arrangement.

BAHA'ISM Iran will always be connected with the Baha'i movement, which is estimated to have six million followers worldwide, but for many the term 'persecution' is too gentle a word to describe the situation in Iran. Officially there are no longer any Baha'is residing in the Islamic Republic of Iran, although it has been suggested that some 330,000 still live there in secret, operating a clandestine system of worship and education – famously, the Baha'is run an online university, with lectures either recorded or provided live by sympathetic scholars worldwide. The Baha'i faith affirms the ultimate unity of all the great religious leaders (Zoroaster, Jesus, Mohammed, the Judaic prophets, Siddhartha Gautama (the Buddha) and Krishna) as historic manifestations of The Word, saying 'the earth is but one country and humanity its citizens'.

Their story begins in the 1840s when a charismatic theologian, Sayyid Ali Mohammed Shirazi, won over many followers by his piety, saying that he was the gate (*bab*) opening the way for the imminent return of the Hidden (12th) imam. His later proclamation in 1848 that he himself was the imam led to his execution in Tabriz, after some 3,000 of his followers were killed. Further persecution followed after a Baha'i assassination attempt on a Qajar shah failed, and to escape the following pogrom many fled to Iraq and Syria and onward to South America, Turkey and Europe. The headquarters of Babaism, renamed as Baha'ism in the 1860s, was established in Acre and Haifa, present-day Israel, which to many Muslims smacked of strong Zionist involvement. In the mid 1950s the Baha'is Tehran offices were severely damaged and the Shah was implicated. Following the 1979 revolution, thousands of Baha'is were rounded up, arrested and executed, the *bab's* house in Shiraz was destroyed, Baha'i cemeteries were desecrated, and all endowments, properties and personal records were confiscated.

EDUCATION

Schooling for both boys and girls is compulsory from the age of seven years to 15, but only in nursery schools are both sexes taught in the same class. Literacy rates, so woefully low in the 1970s, have dramatically improved and a much greater part of the curriculum is now given over to Arabic/Quranic studies, with a few hours per week assigned to English teaching in most secondary schools. With a high youth population and few job opportunities there is a tremendous demand for university education, but many places remain reserved for children of Iran–Iraqi veterans ('Families of the Martyrs'), whatever their pass marks in the national examinations. The number of both state-run and private universities has mushroomed, although few teachers have had research or teaching opportunities outside Iran. Attempts to introduce segregated instruction at this level during the 1980s were not successful, but students sit according to gender. Many of the protestors demonstrating against the stealing of the 'Green Election' in 2009 were university students of both genders. A considerable number of Iranians believe that recent government efforts to curtail the number of women enrolling in higher education are an attempt to punish 'upstart girls', many of them from traditionally pious and conservative families, who were especially outraged by the hypocrisy shown by the government.

Iran leads the world in the field of theological studies at university level along with Saudi Arabia, with student numbers increasing over 500% since the 1970s. The main centres are Qom and Mashhad, where the basic seven-year course (ie: secondary level) includes Arabic grammar, rhetoric and literature, plus studies of the Quran, the Hadith (sayings of the Prophet Mohammed) and Islamic law. Students can then follow another eight years' study and qualify as a *mujtahid* (interpreter of theological law). The teaching method is by convention, instruction and rhetoric, rather than being discursive, hypothetical and analytical.

CULTURE

If there is something that Iranians have over the centuries remained true to, it is their deep-rooted refined culture and the idea of longing for past glory and poetry. According to one of Iran's greatest literary sons, Mohammed Ali Jamalzadeh, Iran in the 20th century lagged behind other countries in terms of literary works. This has not, however, quenched Iranians love of poetry. Mentioning Hafez (see pages 181–2) is a great conversation icebreaker in Iran. Be prepared to hear your driver recite a few verses and even talk about the meaning between the lines. Some have even suggested that Iranian culture is as hard to comprehend as to find the true meaning to any of the Persian poetry. This has also a lot to do with the language itself. While Arabic dominates Persian in religious matters, day-to-day interactions are clearly inspired by Persian, which is a softly spoken language. You are unlikely, for example, to hear people shout or speak loudly. Along the lines of French 'vous', Persian puts strong emphasis on formal vocabulary and, unless the person you are talking to is a child, you must always use polite 'shoma' form. Otherwise, you risk causing offence.

2

Practical Information

WHEN TO VISIT

Visits to the south coast of Iran (eg: Bandar-e Abbas) are best made in the winter months of December, January and February when humidity and heat levels are at their lowest, while spring (March to mid-May) and autumn (mid-September and October) are the best times to travel around central and northern Iran. The summer months of June through to early September are best avoided as the temperature can be in the high 40s (°C), although it is a dry heat except on the south coast.

Take the numerous public holidays (see pages 55–8) into account if your visit is connected with business and/or your time is limited. Try to avoid Ramadan, the first ten days of Moharram (the sacred month) and the first week of the Nou Rouz celebrations, when staffing in offices and government departments will be minimal and all forms of long-distance transport and hotels will be extremely busy. However, during the Nou Rouz and throughtout the high-season summer months, most historical sites and buildings have extended opening hours (until 20.00).

HIGHLIGHTS

- Masouleh and mountains of Gilan province (see pages 141–4)
- Shopping in Esfahan bazaar (see pages 127–8)
- The mountain path to Babak Castle (see page 160)
- Tehran's Milad Tower for exhilarating views (see page 79)
- The historic red mud village of Abyaneh (see pages 114–15)
- Spring flower blossom in Shirazi gardens (see page 183)
- The Gate of All Lands in ancient Persepolis (see page 197)
- The architecture of Kashan's old merchant houses (see pages 109–14)
- The Silk Road trail from Hamadan towards the Iraqi border (see pages 104–8)
- Sunset at one of the Zoroastrian 'towers of silence' in Yazd (see pages 236–7)

SUGGESTED ITINERARIES

The following itineraries presuppose all arrangements have been made in advance, or that a taxi or car will be used. If local bus transport is used, extra time will be needed to organise tickets, and journey times will be longer.

EIGHT TO TEN DAYS One day sightseeing in Tehran; flight to Shiraz for three nights including city sightseeing, a full day in and around Persepolis, and another day in Bishapur or Firuzabad; flight or drive to Esfahan for at least three or four nights there, with two full days city sightseeing; return to Tehran for museum visits.

TEN TO 15 DAYS

Option 1 As above, with the addition of two nights in Yazd and two nights in Kerman (or one in Kerman, the other exploring Mahan and surrounds), and if possible overnighting in Kashan. (However, see page 109.)

Option 2 Before visiting Esfahan and Shiraz, travel to Ardabil from Tehran, overnighting in Bandar-e Anzali (or conversely fly from Tehran to Tabriz); two nights in Tabriz for city sightseeing and a day trip to Maku (Black Church) and Jolfa; return south to stay in Qazvin or Zanjan; then to Hamadan for overnight or to Tehran for Esfahan; then Shiraz.

The shrines of Qom, south of Tehran, and of Mashhad in the northeast will be important visits for any Muslim and will certainly give a wealth of information to any other curious traveller. There are also splendid historic buildings in the vicinity of Mashhad, but these are not located in 'clusters' as in Esfahan and Shiraz. Iranians enjoy visiting the coast and forests of the southern Caspian shores, as well as shopping opportunities on certain Gulf islands (especially Kish and Qeshm).

TOURIST INFORMATION

Theoretically, but not always in practice, every major city in Iran has a tourist information office but these are rarely located centrally and are poorly signposted. Your hotel or any of the local guides mentioned in the book will happily provide you with any information you are looking for. Official road maps are available from well-stocked street kiosks, at airports, hotel bookshops or any bookstore. In different cities you can purchase local maps that identify the approximate locations of petrol stations and tourist inns as well as incorporating new roads. However, the best Iranian-made maps are produced by **Gita Shenassi**, widely distributed in Iran, and from **Stanfords** (*www.stanfords.co.uk*) where other maps more reliably written in English and Farsi with distances and highway numbers are also available.

The British **Foreign and Commonwealth Office** (FCO) issues travel advice (*www. gov.uk/foreign-travel-advice/iran*). Here you will find the latest general and specific area advice as well as information about consular assistance to British citizens in Iran.

TOUR OPERATORS

GENERAL If telephoning from outside Iran, omit the first 0 from the regional code. Despite new regional and city codes, there are no 'official' published telephone directories for Iran, not even for Tehran, and no equivalent of *Yellow Pages*.

UK

Magic Carpet 11 The Poplars, Ascot, Berks SL5 9HZ; \01344 622832; e sales@magiccarpettravel. co.uk; www.magic-carpet-travel.com. Escorted group tours & tailor-made itineraries. They will also deal with the visa procedure for independent travellers for about £120 (see pages 34–6).
Oasis Overland The Marsh, Henstridge, Somerset BA8 0TF; \01963 363400; www. oasisoverland.co.uk. Adventurous overland journeys through Central Asia. See advert on page 108.

Persian Voyages 12d Rothes Rd, Dorking, Surrey RH4 1JN; \01306 885894; e info@persianvoyages. com; www.persianvoyages.com. Offer a number of itineraries or tailor-made solutions; also assist with visa procurement. See advert on page 204.
Wild Frontiers Unit 6, Hurlingham Business Park, 55 Sulivan Rd, London SW6 3DU; \020 7736 3968; e info@wildfrontierstravel.com; www. wildfrontierstravel.com. Founded in 2002, offers a wide range of both group & tailor-made private tours across Iran & the Middle East. See advert on page 89.

Iran

Iran Persia Tour 63 Atlasi Bazaarche, Timsar Fallahi St, Yazd; 📞 0351 6205205; m 091 3351 4460; e info@iranpersiatour.com; www. iranpersiatour.com. Based in Yazd & run by very experienced Iranian guides, offers a variety of tours around Iran. See advert on inside back cover.

Pasargad Tours 146 Africa St, Tehran 19156; 📞 021 22058833/44/55; e info@pasargad-tours. com; www.pasargad-tours.com. All tours are accompanied by a national guide.

Thunder Tour & Travel 488 North Jamalzadeh, Dr Fatemi St, Tehran 14196; 📞 021 66936435, 66433677, 66433678; e info@thundertour.com; www.thundertour.com. Offers several itineraries including trekking & boating tours; can also arrange hotel/air/train reservation facilities as well as customise their package for individual travellers, & arrange the necessary 'letter of invitation' (see page 34) at a nominal cost of US$30. All tours are accompanied by a national guide if required.

SPECIAL INTEREST
UK

ACE Study Tours Babraham, Cambridge CB22 3AP; 📞 01223 835055; e ace@acestudytours.co.uk; www.acestudytours.co.uk. Offers 1 tour each year with a specialist lecturer/leader.

Martin Randall Travel Voysey Hse, Barley Mow Passage, London W4 4GF; 📞 020 8742 3355; e info@martinrandall.co.uk; www.martinrandall. com. Offer lecturer-led itineraries of the major sites.

The Traveller (formerly British Museum Traveller) 10 Bury Pl, London WCIA 2JL; 📞 020 7436 9343; e info@the-traveller.co.uk; www. the-traveller.co.uk. Offers 1 or 2 tours a year to Iran with specialist lecturer & tour manager.

USA

GeoEx, 1008 General Kennedy St, PO Box 29902, San Francisco, CA, 94129-0902; 📞 +1 415 922 0448; within the US +1 888 570 7108; e info@ geoex.com; www.geoex.com. Have been running tours to Iran since 1993 & currently offer cultural 'customisable' Essential Iran & Treasures of Persia tours.

World Affairs Council of Philadelphia (Educational organisation) One South Broad St, Suite 2M, Philadelphia, PA 19107; 📞 +1 215 561 4700; e info@wacphila.org; www.wacphila.org. WACP are scheduled to resume their tours to Iran in April 2014 following suspension of services in 2011.

Iran

Iran Mountain Zone PO Box 15875–3816, Tehran; 📞 021 88883704; e info@mountainzone. ir; www.mountainzone.ir. Runs field trips for the Mountaineering Federation in Tehran, & will organise hill walking & trekking for foreign visitors (min 4 people). The best time is in the spring for the wild flowers. The office can arrange bike rental for mountain biking. Men can wear shorts for this, either knee- or mid-thigh length, but for all trips (except skiing) women must wear full-length trousers (or skirt) & long-sleeved, knee-length shirt or tunic, with, of course, the obligatory scarf. Skiing can also be organised. The office will deal with the visa paperwork for the visit, & reserve any hotel accommodation in Tehran, etc. Certainly the managing director answers email enquiries promptly & Tehran friends recommend the office.

Kassa Tours 27 Naghdi Alley, Shariati St, Tehran 15637; 📞 021 7751 0463–4; e info@kassatours. com; www.kassatours.com.

TIME DIFFERENCE

Iran time is GMT + three hours 30 minutes (ie: 12 noon GMT is 15.30 in Iran). Since 2007, daylight saving has been in operation from late March to late September though this may change, given the post-1979 governments' on and off practice of observing it. One time zone operates throughout the country. To catch BBC or other Western news, tune in on the half-hour.

RED TAPE

Following the 29 November 2011 attack on the British Embassy in Tehran the embassy has closed and the Iranian Embassy in London has followed suit. British citizens or foreign nationals resident in the UK can apply for Iranian visas through the Iranian Embassy in Dublin and once in Iran the Swedish Embassy in Tehran has a British Interests Section, which can assist in the meantime.

VISAS All nationalities except Israelis are allowed to apply for a visa. Anyone domiciled in the USA should approach the **Iranian Interests Section of the Embassy of Pakistan** (*2209 Wisconsin Av, NW, Washington DC, 20007;* \ *+1 202 965 4990/91/92/93/94/99;* e *requests@daftar.org*) or the nearest Pakistani consulate or the **Iranian Mission at the United Nations** (*622 Third Av, 34th Floor, New York, NY 10017;* \ *+1 212 687 2020;* e *iran@un.int*). Those resident elsewhere, however, including US passport holders, should contact the Iranian embassy or consulate in their country of residence for information regarding embassy's opening times, methods of payment and exact visa application details. Although the procedure for British and US passport holders is complex, other nationalities, including those from Germany, the Netherlands, Scandinavia and Italy, have fewer problems in this respect. Women without headscarves will generally be allowed onto Iranian embassy grounds, however, it is advisable and strongly recommended that you do wear a headscarf as it makes a good impression.

If you are going on an **organised tour** you will be able to get a tourist visa by contacting a travel agent in Iran directly (see page 33), who will effectively issue an 'invitation' (or rather confirmation of your tour with them) into the country. You can alternatively contact your local tour operator and arrange the trip through them. Confirmation of your trip printed on official paper or a scanned copy from the agent in Iran would be sufficient for the embassy. You should then bring it with your passport to the local consulate, and fill out the application form; a visa is usually issued within a couple of days. Payment for the travel agent's service varies, but is usually around US$30–50, and it is made to the travel agent on arrival in Iran.

Despite the legalese **individual travellers** not in possession of any pre-booked trip should not encounter any problems applying for a tourist visa. They would only need to explain to the embassy staff their travel arrangements and whereabouts throughout their stay in Iran. This should normally be sufficient, unless requested otherwise. In this case you might have no other choice but to book through a travel agent. Please note that generally single travellers are more likely to arise suspicious and reasons for questioning. It is always best to go to the embassy in person and clarify your application should any additional information be required.

A number of travellers try to avoid the red tape by applying for the visa through the Iranian Embassy in Istanbul. However, do note that there is no guarantee here either. There was a case of a British traveller who had applied for a visa through the Iranian Embassy in Istanbul, where she was informed the embassy had reportedly lost her documents, whereby she was forced to prolong her stay in Turkey following submission of a new visa application. On a different occasion, a Dutch tourist travelled to Istanbul where she was directed to Erzerum 1,220km away. She was then correctly informed that the Iranian Embassy in Ankara (877km of backtracking) had sole issuing authorisation in Turkey; there she was told processing would take more than four weeks after the surrender of her passport. In brief, apply through the closest embassy or consulate first! British travellers are encouraged to apply through the Embassy of Iran in Dublin, well used to processing requests from British nationals.

For the actual visa application, a completed visa form with two photographs, the passport (valid for six months from date of departure, with at least two blank pages and fee (at the time of writing €40 for a tourist visa through the Iranian Embassy in Dublin) need to be sent in to your nearest Iranian consulate.

For **business travellers** wishing to stay in Iran for more than 72 hours, their Iranian business contact needs to prepare an invitation letter filling in correct forms available from the Visa and Passport Office of Foreign Ministry of Iran, after which the visa procedure outlined below will kick in. Only when the reference number has been received will the embassy staff accept the visa application form, photographs and passport. It sounds horrendously complicated but it isn't (unless you hit a cluster of national and religious holidays), though a few extra grey hairs are guaranteed. With other Iranian consulates, this system is not necessarily in operation. In Holland, for example, applicants may write to the consulate requesting a visa without an 'invitation', though apparently less than 50% of such unsupported applications are successful.

For stays of less than 72 hours, the Iranian business contact still has to apply to the ministry for approval and a reference number, but the traveller then picks up the relevant 72-hour visa on arrival at Imam Khomeini International Airport, Tehran. Remember to take a photocopy of the relevant visa notification for the airline check-in desk, to show that your entry has been approved.

Female applicants should wear a headscarf for their visa photographs. Visas are valid for one month's duration after entry. A request for a multiple-entry visa has to be submitted by the sponsor in the 'invitation', not by the applicant at the consulate and is currently only available in the business category.

For the duration of your stay in Iran, you remain the 'invited guest' of the person, company, or institution who/which initiated the procedure. In other words, that sponsor bears total responsibility for your well-being and good behaviour and will bear the brunt of any repercussion.

For a visa extension or amendment, go to the relevant local government office (in Tehran this is the Ministry of Foreign Affairs; outside Tehran go to the local police headquarters) with two photographs (with headscarf for women), a copy of your passport and the flight ticket. The fee of 300,000 rials (around US$10) is payable to the nearest Bank Melli branch. It usually takes three days to get the extension. However, in urgent cases and in smaller towns (i.e. Yazd) you should be able to get it in one day. In the Ministry of Foreign Affairs visa extension office all visitors must leave their cameras and mobile phones with security and women must wear a chador, available to rent from the same security desk. Be warned that any dealing with officialdom will take at least three times longer than you could imagine (see pages 55–8 and 65).

There is a **visa waiver system** (also applicable to US citizens travelling from the UAE) in operation for Kish Island (see pages 221–3) but it is valid only for Kish Island and lasts 14 days; while there, however, visitors can apply for a normal tourist visa to the rest of Iran.

Be warned: Westerners turning up at an Iranian border cannot expect to be issued with a visa (even a five-day transit) over the counter. Stories of successful individual travellers should be rigorously investigated, rather than accepted at face value.

There is a new requirement for travellers to Iran with an **Israeli stamp** in their passport. Applicants may now only be issued an Iranian visa a year after their visit to Israel and Palestine.

Note: Any woman, whatever her nationality, will be refused actual entry into Iran if her dress does not conform to acceptable standards (see pages 67–8). This 'suitable' dress and a headscarf must be donned before approaching the border or disembarking from a flight and retained until leaving Iran. If travelling by an IranAir international flight to Iran, women must check in wearing or showing a headscarf, which can then be removed until entering the boarding lounge; in other words, the IranAir flight is considered Iranian territory.

The above being said, there is hope that it will soon become easier to obtain visa to Iran. The newly elected President Rouhani has recently unveiled his ambition to have the number of visitors to Iran increase to 10 million from the current 4 million. He also seems to be set on improving his country's relationship with the United States.

EMBASSIES, CONSULATES, MISSIONS

There are no UK or US embassies in Iran. When in need of consular assistance in Iran, British citizens should contact the Swedish Embassy and US citizens should contact the Swiss Embassy.

❸ Embassy of Islamic Republic of Iran 415 Av de Tervuren, PO Box 34, B-1130 Bruxelles, Belgium; ☏ 02 7623745; e embassy.iran.bxl@skynet.be

❸ Embassy of Islamic Republic of Iran 4 Av d'Iena, Paris, France 75016; ☏ 01 40697900; e cabinet@amb-iran.fr

❸ Embassy of Islamic Republic of Iran Podbielskiallee 67, PO Box 10439, 14195 Berlin, Germany; ☏ 030 843530; e iran. botschaft@t-online.de. There are also consulates in Frankfurt & Hamburg.

❸ Embassy of Islamic Republic of Iran 72 Mount Merrion Av, Blackrock, Co Dublin, Ireland; ☏ 01 288 0252/2967/5881; e iranembassy@ indigo.ie

❸ Embassy of Islamic Republic of Iran Via Nomentana 361, 00162 Rome, Italy; ☏ 06 86328485

❸ Embassy of Sweden 27 Nastaran St, Boostan St, Tehran, Iran; ☏ 021 23712200; e ambassaden. teheran@foreign.ministry.se

❸ Embassy of Switzerland (Foreign interests section) 39 Shahid Mousavi (Golestan 5th), Pasdaran St, Tehran, Iran; ☏ 2254 2178; 2256 5273; e tie.vertretung@eda.admin.ch

❸ Consulate General of Islamic Republic of Iran Ankara Caddesi 1, Cagaloglu, Istanbul, Turkey; ☏ +90212 33 5138230; www.ircgi.org

❸ Iranian Mission to the United Nations 622 3rd Av, New York, NY 10017, USA; ☏ 212 687 2020

GETTING THERE AND AWAY

BY AIR The main international airport in Iran is currently **Imam Khomeini International Airport (IKA)**, Tehran, but foreigners with valid visas can also enter/exit Iran by way of various Gulf states airports (eg: Abu Dhabi and Bahrain to Shiraz, Bahrain to Mashhad, Dubai to Ahvaz and Bandar-e Abbas). Sometimes officials check your baggage receipt against the tag on your luggage. (For transport from Imam Khomeini International Airport into the centre and other parts of the country, see *Taxis*, pages 48–9.)

There are at present no direct flights from the UK or from/to any American or Canadian airports. British Airways and the international division of BMI, now part of the main British carrier, suspended their daily flights to Tehran in 2012 as a result of the political tensions between the two countries. KLM/Air France and Austrian Airlines suspended their regular flights to Tehran in April 2013 out of economic considerations. **Turkish Airlines** (*www.thy.com*), however, have on the contrary extended their services and now fly regularly via Istanbul to a number of cities in Iran, including Esfahan, Shiraz and Mashhad. Istanbul–Tehran flight duration is around three hours. All flight carrier options listed below, when booked in advance, should not cost more than £500 for an economy-class return fare.

A list of current international cities with services to and from Imam Khomeini International Airport is available on the English version of the airport's website (*www.ikia.ir*), which also contains useful plans showing routes through the airport, positions of banks and lists of available taxi services.

Pegasus Airlines (*www.flypgs.com*), the Turkish low-cost airline, fly to Tehran via Istanbul with connections from various European cities. Expect to pay around £100 for the flight, although prices are seasonal and depend on the city of origin. When it comes to Turkish carriers, getting a connection from Germany is perhaps the most economical option.

Aeroflot (*www.aeroflot.com*) seems to be the favourite route for travellers from Scandinavia. Be warned, however, that despite its 90th birthday in 2013 Aeroflot customer service is not always consistent. Aeroflot has two daily flights from London and its daily evening Moscow–Tehran flight takes only three hours. **Alitalia** (*www.alitalia.com*) should, in theory, have services to Iran as well, but if flying from Rome, it is best to fly **Azerbaijan Airlines** (*www.azal.az*) that offer one weekly flight to Tehran via Baku.

BY ROAD There are border-crossing points from Turkey (via Dogubayezit); from the Republic of Azerbaijan (via Baku/Astara); from Turkmenistan (via Ashkhabad or Sarakhs); and from Pakistan, though the last is not advisable at present. You can get only a five-day transit visa (not extendable) at the border; a tourist visa must be obtained in advance. For documentation required, see pages 34–5.

BY TRAIN Provided you can obtain a visa (see pages 34–5) there is a weekly train, the Trans-Asia Express, from Istanbul to Tehran (twice weekly in summer) leaving on a Wednesday and arriving on a Saturday; The Man in Seat Sixty One (*www.seat61.com/Iran.htm*) provides up-to-date information on timetables, booking, prices and train facilities.

BY SEA Iran can be accessed by sea from Dubai to Bandar-e Lengeh, from Kuwait to Khorramshahr and from Shahjah to Bandar-e Abbas. Ferries are operated by Valfajr Shipping (www.valfajr.ir) with normally two departures per week. Contact one of the company's offices to make a reservation.

HEALTH with Dr Felicity Nicholson

BEFORE YOU GO It is advisable to be up to date with all primary immunisations including **tetanus**, **diphtheria** and **polio** – an all-in-one vaccine (Revaxis) lasts for ten years. You would also be wise to be protected against **hepatitis** A and **typhoid**. Hepatitis A vaccine (eg: Havrix Monodose or Avaxim) comprises two injections given about a year apart. The course costs about £100, but may be available on the NHS; it protects for 25 years and can be administered even close to the time of departure.

Hepatitis B vaccination should be considered for longer trips (two months or more) or for those working with children or in situations where contact with blood is likely. Three injections are needed for the best protection and can be given over a three-week period if time is short for those aged 16 or over. Longer schedules give more sustained protection and are therefore preferred if time allows. Hepatitis A vaccine can also be given as a combination with hepatitis B as 'Twinrix', though two doses are needed at least seven days apart to be effective for the hepatitis A component, and three doses are needed for the hepatitis B.

The newer injectable typhoid vaccines (eg: Typhim Vi) last for three years and are about 85% effective. Oral capsules (Vivotif) may also be available for those aged six and over. Three capsules over five days lasts for approximately three years but may be less effective than the injectable forms as their efficacy depends on how well they are absorbed.

Vaccinations for **rabies** are advised for everyone, but are especially important for travellers visiting more remote areas, especially if you will be more than 24 hours away from medical help and definitely if you will be working with animals. For more information, see page 39.

Visit your doctor or a recognised travel clinic (see below) around eight weeks before you leave.

As on any trip a small medical kit is useful. Consider some or all of the following:

- A good drying antiseptic, eg: iodine or potassium permanganate (don't take antiseptic cream)
- A few small dressings (Band-Aids)
- Suncream
- Insect repellent; anti-malarial tablets; impregnated bed-net or permethirin spray
- Paracetamol or ibuprofen
- Antifungal cream (eg: Canestan)
- Ciprofloxacin or norfloxacin, for severe diarrhoea
- Tinidazole for giardia or amoebic dysentery (see page 39 for regime)
- Antiobiotic eye drops, for sore, 'gritty', stuck-together eyes (conjunctivitis)
- A pair of fine-pointed tweezers (to remove hairy caterpillar hairs, thorns, splinters, etc)
- Alcohol-based hand rub or bar of soap in plastic box
- Condoms or femidoms
- For more remote travellers consider taking a travel thermometer

Should you need any assistance when in Iran, do not hesitate to contact any local pharmacy. These are numerous and usually well stocked.

Travel clinics and health information A full list of current travel clinic websites worldwide is available from the **International Society of Travel Medicine** (*www. istm.org*). For other journey preparation information, consult the **National Travel Health Network and Centre** (*www.nathnac.org/ds/map_world.aspx*). Information about medications may be found on **eMedicine**'s website (*www.emedicine.com*).

IN IRAN In the major cities, it will be said that the water is safe for cleaning teeth as it is heavily chlorinated (neighbouring Tajikistan and Afghanistan suffer cholera outbreaks). However, it is always safer to use bottled water both for drinking and for cleaning your teeth.

Opportunities to strip off and sunbathe are obviously severely limited in the Islamic Republic, but the force of the Iranian sun is powerful and there is comparatively little shade so avoid excessive exertion during midday hours and wear a sunhat. Women should wear theirs over a scarf. Clothing in natural fibres is most comfortable for the hotter months but evening temperatures can drop suddenly, especially in the hills, so take a light sweater too.

Take the usual precautions when walking across rough and stony ground, and through shrubbery and vegetation, against snakes, scorpions, etc. If you are entering a ruined building from broad sunlight, make a noise so that any snakes retreat.

Malaria Malaria is found in areas north of the Zagros Mountains and also in the southeastern provinces of Sistan-Baluchestan, Hormozgan and Kerman. It is predominantly transmitted from March to November. Prophylaxis would usually be with chloroquine and paludrine but you should take advice as the tablets may not be suitable for you. To minimise the risk of nausea, try taking the tablets in the evening with food and wash down with plenty of fluids. It is imperative to complete the prescribed course unless you have been advised by someone suitably qualified to stop. Insect repellents and cover-up clothing can help ward off voracious mosquitoes. These should be used both day and night when mosquitoes are around. Products containing around 50–55% DEET are considered effective and are safe for use in pregnancy and on children. For those who prefer a more natural approach then repellents containing citronella and eucalyptus oil can be used instead but they must be applied every one to two hours. These are still not considered as effective as DEET-based repellents. Mosquito coils and the like can be purchased everywhere. Regarding other insects, avoid flea-pit hotels and very cheap local buses; saving a few dollars can result in great discomfort.

Rabies As in western Europe, there is a danger of rabies. Few dogs in Iran are kept as pets, so they are not domesticated in the same way as in Europe or North America. In particular, avoid sheepdogs as they are trained to see off unwelcome guests. Stand still and if necessary make as if you are throwing a stone in their direction, shouting angrily. If you intend to spend a long time travelling or are staying in rural areas, consider having a course of rabies shots before departure. Ideally three doses of vaccine should be given over four weeks, so careful planning before your trip is required. Rabies is passed on to humans through a bite, scratch or a lick of an open wound. You must always assume any animal is rabid, and seek medical help as soon as possible. Meanwhile scrub the wound with soap

TREATING TRAVELLERS' DIARRHOEA *Dr Jane Wilson-Howarth*

It is dehydration that makes you feel awful during a bout of diarrhoea and the most important part of treatment is drinking lots of clear fluids. Sachets of oral rehydration salts give the perfect biochemical mix to replace all that is pouring out of your bottom but other recipes taste nicer. Any dilute mixture of sugar and salt in water will do you good: try Coke or orange squash with a three-finger pinch of salt added to each glass (if you are salt-depleted you won't taste the salt). Otherwise make a solution of a four-finger scoop of sugar with a three-finger pinch of salt in a 500ml glass. Or add eight level teaspoons of sugar (18g) and one level teaspoon of salt (3g) to one litre (five cups) of safe water. A squeeze of lemon or orange juice improves the taste and adds potassium, which is also lost in diarrhoea. Drink two large glasses after every bowel action, and more if you are thirsty. These solutions are still absorbed well if you are vomiting, but you will need sip it rather than drink it down. If you are not eating you need to drink three litres a day plus whatever is pouring into the toilet. If you feel like eating, take a bland, high carbohydrate diet. Heavy greasy foods will probably give you cramps.

If the diarrhoea is bad, or you are passing blood or slime, or you have a fever, you will probably need antibiotics in addition to fluid replacement. A dose of norfloxacin or ciprofloxacin repeated twice a day until better may be appropriate (if you are planning to take an antibiotic with you, note that both norfloxacin and ciprofloxacin are available only on prescription in the UK). If the diarrhoea is greasy and bulky and is accompanied by sulphurous (eggy) burps, one likely cause is giardia. This is best treated with tinidazole (four x 500mg in one dose, repeated seven days later if symptoms persist).

under a running tap or while pouring water from a jug for a good 15 minutes. Then pour on a strong iodine or alcohol solution. This helps stop the rabies virus entering the body and will guard against wound infections, including tetanus. If you think you have been exposed to rabies then seek medical help as soon as possible to obtain the relevant post-exposure prophylaxis. Those who have not been immunised will need a blood product called Rabies Immunoglobulin (RIG) injected around the wound and four to five doses of rabies vaccine given over 28 days. RIG is expensive (around US$800) and is very hard to come by – another reason why pre-exposure vaccination should be encouraged as if you have had the full pre-exposure course you will not need the RIG and should only need two further doses of vaccine given three days apart following the exposure. And remember that, if you do contract rabies, mortality is 100% and death from rabies is probably one of the worst ways to go.

Ticks There are ticks in Iran and, in previous years (last recorded in 2009), there have been cases of a form of tick-borne encephalitis, which is a potentially fatal disease. It is wise when walking in forested areas, to cover up by wearing trousers tucked into socks and boots, and consider wearing a hat if there are overhanging branches. Always check for ticks at the end of any walk and follow the advice below.

Ideally ticks should be removed as soon as possible because leaving them on the body increases the chance of infection. They should be removed with special tick tweezers that can be bought in good travel shops. Failing that, you can use your finger nails: grasp the tick as close to your body as possible and pull steadily and firmly away at right angles to your skin. The tick will then come away complete, as long as you do not jerk or twist. If possible, douse the wound with alcohol (any spirit will do) or iodine. Irritants (eg: Olbas oil) or lit cigarettes should not be used since they can cause the ticks to regurgitate and therefore increase the risk of disease. It is best to get a companion to check you for ticks; if you are travelling with small children, remember to check their heads, and particularly behind the ears. Spreading redness around the bite and/or fever and/or aching joints after a tick bite imply that you have an infection that requires antibiotic treatment, so seek advice.

Travellers' diarrhoea Travelling in Iran carries a fairly high risk of getting a dose of travellers' diarrhoea; perhaps half of all visitors will suffer and the newer you are to exotic travel, the more likely you will be to suffer. By taking precautions against travellers' diarrhoea you will also avoid typhoid, paratyphoid, cholera, hepatitis, dysentery, worms, etc. Travellers' diarrhoea and the other faecal-oral diseases come from getting other peoples' faeces in your mouth. This most often happens from cooks not washing their hands after a trip to the toilet, but even if the restaurant cook does not understand basic hygiene you will be safe if your food has been properly cooked and arrives piping hot. The most important prevention strategy is to wash your hands before eating anything. The maxim to remind you what you can safely eat is:

PEEL IT, BOIL IT, COOK IT OR FORGET IT.

This means that fruit you have washed and peeled yourself, and hot foods, should be safe but raw foods, cold cooked foods, salads, fruit salads which have been prepared by others, ice cream and ice are all risky, and foods kept lukewarm in hotel buffets are often dangerous. That said, plenty of travellers and expatriates enjoy fruit and vegetables, so do keep a sense of perspective: food served in a fairly decent hotel in a large town or a place regularly frequented by expatriates is likely to be safe. If you are struck, see box (page 39) for treatment.

Medical facilities and pharmacies Every major hotel in the main Iranian cities has doctors or paramedics on call; otherwise, any business contact or friend, or your embassy, will recommend a doctor or dentist. Note that few dentists operate during the 28 days of Ramadan. The hospitals are good, as we (and great numbers of Azerbaijanis flocking to Iran for medical services) can attest, but somewhat basic by Western standards and few medical staff have had any opportunity to study in the West. The Iranian authorities give international 24-hour medical emergency services every assistance, but American citizens should be aware that the current US embargo could be problematic as payments cannot be made with credit card.

Even small towns have well-stocked pharmacies as Iranians vie with the Lebanese as the world's worst hypochondriacs. That said, take adequate supplies of any prescribed drug you need, or at least full details, so the best equivalent can be traced, because most Western brands are not available.

LONG-HAUL FLIGHTS, CLOTS AND DVT

Any prolonged immobility including travel by land or air can result in deep vein thrombosis (DVT) with the risk of embolus to the lungs. Certain factors can increase the risk and these include:

- Previous clot or close relative with a history
- People over 40 (increased risk over 80 years)
- Recent major operation or varicose veins surgery
- Cancer
- Heart disease
- Obesity
- Pregnancy
- Hormone therapy
- Heavy smokers
- Severe varicose veins
- People who are very tall (over 6ft/1.8m) or short (under 5ft/1.5m)

A deep vein thrombosis (DVT) causes painful swelling and redness of the calf or sometimes the thigh. It is only dangerous if a clot travels to the lungs (pulmonary embolus). Symptoms of a pulmonary embolus (PE) include chest pain, shortness of breath, and sometimes coughing up small amounts of blood and commonly start three to ten days after a long flight. Anyone who thinks that they might have a DVT needs to see a doctor immediately.

PREVENTION OF DVT
- Keep mobile before and during the flight; move around every couple of hours
- Drink plenty of fluids during the flight
- Avoid taking sleeping pills and excessive tea, coffee and alcohol
- Consider wearing flight socks or support stockings (see *www.legshealth.com*)

If you think you are at increased risk of a clot, ask your doctor if it is safe to travel.

SAFETY

CRIME Any crime carries severe penalties in the Islamic Republic. It is likely that the greatest danger you will face (other than crossing the road – see below) is having your wallet, purse or camera snatched. Keep photocopies of the most important pages (including the visa if possible) of your passport and air ticket, and spare passport photos separately, and don't flash money or expensive camera equipment ostentatiously. The British Foreign and Commonwealth Office has warned that bogus policemen have approached some visiting foreigners, advising that in such circumstances you should insist on seeing an identity card and inform the restaurant, shop or hotel of the incident. Remember that no Iranian policeman has the right to take or retain your passport unless you are in a police station (see opposite).

Iran is very safe for **women travellers**. Harassment is generally minimal, especially if you wear the *manteau*, as it is assumed you are Iranian and/or Muslim. Be aware, however, that it is very unusual for a single woman to walk unescorted in public at night. Make sure to avoid being alone in the evening in particular in the old town in Yazd, or Ahvaz and Khuzestan generally. If you do feel, however, that you are being harassed, you are strongly encouraged to bring this to the attention of other people present, in particular men (eg: a bus driver). Such behaviour is looked down upon by other members of the society. By expressing your indignation publicly you will be doing other female travellers, and yourself, a great favour. Keep in mind that harassment often happens simply because it is perceived as acceptable.

ROAD SAFETY You are more likely to be in danger if you insist on importing your car. There were 24,000 road deaths and over 80,000 injuries reported in Iran in 2006. During the first eight months of 2012 around 14,000 people lost their lives. The number of deaths, however, seems to be slowly decreasing from the peak of 27,759 deaths in 2005. Leaving aside the nightmare of Tehran traffic, which guarantees road rage and stomach ulcers, be aware that Iranian lorry and coach drivers work very long hours and that few private vehicles have reflectors or working lights and their drivers disregard every rule in the book. Traffic does not necessarily stop at a red light, nor wait until green before setting off, with the exception perhaps of Kish and Qeshm. Regard zebra crossings as merely road surface decorations. Pedestrians take their life into their own hands crossing the road and the sight of their terror-stricken faces forms the chief entertainment for motorists. If a driver flashes his/her lights it does *not* mean it is safe to cross; your presence is being acknowledged, but not necessarily your continued existence on this earth. On the other hand, having started to cross, do not turn tail or break into a run; both actions constitute a personal challenge to the driver to continue the pursuit.

PERSONAL CONDUCT Be aware that it is easy to break an important social convention without realising it and this can affect your safety (see pages 48 and 65–8). For instance, in summer 2004, the smoking of 'hubble-bubble' waterpipes (*qalian*) in public was banned on the grounds that it promoted 'licentious behaviour'. Presently men can smoke in public, but it may be more difficult for women, as most traditional tea houses would not serve *qalian* to women or mixed groups.

If you are confronted with officialdom, do not lose your temper, shout or threaten. Be polite and apologetic if not abject. Women: forget all feminist scruples and cry. Always insist on seeing someone who speaks English (any other Western language will be difficult).

POLICE Various police forces in Iran operate under a central control. The traffic or road police wear white caps and have white cars with a blue stripe while the security police have bright green uniforms with a dark green cap, and white cars with a dark green stripe; some security police wear 'combat fatigues'. The rank is shown by the stars or pips on the shoulder (officers) and by stripes on the sleeve (non-commissioned officers). At present, because there are so few tourists in Iran, the scheme of tourist police is largely in abeyance except in Esfahan.

The emergency telephone number is 110.

NOTES FOR DISABLED TRAVELLERS   *Lieke Scheewe*

Planning an accessible trip to Iran may be challenging, as the required information is not easy to come by. Nevertheless, the ancient beauty of this unique country can very well be enjoyed by anyone, with or without disability. Since the establishment of the Ministry of Social Welfare in the 1970s, public services for people with disabilities have improved, and many disability organisations are active to achieve general inclusion.

PLANNING AND BOOKING There are, to my knowledge, no travel agencies that run specialised trips to Iran for travellers with disabilities. Yet, many travel agencies will listen to your needs and try to create a suitable itinerary. However, the easiest way may be to find local operators through the internet and plan your trip directly with them, as they will also be available for you after arrival.

GETTING THERE At the international airports in Tehran you can expect good assistance and a narrow aisle chair to help you embark and disembark. Lifts and parking lots for the disabled are also common.

VISITING PLACES Tehran is a modern city with many parks and museums where you will find relatively few obstacles to getting around with a wheelchair. To visit the ancient archaeological sites you will often find stairs and rough terrain, but also friendly Iranians to give you a hand.

ACCOMMODATION Finding accessible accommodation is not easy. In general, only top of the range hotels will be largely 'obstacle-free', for example Qapu Hotel Esfahan (*Chahar Bagh St, Esfahan 81346;* +(98) 311222 7979), though I do not know yet of any hotel with grab-handles, roll-under sinks and a roll-in shower.

TRAVEL INSURANCE Most insurance companies will cater for disabled travellers, but it is essential that they are made aware of your disability. Examples of specialised companies that cover pre-existing medical conditions are Free Spirit (0845 230 5000; *www.freespirittravelinsurance.com*) and Age Concern (0845 601 2234; *www.ageconcern.org.uk*), who have no upper age limit.

FURTHER INFORMATION For further information on planning and booking an accessible holiday visit www.able-travel.com, which provides many tips and links to travel resources worldwide. One of these links is www.globalaccessnews.com, where an interesting travel story can be found in the 'Travel Archives' of a couple who travelled through Iran with a wheelchair.

GAY AND LESBIAN TRAVELLERS Homosexuality is forbidden, illegal and carries harsh penalties in Iran.

WHAT TO TAKE

As the authorities and some locals identify backpacks with amoral behaviour, drug taking and the like, it is advisable to use a **case** or **bag** to avoid misunderstanding.

PHOTOGRAPHIC TIPS · *Ariadne Van Zandbergen*

EQUIPMENT Although with some thought and an eye for composition you can take reasonable photos with a 'point-and-shoot' camera, you need an SLR camera if you are at all serious about photography. Modern SLRs tend to be very clever, with automatic programmes for almost every possible situation, but remember that these programmes are limited in the sense that the camera cannot think, but only makes calculations. Every starting amateur photographer should read a photographic manual for beginners and get to grips with such basics as the relationship between aperture and shutter speed.

Digital SLRs come in different formats, which refer to the size of the sensor. The format of the future is the full-size sensor, but at present all full-size sensor cameras are in the higher price bracket. Different lenses are designed to accommodate the camera sensor sizes.

Always buy the best lens you can afford. The lens determines the quality of your photo more than the camera body. Fixed fast lenses are ideal, but very costly. A zoom lens makes it easier to change composition without changing lenses the whole time. If you carry only one lens with a full-size sensor camera, a 28–70mm or similar zoom should be ideal. This corresponds to a 17–55mm or similar for a camera with a smaller sensor. For a second lens, a lightweight telephoto zoom will be excellent for candid shots and varying your composition. Wildlife photography will be very frustrating if you don't have at least a 300mm lens. For a small loss of quality, tele-converters are a cheap and compact way to increase your focal length: a 300mm lens with a 1.4x converter becomes 420mm, and with a 2x it becomes 600mm. Note, however, that 1.4x and 2x tele-converters reduce the speed of your lens.

For wildlife photography from a vehicle, a solid beanbag, which you can make yourself very cheaply, will be necessary to avoid blurred images, and is more useful than a tripod. A clamp with a tripod head screwed on to it can be attached to the vehicle as well. Modern dedicated flash units are easy to use; aside from the obvious need to flash when you photograph at night, you can improve a lot of photos in difficult 'high contrast' or very dull light with some fill-in flash. It pays to have a proper flash unit as opposed to a built-in camera flash.

The resolution of digital cameras is improving the whole time and even the most basic digital SLRs are more than adequate for ordinary prints and enlargements. For professional reproduction, cameras with a resolution up to 24 megapixels are available.

Memory space is important. The number of pictures you can fit on a memory card depends on the quality you choose. Calculate in advance how many pictures you can fit on a card and either take enough cards to last for your trip, or take a storage drive on to which you can download the content. A laptop gives the advantage that you can see your pictures properly at the end of each day and edit and delete rejects, but a storage device is lighter and less bulky.

Luggage has to be securely locked for intercity bus trips and internal flights, and padlocks are readily available. A **torch** is useful for exploring ruined buildings, etc, and because street lighting is erratic. The water is heavily chlorinated and very hard; a **moisturising cream** may sound effeminate but is a godsend, as is **lip salve**. As Muslim law stipulates washing under running water, bath and basin **plugs** are not usually provided. For the same reason, **toilet paper** is usually found only in the better hotels and restaurants (to be deposited in waste-paper bins, as Iranian

Bear in mind that digital camera batteries, computers and other storage devices need charging, so make sure you have all the chargers, cables and converters with you. Most hotels have charging points, but do enquire about this in advance.

DUST AND HEAT Dust and heat are often a problem. Keep your equipment in a sealed bag and avoid excessive exposure to the sun. Digital cameras are prone to collecting dust particles on the sensor which results in spots on the image. The dirt mostly enters the camera when changing lenses, so be careful when doing this. To some extent photos can be 'cleaned' up afterwards in Photoshop, but this is time-consuming. You can have your camera sensor professionally cleaned, or you can do this yourself with special brushes and swabs made for the purpose, but note that touching the sensor might cause damage and should only be done with the greatest care.

LIGHT The most striking outdoor photographs are often taken during the hour or two of 'golden light', after dawn and before sunset. Shooting in low light may enforce the use of very low shutter speeds, in which case a tripod might be required to avoid camera shake. Some top digital SLR's now give good results with minimal grain when shooting at very high ISO settings which makes low light photography a lot easier and reduces the need of a tripod in many situations.

With careful handling, side lighting and back lighting can produce stunning effects, especially in soft light and at sunrise or sunset. Generally, however, it is best to shoot with the sun behind you. When photographing animals or people in the harsh midday sun, images taken in light but even shade are likely to be more effective than those taken in direct sunlight or patchy shade, since the latter conditions create too much contrast.

PROTOCOL In some countries, it is unacceptable to photograph local people without permission, and many people will refuse to pose or will ask for a donation. In such circumstances, don't try to sneak photographs as you might get yourself into trouble. Even the most willing subject will often pose stiffly when a camera is pointed at them; relax them by making a joke, and take a few shots in quick succession to improve the odds of capturing a natural pose.

Note that cameras are not welcome in official buildings, such as military or police. Avoid taking pictures at gatherings or demonstrations. In shrines you will have to leave your camera equipment before being allowed in. Camera phones are, however, permitted.

Ariadne Van Zandbergen is a professional travel and wildlife photographer specialising in Africa. She runs The Africa Image Library. For photo requests, visit www. africaimagelibrary.com or contact her by email at e info@africaimagelibrary.com.

soil pipes have small diameters); you may not fancy using the toilet's cold-water douche. Feminine **sanitary products** are expensive and difficult to obtain outside urban centres. Take an electrical **plug adaptor**; the voltage is usually 220 and the plug is the two-pin rounded variety as found in France (though at least one Tehran hotel has been refurbished with three-pin square British style plugs). **Camera** batteries and extra memory for digital cameras are easy to find in big cities such as Tehran and Esfahan but slide (diapositive) films and some lithium batteries for 'conventional' cameras are difficult to obtain. Don't forget **sunglasses** and extra supplies of **prescribed medication** (see page 41).

Where possible, in *Part Two* of this guide we have given Quranic references for building inscriptions (we like knowing what the calligraphy says), so if you share this interest pack a paperback translation of the **Quran**, with chapter/verse notation.

As you will meet friendliness and kindness throughout Iran, why not take some local **postcards** from home to give as small mementos? They give pleasure to adults and children alike.

Finally, with regards to **clothes**, it really depends on the season and the area in Iran you are travelling to. For Eastern Azerbaijan or Tehran in winter you will need warm clothes suitable for continental European winters and preferably waterproofs if you decide to go hiking. Also, bring a warm hat and a pair of gloves. For the Persian Gulf region and Khuzestan, lighter, preferably linen, clothes and a pair of flip-flops will be sufficient all year round. Central areas, such as Esfahan and Shiraz, are hot in summer and cool in winter, and spring is easily the best season to travel here. Generally speaking, it is important to bring with you good ventilator **hiking shoes**, one jumper and a light jacket for travelling on the bus or sleeping in the desert. It gets a little more complicated for female travellers who must ensure that whatever clothes they wear, the lower part of their torso is covered at all times. Please see pages 67–8 for advice on more specific **dress codes**.

EXPORT AND IMPORT RESTRICTIONS

The export of **gold** over 150g in weight, antiques (interpreted as items over 50 years old) and certain electrical goods is technically forbidden. Some export restrictions remain on **carpets and rugs**, largely relating to the place of production, size (totalling a maximum of 12m²) and value. If you are with a travel company, the Iranian guide will advise; otherwise it is best to have a friend or colleague accompany you to the airport so that, if the customs officials object, you can hand the offending article to your friend and try another time. The duty-free section on departure from Tehran's Imam Khomeini International Airport sells such items as art or history books published in Iran, CDs, Iranian caviar and American cigarettes; all purchases are priced in US dollars and rials.

Concerning imports into Iran, the usual restrictions on narcotics, weapons and pornographic material such as videos, DVDs, tapes and books, etc apply, but the customs officer's definition of pornography may include material at the level of Louisa May Allcott's *Little Women* if you prove irritating. Even *Elle, Vogue* and *FHM* can be offensive; leave any lurid dust jackets at home. No **alcohol** may be imported into the Islamic Republic of Iran, even for private use; if supplies are found in your baggage you, your companions and your sponsor will suffer. Do note that all luggage is scanned at the baggage reclaim section before you exit to the arrivals hall.

If importing your **car** temporarily, you will need a current international driving licence, a *carnet de passage*, car registration, third party insurance (valid for Iran), a nationality badge, a red warning triangle and spare parts. Iranian customs officials will not believe any story of theft or vehicle write-off unless you have proof. They will assume you have sold it and fine you accordingly.

Currently it is forbidden to import and/or export Iranian rials (IRR).

MONEY

Notes are printed in denominations of 50,000, 20,000, 10,000, 5,000, 2,000, 1,000, 500, 200 and 100, and coins 500, 250, 100 and 50. You may sometimes get sweets or chewing gums in return if shops do not have the exact change. Although the rial is the stated currency, Iranians frequently refer to *tuman* (ie: 10,000 rials) thus something priced as 100,000 rials is generally spoken of as costing 10 *tumans*, so do clarify before agreeing to purchase. For small purchases such as fruit, nuts and so on a basic recognition of Farsi numeral symbols is useful (page 272).

WHAT TO CARRY Short-stay visitors will find it much easier to take quantities of US dollars, pounds or euros in **cash**, in large and small denominations. Memories of the large-scale forgery of dollar bills in ex-Soviet territories in the early 1990s still linger, so new, post-1996 bills are essential. **Travellers' cheques** (but not those of American banks) can in theory be exchanged but cannot be used for any direct payments and are thus best avoided. If you can change them, a commission of 4% will be levied. **Credit cards**, like travellers' cheques, are of little use though some, such as MasterCard and Visa (but excluding American Express because of the US embargo) may be used for purchasing carpets, but billing may be processed through Dubai, Switzerland or Germany at an extra charge. There are no ATM machines available for transactions involving foreign bank accounts. Credit cards are not accepted for payment in hotels; payment is in rials only.

CHANGING MONEY There are two foreign currency exchange rates: the official and the 'free market' one, and the former, quoted in banks and press (including local English language newspapers), is about one-third of the free market value. It drops considerably during Nou Rouz holiday season when Iranians plunge into excessive spending. You can exchange money in any street kiosk or any of the

SOME PRICES OF INTEREST

Single local bus ride without changing	2,000 rials
Single metro ticket	3,500 rials
'Bavaria' beer (non-alcoholic, of course)	35,000 rials
4 AA batteries	12,000 rials
Fuji film ASA100	60,000 rials
8GB camera card	600,000 rials
CD (original, not pirated)	30,000–50,000 rials
Cinema ticket	25,000–35,000 rials
'Pizza' Iranian style	70,000–90,000 rials
Double hamburger	70,000 rials
Carton of Winston cigarettes	70,000 rials
Cup of 'Nescafé' (instant coffee)	30,000 (more in five-star hotels)
A litre of petrol (car)	4,000 rials for rationed petrol
	7,000 rials for free market petrol

numerous jewellery stores; Iranians save their money buying large quantities of gold and coins. 'Free market' exchange kiosks are available on main streets of major cities. If you are short on cash, gold shops can equally exchange foreign currency at the same 'free market' rate valid across the country. Please note that the only 'free market' exchange kiosk in Tehran's Imam Khomeini International Airport is on the first floor at the departures area. Do not attempt to exchange foreign currency with illegal street traders. If you are caught, you will be arrested. Flights and accommodation purchased through an Iranian travel agent must be paid in rials.

Money transfers from abroad to an Iranian bank cannot be arranged at present.

BUDGETING

The following is a rough approximation of a daily budget for a single independent traveller – who has not prepaid for any domestic travel and hotel/meal arrangements – intending to visit one important and one minor tourist site each day. Note that stays, meals and visits in tourist centres such as Tehran, Esfahan and Shiraz will be more expensive than in other less-visited towns.

In March 2013 the Iranian government reintroduced a double pricing system, whereby foreign tourists pay higher admission rates to museums and historic sites. The average ticket price at present stands at 100,000–150,000 rials. However, some smaller museums (eg: the Water Museum in Yazd) charge a fraction of that.

Hotel overnight	US$20
Three meals, including tax	US$15
Transport (eg: intercity bus or half-day taxi)	US$20
Site/museum charges	US$7
Other (eg: soft drinks, laundry, photocopy)	US$3
Total	**US$65**

GETTING AROUND

On all forms of public transport that are not pre-segregated already, and excluding planes, men will probably be asked to change their seats to avoid sitting next to female strangers.

When travelling around, a copy of the Iranian solar calendar might come in handy and save a lot of time when planning your travel. See pages 56–8. Note that costs given are approximate.

CITY TRANSPORT Tickets (2,000 rials for a single direct journey) for **public buses** are purchased before boarding, at kiosks and/or shops nearby. All tickets should be given to the driver. This is easier for men, who get on at the front, than women who have to give their ticket to the driver after the journey. Women must leave through the back door and then come up to the front and pay the fare. On some occasions, however, when the bus is not full and there is no barrier separation, it is acceptable to come up to the driver through the bus without having to get off. If travelling with a companion of the opposite sex, agree beforehand on a meeting place as you may well get separated in the crush. An electric **trolley bus** service operates at the same fare as the bus. *Taxi khatteh*, the equivalent of the Turkish *dolmus* (shared taxi or minibus), operate on agreed routes within towns, and also in the outskirts; you pay the assistant. A short, shared taxi ride along Vali Asr Street, for example, costs around 10,000 rials.

Please note that unlike Europe, intercity bus and train stations are located on the outskirts of the city and will always require a taxi to town. Keep an eye on your wallet/purse on buses and trains. Pickpocketing is a regular occurrence.

Tehran metro (*www.tehranmetro.com*) has five different lines, each colour coded and two more are under construction. Parts of the system run above ground and parts underground; the system has its own website with up-to-date information in English. The cost of a single metro ticket in Tehran is 3,500 rials but there are also cheaper options such as a return trip, blocks of tickets for ten journeys and various types of season ticket for three or seven days or one month. Metro station maps and displays within carriages are in both English and Farsi. See page 286 for an English-language version of the Tehran metro map.

Private taxis are hailed from the roadside, and it's best to use the locally registered ones with a taxi sign. As the driver swerves towards you, yell out your destination; if he brakes, he's willing to go that way. Before the journey, ask colleagues or hotel staff the approximate cost of the journey and get written or verbal directions, unless the ride is to a notable landmark; taxi drivers do not undergo the same rigorous tests as, say, London cabbies. Outside Tehran consider hiring a taxi for a day or half-day, especially in Ahvaz, Esfahan, Mashhad or Shiraz, as it is the cheapest and most convenient form of transport offering freedom of routes and stops. You would need to go *darbaz* if you are the sole passenger and your route is curvy; **shared taxis** are called *savari* and these drive in a straight line across the city. Bus companies also regularly use *savari* taxis for distances up to 200km (eg: Tehran–Qazvin) whereby a front seat usually costs up to 20–30% more.

A private taxi from Imam Khomeini International Airport into the centre costs approximately 400,000 rials (US$12) and there are no 'shared' taxis from the airport. *Never* accept lifts in 'unofficial' taxis. The metro is being extended towards the new airport but currently only reaches Khomeini's tomb at Behesht-e Zahra. From the airport you can also order a taxi to other parts of the country. A taxi to Esfahan, for example, 421km away, costs around 2,000,000 rials (US$56).

INTERCITY ROAD TRANSPORT There are usually two types of **bus** service: VIP and *mamouli*. The price difference is negligible but the level of comfort isn't, so treat yourself. If VIP is not available it is acceptable to pay for two seats for some leg room. The VIP bus service includes small snack packs, tea and fresh water. The 895km drive from Shiraz to Tehran by 'deluxe' Volvo costs up to 400,000 rials (US$12). Seats are numbered and assigned according to gender or family groups. Tickets can be purchased up to a week in advance or on the same day from the bus station or bus company's city office, with three or four departures an hour on the busiest routes, although there are no timetables in circulation. During Ramadan and Nou Rouz, reservations must be made well in advance.

The **bus terminal** (with toilets located near the *namaz khaneh* or prayer room – where you are welcome to rest in case of a long wait) is generally located on the outskirts of town but large cities have more than one, so check which terminal your bus leaves from. Short stops are made every five or six hours (ensure you know the departure time) but it's best to take some food/drink with you. In case of an overnight journey with a departure time after 17.00, buses stop at a local restaurant for dinner at around 21.00. As in pre-revolutionary times, all public vehicles have to register at the police control points entering and leaving city limits, so carry your passport in your hand luggage in case it is required. The only time, however, when your passport might be inspected is in Kerman province due to rigorous anti-drug smuggling checks. All items going into the baggage holds should be padlocked.

When travelling to distant places around and in between relatively close towns (eg: Hamadan and Kermanshah), there are usually **minibuses** (often called minibus *mahalli*, meaning local), but such journeys take longer.

BY RAIL There are four main (overnight) services: Tehran–Mashhad, Tehran–Tabriz, Tehran–Esfahan–Kerman and Esfahan–Yazd–Tehran–Mashhad. As with intercity buses the price difference between first and second class is minimal but the standard of comfort is significant. Train tickets are usually sold out well in advance.

A single ticket from Tehran to Mashhad costs around 400,000 rials (US$12) (including a light snack) and Tehran to Tabriz costs around 300,000 rials. A train ticket from Esfahan to Mashhad is 500,000 rials (US$15). The service isn't fast and the timings of arrival/departure are often inconvenient. Tickets are sold at travel agencies with day tickets only available from the mainline station. The **Iran Rail** website (*www.raja.ir*) also has an English version accessed by clicking on the house image and then the word English top right; it displays timetables and prices.

BY AIR Internal air travel is reasonably priced and, as well as **IranAir**, there are private airlines available on some routes. IranAir does, however, allow a 50% discount on one internal flight if your international flight was with them. A one-way ticket from Shiraz to Tehran costs approximately US$41, and from Yazd to Tehran US$33 (see pages 36–7). Apart from the Iranian flag carrier, **Iran Aseman Airlines** and **Kish Air** both operate a number of services across the country and even internationally. You can, in theory, book tickets for Aseman online, but it is best to do so through a local travel agent.

To purchase a domestic flight ticket in Iran, you will need to book in advance, take your passport and pay in rials. Organising this takes time and patience so, unless you have time to waste, consider booking in advance (eg: through Magic Carpet Travel, page 32) or using an agent such as Thunder Tour (see page 33). The agent will keep the booking active and will also confirm and reconfirm your ticket at the local IranAir office.

Allow plenty of time to get to the airport (particularly in Tehran where traffic is frequently gridlocked) and to check in. On entry to any airport terminal building there is a security check: men with all their baggage go through one door, and 'sisters' with theirs through another. At the check-in desk abandon any idea of polite queuing; block all-comers and use elbows forcibly. You may be required to show your passport on passing to the next security check – again arranged according to gender – leading to the departure lounge.

An airport porter will expect at least 5,000 rials per case to/from the baggage hall and car or taxi, and more if he is required to 'negotiate' with the authorities on your behalf.

Some of the aircraft used on domestic **IranAir** (*www.iranair.co.uk*) flights are nearing the end of their serviceable life, especially those purchased from ex-Soviet republics whose service history cannot be guaranteed. The last major crashes were in July 2009; both involved Russian-made planes and the first killed 168, the second 17. Think twice about using any non-Boeing, non-McDonnell Douglas, non-Fokker or non-Airbus plane for internal flights. The state seems to be, however, monitoring the conditions of the internal airlines air fleet. In April 2013 Iranian Saha Air was forced to stop its operations. It was the last airline in the world using Boeing 707 planes more than 36 years old. Note that no alcohol is permitted on board flights, and that women should dress suitably (see pages 67–8).

BY PRIVATE CAR It is now possible to rent a car in Iran. **Europcar** (✆ *021 88366614; www.europcar.ir*) have offices in Tehran (IKA Airport), Esfahan, Yazd, Shiraz, Mashhad and Kish and payment can be made with Visa or MasterCard. They can also arrange car rental in Dubai at a lower rate than in the United Arab Emirates (UAE), in case you are continuing your journey to the Persian Gulf (which is not unlikely, as a number of foreign tourists fly to Iran via Dubai). A car can be rented for a minimum of 24 hours at a daily maximum of 250km; an extra per-kilometre charge applies for distances above this limit. Daily car rental costs are approximately €32/US$42 and there is also an additional charge for a car drop-off in a different city. Alternatively a **private taxi** can be hired for a day or longer (see page 121) through a hotel or directly from the taxi driver.

The cost of rationed petrol is 4,000 rials with an allowance of 100–120 litres per car per month depending on the season. Free market petrol sells for 7,000 rials a litre. Even with experience of other chaotic cities, we would not choose to drive in Iranian cities, especially Tehran. Iranians have a habit of driving in between two lanes. That said, the roads are well engineered with very few pot-holes, except perhaps in Gilan and Mazandaran, and with good road signs (in both Farsi and the Roman alphabets). Petrol stations, however, might be hard to find in more faraway regions of the country. Motor spares, especially for foreign-made cars, are difficult to find (the US embargo again) even in the main urban centres. Petrol station toilets are usually poor; more preferable are *namaz khaneh* (roadside prayer room) washrooms.

It is compulsory to wear seat belts, although many drivers and front-seat passengers don't. Speed limits are in operation, at least in theory: up to 120km/h (but mostly 110km/h) on motorways, and 85km/h at night; country road 85km/h day and 75km/h night. Some roads have speed cameras in operation. Motorcycle riders are expected to wear helmets. Most motorways in Iran are toll roads and you will be required to pay between 2,000 to 15,000 rials depending on the road. Several towns operate commercial vehicle and/or bus drive zones, and police seem to operate on a fine-incentive system. Driving at night is extremely hazardous (see page 42). If you break down, display the obligatory red warning triangle some distance behind the car, and ask passing vehicles to summon police, garage assistance or both.

As the driver, do not even think of leaving the scene of any accident before police agree to your departing. Any incident involving a person will probably mean imprisonment until the matter is investigated, especially if it resulted in a fatality; considerable financial compensation will have to be deposited for possible payment to the victim's family *before* any release can be contemplated. If your car is badly damaged, obtain an official report (especially necessary for the frontier customs if you have imported it; see pages 46–7).

The emergency police number is 110. Traffic police have white caps, and their cars are white with a dark blue stripe.

One small note regarding street names: since the revolution many street names have been changed predominantly in honour of *shahid* (martyrs who died in the Iran–Iraq war) and religious figures. Keep an eye and ear open, as what you hear might not be on the map: the pre- and post-revolution names may be used interchangeably (eg: most Tehranis will direct you to Adan Street, which is in fact called (Shahid) Azodi Street).

ACCOMMODATION

There are various types of accommodation across the country and major Iranian cities are awash with hotels. Iranians themselves travel a great deal within Iran and traditional Tourist Inns offer very reasonably priced and suitable rooms.

Remember that since no travellers' cheques, foreign currency or credit cards are accepted for payment of bills (eg: rooms, meals) by hotels or restaurants, individual travellers making their own arrangements must have enough Iranian currency.

Hotel rates in Iran are seasonal and prices vary significantly:

Low Season	High Season (up to 50% extra)
January	Second half of March
February	April
First 15 days of March	May
June	First 15 days in August
July	Second half of September
End of August	
First 15 days in September	
November	
December	

There is a 6% (increased from 5% in April 2013) tax on all accommodation bills, but this is often included in the price quoted initially. Refer to sections in this book on individual towns for recommended hotels but note that the prices relate to spring 2013, and all include breakfast, unless mentioned otherwise. Foreign nationals are allowed to share the same room irrespective of their marriage status.

The *mosafirkhanehs* (literally 'traveller's place') catering for Iranian nationals are sometimes willing to take foreign budget travellers but may refuse them, especially independent women travellers, knowing that local police will object. If *mosafirkhanehs* are what you're after, ask a taxi driver to take you to the nearest place – expect to pay up to US$10 per night and be aware that toilets are more likely to be of the squat variety and unlikely to be en suite. Check the room and think whether saving a few dollars is really worth it (though you could always have a scrub-down next day in the local *hamam* or bathhouse; a real cultural experience – see box on page 239). Good value and generally much cleaner are the official **Tourist Inns** (hotel *jahangardi*), which offer basic but adequate accommodation, usually with private facilities.

Then there are **hotels**. Most 'two-star' (very basic) hotels will have rooms with private (mainly squat style) facilities. Prices are fixed according to demand rather than a regulated system linked with an internationally recognised hotel 'star' rating.

In the rooms there will be a symbol (an arrow, a picture of the Ka'ba in Mecca, etc) indicating the *qibla* direction for prayer, a prayer mat, a *mohr*, small clay tablet for Shi'a prayer prostrations and a Quran; no Gideon's Bibles here. Until recently, some bathrooms in a certain Esfahani five-star hotel bore evidence of a theological directive requiring toilet pedestals to be relocated to avoid the occupant facing towards or against the *qibla* direction during usage. If plastic mules or sandals are provided in the room, these should be used for the bathroom and left by its door.

HOTEL PRICE CODES

Prices indicate the cost of a double room per night.

$$$$	US$70+ (2,450,000 rials+)
$$$	US$50–70 (1,400,000 rials–2,450,000 rials)
$$	US$20–50 (700,000–1,400,000 rials)
$	US$10–20 (350,000–700,000 rials)

No youth hostels affiliated to Hostelling International are available in Iran, and camping or staying in a stationary vehicle overnight will arouse great suspicion. If you are caught without accommodation in a rural area, ask for help from local police, who will assist (either by putting you up in a family home or in police grounds). There are backpacker hostel-type **dormitories** or **guesthouses** (*mehman pazir*) available in some cities. These are generally very basic, but clean and centrally located. It is possible to stay overnight in the desert, but this is better arranged through a local guide, who can leave you alone there if you wish. Contact Mohammed Jalali for details (see page 117).

Not all hotels offer single rooms, but single travellers can expect to get a 20% discount for a double-bed room (eg: Ehsan Historical Guesthouse offers a 200,000 rials discount). While most hotels advertise their rates in rials, in 2013 some hotels started switching to double pricing (ie: US$ for foreign tourists; rials for Iranians).

EATING AND DRINKING

If accepting an invitation to visit a family home, it is usual to take a small present (see page 66).

In local restaurants and cafés, the portions are quite large and it is acceptable in more upmarket restaurants to ask for a doggy bag. All you need to say in this case is *meesheh yek zarf bedaheed ke gazaa ra meekham bebaram* ('Could you please bring me a bag to take food home?'). Restaurants in larger hotels serve Western dishes. All the meat served is halal (slaughtered according to Muslim law; ie: without pre-stunning); pork products are not available except to Armenian Christian families resident in Esfahan (check Ararat supermarket for some imports from Armenia), so all sausages, salami and mortedella are made from beef or lamb. Forks and spoons, but not knives, form the usual table cutlery and, as in other Muslim countries, the right hand is used for taking bread, etc. Drinks are normally served with the food and you will have to wait until the meal is ready, unless you ask for it to be brought in advance.

In town and village restaurants, women or mixed company will be directed to the 'family' area, whereas men without female companions will sit in a male-only section. Whether in a café or family house, men and women tend to sit according to gender rather than relationship. In a private house in villages, you may eat at floor level rather than at a table, so prepare for aching leg muscles. The kitchen is considered the women's domain so men should not enter unless invited.

Managing to pay for a restaurant meal with Iranian friends is a major problem. The habit of 'going Dutch' is simply not an Iranian convention, and if you are a woman, the problem is compounded. It may sound like a freeloader's paradise but of course it is not. One possible answer is to talk to a sympathetic waiter to ensure that you get the bill, and have extra cash in case other friends or relatives join your table.

There are enormous difficulties finding a café or restaurant open during the daylight hours of Ramadan (see page 57), when it is very important not to be seen in public smoking, drinking or eating.

DRINKS All alcohol is banned in Iran although the Christian communities, in Esfahan for example, are allowed wine strictly for communion use. However, Iran's famous vineyards are now being recultivated after most were uprooted in revolutionary zeal; the grapes are for eating, and for the production of grape juice, syrups and vinegar. Iranian (non-alcoholic) beer is terrible, though Delster is just about palatable if well chilled. A very passable non-alcoholic 'lager' is Bavaria, now

2

Prices indicate the average price of a main course for one person.

$$$	US$20+ (700,000 rials+)
$$	US$10–20 (350,000–700,000 rials)
$	Up to US$10 (up to 350,000 rials)

imported from Dubai. It's available only in large centres at about 35,000 rials from local shops (US$1) but more in restaurants and hotels – just slightly more than the Iranian bottled beer but worth every rial.

Local carbonated soft drinks, such as cola, Fanta and Sprite, tend to sweetness, and the fruit juices, either freshly pressed or in cartons, are more thirst quenching, such as pomegranate juice, *talebi* (cantaloupe melon) juice, and carrot juice with a scoop of ice cream from fruit-juice shops. The refreshing, pressed-lime sodas of pre-revolutionary Iran are unfortunately no longer available (presumably because the soda isn't) but another refreshing drink, *doogh* (yoghurt and water, like Turkish *ayran* or Indian *lassi*), is available.

As for drinks, local Iranian Zam Zam producer makes cola and Fanta-like drinks – and tea is consumed continually.

FOOD Iranian cuisine is one of the world's finest, an intriguing mixture of sweet and sour that owes nothing to the Chinese version. Iranian *khoresht* – stewed dishes of meat and fruit – may sound uninspiring but wait until you've tried duck or chicken in pomegranate and walnut sauce (*fesenjan*), lamb with morello cherries or apricots, beef or lamb with spinach and prunes (*aloo*) and chicken and *zereshk* (barberries), etc. Delicious. Also try *abgoosht* (literally water-meat), or *dizzi* stew served in a jug-like container with a pestle and commonly available even at bus station restaurants. This is a concoction of slowly simmered pulses, meat and vegetables. When in Esfahan, try *beryani*, boiled lamb meat minced and fried with onion and spices. Saffron (in particular from Mashhad) itself is a very common ingredient that you will even taste in chicken kebab and rice.

White rice and bread are the staple foods. A delicious change is rice with butter slowly steamed until a crunchy, caramelised layer is formed. Traditional Iranian salads or servings of fresh mint leaves are called *sofreh* and traditional restaurants are then often called *sofreh knaneh*, meaning a 'house of sofreh' in Persian.

Fresh fish such as trout from the many farms, prawns and shrimps from the south and north coast, and sturgeon from the Caspian Sea are flown in every day to the major cities.

The Iranian equivalent of British fish and chips, or American hamburger and French fries, is *chelo-kebab*, a skewer of grilled lamb, served with plain rice, with or without a raw egg on top. There is also Iranian coleslaw, which is often available in restaurants in place of salad or in addition, and is called *salad-e kalam* (cabbage salad). *Zorat-e mekziki* (Mexican corn) is the the all-time favourite snack on sale practically everywhere in major cities.

And of course there's the originally Shirazian sweet delight of *falludeh* ice, a sorbet with wispy 'noodle'-like strands, served with lime juice and ice cream. One of the joys of visiting Iran is sitting eating *falludeh*, sipping tea or smoking a pipe in the attractive surroundings of a historic tea house. *Gooshfil* deep fried and *poolaki* caramelised sugar sweets are also widely popular.

Meals Breakfast is usually bread, a white *feta*-like cheese with green herbs, *mast* yoghurt (which in Shiraz has a smoky flavour), and tea taken without milk. Coffee, also taken without milk, is imported and thus is not widely available outside cafés and luxury hotels, where a wider breakfast menu is also served. There are four main types of bread: *lavash* is a thin, flat white bread, best when very fresh as otherwise it looks and tastes like a bathmat; *sangak* is made from brown flour, and is thicker and oval in shape (but check for any stones that have become embedded during the milling/baking process); *taftun* is crispy and round; and lastly, there's *barbari*, a deep oval white loaf with a crispy crust. A rough price for breakfast in a four-star hotel would be up to US$4 plus tax, or half this in a two- or three-star hotel.

Lunch, taken around midday, is generally a rice and meat dish, often *chellokebab*, served with a dish of either green herbs, or cucumber, spring onions and tomatoes and usually with a sweetened yoghurt dressing, often luridly coloured like some American-style bottled dressings. In a good tourist restaurant, the main dish at lunch will cost around 100,000 rials; fish is more expensive.

Dinner, eaten after 20.00, is generally at least three courses, consisting of thick barley or lentil soup, perhaps an appetiser, then a meat or fish dish with rice and a side salad, before finishing with seasonal fruit. Expect to pay 150,000–200,000 rials, though in smart Tehrani locales it can be double that or more. Few Iranians will take hot tea after eating chilled melon, and for most foreign visitors drinking iced or chilled water just after eating watermelon is a guaranteed stomach-churning combination. Thick black coffee akin to Turkish or Arab coffee, served in a small cup and always without milk, is occasionally available. As sugar is added during its making, specify the amount of sugar required as you order: *sa'adeh* (without sugar) or *kam shekar* (with a little sugar). Instant coffee (known as 'Nescafé' or 'American coffee') and 'French' coffee are usually available only in luxury hotels and restaurants, but milk will not generally be included unless requested.

There is generally no tipping in Iran but most upmarket places in Tehran would add a compulsory service charge to the bill (see also pages 68–9).

PUBLIC HOLIDAYS

Holidays such as Republic Day and Nou Rouz will always fall on the same days of the Gregorian solar calendar (although Nou Rouz, celebrated on the exact moment of the vernal equinox, sometimes starts on 20 March rather than the next day). Lunar holidays, on the other hand, vary, changing by about 11 days each year. To try and make things more accessible we have tried to give the names of the Muslim months in which some of these occur – we already use Ramadan and Moharram, for example, which are the names of the months. You can also refer to a website that gives the main dates (but not all the particular Shi'a ones necessarily) such as www.bbc.co.uk/religion/tools/calendar/faith.shtml?muslim.

IN 2014/2015 Iran has national holidays (NH) and religious holidays (RH) (feast or mourning ceremonies). On mourning occasions all sites will be closed. Those marked with ★ below mean that the behaviour of foreign visitors must be low-key and extremely decorous.

2014	2015	Description
2 Jan		Martyrdom of 8th Imam Reza (RH). Sites are closed.

19 Jan	8 Jan	Milad al-Nabi (Birthday of the Prophet Mohammed. Note that if Sunni Muslims mark this event, they do so some five days earlier but many of them regard its celebrations as a religious innovation) and 6th Imam Sadeq (RH)
20 Mar	20 Mar	Nou Rouz – Iranian New Year Holiday (NH)
28 Jun	18 Jun	Ramadan (the Muslim month of fasting) (RH) begins
19 Jul	8 Jul	Martyrdom of first Imam Ali (RH). Sites are closed.
29 Jul	18 Jul	Eid al-Fitr (RH) – the end of Ramadan when Muslims celebrate the end of fasting and thank Allah for his help with their month-long act of self-control
22 Aug	11 Aug	Martyrdom of sixth Imam Sadeq (RH). Sites are closed.
5 Oct	24 Sep	Eid al-Adha (in Iran called Eid al-Qorban) – Festival of Sacrifice marking the day after Arafat (RH). The Day of Arafat is the most important day in the hajj ritual. This is a four-day holiday.
13 Oct	2 Oct	Religious feast Eid al-Qadir (RH)
24 Oct	13 Oct	Al-Hijra – Islamic New Year (RH). Marks the migration of the Prophet Mohammed and his followers from Mecca to Medina.
2 Nov	23 Oct	Tasua – mourning holiday for martyrdom of third Imam Hossein (RH). Sites are closed.
3 Nov	24 Oct	Ashura – Islamic holy day observed on the 10th of the Islamic month of Moharram (RH). Shi'a Muslims regard it as a major festival marking the martyrdom of the Prophet's grandson, Hossein. ★
13 Dec	3 Dec	Mourning bank holiday for Arbaeen of Imam Hossein (RH). Sites are closed.
22 Dec	12 Dec	Martyrdom of eighth Imam Reza (RH). Sites are closed.
	29 Dec	Milad al-Nabi (Birthday of the Prophet Mohammed) (RH) and sixth Imam Sadeq

Organising travel, accommodation and any business appointments during lengthy holidays such as Nou Rouz will require much planning and repeated confirmation to keep the bookings active. During Nou Rouz and Ramadan many offices, especially government departments, will be minimally staffed and keep erratic and shorter hours. It will be difficult during the daylight hours of the 28 days of Ramadan to find restaurants and tea houses open except in four- and five-star hotels, and few dentists will accept patients (to avoid giving mouthwashes). Fasting inevitably means tempers are shorter, and little work is achieved. Try to avoid such times.

There are two main types of other holiday, those in the **solar calendar** and those relating to the **lunar calendar** (11 days or so fewer than in the solar year, and linked to the sighting of the new moon).

SOLAR These are national days, that are not necessarily holidays, falling on the same day each year:

10 Feb	Revolution Anniversary
11 Feb	Khomeini assumed control in 1979
20 Mar	Mossadegh's nationalisation of oil and petroleum companies
1 Apr	Establishment of the Islamic Republic in 1979
2 Apr	Nature Day
4 Jun ★	Death of Khomeini in 1989
5 Jun ★	Khomeini's arrest in 1963 and consequent anti-Shah demonstrations

The **one-week** Nou Rouz (Iranian New Year beginning on the night of **20 March**), the spring equinox, is also calculated in accordance with Solar calendar. The official state holiday closure is, however, only for four days, but most people are off for two weeks. Originally a Zoroastrian festival, and an established part of Iranian life, it is a time for wearing new clothes and giving gifts, so if visiting or staying with friends it would be wise to get a supply of new banknotes for the children of friends, janitors, cleaning staff, etc. The first week is usually observed with family visits following a strict, unstated protocol. There is a total closedown of services on the first day, and thereafter reduced services which slowly improve as the days go by. Most businesses close for two weeks, and all schools and universities close for the whole three weeks.

Conversely, the winter solstice on the night of 21 December, **Shab-e Yalda**, is considered an inauspicious time, so many people stay at home or pass the time with friends.

LUNAR All of these are Muslim holy days; the shorter lunar calendar means the holiday date advances approximately 11 days each year. Under the Pahlavi regime most of these were officially ignored but they are now observed; some are specifically Shi'a in character. Such holidays can mean office (including Iranian consulates abroad), bank and shop closures.

Ramadan (in Persian pronounced as 'Ramazan') Twenty-eight days from the sighting of the new moon. During this time, all Muslims with very few exceptions must refrain from drinking, eating and smoking during daylight hours. Even non-Muslims must not be seen in public doing any of these things; the consequences will be very serious. No weddings are held in this month.

Eid al-Fitr Important three-day feast marking the end of Ramadan with gifts given. Full-day closure on first day.

Moharram ★ A full 28 days commemorating the tragic death of the third imam, Hossein. Radio and television programmes will be subdued during the first ten days, and women wear more sombre clothing. Locals, however, enjoy the celebrations and dishes are served to people and mourners in the streets for free.

Tasua and Ashura ★ On the ninth and tenth day of Moharram, marking the eve and actual day of Hossein's death with performances of the 'mystery play' retelling the Karbala story (see box, page 58). On the ninth day in Yazd and Abyaneh, for instance, processions of athletic young men carrying the giant wooden *nakhla* (a large structure shaped like a palm leaf) are avidly watched by girls. Attend plays or procession *only* if invited and accompanied by friends, and leave your camera behind.

Eid al-Qorban (Also known as Eid al-Adha) This feast marks the end of pilgrimage season; sheep are sacrificed in the Muslim month of Dhu al-Hijjah.

Eid al-Qadir Khom Held on the 18th day of Dhu al-Hijjah. The day Prophet Mohammed appointed Ali as his successor.

Ruz-e Qatl-e Ali Iman Ali's martyrdom, 21st day of Ramadan.

Imam Sadeq's martyrdom Held on the 25th day of the Muslim month of Shaval.

Hossein, the younger son of Ali and Fatima, was born in Medina (in today's Saudi Arabia) in 626 CE. On the death of the (Umayyad) Caliph Muawiya in 680, recognised as the leader of all Muslims by the Sunni community, Hossein was 'invited' by the Medina governor to take an oath of allegiance to his successor, Yazid. Aware of imminent danger, Hossein, advised by Medina citizens to avoid taking this oath, left the city for Mecca and then Kufa in Iraq. Pursued by the Umayyad army, he told his supporters, numbering 72 excluding women and children, to leave him to his fate but they refused to desert him. The Umayyad forces poisoned the waterholes *en route* and Hossein's relative, Abbas Abu'l Fazl, volunteered to find drinkable water, losing both hands in the process. The small force reached Karbala on the second day of Moharram and again Hossein ordered his men to flee. They refused and battle commenced. Hossein, the third imam, and all 72 supporters were killed on 10 Moharram 61 AH (680 CE).

Arba'in-e Hosseini ★ The 40th day after Hossein's death.

Imam Hassan's Martyrdom and Prophet Mohammed's death Held on the 28th day of the Muslim month of Safar.

In addition, government offices and institutions, and some shops will also be closed on the following days:

Birthday of the 12th Imam On the 15th day of the Muslim month of Sha'ban.

Imam Reza's birthday On the 11th day of the Muslim month of Dhu al-Qa'da. The city of Mashhad is especially busy.

Imam Sadeq and Prophet Mohammed's birthday On the 17th day of the Muslim month of Rabi-al Awwal; but note that Sunnis celebrate the Prophet's birthday on a different date.

SHOPPING

Shopping hours are generally 09.00–13.00 and 16.00–20.00 (later in the summer); shops are usually closed on Fridays. During Nou Rouz, Ramadan and Moharram, expect shorter opening hours, especially in the bazaars.

For daily supplies, small **corner shops** sell everything, but check the expiry dates. In the large cities there are a few **supermarkets**, such as Rifah in Tehran, which stock household items and furniture. Prices, especially of luxury and electrical goods, can range widely depending on whether the supplier is a small-scale importer or a franchise operator for a government registered charity (see page 70); certain cheaper items (eg: motor car spares) may be counterfeit. For **books** in the English language, there are plenty of stores around Enghelab Square in Tehran.

The **bazaars** of Iran have well-earned reputations both as rabbit warrens and for haggling. Very few (eg: Tabriz and Zanjan) are located within a defined block; most (eg: Esfahan) have developed over the centuries to no predetermined plan. The medieval system which facilitated market inspection for weights and measures, pricing and quality, by gathering like trades in sectors (eg: coppersmiths in one quarter, goldsmiths in another, booksellers elsewhere) has been largely retained, so it is a matter of finding the correct section. Never presume you will easily find it or the actual shop again, so take the trader's business card and next time ask directions; usually another trader will assign a small boy (who will expect a small tip) to take you there. Almost all traders have electronic calculators that facilitate bargaining for foreigners. Check whether rials or tumans are being quoted (see page 47). The best souvenir bazaars are in Esfahan and Shiraz. In Tehran, Babhomayoun Street near Maydan-e Imam Khomeini has a wonderful variety of men's formal wear shops.

If you loathe haggling then the **Iranian Handicrafts Organisation** (IHO) shops are strongly recommended. Prices are fixed in rials/tumans, but do check what exchange rate is being used, as it can be extremely disadvantageous if the local manager is ignorant of current rates. A visit to an IHO at least gives an idea of local prices, and Iranians often frequent these centres too.

The **gold** (18 carat unless specified otherwise) and **silver** prices are published in newspapers every day, so the jeweller will weigh the piece and add something for the workmanship. The gold is of a high quality but often set with paste and semi-precious stones. It is unlikely that one can find a bargain without active participation by an Iranian friend, as gold is the established hedge against inflation and Iran has no gold mines of its own.

We cannot stress enough how useful, comfortable and cheap women's *manteaux* are (see page 68). There is a universal size, though the length may need adjusting. The price is about US$10 or upwards depending on the quality of fabric, colour, trimmings, seasonal weight, etc.

Carpets, miniature paintings, printed cottons, marquetry work (eg: picture and mirror frames, pen and cigarette boxes) and leather goods are popular purchases, but consider too a pair of cotton *giveh* (slippers), *gaz* (nougat), pistachio nuts and dried apricots or limes, spices like saffron or *sumak* (*Rhus coriaria*), or pomegranate juice to make *fesenjan* at home. As will be noted in the relevant sections, some towns are famous for certain products, for instance the rose water of Shiraz and the sweetmeats or *termeh* cloth of Yazd. Esfahan is known for its block-printed cottons; the price range reflects the fabric quality, the number of blocks and dye/mordant baths involved; salted cool water is recommended for the first washing. Good-quality Kerman embroideries (on scarlet wool fabric) and Rasht patchwork are now difficult to find; look and compare. Miniature paintings are produced by college-trained artists in traditional styles; the finer the detail, the higher the price. Painting on 'bone' is always more expensive as tourists seem to prefer such work. Forget about acquiring an antique example of classical Persian painting. Firstly, export authorisation will be needed, and secondly there is a lively market in buying antique paper, washing it and painting on top.

As for handmade **carpets**, as distinct from machine-made, there are essentially two types and two pattern compositions. In both, look for secure fringes, good firm weft-edges and selvages or cords (clumsy over-sewing can hide cut edges). *Ghelims* are plain weaves without any pile knotting, involving less yarn and production time and cost less. The quality can range from the very fine (used as throws, drapes) to thick and hard-wearing. Complex and fine pattern detail means extra weaving time, which will be reflected in the price. *Ghelims* with long weave-slits in the pattern are more prone to future wear and tear. The second type incorporates pile-knots over the whole or part of the surface, which involves more work and yarn, so these carpets attract higher prices than *ghelims*. The official ban on exporting pile carpets was lifted a few years ago, but on your departure custom officials may ask to see your carpet, and the receipt (see page 46).

There are two essential pattern compositions: one is based on classical 'court' designs characterised by curvilinear motifs carried on arabesque scrollwork, and the other on 'tribal' patterns which have a more angular, geometrical appearance. The variations in patterns are infinite, as are their prices, quality and indeed the number of books about carpets. Always remember that so-called vegetable dyes and countless hours of work cannot transform a bad design into a work of art. You are more likely to get a bargain (though not necessarily 'authentic' Persian production) at home rather than from Esfahan, whose carpet dealers are notorious among Iranians.

With expensive purchases such as carpets (see above), avoid going into a carpet shop with a group to buy and don't be hassled into deciding within 30 minutes. If you do buy, it is safe to get rugs sent home (probably routed through Italy or Germany), and if you pay by credit card the billing will probably travel the same route (the US embargo again), and you'll have to the cover the card fee.

CULTURE AND ENTERTAINMENT

Social life in Iran tends to be firmly family orientated; 'friends' are usually members of the family.

In the first years of the Islamic Revolution, most of the theatres, the Tehran Opera House, cinemas and, of course, discos and nightclubs were closed, as it was considered that such entertainment was morally reprehensible, tainted by 'Westoxification' (see page 16). But in recent years Iranian **theatre**, and especially **film**, with directors like Kiarostami, Ibrahimifar, Mehrjui, Bahmalbar, Farhadi et al, have blossomed. Films such as *Children of Heaven*, *The White Balloon*, *Taste of Cherry* and *A Separation* have all been nominated for or won prizes abroad. Subjects range from women in Islamic society, modern life and religious devotion, to Iran–Iraqi war themes and child abuse. The **Iranian International Film Festival** aka the Fajr Film Festival (*www.fajrfilmfestival.com*) takes place annually in Tehran, usually in late January to early February to coincide with the anniversary of the Islamic Revolution. During this time, there are also important music and theatre festivals, which take place around Tehran.

During the Pahlavi regime (1926–79) the traditional annual *taziyeh* or 'passion play' performed during Moharram (see pages 55–7) was officially banned. Today most towns organise a performance that retells the tragedy of Ali's son, Hossein, and his family in their final hours at Karbala. Casual foreign visitors are not appreciated on these occasions, so attend only if specifically invited by a close Iranian friend. This advice also applies to the Moharram processions.

In the early years of the revolution only martial music, recitations and chanting of religious works were allowed but shortly before Ayatollah Khomeini's death it was announced that the sale and purchase of musical instruments were permitted. **Musical performances** now take place (with certain provisos), and since August 1999 the import of 'Western' instruments, such as pianos, has been allowed. In 2000, *The Phantom of the Opera* could be heard on the tannoy system in an Esfahani five-star hotel and music with a Latin American beat was being transmitted on radio and television. However, official disapproval of American and Western rock, reggae, etc, remains. Clandestine recordings of favourite émigré Iranian singers and musicans, along with upbeat Indian pop, can be bought on the black market, and there is a growing home industry promoting young singers who sound like the émigré stars. In the mid 1990s it was not permitted for men to listen to female singers (passions would be inflamed) so it was usual practice, while driving, to change CDs as one drove up to and departed from road checkpoints.

CRAFT Iran has a long tradition of art and craft, dating back centuries and even thousands of years. Persian **carpet making** is easily its most long-standing craft and dates back to the Achaemenid Empire (550–330BCE). **Persian miniature**, popular since the 13th century, with wonderful painted representations from the *Shahnameh* epic or the classic *gol-o morgh* (flower and bird) motif, can be seen as museum exhibits and souvenirs, while beautifully decorated **wooden items** such as pen boxes, known in Persian as *qalamdan*, or backgammon boards are simply exquisite.

SPORT Sports in Iran are strictly gender-segregated so public attendance is limited to male spectators, except where segregated seating (rarely found) has been installed. Interestingly enough, in 2006 president Ahmadinejad tried to change the rules that banned women from watching football matches, but his attempts failed due to clerical opposition.

When it comes to sports facilities, while you will be pleasantly surprised to see a wide range of exercise equipment installed in parks all around the country. At present you will also notice a few women hill walking (especially in northern Tehran) and there are, of course, sports training grounds for women in large cities, but access to facilities beyond that is quite limited. Indeed, medical concern has been voiced over women's health, and ex-president Rafsanjani's daughter, Faizeh, was a prominent campaigner in the late 1990s for greater access to facilities for women.

A major problem for women in sports has been the absence of a 'proper' sports dress design which is acceptable in all quarters, and which would allow the televising of women's team events and full participation in international events abroad. In September 2005 Tehran hosted the fourth Women's Islamic Games which included participants in at least two disciplines from Britain, the first non-Muslim state to compete. At the 2008 Beijing Olympics, Iran's team included about 15 women all kitted out in headscarf and *manteaux* for the opening ceremony but clothed in more regular sports attire with headscarf for competition. More recently an Iranian woman who refused to remove her headscarf in an international karate competition and was excluded from the *tatami* mat as a consequence, was awarded a new car by the president in a public ceremony. However, the strict dresscode is not acceptable in all quarters and does exclude female athletes from various competitions. In 2011, for example, the Iranian women's football team was banned from playing against Jordan in the London 2012 Olympics qualifier match. FIFA banned the wearing of hijab in 2007.

Iranian men are sports mad, especially for football – as seen in the 1998 World Cup – volleyball and basketball. Tehran's national Azadi stadium is the fourth largest in the world by capacity. Interest has revived in wrestling, and the 1998 visit of a US team marked the beginning of a new diplomatic interchange, soon dropped, between the two administrations. If you have the opportunity, visit a local *zurkhaneh* (see box, page 120) to see the rigorous calisthenic routines the wrestlers perform. Many *zurkhaneh*s were closed by the late Shah to curb the spread of anti-royalist propaganda, but have now reopened; even the most intellectual Iranian males know all the vocal audience responses for the sessions.

Camel riding has its supporters, especially in the south, while in the north and west **shooting** and **horseriding** are popular. The London 2012 Olympics also saw two female Iranian athletes compete in shooting and one Iranian woman has taken part in the 1996, 2000 and 2012 Olympics archery competitions. Once a year in early June there is a women's horse race near Khorramabad. Tehran has a **tennis** club and 18-hole **golf** course. **Skiing** is popular in Tehran, Hamadan and Tabriz from January to the end of March, especially during Nou Rouz (see pages 56–7) and at weekends, particularly Thursday and Friday. The main ski resorts are Darbansar (for beginners), Shemshak, Ab-Ali and Dizin (fashionable) at Shaleh; equipment hire is cheap. With the exception of Mount Tochal – which has chair-lifts – the slopes are gender-segregated.

Mountain climbing, north of Tehran, Hamadan and in the Azerbaijan region, is both exciting and popular. The usual safety rules apply: wear suitable clothing for any unexpected weather conditions and always tell people of your route, estimated arrival and return times. It is wise to obtain official permits, and the tour company Kassa (e *info@kassaco.com*) (see page 33), which organises trips for the Mountain Federation of Iran, is very helpful. Useful information is available on the website www.mountainzone.ir. Perhaps more popular among young Iranians (as it offers rare 'boy-meeting-girl' opportunities) is *kuh navardari* or **hill walking** in the mountains, especially along the paths of Darband, Tochal and Kolok Charl, north of Tehran, which are dotted with rudimentary tea houses ideal for short breaks. Again Kassa can assist with routes and maps.

As for **swimming**, there are certain segregated pools or designated times/days for male or female use. At the sea, women sit on the shore in a certain area and enter the water fully clothed, including the headscarf; foreign women are also expected to swim full clothed, with the exception of specially segregated beaches on Kish Island, for example. Bathing shorts, but not thongs, are permitted for men on public or male-only beaches. **Scuba diving** is possible off Kish Island, where there is a good beach open to tourists, with showers, toilets and a (dry!) bar – swimsuits are permitted, but take your passport. There are **sailing** and **waterskiing** facilities on the Caspian and at Amir Kabir Dam (north of Karaj, Tehran).

BOARD GAMES All gambling, such as cards, dice-playing and backgammon, is prohibited under Islamic law. The revolutionary proscription on the sale and purchase of chess sets was lifted in 1989, and now chess competitions do take place and you may witness an occasional game of backgammon in local cafés. Esfahan bazaar around Maydan-e Imam has a wonderful variety of lacquered and beautifully painted backgammon boards.

HAMAMS Particularly if you are staying in very modest hotels, think of visiting a *hamam* (public bath); those still in operation are open to men only. Always go before, not after, eating a meal. You will emerge squeaky clean and scoured to one surviving millimetre of skin. The desk person will organise your session after you decide whether to have a massage or shampoo as well as the 'bath' (somewhat of a misnomer because hot and cold water are sloshed over you). 'Plunge pools' are available only if the *hamam* is in a special spa area. Your clothing and valuables can be secured under lock and key, but never undress to the point of nudity. Towels, bath wraps, soap and shampoo can be provided at a small extra charge, as can tea and coffee.

MEDIA AND COMMUNICATIONS

POST Postage is inexpensive: to send a postcard to anywhere in the world will cost 20,000 rials; the service takes about a week. Postboxes are located near to post offices, where stamps are obtained. There are very few postboxes anywhere else. Letters or parcels that require weighing involve a visit to the post office, and many good hotels will undertake this kind of service on the traveller's behalf.

In July 2004, the offices of the Iranian Cultural Heritage Organisation (ICHO) and the Iranian Touring & Tourism Organisation (ITTO) were brought under one umbrella and immediately it was announced that entry charges for foreigners to all the ICHO monuments would be reduced to the same level as those for nationals. This policy remained in operation until March 2013 when double pricing was reintroduced. With the exception of some smaller museums (eg: the Water Museum in Yazd) expect to pay up to 150,000 rials (US$5) at each site.

TELEVISION AND RADIO Iranian television has eight channels: the first two are general, the third is a sports channel, the fourth has mostly cultural programmes, while the fifth is provincial and varies in content from region to region. Channel six is a news network and channel seven is reserved for instruction particularly in the religious field. Perusal of the website http://english.irib.ir/ will lead you to the current schedules for English-language news broadcasts.

Until recently, Iranian television films were increasingly based on historical themes, or recalled the heroic sufferings of the Iraqi conflict. The pace was never more than slow and there was always an unambiguous moral to the plot. Satellite dishes were banned in 1995 as the authorities feared unsuitable programmes were being received (reportedly the American *Baywatch* series, with its silicone-endowed females, was very popular); now watching satellite television is permitted only to those with government permits, such as the guardians of public morals. But depending on one's geographic location in Iran, Turkish or Arab channels can be received. DVDs can also be obtained.

Regarding radio, tune into BBC Radio World Service/VOA on the half-hour for news broadcasts. Nowadays many people watch the VOA Farsi channel on the Hot Bird satellite and the BBC has started a television service (*www.bbc.co.uk/persian/*)

NEWSPAPERS AND BOOKS Four newspapers, under direct or indirect government control, are printed in English: *Kayhan International, Tehran Times, Iran Daily* and *Iran News*. It is also possible to read the *Iran Daily* (*www.iran-daily.com*), the *Tehran Times* (*www.tehrantimes.com*) and *Kayhan International* (*www.kayhanintl.com*) online. All are published and printed in Tehran. There has been a marked change in content and criticism since the elections in February 2000, when there was full coverage of the notorious vote-counting muddle, offering a wide diversity of views. A crackdown in press coverage ensued and another followed in 2004, after public disquiet over the disqualification of some 2,000 parliamentary candidates from standing for election. Over 20 newspapers and magazines have been closed by the Council of Guardians and the standard of reporting now verges on the innocuous. Parliamentary requests for an official investigation into press closures have been rejected by the Supreme Leader as being against Islamic law.

Other than TEFL (Teaching English as a Foreign Language) and computer manuals, few English-language publications are available except pirated, ex-copyright versions of pre-1979 Western works on Persian art, history and archaeology. The Iranian-published English translations of such important Persian poets as Omar Khayyam, Hafez and Saadi are generally extremely poor. There is now a Penguin edition (2007) of the Iranian epic, *Shahnameh*, translated by Dick Davis and recitations from it (in Farsi) can now be heard again in *chay-khanehs* (tea houses). Modern novelists – all established writers before 1979 – include Sadeq Hedayat (who wrote the classic *The Blind Owl*), Simin Daneshvar and Dawlat Abadi.

MOBILE PHONE AND INTERNET These days most travellers have a **mobile telephone** but as roaming charges are high, you may prefer to buy a local SIM card from a phone shop. You can buy a 'secondhand' SIM card for 200,000 rials. A brand-new one costs around 350,000 rials and you need to register it in the so-called *mukhabarat* government office before you can start making calls. Ask at the phone shop you are buying the card from for the nearest office. The registation process is tedious and might take easily over an hour. You need to be patient and it is best to bring a friend who speaks Farsi. Bring your passport, and you will be required to leave a copy of your fingerprint and pay a service charge of around 20,000 rials. The cost of calls and texts is reasonable and phone top-ups can be easily purchased from convenience shops anywhere in Iran.

The **internet** is widely available, though be aware that some sites may be blocked and the connection may not be very fast; Hotmail is particularly slow. Hotels generally have Wi-Fi and in most towns and cities it will be reasonably easy to find cheap internet access. Do note that Facebook is officially blocked, but the young and creative have their ways around it. Some internet cafés in larger cities have Facebook on their PCs. Alternatively, ask an Iranian friend to help. Some smaller hotels in Iran still have a fax machine as opposed to email or a website. In this book we supply a fax number when there is no email address or website available.

A BUSINESSMAN'S VIEW   *'Fluvius'*

One of the perks of being a businessman involved in overseas work is that glowing feeling that someone else is paying for the travel and accommodation. Even better when the destination is unusual and redolent of the mysteries of faraway lands. Iran will not disappoint the attentive traveller: it has a rich history and cultural traditions. Above all, it is very different from Europe and America. Scratch beneath the surface of modernity and you will find a world of cultural nuance, literary allusion and a history to match any, involving the sweeps of empire and transition.

There are several issues of business culture in Iran to rapidly absorb. In general, overseas business travellers may talk of prevarication as an artform in the Middle East but it will mostly come down to doing the homework about what the client requires and whether there are funds in hand. Business in Iran is booming and contracts are being placed all the time so somewhere the prevarication is replaced by action. The savvy will be able to spot the drift of an opportunity by asking firm questions and getting their Iranian counterparts to follow agendas and sign minutes of meetings. Politeness and warm greetings are no substitute for serious and contested negotiations. As a measure of development of the business, the strength of the discussions – as opposed to mere civility – will tell the businessman he is on the right track.

Iranians are practised negotiators from birth. Children will be seen haggling over prices in the corner grocery store. Negotiation is a national sport that most Iranians love. It is a highly entertaining form of conversational jousting with (often) considerable humour. Just listening to two Iranians twist and turn to gain the upper hand in settling a price is a delight. So the overseas businessman brought up on fixed prices and glacial, or simply bored, stares from shop assistants is an innocent waiting to arrive.

BUSINESS

The working week is theoretically around 40 hours long, with annual leave of about 30 days per annum. Most government offices are open 08.00–14.00 Saturday–Wednesday and 08.00–12.00 on Thursday, with other offices, workshops, bazaars, etc generally having longer working days; bazaars close between 13.00 and around 16.00.

There is a confusing multiplicity of public holidays (see pages 55–6) when offices, government departments and bazaars are shut. If visiting Iran for business, do allow at least three times the number of days you think necessary to see people – even if appointments have been confirmed. To cope with inflation and low wages, many Iranians may have more than one job, which usually involves crossing town and meeting the inevitable traffic jam, so appointments are often subject to long delays or last-minute cancellations.

CULTURAL ETIQUETTE

Just to repeat: no eating, drinking or smoking in public during daylight hours of the 28 days of Ramadan (see page 57). The repercussions otherwise will be very serious for you and your sponsor. You'd also do well to abide by the following.

SHOES Entry into a 'working' religious building or into a private home entails removing shoes at the edge of the carpet, rug or floor covering in order to prevent

The overseas businessman must prepare for this sport. Practise a sour or disappointed look at the first mention of a discount. Work at this in front of the mirror. Until tears roll down your cheeks looking at your reflection, you have not practised enough. Even with this new skill you will need resilience, patience and determination.

The business traveller should be aware that the Iranian authorities take a dim view of foreign travellers wandering off to remote and possibly sensitive spots such as border regions. Stick to the beaten path of tourism; it is not overly patronised, contains plenty of interest and means you avoid coming under suspicion.

Other helpful hints (purely random) would be:

- Always look both ways before crossing a one-way street.
- Do not believe zebra crossings are there for the pedestrian to cross unharmed.
- Do not blow your nose in public.
- However inappropriate for the weather, wear a collar and tie as far as possible, because it fits the Iranian idea of a foreign male businessman.
- Men should not try to shake the hand of a woman.
- Be careful where you take photographs (see pages 44–5).

Most of all I would recommend that the businessman should expect to be surprised. We all get jaded travelling around the world from one concrete and glass bunker to another; Iran will definitely not be like that. Try the local food; go beyond the delicious kebabs and fruit juices and revel in the difference. This guide outlines so many fascinating places to see around Iran and hopefully the business traveller can be encouraged to experience some of them.

street filth being brought in. Feet (especially women's) should be covered with socks or nylons which should be put on discreetly beforehand – it has been argued that ladies' bare toes may drive men to thoughts of sexual fantasy. Shoes are removed just at the transition of pavement or earth to floor covering. *Not* before. *Not* after. By all means untie or slacken shoes before, but remove shoes/sandals only at the transition point and likewise on leaving, when you slip on your shoes; they can be fastenend up later at leisure. Ignoring this convention causes great disquiet and disgust, perhaps akin in Western society to excavating one's nasal passages in public and examining the contents minutely before consumption.

If visiting a family house (removing your shoes in the entrance hall) and using the bathroom or toilet, slip on the sandals placed near the bathroom door and return them when re-emerging. Such footwear is not worn elsewhere in the house.

TOILETS The toilet won't necessarily have toilet paper, but if you take some with you, this and any other used sanitary product should be jettisoned into the waste-paper bin as the small waste pipes become easily blocked.

TRANSPORT In taxis, long-distance buses and so on passengers sit according to gender or family. On city buses, men go to the front, women to the back section. Some buses have separation barriers in between and, if you are travelling with a companion, agree where to meet before you are separated! On the buses without a barrier and outside rush hour you can travel together in the middle of the bus.

CONTRABAND All forms of pornography are banned, and of course the definition of 'pornography' never lies with the owner. All publications by Salman Rushdie are banned, along with all alcohol (see page 53) and drugs. The authorities are very determined to stamp down on the growing drug problem (Iran has the highest addiction rate in the world), so lorries, intercity buses, etc are often searched; penalties are severe. As in China, homosexuality 'does not occur' in Iran and such behaviour is forbidden and illegal, carrying harsh penalties. Men often hold hands and embrace each other, but this is a sign of friendship and has no sexual connotations.

INTERACTING WITH PEOPLE Apart from close family relatives (eg: husband/wife, parent/children, brother/sister) it is not done for a Muslim to touch the opposite sex except in an emergency or danger. Thus if an Iranian ignores an outstretched hand, this is not rudeness: strictly speaking, handshaking between the sexes is not acceptable. Remember that a German businessman was detained for years on the grounds of 'having knowledge' (British Foreign and Commonwealth Office biblical coyness!) of an unrelated, unmarried Iranian woman (see page 21). If asked out by a member of the opposite sex, you should enquire who else (eg: another friend or relative) will be coming.

Visiting Iranian friends or a family, it is customary to take flowers, sweetmeats or chocolates, etc and, if possible, wrap them. To show you are more important than any gift, your host will probably place it unopened to one side but the gesture has been really appreciated. By all means praise the house, the food and hospitality offered but never a household item (eg: dish, glass) unless you are sure it is nailed to the floor or otherwise permanently fixed, or you could be deeply embarrassed having to accept it as a gift (and having therefore to part with a prized possession when the visit is reciprocated).

At a family meal, even your third refusal to eat or drink more will not be accepted, but persevere.

As in visiting any Muslim household, foreign women should expect to be closeted with the women, although they may be treated as 'honorary men' for the visit. Similarly, foreign men might not see the women of the household during their stay.

For any appointment, arrive on time but with little expectation that others will do the same; often business appointments or meetings will be cancelled with little or no notice.

Iranians are knowledgeable and intensely proud of their country, its history and cultural heritage, and rightly so. They often make very amusing and critical jokes about themselves, their society and public personalities, but can be quickly hurt or insulted by any jokes or denigration expressed by a foreigner. Just be an appreciative audience, not a commentator.

Even the sweetest-tempered Iranians tend to be irritable during Ramadan (see page 57).

If you wish to compliment someone on a child, a new baby, a new possession, etc, it will really be appreciated if you precede or supplement your compliment with the phrase *ma'shallah*, which asks for Allah's blessing, so thwarting evil.

If in need of help or assistance, it is best to approach a person of the same gender, unless you wish to complain about harassment. Here only another man can rightly put the culprit in his place. As previously mentioned, single women should avoid walking unescorted in public at night; it will be assumed they are prostitutes.

DRESS
Men Before 1997 full-length shirtsleeves were required but now elbow-length is deemed acceptable. Garish colours and vivid Hawaiian shirts should be avoided. Shorts, even knee length, are not acceptable, except for mountain biking. Ties are not widely worn by Iranian men; during the first years of the Islamic Revolution some believed that the *kravat* was a hallmark of anti-revolution intellectuals, similar to how the Red Guard in 1970s China viewed spectacles. However, in May 2004 at least one north Tehran clothing store put ties in its window display. Designer stubble is still 'in' (formerly the mark of a revolutionary), but most Iranian men visit a barber every other day or so for a shave; it is cheap (US$3–5 including tip in Esfahan) and very relaxing, we are told, although perhaps best avoided unless you are sure that the conditions are totally hygienic.

Women Spring 2007 saw the first 'fashion' show in a hotel, with the state saying it was 'happy' (undefined) as long as the garments and colours were modest. The dress code is simple and inexpensive, but to ignore or flout it is guaranteed to upset people, even if this is not expressed in words, and Iranian women clearly and warmly appreciate foreign women making the effort. The scarf, to be worn all the time except in the privacy of the hotel bedroom, should be at least 1m² so that the nape of the neck and the ears are concealed; long cotton ones may be best with the ends over the shoulders. A nun-like coif is not needed; Iranian women will soon warn you if too much hair is showing. At holy sites in Qom and Mashhad, women will also be reminded to cover their hair fully.

As for the actual dress, the essential requirement is to conceal distracting feminine bumps and curves and any bare skin save hands and face. Forget the semi-circular *chador*, which takes years of practice to wear successfully, especially when carrying bags, cameras and packages. (It is, however, required in some shrines such as Shah Cheragh in Shiraz, and the Qom and Mashhad precincts, but may be hired or borrowed.) Instead, wear the loose-fitting *manteau* (or *rupush*), a full-length, long-sleeved 'coat' made of lightweight cotton, poplin, etc for summer, and thicker fabrics for winter. In April 2006 President Ahmedinajad warned that some garments were too tight and that steps would be taken to enforce the rules. *Manteaux* can be purchased easily for US$10; many visitors buy several to use as theatre or evening coats back home. If you are on an organised tour though, beware, as it is not always possible to buy a *manteau* immediately on arrival and it may be advisable to search out an 'overall' before leaving home, perhaps from a shop supplying uniforms; alternatively Indian-style dress of *salwar kameez*, basically baggy trousers and tunic, is acceptable. If you are saving every penny, a knee- or lower thigh-length, long-sleeved, loose tunic works, but only if worn with an ankle-length skirt or loose trousers underneath. The *manteau*, however, is so much cooler and more comfortable in high temperatures. The fabric should be opaque, of course, and plain or discreetly patterned; 'Jackie Collins'-styled padded shoulders are still fashionable. Other than during Moharram (see page 57), when more muted colours are generally worn, pastel colours such as rose pink, powder blue, beige and old gold are popular. White (a mourning colour), and emerald green (recognised as the Prophet's colour) are best avoided.

Women are advised to refrain from **smoking** in public; it is considered vulgar with all sorts of negative connotations attached.

TIPPING As a general rule you are not expected to tip in restaurants, especially not in local ones. In others (eg: Monsoon in Tehran) there is a compulsory 15% service

LIVING IN IRAN

Frances Harrison, former BBC Tehran correspondent 2004–07

It's the traffic that hits you first in Tehran. I was amazed that even the British Foreign Office travel advisory warns visitors that they may have trouble with the style of driving. Huge six lane highways, named after ayatollahs who would otherwise have long been forgotten, teem with pollution-spewing, Hillman Hunter taxis interspersed with Mercedes and 4x4 jeeps and the odd pick-up truck with a bleating sheep being transported for slaughter. Late at night Iranians play real life speed cars – inspired by computer games – chasing strangers on the highway. You can't live in Tehran without experiencing a few car accidents – sometimes all on one day. Friday lunchtime when everyone goes out for kebabs because it's the weekend is one of the most dangerous times because the roads are a little less clogged with commuters going to work and so drivers can go faster. I've seen several dead bodies and appalling pile ups in Tehran – even a man writhing in pain after his foot was run over by a woman driver.

Statistics for road accidents in Iran are horrific and exceed death rates for major earthquakes. Most Iranians will think nothing about driving at speed the wrong way down a one-way road or reversing down a main thoroughfare if they've missed a turning. Once you get used to the style it's very hard to adjust to driving in somewhere like London again. It's frustratingly sedate.

Transport aside, it's pretty safe if you're not involved in politics. When I first arrived and went out shopping I stood in a queue for ice cream for my son and was amazed to find the man in front of me insisted on buying the ice cream for him. He was a total stranger but realised we were foreigners and wanted to be friendly. Personal hospitality is deep rooted even though the revolution has led to officials being staggeringly rude at times. Clerks will hardly look up from their TV screens or ledgers and often throw the relevant bit of paper at you without charge. Hotel porters will be satisfied with 5,000 rials for each bag or case, while airport porters will expect 5,000 rials and more if you want help through customs. For toilet attendants, perhaps 1,000 rials is sufficient. Mosque and tomb guardians unlocking doors, etc should be given upwards of 10,000 rials, depending on their help. As for taxi drivers, if you have negotiated the price already (eg: a half-day trip), he will hope this does not include a tip; if he has been extra helpful, why not add 10% extra? For an Iranian tour guide, so much depends on the time, effort and work he or she puts into the job, but think of at least US$1 a day from each person if it's a large group, or US$5–7 a day each if travelling by yourself or with one or two friends; the driver might be given about a third less, but again much depends on whether he has been particularly helpful.

Remember that wages are low and inflation high, and the benefit system for the mentally ill, disabled and elderly is not as generous in Iran as it is in the West.

TRAVELLING POSITIVELY

The concept of 'charity' differs in each culture, and both Iranian officials and individuals will be affronted by any action they see as patronising and interventionist. On all streets, there are metal charity-box stands, often decorated with a rose or tulip symbol, placed by the kerb. If you wish, you can contribute money. These boxes are usually for the **Emdad** organisation for orphans and the poor; its administrators

even making eye contact. But the most intimidating woman in a black *chador* at a security check post will melt when she realises you are a foreigner and especially if she finds you speak a few words of Farsi. Even demonstrators shouting 'death to England' will find it hard to be really rude and unpleasant to an individual Englishman or woman.

There are many pleasures in living in Tehran: the snow-capped Alborz Mountains on a sunny spring day with the mountain water running down the open drain channels (known as *jubs*) on either side of the roads, or whole families barbequing elaborate meals for picnics in parks and even on spare strips of grass alongside motorways.

Iranian food helps the quality of life. On the way to my house there was a small corner shop selling pomegranate juice – freshly squeezed as you wait and decanted into used plastic water bottles. Few know Iran produces its own brand of mozzarella cheese, and sour cream and chives crisps that would rival anything you'd find in a giant Western supermarket. Getting away from global consumerism isn't entirely possible in Iran but there is no McDonald's – just an Islamified burger joint, Mac Marshallahs. There are traditional restaurants in the foothills of the mountains – retreats from the summer heat where you can lounge on carpet-covered beds while drinking mint-flavoured yoghurt and nibbling on fresh herbs, goats cheese and hot flat bread. Afterwards it's traditional Persian ice cream – something you can't find anywhere else in the world – sticky, chewy and served sandwiched between wafers. Even 18th-century European travellers to Persia commented on how obsessed the locals were with talking about their cuisine. I have sat at dinners where 80% of the conversation has been about the food – the process of cooking, the quality of the raw materials, the price of ingredients and so on. The other 20% is about how awful their journey was to get there.

are responsible to the Supreme Leader. An important series of charitable trusts is **Bonyad** (one of which is the Organisation for the Oppressed and Disabled of the Islamic Revolution), which administers most of the Iranian property and holdings of the late Shah's Pahlavi Foundation charity, and of former high-ranking courtiers. (Thus a number of tourist hotels are run by Bonyads.) Said to be the franchise holder of Mercedes, BMW, Volkswagen and Toyota, the full scale and financial value of the Bonyad assets is not known as there is no legal requirement to make its annual accounts public; its head answers only to the Supreme Leader and over 40,000 people are in its direct employment.

There is also the *vaqf*, or religious endowment, for mosques and other religious buildings. Since early Islamic times, individuals and businesses have assigned property and/or rents over to a building to pay for its upkeep, repairs and equipment. Thus a popular monument might be awash with funds but another falling into terminal decline. For instance, the person heading the *vaqf* administration for the Shrine of Imam Reza, Mashhad, is responsible for donations and also for investment in all associated economic activities such as manufacturing, farming, housing projects and food-processing plants. It is one of the most influential and wealthy institutions and, as with the Bonyad, its head reports to the Supreme Leader and there is no legal requirement for the publication of annual accounts.

From talking to people in Iran and asking them about 'travelling positively', the reaction is always the same: tell your friends and family how much you enjoyed your visit to Iran. So the greatest gift to them will be in disseminating accurate information rather than hyperbole about the current situation in Iran, arguing for and promoting a better understanding. And, of course, redistributing some of your hard-earned money in the bazaars of Iran will improve the lot of everyone.

Part Two

THE GUIDE

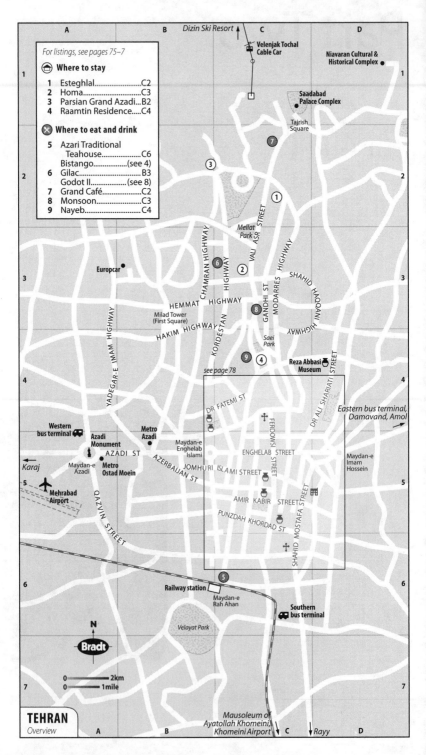

For listings, see pages 75–7

Where to stay
1 Esteghlal.....................C2
2 Homa...........................C3
3 Parsian Grand Azadi...B2
4 Raamtin Residence......C4

Where to eat and drink
5 Azari Traditional
  Teahouse...................C6
  Bistango.................(see 4)
6 Gilac............................B3
  Godot II..................(see 8)
7 Grand Café...................C2
8 Monsoon......................C3
9 Nayeb..........................C4

Dizin Ski Resort ↑

Velenjak Tochal
Cable Car

Niavaran Cultural &
Historical Complex ●

Saadabad
Palace Complex

Tajrish
Square

Mellat
Park

VALI ASR STREET

CHAMRAN HIGHWAY

HIGHWAY

MODARRES HIGHWAY

SHAHID HAQQANI HIGHWAY

Europcar ●

HEMMAT   HIGHWAY

Milad Tower
(First Square)

HAKIM HIGHWAY

KORDESTAN HIGHWAY

GANDHI ST

Saei
Park

see page 78

Reza Abbasi
Museum

DR ALI SHARIATI STREET

Eastern bus terminal,
Damavand, Amol

Western
bus terminal

Azadi
Monument

AZADI ST

Metro
Azadi

Maydan-e
Azadi

Metro
Ostad Moein

AZERBAIJAN ST

Maydan-e
Enghelab
Islami

JOMHURI ISLAMI STREET

DR FATEMI ST

FERDOWSI STREET

ENGHELAB STREET

Maydan-e
Imam Hossein

Karaj ←

Mehrabad
Airport

QAZVIN STREET

AMIR KABIR STREET

PUNZDAH KHORDAD ST

SHAHID MOSTAFA STREET

Railway station

Maydan-e
Rah Ahan

Southern
bus terminal

Velayat Park

N

Bradt

0 ___ 2km
0 ___ 1mile

TEHRAN
Overview

Mausoleum of
Ayatollah Khomeini,
Khomeini Airport

↓ Rayy

3

Tehran and the Road South

Telephone code 021

Looking at the sprawl of modern Tehran spreading up into the Alborz foothills, it is difficult to believe that before 1795, when it became the Qajar capital, it was an insignificant village 'possess[ing] nothing, not even a single building, worthy of notice' (Thomas Herbert, 1627). Then, there were unimpeded views of Mount Damavand (5,610m) and the Alborz. By 1850 the city's population had escalated to around 90,000, more than a fourfold rise in 50 years, enjoying its improved water supply, extended bazaars and newly built caravanserais. In late 1867, inspired by the urban planning in St Petersburg and the work of Haussmann in Paris, Shah Naser al-Din ordered the French military engineer General Buhler to tear down the city walls, fill in the defensive ditch to form thoroughfares wide enough for European-style carriages, and extend the walls of the Arg (citadel) and double the number of gates to 12 (of which all have since been destroyed). By 1920, the population was estimated at 210,000 and it then quadrupled again by 1946. Since then the figures have soared: a conservative estimate in 1992 was over 6.5 million in the immediate centre with half again in the outlying suburbs. According to the 2011 census the population of Tehran is over 12 million, which is just over one sixth of the country's total population. While population growth in Iran from 2006 until 2011 has only been around 1.3%, the general urbanisation rate has now passed 70%, which may suggest further growth of the capital as more people from the villages are moving here in search of employment. Currently Tehran accounts for more than half of the country's economic activity and is set to grow further. The inner areas of the city are home to around 50 colleges and universities, making it the most dynamic student city in the country.

Today, with the number of private cars almost doubling since 1985, low-lying smog usually hides the mountains two hours after sunrise. A weather phenomenon known as 'inversion', which happens when a thick layer of smog is trapped over the city by colder weather from the surrounding mountains, is also regular here. A particularly servere occurrence happened in February 2013, when schools and government offices were closed. No wonder the citizens of Tehran escape when they can to the hills and the Caspian region to breathe fresher air.

Tehran is a wonderfully diverse and vast city with a vibrant café culture and pleasant parks scattered around the city perimeter. While its southern parts (around Golestan Palace) offer, or rather conceal from the general view, a vast range of historic monuments, the upper affluent northern Tehran (Alborz foothills) is the place for an evening stroll or weekend mountain hiking (Tochal). It is easier to get around if you think of Tehran, as one never-ending Vali Asr Street and everything else springing from it, like branches from a tree. When flagging down a taxi, make sure to give the driver not the house number, but the Vali Asr Street intersection.

GETTING THERE AND AWAY

BY AIR Tehran is usually the first stop on any visit to Iran. Despite the distant perceptions of Iran, its capital is located at a surprisingly short flying distance from major European capitals and Istanbul. Over the past couple of years numerous European airlines, such as British Airways, KLM/Air France and Austrian have regrettably suspended their direct flights to Iran, but you can still get here with **Azerbaijan Airlines**, **Aeroflot**, **Lufthansa**, **Pegasus Airlines** and **Turkish Airlines**. The Turkish national carrier has numerous services to various cities across Iran and is perhaps the most reliable and flexible option. Tehran is also well serviced by regional routes from the United Arab Emirates, Ukraine, Belarus, Georgia and particularly Azerbaijan.

Imam Khomeini International Airport (IKA) is located some 30km south of Tehran on the road to Qom. A joint venture with Austrian and Turkish companies, it was completed at a cost of £260 million, but shortly after the airport's opening in 2004 it was forced to close by a section of the Iranian army, concerned about such an important national symbol being under a foreign, namely Turkish and Austrian, 'authority'. This airport now deals with all international and some internal flights, and **Mehrabad International Airport**, 12km west from the city, formerly the only airport serving Tehran, is used essentially for internal flights. Mehrabad serves 20 Iranian centres (see individual cities in this guide); some international flights also depart from here during the month of the hajj.

A taxi from IKA airport into the centre will cost about 400,000 rials (prepay at the airport kiosk or directly to the taxi driver outside the arrivals hall; either way is acceptable, as prices – depending on the type of car you choose – are listed in English at the taxi rank) and take 45 minutes; from Mehrabad, this cost is 150,000 rials. Do not take an unofficial 'taxi' as there is a risk of mugging. Also do not queue; queuing is not the custom in Iran and you will simply be overlooked. Observe for a second how locals behave and do likewise – just head directly to the driver or kiosk sales person. There are numerous intercity buses operating to and from the three terminals at Mehrabad Airport. The metro station at the airport itself is soon to be completed and will become the most comfortble way of getting into the city centre.

BY TRAIN The railway station is located at Railway Square (Maydan-e Rah Ahan) and it is usually the final stop of the buses running along Vali Asr Street. The ticket office is not in the station but in a building to the left. Allow at least 60 minutes before train departure time. This is not an area to wander around in.

GETTING AROUND

BY BUS Women normally go to the back and men to the front of the bus, but on some routes in Tehran this arrangement is reversed. It is worth mentioning, however, that buses are quite efficient in Iran and it is by far the most preferred transport for women, who deem it safer than taxis.

Buses operate throughout the city but timetables and routes are not readily available. Bus stops, in particular along Vali Asr Street, are clearly marked and numerous. Otherwise, you can ask a passerby for the nearest stop. Day services are frequent, but in the evenings (some buses do not run after 21.30) and on Fridays these are more sporadic. Always buy a ticket either at the kiosk or from the driver himself, paying at the end of the journey. Female travellers may need to exit the bus and then come up to the driver at the front to pay for the ticket (around 3,000 rials).

BY METRO The first line of the Tehran metro opened in February 2000. There are now five lines in operation connecting the far-flung parts of this huge city. One-way and return ticket costs are 3,500 rials and 5,500 rials respectively, regardless of the distance. Travel passes are the cheapest way to use the metro and useful if you plan to use trains regularly. Like the Oyster card on the UK London underground, you purchase a card at the ticket office and charge the card with funds and swipe in and out of the barriers at the stations. Rush hours, best avoided, are from 06.00 to 09.00 and 14.00 to 17.00. Metro carriages are also gender-segregated, but metro travel is safe and efficient and indications are written in both Persian and clear English. While metro services are not as frequent as in European cities, the carriages are clean and you can always purchase a little something from one of the sellers along the way. See page 286 for a map of the metro.

BY ROAD Travelling by **taxi** in Tehran is easy and inexpensive. A shared taxi (*savari*) costs around 5,000–10,000 rials and private hire (*darbaz*) costs up to 80,000 rials, depending on where you are going. Do remember that Tehran is not a pedestrian-friendly city and a short *savari* ride up Vali Asr Street may save a great deal of energy.

It is now possible to **rent a car** in Iran and there are a few options in Tehran for those who are fearless and compelled to take this chance. **Europcar** (operated by TASCO) (e *info@europcar.ir; www.europcar.ir*) have two offices in Tehran: at IKA airport (✆ *51007539*) and in the city centre (*Unit 1, 2 11th St, Falamak St, Shahrak-e Garb;* ✆ *88366615*). Alternatively, you can rent a car from a smaller local firm, such as Royal Taxi Service (*Karim Khan Zand St, 6 1st Qaem Maqam Farahani St;* ✆ *88823800, 88820241, 88308671, 88836162*).

TOUR GUIDE For cultural and nature tours in Tehran and around, contact English-speaking guide Houman Najafi (m *091 2202 3017;* e *houman.najafi@gmail.com*).

🏠 WHERE TO STAY

The Tehran International Fair (www.iranfair.com), usually held in the last week of September or the first week of October, means all hotels in Tehran are busy and often room charges are increased during this period. In addition to the hotels mentioned below, there are over 20 **mid-range** and **budget** hotels along Amir Kabir Street and South Sadi Street. Toilets, however, are mainly squat style and not always en suite. Do note that while the area during the day is a bustling car-parts market, it is not the place to walk around after dark, especially for single female travellers. For location of listings see the map on pages 72 and 78, unless otherwise stated.

LUXURY

🏠 **Esteghlal** (formerly the Hilton) (552 rooms) Vali Asr Intersection, Chamran Highway; ✆ 22660011–25; e reservation@esteghlalhotel. com; www.esteghlalhotel.com. All the facilities you would expect from a hotel of this calibre. It is rather remote from the centre's attractions, but the views from the rooms are spectacular. Established in 1962 it boasts a number of international cuisine restaurants & offers an exclusive hotel service. **$$$$**

🏠 **Homa Hotel** (172 rooms) Nr Vanak Sq; ✆ 88773021–39; www.homahotels.com. One of the most luxurious hotels in Iran with indoor swimming pool & impressive décor. The cherry of the Homa Hotel Chain it is also its most expensive one. Rooms are spacious & bright & staff are courteous with pleasant manner. **$$$$**

🏠 **Laleh** (formerly the InterContinental) (380 rooms) Dr Fatemi St, PO Box 14155–1771; ✆ 889650219/660219, 89670219; e reservation@ lalehhotel.com; www.lalehhotel.com. This is the most central 5-star hotel (& a favourite with Western correspondents reporting the early days of the Islamic Revolution in the late 1970s). The lobby is pleasant, but the décor is a little effete & old-fashioned. The outside garden is lovely, but the pool has regrettably fallen into disuse. The staff are polite & share with the hotel a slightly decadent charm. **$$$$**

🏠 **Parsian Grand Azadi Hotel** (482 rooms) Chamran Expressway, Yadagare Imam Crossroad; ✆22344444; e reservation@azadihotel.com. It is hard to miss this highrise hotel near the Alborz Mountains. One of the largest hotels in Iran, it comes with all kinds of frills: spa, Western cuisine, you name it … Views of the mountains are superb, although the location is a little less central than other hotels in the same price range. **$$$$**

🏠 **Raamtin Residence Hotel** (50 rooms) 2153 Vali Asr St; ✆8872 2786–8; e info@raamtinhotel.com. This business-style boutique hotel is simply classy & comes with excellent service. No opulence or frills here, but a sharp & minimalist interior that was recently renovated with taste. Rooms are spacious & comfortable & the basement restaurant offers great food in case you miss a good Western meal. The location is superb, just a few mins away from Saei Park in northern Tehran. **$$$$**

ABOVE AVERAGE

🏠 **Ferdowsi Grand** (182 rooms) Ferdowsi St; ✆66727026–31; e info@ferdossihotel.com; www.ferdoswsihotel.com. Within walking distance of the National Archaeological Museum, the Golestan Palace, the Ministry of Foreign Affairs, the German & Turkish embassies, it boasts a rather glitzy lobby, but also a highly recommended, traditional restaurant run by the locally known Mr Alizade. Also has a patisserie shop (with ice-cream sundaes!). **$$$**

🏠 **Hoveyzeh Hotel** (formerly the Waldorf) (178 rooms) 115 Taleghani St; ✆88804344–58; www.howeyzehhotel.com. With exceptional views over the city & the mountains, the hotel

has nevertheless seen better days. The facilities are a little shabby & windows could do with some washing. The main lobby is pleasant & bright, though, overlooking wide Tehrani steets. The staff are professional & most pleasant. **$$$**

🏠 **Iranshahr Hotel** (48 rooms) 81 Iranshahr St; ✆88310335/7/9, 88820914; e info@hotel-iranshahr.com; www.hotel-iranshahr.com. One of the best hotels in Tehran with a lot of character & super-smooth staff. The rooms are impeccable & the location superb, despite the rooms being a little dark. Room rates for foreign tourists are slightly higher & quoted in US$, but payment can be made in rials. **$$$**

MID-RANGE

🏠 **Firouzeh Hotel** (26 rooms) Amir Kabir St, Dowlat Abadi Alley; ✆33113508; e info@firouzehhotel.com; www.firouzehhotel.com. Cheap & clean with old-fashioned décor & stylish staff. The clientele here is quite diverse: from photographers to backpackers. A good choice if you plan to spend most of your time outdoors. **$**

🏠 **Khayyam Hotel** (45 rooms) 3 Navidi Alley, Amir Kabir St; ✆ 33911497, 33920218, 33116368–3757; e hotelkhayyam@hotmail.com; www.hotelkhayyam.com. Rooms are small & a little dark, but pristine. The staff are jolly & the talkative parrot Peyman adds charm to this very pleasant place. By far, the best mid-range/budget choice in town. Has reasonably fast Wi-Fi & a lovely lobby with Peyman & other birds singing. **$**

BASIC

🏠 **Nader Hotel** (20 rooms) 22 Qaem Maqam Farahani St; ✆88841657, 88308681; e naderhotel@yahoo.com. Large rooms that may need an extra layer of plaster, but the location is superb: 2mins' walk from the Haft-e Tir metro station & some of the nicest cafés in town. Lovely walk in the evening for a nearby ice cream & fresh juice is a must. There is regrettably no Wi-Fi & the main lobby is rather uninviting. **$**

✕ WHERE TO EAT AND DRINK

Apart from fancier restaurants, Tehran has a huge variety of fast food restaurants serving all kinds of halal food, and traditional tea houses that also serve delicious and filling local meals. All restaurants below are open for lunch from 12.00 until 15.00 and for dinner from 19.00 until 23.00, unless stated otherwise.

Iran also has a lively café scene, but it is somewhat hidden from an ordinary traveller. Cafés, though, are where you can find young Iranians chatting and sipping caffè lattes to the sounds of untraditional music. For Iranian-style tea houses, note that female or mixed groups of travellers may not be admitted, as some are essentially for waterpipe (*qalian*) smoking, which is generally for men only. Ask in advance if *qalian* is what you are after.

For location of listings, see maps on pages 72 and 78, unless otherwise stated.

LUXURY

✗ **Nayeb** 2220 Vali Asr St, across road from Raamtin Hotel below; ☏ 88713474; www.nayebsaei.com; ⏲ lunch & dinner. This much-loved family-run restaurant features a wonderful traditional Iranian menu & the food is served in style. The interior is modern with a touch of French glamour. **$$$**

✗ **Bistango** Raamtin Residence Hotel, 2153 Vali Asr St; ☏ 88554409; www.bistangorestaurant.com; ⏲ lunch & dinner. The ambience, cuisine & décor are completely European. Staff are professional & service is top-notch. **$$**

✗ **Gilac** 15 Parc des Princes, Kordistan Highway; ☏ 8052998, 8048291; ⏲ lunch & dinner. Caspian fish specilialities are on the menu at this gem of a restaurant. **$$**

ABOVE AVERAGE

✗ **Farid** 39 (Shahid) Sareni St (formely Adan-e Jonubi St); ☏ 88904104–6583; ⏲ lunch & dinner. Located in a pleasant & relaxed corner of Tehran, but just a 5min walk from the busy Vali Asr Street. Serves a speciality of steamed 'blue fish'. **$$**

✗ **Monsoon** 8 Gandhi St, Shahid Gandhi Shopping Centre (note that neither the street nor the shopping centre are named after the leader of Indian nationalism); ☏ 88791982; ⏲ 12.00–23.00. Asian fusion restaurant where dishes range from sushi to Thai curry, all prepared Iranian style. The food is good, but apart from the 2 bonsai trees the décor is disappointingly European & the atmosphere is spiced up with Abba tunes. Compulsory 15% service charge. **$$**

MID-RANGE

✗ **Hani** Vali Asr St, cnr of Motahhari St; ☏ 88932020; www.hanitarighat.com; ⏲ 12.00–23.00. This buffet-style restaurant offers a spectacular range of the most delicious traditional Iranian specialities. Watch out for that extra serving of saffron rice! Very busy during lunch. **$**

CAFÉS AND TRADITIONAL TEA HOUSES

⛾ **Azari Traditional Teahouse** 1 Vali Asr St, Rah Ahan Sq; ☏ 55390710–11; e info@azariteahouse.com; ⏲ 12.00–23.00. Great local atmosphere, full of chatty old men. A little far from the centre, but perfect to have a break while waiting for your train. Enquire about *qalian*.

⛾ **Godot II** 8 Gandhi St, Shahid Gandhi Shopping Centre. A wonderfully hip café infused with Samuel Beckett keeping an eye on its clientele: young & pulsating middle-class Tehranis.

⛾ **Grand Café** Vali Asr St, across the road from the Ladan Pastry, Alley Saadi, ☏ 22716876. This cool, new & upbeat cellar café might seem more like a Western-style wine bar, but milkshake would be its fanciest cocktail. The staff are hip, the music alternative & Wi-Fi fast.

⛾ **Iran Tak** 431 Vali Asr St, Enghelab St intersection; ☏ 66959847, 66407351; ⏲ 12.00–23.00. This traditional cellar tea house is always full of young people, as *qalian* smoking is permitted for both men & women alike. Food menu is traditional filling Iranian dishes.

⛾ **Bijan Café** 132 22nd St Qaem Maqam Farahani St, metro Haft-e Tir, walk up past Sho AA Sq; ☏ 88842181. Excellent café, always full of young Tehranis. Serves by far the best Americano in town. Very arthouse & cultural atmosphere, where the *hijab* is the least of the ladies' worries.

WHAT TO SEE AND DO

Tehran is not a pedestrian-friendly city and while major palace complexes are compact, other sites may be separated by some distance. It is usually best to travel

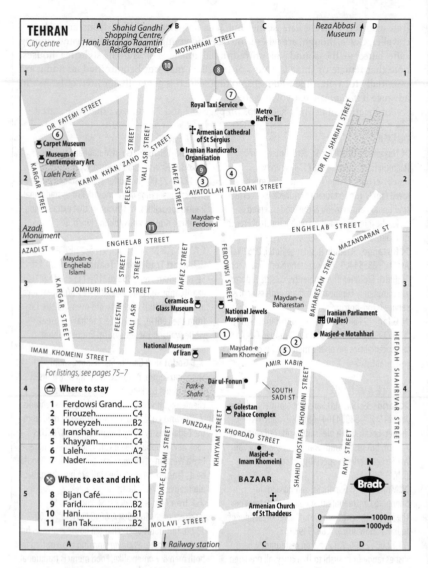

TEHRAN
City centre

Shahid Gandhi
Shopping Centre,
Hani, Bistango Raamtin
Residence Hotel

Reza Abbasi
Museum

MOTAHHARI STREET

DR FATEMI STREET

Royal Taxi Service ●

Metro
Haft-e Tir

☩ Armenian Cathedral
of St Sergius

● Iranian Handicrafts
Organisation

Carpet Museum

Museum of
Contemporary Art

Laleh Park

KARIM KHAN ZAND STREET

FELESTIN STREET

VALI ASR STREET

HAFEZ STREET

DR ALI SHARIATI STREET

AYATOLLAH TALEQANI STREET

Maydan-e
Ferdowsi

Azadi
Monument

AZADI ST

ENGHELAB STREET

ENGHELAB STREET

MAZANDARAN ST

Maydan-e
Enghelab
Islami

JOMHURI ISLAMI STREET

KARGAR STREET

FELESTIN

VALI ASR

HAFEZ STREET

FERDOWSI STREET

BAHARESTAN STREET

Ceramics &
Glass Museum

National Jewels
Museum

Maydan-e
Baharestan

Iranian Parliament
(Majles)

● Masjed-e Motahhari

IMAM KHOMEINI STREET

National Museum
of Iran

Maydan-e
Imam Khomeini

AMIR KABIR

HEFDAH SHAHRIVAR STREET

Park-e
Shahr

Dar ul-Fonun ●

SOUTH
SADI ST

SHAHID MOSTAFA KHOMEINI STREET

Golestan
Palace Complex

PUNZDAH

KHAYYAM STREET

KHORDAD STREET

RAYY STREET

● Masjed-e
Imam Khomeini

VAHDATE ISLAMI STREET

BAZAAR

N

Bradt

☩
Armenian Church
of St Thaddeus

MOLAVI STREET

↓ Railway station

For listings, see pages 75–7

⊖ **Where to stay**

1	Ferdowsi Grand.....	C3
2	Firouzeh..................	C4
3	Hoveyzeh................	B2
4	Iranshahr.................	C2
5	Khayyam................	C4
6	Laleh......................	A2
7	Nader.....................	C1

⊗ **Where to eat and drink**

8	Bijan Café..............	C1
9	Farid......................	B2
10	Hani.......................	B1
11	Iran Tak.................	B2

0 ——— 1000m
0 ——— 1000yds

by metro or taxi between the sites. If you fancy a walk, leave it for one of the numerous city parks.

AZADI ('FREEDOM') MONUMENT (*Western end of Azadi St, next to the Western bus terminal; metro Azadi; lower gallery & viewing gallery are now closed to tourists*)
Standing 45m high on a huge roundabout on the western approach road to Tehran, the monument is an unmistakably noticeable building. It was designed by an Iranian architect and built by a British construction team as part of the late shah's '2,500th' extravaganza in 1971. The influence of 14th-century Timurid architecture is evident in the intersecting rib network, while the turquoise-coloured glazed brick emphasis on the white Hamadan granite is derived from late 12th-century Seljuk decoration. In the 1970s there were two museums in the building, a permanent

display upstairs with visitors carried on a travelator, and temporary displays in the basement galleries. At present, however, the tower is visibly neglected and poorly maintained. It is suffering from humidity and internal water damage. Repairs in 2010, in particular, appear to have caused more damage than good. It is best to walk here from the Azadi bus terminal. Reaching the monument from Azadi Street calls for rock-steady nerves, as pedestrians have to cross six moving lines of traffic – not for the faint-hearted.

MILAD TOWER (*Sheikh Fazl Allah Nouri Expressway; www.tehranmiladtower.ir;* ☉ *09.00–23.00 daily; entry 50,000–250,000 rials, depending on the deck you are visiting*) Built in 2007, at 435m high the tower is the tallest in Iran and the sixth tallest in the world. It is unmistakably noticeable from wherever you approach Tehran. The views of the city and the surrounding mountains, especially during sunset from one of its observation decks, are breathtaking. At the base there is an international convention centre and a shopping centre with restaurants. The easiest way of getting here is by taxi, or by metro to Shahid Hemmat station and then along the motorway by a *savari*.

CARPET MUSEUM (KAREGAR-E SHAMALI) (*At the north end of Laleh Park, a short distance from Laleh Hotel;* ✆ *88962703; http://carpetmuseum.ir;* ☉ *09.00–17.00 Tue–Sun; entry 100,000 rials*) About 100 carpets and rugs are usually on show in this museum, opened in 1977. The ground-floor display is arranged more or less in chronological sequence, working in an anticlockwise direction, beginning with a replica of the Pazyryk rug (c5th century BCE, the oldest known knotted carpet found in Siberia in the 1940s, now held in the Hermitage Museum, St Petersburg, Russia). It includes superb examples of 16th- and 17th-century Safavid rugs including the so-called Polonaises, which caused a sensation at the 1867 Paris Universal Exposition. But you may prefer decoding the 18th-century 'garden' carpets with their stylised irrigation channels (including fish) and chenar plane trees (see page 183). The impact of European art and taste on 19th-century Persian carpet design grows more marked as you walk around, whether it is the reproduction of a Watteau oil painting or a large 'family tree' of American presidents with a 1904–05 date (presumably made for the 1904 Louisiana Purchase Exposition, St Louis). The upstairs gallery serves as a temporary exhibition space, but generally includes more 'tribal' work. There is also a small cafeteria to the left of the entrance and a bookshop in the first gallery, both with the same opening hours as the museum.

MUSEUM OF CONTEMPORARY ART (HONAR-E MO'ASER) (*In Laleh Park, Kagar St;* ✆ *88965411;* ☉ *09.00–18.00 Sun–Thu, 14.00–18.00 Fri; entry 100,000 rials*) This gallery is always full of young people eager to hear your reactions to the paintings displayed both in the main galleries and in the temporary exhibition section in the basement, the latter housing shows organised by foreign cultural associations. Art students in Iran can major in 'traditional' or 'modern' schools or styles, though instruction and practice in both are encouraged. As Islamic art historically favoured two-dimensional work (some theologians argued against the relevance and legality of three-dimensional work outside architecture), it is not surprising to find the emphasis here is on oil painting rather than sculpture, but there is a wide diversity of approaches from the figural to the 'soft' abstract (ie: action painting is out but op art is in).

NATIONAL JEWELS MUSEUM (formerly Crown Jewels Museum) (*Ferdowsi St, in an underground section of the Bank Melli central office, through the black gate;*

✎ 64463785, 64463869, 64463870; ⊕ 14.00–16.30 Sat–Tue; entry 30,000 rials; no children under 12; strict security means no bags of any size allowed) The labelling in English and Farsi is minimal and engraved on unpolished brass plaques, making it difficult to read, but the glitter and colour of the pieces set against a crimson red fabric are eye-catching. Perhaps the most interesting pieces are the crowns, as one works out the historical artistic antecedents of the Kiani crown worn by Fath Ali Shah (d1834) with its 1,800 pearls (see opposite), and the one made for Reza Shah's coronation in 1925 with their clear allusions to Sassanid diadems (3rd–7th century CE). Another exhibit not to miss is the world's largest pink diamond (182 carats), the Darya-e Nur (Sea of Light), sister to the Kuh-e Nur in the British crown jewels; both were part of the booty plundered by Nader Shah Afshar during his 1739 Indian campaign (see page 263).

Surely the ugliest and most preposterous bejewelled object is the Globe of Jewels made for Qajar shah, Naser al-Din in 1869 or 1875. The wooden stand and frame are covered with gold sheet and smothered in jewels, while the globe itself has the land masses picked out in diamonds and rubies, the oceans in emeralds; altogether there are over 51,000 gemstones totalling 18,200 carats.

CERAMICS AND GLASS MUSEUM (ABGINEH) (Si-ye Tir St; www.glasswaremuseum. ir; ✎ 6708153–4, 6716930; ⊕ 09.00–17.00 Tue–Sun; entry 100,000 rials) Opened in 1980, the museum is housed in the 1915 mansion of a former prime minister in Reza Shah's government, and from 1953–60 it functioned as the Egyptian Embassy, so the building itself has architectural merit. There are two floors of displays that include dramatic 'Nishapur' slip-painted ceramics of the early medieval period, glass works from the 12th–13th century, known as the Golden Age of glass-making in Iran, lustreware from the Gorgan and other excavations, 14th-century pottery from Takht-e Soleyman and some later Safavid and Qajar ceramics. Most of the glass, however, some 260 pieces, is exhibited on the ground floor.

NATIONAL MUSEUM OF IRAN (Iman Khomeini St; ✎ 66702061; ⊕ 09.00–18.00 Tue–Sun; www.nationalmuseumofiran.ir; entry 150,000 rials) This museum is the main archaeological museum of Iran (formerly Iran Bastan Museum) and the brainchild of André Godard (d1965), the French archaeologist and architect who was its first director. (He also established the first school of architecture in Tehran, based on the French system, and designed a number of 'national' tomb monuments in Shiraz, Ferdowsi, etc.) The vaulted brick entrance was designed to recall the famous Sassanid audience hall at Ctesiphon, Iraq. After its completion in 1936, the pre-Islamic collection of artefacts was displayed on the ground floor, with Islamic art exhibited on the first, but today the Islamic collection is housed in a building to the right of the entrance (see opposite).

In the 1936 building, the first cabinets display ceramics dating from the 4th millennium BCE, but visitors are always attracted by the superb unglazed zoomorphic vessels from the 1000BCE Marlik settlement on the Caspian. Remember to look out for the polished reliefs, capitals and statues of the Achaemenid period (6th–4th century BCE); this gleaming, rich brown colour is how the real Persepolis stone quality should look (see page 195), not today's grey, pitted surface. In the bay before it stands the lower half of the famous Darius the Great statue found at Susa (see pages 209–11) in 1972, recording his victorious campaigns in Egypt and declaring 'This is the stone statue which Darius ordered to be made in Egypt so that in the future, he who looked on it would know that the Persian Man held Egypt'. On the side walls there are two panels of glazed, moulded brick from Achaemenid times, reminding visitors that their palaces had richly decorated tiled and painted walls. Further on is a feat of 1st- and 2nd-century CE bronze casting, the moustached and bearded Parthian warrior (1.94m high), found at Shami (see pages 9 and 216). A new cabinet shows the remains of a 3th–4th-century CE man found in a salt mine near Zanjan, north Iran, probably from the Parthian era. In the current arrangement the Sassanid period is poorly represented: the gold and silver gilt platters decorated with scenes of hunting and courtly entertainment displayed in the 1970s have been removed and all that are shown are examples of carved and moulded plaster of Paris, stone capitals and some mosaics from Bishapur. The museum shop here is virtually non-existent.

Islamic Art Museum (*Within National Museum compound; closed with no definite reopening date*) The museum houses a collection of Qurans as well as other manuscripts showing calligraphic styles and paintings in surrounding cases. House textiles, ceramics, etc are displayed in other sections of the museum.

GOLESTAN PALACE COMPLEX (ROSE GARDEN/KAKH-E GOLESTAN) (*Arg Sq;*
☏ *33113335; www.golestanpalace.ir;* ☉ *08.30–17.30 daily; 12 museums with separate tickets, garden entry fee 150,000 rials, 50,000 rials for each museum*) All traces of mid 18th-century construction by the Zand regime were almost totally obliterated by the early Qajar shahs and, rubbing salt into the wound, Agha Mohammed ordered the bones of Karim Khan Zand to be exhumed from his Shiraz grave and placed under the main threshold to be trodden on by all. The palace pavilions then built by Fath Ali Shah were in turn largely torn down during the extensive and lengthy construction programme (1867–92) of Naser al-Din Shah, although two main sections were saved: the Talar Divan Khaneh or Audience Chamber of the Marble Throne (Takht-e Marmar) and the Emarat-e Badgir (Wind Tower) in the south. But the work of that shah suffered too. The huge Taziyeh hall, used for

---

BLAZING MAJESTY OF A QAJAR SHAH

Fath Ali Shah (d1834) was … one blaze of jewels, which literally dazzled the sight on first looking at him … A lofty tiara of three elevations was on his head, which shape appears to have been long peculiar to the crown of the Great King. It was entirely composed of thickly-set diamonds, pearls, rubies and emeralds, so exquisitely disposed, as to form a mixture of the most beautiful colours, in the brilliant light reflected from its surface … His vesture was of gold tissue, nearly covered with a similar disposition of jewellery; and, crossing the shoulders, were two strings of pearls, probably the largest in the world … But for the splendour, nothing could exceed the broad bracelets round his arms, and the belt which encircled his waist; they actually blazed like fire, when the rays of the sun met them … The jewelled band on the right arm was called The Mountain of Light; and that on the left, The Sea of Light; and which superb diamonds, the rapacious conquests of Nader Shah had placed in the Persian regalia … [There was the throne] platform of pure white marble, an apt emblem of peace, raised a few steps from the ground, and carpeted with shawls and cloth of gold, on which the King sat in the fashion of his country, while his back was supported by a large cushion encased in a net-work of pearls.

From R Ker Porter, *Travels in Georgia, Persia, Armenia* … 1821, vol I,
pp 325–7, describing the Nou Rouz royal audience, Golestan Palace, in 1818

for Moharram performance and inspired by the Royal Albert Hall in London (as seen by the Shah during his 1876 state visit), was destroyed in 1946, and his 1891 Kakh-e Abyad (White Palace) was razed to make way for offices of the Ministry of Finance, the Bank Melli and the Ministry of Roads. Also inspired by the Shah's 1873 visit to Europe, which included Versailles with its famous mirrored gallery, is the Hall of Mirrors within the UNESCO-listed Golestan complex which served as the coronation room for both Reza Shah and his son; it remains intact.

If you do not have time to visit all 12 museums, do buy a ticket for the Marble Throne veranda and the art gallery, followed by a walk in the courtyard to look at the various tiled panels, all extremely decorative with the distinct Qajar palette of yellows, pinks and blues. There is a good but expensive giftshop next door to the (currently closed) Ethnographic Museum. The Marble Throne veranda (Ivan-e Takht-e Marmar), straight across the courtyard from the main gate, is decorated with mirrors and other goodies seized by Agha Mohammed from the Zand palace buildings. The throne-couch itself, not the most beautiful artefact made by man, was carved by Esfahani craftsmen in 1807 or 1841 (depending upon who you read) and was where the shah sat during public audiences; Reza Shah Pahlavi was the last ruler to receive birthday and Nou Rouz greetings from his courtiers on this throne. On the veranda a door leads into a small portrait chamber decorated with oil paintings of rulers, historic and mythical, a bevy of European ladies and garden scenes; Fath Ali Shah's portrait is over the chimney. The main art gallery (Negar Khaneh) is next door, including mainly 19th-century oils, some the work of Kamal al-Molk, the leading court painter to Naser al-Din Shah, and then come the 1875 hall of mirrors and the European Art Gallery. The twin-tower pavilion is the Shams al-Emerah built by Naser al-Din, which now houses a small collection of calligraphy (no labels in English) in a splendour of mirrors and plasterwork. This was the first five-storey building to be constructed in Tehran, which Lord Curzon described in 1892 as 'a very creditable specimen of the fanciful ingenuity that still lingers in modern Persian art'. Continuing around this gaily tiled courtyard you come across the photography gallery and archive, the Tent House, now used for conferences, and the so-called Diamond Room, a tea house and toilets.

MASJED-E MOTAHHARI (formerly Masjed-e Sepahsalar, 'Commander in Chief') (*East of Golestan Palace, on the south side of Maydan-e Baharestan, northeast of Maydan-e Imam Khomeini; admittance to the public is generally not allowed, if you are with a guide an exception can be made*) This, along with its adjacent madrasa, is one of the most photogenic historic mosques in Tehran. The official policy promoted by Reza Shah Pahlavi in the 1930s led to most of Tehran's mosques closing down along with the madrasas; it has been estimated that by 1942 only 24 mosques were open and operating in the capital. That is certainly not the case today. As the Madraseh va Masjed-e Motahhari, it is now a fully functioning theological college again. The main entrance portal and the façade are quite distinctive Qajar style. Built by two high-ranking officials in the court of Naser al-Din Shah in 1879–81, when its location was just inside the city walls, for many years it was one of the largest four-*ivan* mosques in Tehran. Two massive minarets flank the recessed entrance, which leads into a courtyard surrounded by twin-storeyed arcades of college rooms; in all there are some 60 chambers. Tiles with full-blown floral motifs in typically flamboyant Qajar style decorate the courtyard, while a tile inscription band gives details of the original endowment. The prayer hall dome, 37m in height, is supported by 44 columns. Right behind the mosque is the new parliament (*majles*) building.

MASJED-E IMAM South of Maydan-e Baharestan in the main bazaar area is the Masjed-e Imam Khomeini (formerly Masjed-e Shah), built according to inscriptions in the qibla *ivan* in 1808–13 on the orders of Fath Ali Shah (d1834); at that time it faced the main citadel. Much of the mosque, its central courtyard with the four-*ivan* layout and the *muqarnas* vaulting in the *ivans* recalls the royal buildings of 17th-century Esfahan, but the tile decoration is in the gloriously flamboyant Qajar style. It was repaired by Fath Ali Shah's grandson Naser al-Din Shah some 60 years later.

BAZAAR AND AROUND The bazaar is located within the block edged by Khayyam Street (in the west), Panzandah Khordad Street (north) and Shadid Mostafa Khomeini (east). Traffic around this area is horrendous. The first higher education establishment in Tehran, Dar ul-Fonun, founded in 1851 for upper-class Persians, is located nearby on Naser Khosrow Street. An Armenian church, St Thaddeus (Kelisa Talavus), one of the handful in the capital, is located to the southeast section, off Shadid Mostafa Khomeini, on Shahid Mostavi running west. There is also the 19th-century Armenian Cathedral of St Sergius (Kelisa Sarkis) (*north end of Shahid Ostad Nejatollah, just south of Karim Khan Zand St;* \ *88897980;* ⊕ *13.00–18.00 daily*). Ostad Nejattollah Street, running south, boasts a large number of souvenir shops, including an Iranian Handicrafts Organisation shop.

REZA ABBASI MUSEUM (*892 Dr Shariati St;* \ *88513002; www.rezaabbasimuseum. ir;* ⊕ *09.00–17.00 Tue–Sun; entry 100,000 rials*) Do make every attempt to visit this museum: it is the place to see some of the masterpieces of classical Persian book painting from the 14th century and other eye-catching archaeological treasures. There are five galleries, with the top floor displaying some of the most important finds in gold and silver. Vessels from Ziwiyeh and Marlik dating from the 1st millennium BCE, as well as treasures from other Achaemenid sites, feature alongside the silver-gilt 'hunting' platters of the Sassanid dynasty. The displays on the second floor concentrate on Islamic ceramics and metalwork up to and including the Qajar period. The Painting Gallery is located on the first floor and manuscript illustrations range from the separate leaves from early Shahnamehs to the album studies of the late Safavid period. Each is labelled in Farsi and English. More detailed information is available in Farsi only. The ground floor is where temporary exhibitions are shown. Getting here may prove to be a challenge. Make sure to give directions to your taxi driver. The museum is located across the road from the K H Toosi University of Technology on the corner of Mir Motahhari Street and before the high suspension car bridge.

SAADABAD PALACE COMPLEX (Kakh-e Saad Abad) (*Vali Asr St, Taheri St;* \ *22752031; www.saadabadpalace.org;* ⊕ *09.00–18.30 daily; 19 different museums with separate tickets; entry 50,000 rials each, 150,000 rials for the garden complex only; free minibus service within parts of the complex*) An enjoyable, unrushed half-day can be spent exploring Saadabad Palace and its 110ha of grounds, constructed to house the Pahlavi family and officials. If nothing else, such a visit reminds one how the late Mohammed Reza Shah (d1980) removed himself from the everyday life of Tehran. Today, of course, residential housing has spread on to this previously isolated hillside. Some of the palace-mansions now function as headquarters for various municipal services (eg: water), others house art collections and before President Ahmadinejed took office, visiting VIPs were occasionally accommodated here, which meant certain areas were out of bounds, but currently such guests are housed elsewhere. If you do not have time to visit all the museums, do find time for the **Mellat Palace** ('White

Palace') with a pair of giant bronze boots – all that remains of a huge stature of Reza Shah (d1941) – standing by the side of the steps. It was said that the army life so conditioned Reza Shah that he preferred sleeping on the floor rather than in a bed, and certainly this house does not feel lived in. During Nou Rouz outside the palace there are concerts and a small local market with a traditional tea house.

Further up the hill from Mellat Palace is another must-see museum. The Green Palace is so called because it is faced with a distinctive special greenish-yellow marble, which reminded one visitor of 1950s Fablon plastic coverings. Reza Shah ordered this construction in 1925 and certainly his small office has a more personal ambience than the Mellat. Elsewhere the excess of mirror-work, blue brocade silk curtains with silver metal thread fringes, tassels in the bedrooms and the crimson silk dining rooms speak more of the excesses of his son, Mohammed Reza.

NIAVARAN CULTURAL AND HISTORICAL COMPLEX (KAKH-E NIAVARAN)
(*Pourebtehaj St;* ☏ *22282012;* ⊕ *09.00–18.30 daily; entry 150,000 rials; 7 museums with separate tickets; entry 50,000 rials each apart from the Niavaran Palace – 100,000 rials*) Initially a Fath Ali Shah summer residence, the palace complex buildings, built in the Qajar and Pahlavi periods on this 11ha land, now function as museums. The most interesting, however, is the more recent **Niavaran Palace** completed in 1968; it served as the residency of the royal family and it is from here that in January 1979 Shah Mohammed Reza Pahlavi went into exile, two weeks before the proclamation of the Islamic Republic in Iran. It is wonderfully modern, but the interior, designed by French architects, is classic. On the first floor there is fine French 18th-century tapesty and the Marc Chagal *Azure Shore* painting. **Ahmad Shah Pavilion**, built in the final days of Qajar rule as a private house for Ahmad Shah the seventh and the last Qajar monarch, and was subsequently used by Reza Pahlavi as his residency and office, is another must-see in this complex.

MAUSOLEUM OF AYATOLLAH KHOMEINI (*Behesht-e Zahra cemetery, southwest Tehran, visibly unmissable when coming along the Besat motorway from the IKA airport, around 20km from Tehran; metro Haram-e Mottahar; entry free; shoes, bags, etc must be left at the mausoleum entrance & photography is not allowed; women enter to the left, men to the right; no chador necessary*) The complex is situated adjacent to the huge cemetery, Behesht-e Zahra, named after an epithet of Fatima, the Prophet's daughter and wife to Ali, the first imam. In the late 1970s, this cemetery became closely associated with the revolutionary movement against the Pahlavi regime, as many of those killed in the 1978 demonstrations were buried here; after the 8 September 1978 demonstration over 4,290 burial certificates were issued for this site. No wonder this was the place selected by Ayatollah Khomeini for his first public speech six months later. Many of the soldiers killed during the Iran–Iraq war were also buried here and photographs of the central fountain which once ran with blood-red coloured water (symbolising the martyrs' sacrifice) featured on the front page of many Western newspapers.

The mausoleum of Khomeini is still not finished but it already dominates the landscape, particularly at night when the central golden-domed tomb and the surrounding buildings on each corner of an enormous 'terrace' are illuminated. The floor area of the actual tomb building is equivalent in size to twice that of London Heathrow's terminal 4 check-in area, and has similar exposed pipes and structural girders. Acres of green onyx slabs cover the vast floor while a glass drum adorned with giant, fat, blood-red tulip motifs (blood of the martyrs) sits uneasily over the cenotaph grille.

DAMAVAND AND SKI RESORTS AROUND TEHRAN In proximity to the Iranian capital there are numerous mountain-hiking areas and ski resorts, where you can easily spend a full day walking or even stay overnight if you decide not to return to Tehran the same day.

Damavand, at 5,610m, is Iran's highest summit, covered with snow all year long. The area surrounding this volcanic mountain is rich in natural hot springs, and small rocks of volcanic formation scattered along the area's curvy roads are used in Iranian households. About 50km northeast from Tehran towards Damavand along the Haraz road lies a small ski resort and the wealthy Tehrani holiday-home conglomeration of **Abadieh**. Continuing along the road you pass through **Imamzadeh Hashem**, famous for its kite games due to strong wings at this altitude. The next town in the area is **Polur**, known for its freshwater trout and salmon hatcheries and fish market. One of the local fish restaurants here would be a good choice for lunch before you continue on towards the village of Rineh, where the Iranian army kept Iraqi prisoners of war. The town of **Larijan**, the namesake of the current chairman of the parliament of Iran, is known for its hot springs and has numerous apartment-style, essentially budget, hotels with a hot-spring bath. The best and by by far the largest in the area is Pasargard Hotel (*36 rooms;* \ *0122 23362364–5;* e *info@hotel-pasargad.com; www.pasargadhotel. com*). Hotel Parsian (\ *0122 3362091, 3362502*) and Negine Hotel (\ *0122 3362170*) are the cheaper options if you decide to stay here overnight. If returning to Tehran along the same road, swerve in by the **Latiyan Dam**, 10km away from the capital. Here you can take a break and have a picnic by the blue lake amid the mountain range.

The northern suburb of Velenjak is home to **Tochal** ski and hiking resort (\ *22404001–5; www.tochal.org*). Known as Bam-e tehran, 'the roof of Tehran', Tochal (3,964m) is the most popular and central Tehrani hiking spot. Getting here requires a taxi ride (up to 180,000 rials) to the corner of Velenjak Street and Daneshju Boulevard. Consider this the '0' station. From here it is a short walk through the parking lot and past a café area to where you can take a bus (5,000 rials) or walk around 2km to the first station. From here, yet again you can walk 3.5km up or take the cable car (*70,000 rials one-way;* ⊕ *08.30–00.30 Tue–Sat*) to the second station, where you need to change and purchase another ticket if you wish to continue on to the final, seventh station.

Higher yet again, around 1.98km from the seventh station is the famous Tochal Hotel (*30 rooms; Shahid Chamran Expressway;* \ *22418000; $$$*). The area offers exceptional skiing opportunities seven to eight months of the year. The total distance between the first station and the Tochal Hotel is 17.08km and there is a walking path all the way up for those in good shape and spirits. There are toilet facilities and a rest area at each of the stations. If you've left your skis at home, do at least come here for the breathtaking views over Tehran.

Another popular and highly recommended ski resort is **Dizin**, 20km north of Tehran on the way to Chalus after the small village of Pol-a Zanguleh. There is an internationally recognised ski slope here, but coming here would necessitate a taxi or private car hire. Dizin skiing season is from mid-December until May and there is the pleasant **Gajereh Grand Hotel** (*120 rooms; Bokharest St, 15 8th St;* \ *88754944–6;* e *info@gajereh.ir; www.gajereh.ir; $$*). With large and clean rooms in two separate buildings, comfort depends on the price. Cheaper rooms are not unlike other budget hotels around Iran, but more expensive options are better. The hotel has a restaurant, coffee shop and a spacious and bright lobby.

3

SOUTH OF TEHRAN

RAYY AND AROUND Before the 19th century, biblical Rhages (a name of Greek origin), known in Iran as Shahr-e Rey, was a more important town than Tehran; it lies 16km south of the capital but Tehran has now engulfed it and the metro has stretched all the way from the city centre to here. Said to be the 12th city of the world to be created by Ahura Mazda, and the place where Tobias and the angel stopped after the wedding in Hamadan (see page 211), the town was rebuilt and renamed as Europos by Seleucus Nikator (c300BCE), the same person responsible for Apamea and Dura Europos in Syria. There were important Parthian and Sassanid settlements here and Harun al-Rashid, the famous Abbasid caliph whose son was later to be involved in the sudden death of Imam Reza (see page 260), was born here in 763CE. It became an important administrative centre under the Seljuk sultanate when it became known as 'the most beautiful city of the East', second only to the Abbasid centre of the Islamic Empire, Baghdad. Very little of that remains, as Rayy (as it is usually transliterated today) was almost totally obliterated by the Mongol armies in the 1220s.

Getting there Rayy is located around 16km south from Tehran and is accessible by metro (Shahr-e Rey station).

What to see and do To many Iranians, the most important monument in Rayy is the **Shrine of (Shah) Abd al-Azim**, which houses the graves of the descendants of the second and fourth imams, and Hamzeh, a brother of the eighth imam. During the late shah's time, non-Muslims were not permitted to enter but could catch glimpses into the first courtyard from the 1950 concrete memorial-tomb of Reza Shah, who died during his South African exile, its monumental proportions reminiscent of certain Lodi tombs in Delhi, India; it was one of the first Pahlavi monuments to be destroyed in 1979. The shrine itself was lovingly repaired and decorated during the Safavid period, with additions including the mirror-work in the 19th century. It was here, on leaving the shrine, that Naser al-Din Shah was assassinated in 1896.

To the north of the shrine are the heavily restored remains of a Seljuk tomb tower locally known as Toghrol after the sultan Toghrol Beg (d1063), although it was built over 60 years later. It stands about 20m high, with a diameter of about 16.5m, but it has lost its original conical dome. In the hills behind is a Qajar rock-cut relief depicting the unfortunate Qajar shah, Naser al-Din, with his ten sons, and another earlier panel showing Fath Ali Shah with some members of his enormous family (he was said to have fathered 189 children). This is Chesmeh Ali (Spring Water of Ali) whose pure soft water has ensured its reputation as a carpet-washing centre over the last two centuries.

It was near here that, during the 1920s and '30s, American archaeological teams excavated the site of Nagareh Khaneh and found, among other items, remnants of woven silk fabrics, thought to date to around 900–1220CE. The textile world was astounded by the discoveries and when further pieces came on to the open market during and after World War II, they were eagerly snapped up by the major museums in the West; in the late 1970s scientific analyses revealed that many of the newly acquired 'Buyid' pieces were in fact clever forgeries. This is also the location of the Shrine of Bibi Shahrbanu. The story of this shrine is closely linked to that of a Zoroastrian shrine outside Yazd, in southeastern Iran (see page 236), and similar to that of St Tikla of Maaloula, outside Damascus, Syria. It is said that a daughter of the last Sassanid shah, Yazdegerd III, married to the third imam,

Hossein, grandson of the Prophet Mohammed, fled here to escape the overtures of an Umayyad general. At her behest, the mountain opened and then closed around her, saving her from a fate worse than death. Probably this was originally a shrine to Anahita, the Zoroastrian divinity. Evidence of 10th-century building work has largely disappeared under continuous rebuilding from the 15th century onwards.

Continuing south some 10km will bring you to the remains of a huge brick complex, Tappeh Mil, dating from Sassanid times. It is thought this was an important fire temple with royal audience halls and associate buildings. Little was readily identifiable in the mid 1970s and today it is more of a monument to modern reconstruction skills.

It is about 20km further on to **Varamin** which is home to the heavily restored tomb tower of Ala al-Din (c1289), whose exterior is decorated with 32 angled flanges, and an early 14th-century Masjed-e Jame, built on the four-ivan plan. It is thought that the Ilkhanid ruler, Oljeitu, paid for this mosque, which was then completed by his successor in 1322. Almost a century later it needed attention as two panels in the prayer chamber refer to the Timurid ruler, Shah Rukh (see box, page 254). A great deal of restoration and rebuilding work was undertaken in the 1970s. Enough of the strap-brickwork decoration in turquoise and cobalt blue and the carved plasterwork remains to allow the imagination to picture the original scheme of decoration and the clean proportions. There are the remains of two other Ilkhanid structures in Varamin. One is just a portal to the Masjed-e Sharif of 1307, not far from the Masjed-e Jame, and the other is the Imamzadeh Yahya, whose splendid tile-*mihrab*, now in the Hermitage Museum, St Petersburg, gives a late 13th century date for the buildings itself.

QOM AND AROUND (pronounced Ghom; population 1,100,000) Located 154km southwest from Tehran, this city is the second most sacred place in Iran after Mashhad, because it was here that Fatima, the sister of the eighth imam, Imam Reza (and not Fatima, the Prophet's daughter and wife of Ali) fell ill on her way to Mashhad and died in 816CE. The city has grown extensively since the early 1970s, with a road and traffic system designed to cope with a daily influx of pilgrims and visitors.

When the town was established is unclear, for its water supply has always been poor and brackish so there was little logic for a settlement. Perhaps it was founded by the Arab Muslims after conquering the region in 644CE but possibly there was a sizeable settlement in existence then, for we know Zoroastrianism remained influential here until 901CE. By then Qom was also known for its Shi'a theologians although there was no sign of a special tomb to commemorate Fatima. It was rumoured this was the birthplace of that powerful political figure, Hassan al-Sabah, leader of the Ismaili sect, the Assassins (see page 94). Perhaps that was why the Mongols exacted such a fierce revenge on the small town, as it was then, massacring most of the population in 1221. In the 14th century it was best known for its hunting, and many Iranian rulers wintered here; a shrine for Fatima was in existence, but by all accounts it was a modest complex. All that changed with the Safavid regime (1501–1735). As champions of Ithna 'Ashari Shi'ism, the Safavid shahs undertook a programme of construction and repairs to the Qom shrine, as they would do with those of Karbala, Ardabil and Mashhad, perhaps hoping to persuade Iranians and other Shi'as to forego the hajj to Mecca and Medina. The rebel Afghans exacted their revenge and even with royal Qajar patronage, Qom's population in 1872 was a mere 4,000.

Today the population stands at approximately 1.8 million, owing much of its reputation as a theological teaching centre to the charismatic theologian, Ayatollah

Haeri-Yazdi (d1935), one of Ayatollah Khomeini's teachers. As for the town's water, new reservoirs were constructed soon after the revolution.

Getting there Regular **buses** to Qom depart from Tehran's Terminal-e Jonoob (South Terminal). There is, however, no bus terminal in Qom and when returning or going further south the taxi will drop you at 72 Tan Square or Vali Asr Square respectively from where buses depart as soon as all seats are filled.

What to see and do The golden dome and twin minarets of Fatima's shrine, **Hezrat-e Ma'sumeh** (shrine of Fatima, sister of Iman Reza, see page 260) (⊕ *always; grounds accessible to non-Muslims but women must wear a chador, available to rent in the women's entrance hall, & must ensure that hair is covered entirely & at all times, otherwise it will not be long before one of the guardians points it out*), dominate the skyline. It is, as Lord Curzon said, the 'Westminster Abbey of many of her kings', for the shrine houses the remains of four Safavid shahs (Safi I, Abbas II, Soleyman I and Sultan-Hossein) and two Qajar rulers, Fath Ali Shah (with two of his sons) and Mohammed Shah along with countless high officials of the Qajar court. There is a large *maydan* in front surrounded by a bazaar, souvenir shops and sweet shops selling the local delicacy, *sohan*, a thin butter 'brittle' with pistachios. Just before the main entrance to the first courtyard, the tiled doorway on the right marks the entrance into the madrasa where Ayatollah Khomeini studied. The city has been, and still is, witness to some of the liveliest and most thought-provoking theological debates, discussing the role of the *ulama* (clergy) in revolutionary Iran,

A short description of the complex follows but note that it is based on information and maps published in the late 1970s; no account of any repairs or construction appears to have been published since then. An earlier arrangement of four courtyards in the complex was revised in Safavid times, when the Madrasa Faydiyeh was built over two of the courts, with a small hospital (Dar al-Shifa) behind. In the late 19th century a huge courtyard, Sahn-e Jadid, was constructed to cope with pilgrims. Several madrasas, including that of Jani Khan, were extensively repaired at this time, and the dome and drum over Fatima's cenotaph were gilded and the chamber extensively clad in mirror-work. Such funding dried up as the Qajar regime faltered. Increasingly, during the first half of the 20th century, theological studies and the colleges involved in their teaching received markedly less royal patronage and funding. However, with increasing secularism in Ottoman and then Kemalist Turkey, Shi'a theologians returned to Iran, and particularly to Mashhad and Qom. Disused madrasas in the sacred precinct were repaired and reopened, and with the installation of Ayatollah Haeri-Yazdi from Arak and his numerous students, the rejuvenation of Qom as a teaching centre and a pilgrimage place really began.

From 1975 onwards, the main entrance has opened immediately into the Sahn-e Jadid, renamed Nou Atabaki, where the festival prayers are held. Directly opposite on the far side is the passageway, which leads to the Old Treasury. To the left is the tomb of Shah Safi (d1642) and, behind, that of Abbas II (d1666) along with the entrance into the Masjed-e Bala Sar, which formerly housed the museum. To the right a passage leads into the Sahn-e Kuhneh, where Fath Ali Shah is interred at the far end. Behind this courtyard are the Madrasa Faydiyeh and the Dar al-Shifa.

Some locals say that there are around 400 *imamzadehs* in Qom, but historical monuments here are few. The 8th-century **Gonbad-e Sabz** (the Green Domes Historical Complex) (⊕ *07.30–17.00, but mostly closed*) is across the road from

Imamzadeh Ali Ibn Jafar, which was built in 1360 for a local amir and his family by a craftsman who went on to erect three other mausoleums. Its 12-sided exterior (but octagonal interior) once supported a double dome, hemispherical inside and tent-like on the outside, but today they have been replaced. The carved plasterwork on the exterior was originally colourfully painted.

From Qom, it is about 100km south to Kashan (see pages 109–14). Along this road, 6km from Qom is another important pilgrimage monument, the **Jamkaran Mosque**, built on the site where it is believed the 12th imam once appeared. When looking at a road map it is always intriguing to note the Iranian village given as Naufel Le Chato on some early 1990s maps (the spelling on later maps is often 'Neufle'). This settlement wished to honour Ayatollah Khomeini, and so redesignated itself after the French town outside Paris where the Ayatollah lived in exile, Neauphle-le-Château.

Southwest of Qom is **Saveh**, 112km from Tehran, associated with a type of lustre and enamel-painted ceramics which was thought to have been made here in the 13th century, and more importantly for its double-spiral staircased minaret in the centre of town, considered to be the earliest still standing in Iran, linked to the Masjed-e Maydan of 1062. Further down the same road is another early minaret with splendid brickwork patterning, this time belonging to the Masjed-e Jame of 1111. The prayer hall of this second mosque was probably constructed at the same time but much restoration and rebuilding was carried out in both the Mongol and later Safavid periods.

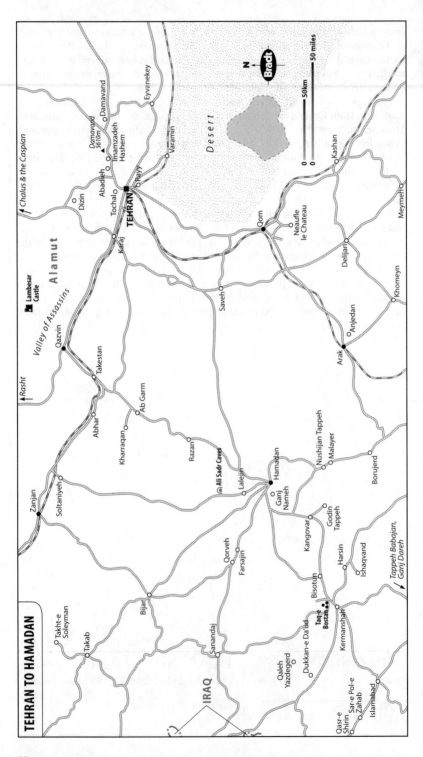

TEHRAN TO HAMADAN

West of Tehran: Qazvin and Hamadan

QAZVIN *Telephone code 0281*

About 152km west of Tehran lies Qazvin (pronounced as Ghazvin, population 464,000), founded by the Sassanid shah Shapur I (d272) on the great central plain criss-crossed by caravan routes to the Zagros Mountains and Mesopotamia (Iraq), the Caucasus and the Caspian. The town quickly fell to the Arab Muslim armies in 644 and prospered as the trade routes were made secure, with members of the Abbasid caliphate visiting the town *en route* for eastern Iran. In the 12th century the regional administration became destabilised as the Assassins established strongholds around Alamut to the north. Order was restored by the Seljuk sultanate, but then the city suffered at the hands of the Mongol armies in 1220 and 1256. The political rivalry between the Ottoman and Safavid empires in the early 16th century was translated into military confrontation and Tabriz, the first Safavid capital, proved too close to the battlefield. The court moved down to Qazvin in 1555 until the Ottoman threat forced it to relocate to Esfahan in 1597, leaving behind the royal gardens, pavilions and offices. Even so, in 1628 foreign visitors reported that the city extended over 11km, with a population of about 150,000. By 1700 Ottoman incursions and earthquakes had left Qazvin in ruins, with few defences to withstand Afghan attacks against Safavid authority. Prosperity returned to a degree with Qajar rule, but again the city's location made it strategically important to Russian and then Soviet occupying forces during both world wars. Qazvin Islamic Azad University, which is second after Tehran as the most popular choice among foreign students for studying Persian, is located here.

GETTING THERE AND AROUND Frequent *savari* taxis leave the Azadi (Western) Terminal in Tehran and get here within 90 minutes. Tickets cost 70,000–100,000 rials and can be easily purchased right before departure. **Buses** depart from the same terminal, but are less regular and you are more than likely to be intercepted by a *savari* section employee who will take you to the *savari* departures area.

Once you are in Qazvin, as the town map on page 93 indicates, most of the sights are within walking distance of each other and the two hotels recommended are conveniently located near the historic city centre.

TOURIST INFORMATION Qazvin's **tourist office** (*Naderi-e Shomali St, next to Mir Imam Sq, in the park;* 3354708; 08.00–20.00) can organise tours and open closed doors, such as those of the Qajar-period Russian Orthodox Church (see page 95).

WHERE TO STAY AND EAT Qazvin is the best place to stay overnight if you wish to visit the Alamut region, and the two hotels below are more than adequate. For locaton of listings see map, page 93.

⌂ **Hotel Marmar** (50 rooms) Ayatollah Khamenei Bd; ☎2555771–5, 2565771–5. Self-described as 'the best & the largest city hotel' it has certainly seen some glory days. Lobby décor is Qajar mixed with tourism grandeur ambitions, but the rooms are large & clean, albeit a little dark. Staff seem a little bored, but the street outside is one of the busiest in town, full of coffee & ice cream shops. **$$**

⌂ **Alborz Hotel** (36 rooms) Taleqani St; ☎2226631; e info@alborzhotel.com; www.alborzhotel.com. A budget traveller's dream, this recently renovated hotel has a large lobby with small balconies overlooking the main street. Each room is immaculate & spacious. Wi-Fi is fast, but available in the lobby only. B/fast is excellent &

staff most accommodating. Easily the best choice in town. **$**

✕ **Hamam Safa** (formerly Haji Mohammed Rahim) Molavi Jonubi St; m 091 26823055; ⊕ for tea 12.00–23.00, for meals 12.00–15.00 & 19.00–23.00. This 19th-century *hamam*, formerly a museum, has recently been converted into a lovely traditional restaurant. It serves standard Iranian dishes & *qalian* is allowed for men & women alike. **$**

✕ **Yas** Taleghani St, across the road from Alborz Hotel; ☎2222853; ⊕ 12.00–15.00 & 19.00–23.00. Serves good food fast. Do not expect to be served any exotic local specialities, but chicken kebab & lamb shank are recommended. **$**

WHAT TO SEE AND DO Very little remains of the pre-20th-century walled town of Qazvin except for the Qajar-period **Tehran Gate**, decked out in its 19th-century yellow, blue and black tiling, looking rather lost and forlorn standing alone in the street. Most visitors make their way immediately to the **Imamzadeh Hossein**, which enshrines the remains of Hossein, a son of the eighth imam (passing at the top of the road, a *zurkhaneh* or wrestling gymnasium (see box, page 120) identified by the external tiled cornice of wrestlers and 'Indian clubs' – the caretaker happily shows people around). The main entrance vestibule into the *imamzadeh* is also decorated with 19th-century Qajar tiles in pastel shades depicting full-blown roses and other flowers. This brings the visitor into a huge octagonal courtyard (representing the four quarters of the world overset with the four gardens of paradise). In the centre stands the shrine with its mirrored-glass veranda. There should be no problem entering through the shrine's massive silver doors, women using the left-hand door and men the right, leaving shoes at the attendants' desks. Women must wear *chadors*, which are available for rent when passing through the main entrance. Note that no photography is allowed inside. The shrine was clearly active during Safavid times because an inscription records that a daughter of Shah Tahmasp paid for restoration work in 1630, but most decoration is much later. On Fridays and holy days many families come here on pilgrimage, having lunch as they sit in the courtyard alcoves. As you walk round the exterior of the building, look at the paving stones, especially those to the left of the main veranda. Some of these are gravestones bearing emblems denoting the gender and profession of those commemorated.

A short walk from here is the **Masjed-e Jame**, also known as **Masjed-e Atiq** (*entry 100,000 rials*), slightly set back from the main road. Head down the passageway and into the courtyard of this four-portal mosque. The inner arcades of the courtyard, with the characteristic Qajar pink and yellow tiles on their façades, have been extensively restored in the last decade, and there has also been 19th-century 'prettification' following on from extensive late 17th-century repairs to two of the four ivans. The real reason for visiting is the main prayer hall to the left. It is thought to have been built over a ruined Zoroastrian fire temple, but in recent years repairs and a forest of scaffolding have prevented access to this chamber. However, in case the restoration is completed soon, it might be useful to include a brief description of this early 12th-century chamber (15.25m²). It is dominated by a huge, 19m, hemispherical dome

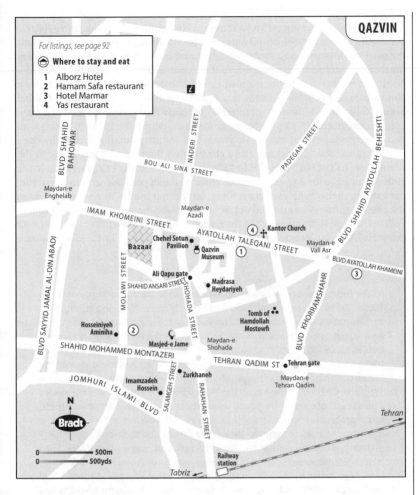

For listings, see page 92

⊜ **Where to stay and eat**

1 Alborz Hotel
2 Hamam Safa restaurant
3 Hotel Marmar
4 Yas restaurant

BLVD SHAHID BAHONAR

NADERI STREET

BOU ALI SINA STREET

PADEGAN STREET

BLVD SHAHID AYATOLLAH BEHESHTI

Maydan-e Enghelab

IMAM KHOMEINI STREET

Maydan-e Azadi

Kantor Church

4

AYATOLLAH TALEQANI STREET

BLVD AYATOLLAH KHAMEINI

Chehel Sotun Pavilion

Bazaar

Qazvin Museum

Maydan-e Vali Asr

1

3

BLVD SAYYID JAMAL AL-DIN ABADI

MOLAWI STREET

Ali Qapu gate

SHAHID ANSARI STREET

SHOHADA STREET

Madrasa Heydariyeh

BLVD KHORRAMSHAHR

Hosseiniyeh Aminiha

2

Masjed-e Jame

Tomb of Hamdollah Mostowfi

Maydan-e Shohada

SHAHID MOHAMMED MONTAZERI

TEHRAN QADIM ST

Tehran gate

JOMHURI ISLAMI BLVD

SALAMGEH STREET

RAHAHAN STREET

Zurkhaneh

Imamzadeh Hossein

Maydan-e Tehran Qadim

Tehran

N

Bradt

0 ———— 500m
0 ———— 500yds

Tabriz

Railway station

supported on four large squinches. A monumental, floriated, Kufic brick inscription around the dome-base states that the Seljuk governor of Qazvin, Khumartash (d1136), ordered its construction in 1106, finishing nine years later. Given that the Seljuks were staunch Sunni Muslims, it is intriguing that there is also an unusual reference to Ali, the son-in-law of the Prophet Mohammed. Slowly the eye adjusts to the understated decoration of subtly coloured brickwork and carved plaster, once colourfully painted. A lengthy inscription band (Q3:133; 27:40; Q16:34; Quran reference, explained under *What to take*, page 46) snakes over three walls in a series of giant trilobed meanders, while other inscriptions record the list of endowments to the mosque from shop rents, villages taxes and so on.

If on site, the architect in charge of works welcomes visitors into his office in the far-left corner of the courtyard. Speaking a fluent mixture of French, German and English, he delights in showing photographs (some pre-1960), drawings and maquettes of the mosque and other local monuments. Try not to disturb the male students working in the library directly opposite. The 19th-century winter hall downstairs has pleasing proportions but this has now been converted into a library for female students, who are happy to let foreign women (but not men) invade their space.

Behind the mosque just off Molavi Street, is **Hosseiniyeh Aminiha** (*entry 100,000 rials*), built during the 19th century to house the Moharram 'mystery play' that retells the story of Hossein's tragic death at Karbala and is performed every year. Turning north along Molavi takes one towards the bazaar and the 19th-century Masjed-e Nabi, and further east to the main square of Maydan-e Azadi. On its south side, almost concealed by bus shelters, is a small Safavid garden pavilion, the **Chehel Sotun** (Caligraphy Museum) (⊕ *09.00–17.00; entry 50,000 rials, the garden is free*), constructed around 1545 possibly by or for Shah Tahmasp (r1524–76) along with two other pavilions that haven't survived. This intimate building, originally open on four sides (now glassed in), and a chamber on the ground floor, served as the 'coronation' hall of Shah Ismail II in 1576, and of Shah Abbas I 12 years later. In the 19th century, the local Qajar governor repaired the upper floor structure covering the exterior arches with exuberant tiling, but during the 1970s restoration, when the present garden was also laid out, some original Safavid decoration was found. Follow the large sign at the back of the garden to **Qazvin Museum** (⊕ *09.00–18.00; entry 50,000 rials*) founded in 1957. It was initially located in the Chehel Sotun

THE ISMAILI ASSASSINS

As the Fatimid regime of Egypt and Syria began to crack and fragment in the 1060s, the Ismaili community in Iran began to dig in, securing strongholds to defend their villages and land. This valley of the River Alamut soon gained an international reputation as the 'Valley of the Assassins', with its chain of impregnable fortresses dominating the trade routes, and its team of highly trained men willing to sacrifice their own lives to safeguard the leaders of the Ismaili community, such as Hassan al-Sabbah in Iran and Rashid al-Din Sinan in Syria (the 'Old Man of the Mountains' as described by the Crusader chronicler, Joinville). These were the young men whose clandestine activities spread terror among the Crusaders and Muslim military leaders as they infiltrated inner court circles to 'remove' those who threatened their own community – leaders like the Seljuk sultan and champion of Sunni Islam, Malik Shah (r1072–94), his vizier Nizam al-Molk (assassinated 1092) and Richard Coeur de Lion. As recorded by Marco Polo, rumours spread that Hassan al-Sabbah could instil such loyalty and single-mindedness only by drugging his followers (known as *hashashiyya*, from which comes 'assassin') and promising them the delights of paradise. The reality was that this was a tight-knit community with a rigid hierarchy under a charismatic leader, renowned for his scholarship and library. His death in 1125 resulted in serious disquiet within the community, and without the protection of the strongholds such as Alamut, perhaps its very survival would have been threatened. Later successors followed more pragmatic policies, establishing links with neighbouring political powers, but the Mongol invasions changed all this. Circumstances allowed Hulagu, the Mongol commander, to seize and imprison the leader of the Iranian Ismaili community in Qazvin in 1256, heralding a massacre in which the fortresses were surrendered.

The community scattered throughout Iran but in the 1770s it was in control of Kerman and Bam, with the blessing of the Zand family. The leader of the Ismailis was honoured with the title of agha khan by Fath Ali Shah, but by 1840 the religious atmosphere had so changed that the community left for India.

pavilion, but moved here in 2004. Its archeological exhibits are worth a look if you are in the gardens already.

Close by is the only other Safavid building surviving in Qazvin, the 17th-century **Ali Qapu** (pronounced Ghapu) or monumental entrance into the former palace complex. For over 40 years it has been the police headquarters, so neither access nor photography is permitted. About 250m southeast and not far from the Masjed-e Jame, geographically and chronologically speaking, are the remains of a two-ivan **Madrasa Heydariyeh** located in a school yard; the guardian may seem reticent, but only because foreign visitors create intense excitement among the schoolboys. Modern buttresses and a dome support the prayer hall, built c1115, probably just after the Masjed-e Jame, while a 'new' basement successfully combats rising damp (many restoration programmes have involved a generous use of concrete which has resulted in serious damp problems). Much remains of the early 12th-century brickwork with its subtly fired colouring, touches of turquoise and cobalt-glazed brick inserts, together with a fine plaster *mihrab* decorated with florid motifs and floriated Kufic. If time permits, the 14th-century **Tomb of Hamdollah Mostowfi** (*entry 100,000 rials*) not far from the Tehran Gate, is worth seeing. Although heavily restored, this tomb of a famous historian and geographer with its tiled, pointed, conical dome, has sufficient originality to satisfy the visitor.

One of the remnants of a more recent past is the Qajar-period **Kantor Russian Orthodox Church** (*off Daraee St & just a 2min walk from the Alborz Hotel*), known for its distinctive bell tower around 11m high and the two courtyard gravestones: one for a railroad engineer, dated 1906, and the other for a Russian World War II pilot. The church is permanently closed, but you can contact Qazvin Tourist Office (see page 91) to arrange a time to view the inside.

Around Qazvin
Around 60km northeast from Qazvin the **Alamut** region begins, encompassing fertile valleys, hillside villages and beautiful mountains. **Lambesar Castle** is about 25km along the road to the left once you arrive in the first town in Alamut. Follow the first and only sign and after that ask one of the local farmers for further directions. **Alamut Castle** (*entry 100,000 rials*), however, is another 60km further afield. The road is good, but mountainous and curvy and takes a long time. Another famous natural attraction neaby is the picturesque **Ovan** village by the lake of the same name. Plan to spend a full day exploring this scenic area; bring your lunch box with you. A full-day taxi can be arranged at your hotel for around 1,200,000 rials. Today, Alamut itself is not in a good state of repair, but **Shamran** in the valley and another fortress at Soru, 100km east of Tehran, still retain something of their multiple defence walls and round towers.

If you are interested in patterned brickwork, there is a cluster of fine medieval examples near Qazvin. The first is in the outskirts of **Takestan**, southwest of Qazvin on the road to Hamadan. This is the **Imamzadeh Pir**, built c1100 in what is a rather unattractive location. The plan is square both inside and out, with engaged columns flanking the single entrance and a single dome on squinches. Clearly the ground level around the *imamzadeh* has risen by over 1m because you have to walk down to see the north-facing frontage, grimy but still original. The interior, now firmly padlocked, should be covered with plaster decorated in strapwork designs, with details similar to those found in Qorveh's Masjed-e Jame, some 35km away, but we could make out only rows of bricks in the gloom. The second example is **Imamzadeh Abdullah**, a 15th-century tomb in the village of **Farsajin**, just before Qorveh. Its octagonal exterior is echoed on the inside, and it has a double dome, hemispherical over the interior and an external tent or pyramidal form. At some point an entrance portal and vestibule were added. In **Qorveh** itself, ask for the **Masjed-e Jame**, to the northwest on the old Soltaniyeh–Zanjan road. A faded, painted inscription beneath its prayer dome dates this chamber and the two barrel-vaulted side rooms to 1023, perhaps reusing material from an earlier Sassanid fire temple judging from some very large bricks in the lower dome area. The *mihrab* probably also dates from the early 11th century, though alterations were made about two or three centuries later when repairs were made to the dome. Remains of painted plaster decoration in the drum and squinches supporting the dome probably relate to another inscription dated 1179. Like many early Islamic buildings in Iran, the visual impact is not immediate but its charms slowly reveal themselves.

The real delight, however, is on the horizon. Returning to the main Qazvin–Takestan–Hamadan road, drive about 35km towards Hamadan, turning west just before **Ab Garm** to **Hesar-e Armani** for **Kharraqan** (125km northeast of Hamadan). After about 30km on this recently upgraded asphalt road, two splendid Seljuk **Kharraqan tomb towers** (Gonbad-e Kharraqan) located in a small cemetery come into view. Both were badly damaged in the 2002 earthquake but prompt action by the local gendarmerie using available timber saved them from complete collapse. Just look at their superb brickwork patterning. First recorded only in 1963, the tower to the east was constructed in 1068 while its companion, also octagonal inside and out, is thought to be slightly later in date. A staircase in the buttress to the left of the door went from the crypt to the roof space between the two domes (approximately 7m in diameter) presumably for later repair work. Little remains now of the original painted plaster on the interior, which depicted hanging mosque lamps, a stylised tree with a bird stiffly sitting on each branch, and an inscription reading 'Blessings on its owner' but it is the external brick decoration that is such a joy. There are over 30 patterns in recessed and relief brick, including a Quranic inscription (Q59:21–4) and its date makes this one of the earliest (securely) dated double-dome constructions in Iran. The second tower, with even more glorious brick decoration and with each blind niche divided into three zones, was built in 1094. The Quranic quotations here are Q59:21–4 under the exterior dome, and Q23:115 on the door frame: 'What, did you think that We created you only for sport, and that you would not be returned to Us?' Again double-domed, it too has a staircase going up into the roof space concealed in a buttress. There is nothing to identify who was interred in either tomb but because of visual similarities with that 10th-century masterpiece of brickwork –the tomb of Ismail Samanid in Bukhara, Uzbekistan – scholars believe the Kharraqan towers were constructed for a local military commander, perhaps originating from central Asia, by a local Zanjani mason.

Back to the main road, another 65km towards Hamadan takes you through **Razan**, which possesses two more (so-called Darazin) tomb towers, the Gonbad-e Hud thought to be Seljuk and the Azhar about 3km further east, possibly a Mongol/Ilkhanid construction. Continuing towards Hamadan, you might note the signs for Ali Sadr and Lalejin. The caves of **Ali Sadr** were 'discovered' in the 1970s, although they were used in Safavid times to house refugees (perhaps fleeing from Ottoman incursions), and one hires a pedalo to view the magnificent natural beauty of stalagmites and stalactites. You could also enjoy a visit to the local potteries of **Lalejin**, whose production was very well regarded in pre-revolutionary Tehran.

HAMADAN   *Telephone code 0811*

It is best to overnight in Hamadan (altitude 1,850m, 322km from Tehran), formerly the ancient 7th–century BCE Median stronghold and then the Achaemenid summer capital, Hagmatana/Ecbatana, in the foothills of the Zagros Mountains which link Iran with Iraq (Mesopotamia).

Its location near Mount Alvand (3,575m) and the pass across the Zagros always gave it a mercantile and strategic importance. In 550BCE the Achaemenid Cyrus the Great defeated the Medes and took control of the region and this city, which according to Herodotus was defended by seven walls, the last two being of silver and gold (a clear allusion to great commercial prosperity). Alexander the Great was its next conqueror in 331BCE but he paid heavily with the death of his friend, Hephaestion. The city flourished under the Parthian regime as an important cultural centre but then was neglected in Sassanid times. By 645CE, the Arab army had swept through bringing Islam; at first the town profited from the new political order but the 10th century brought a series of disasters: in 931CE large numbers of the inhabitants were massacred by a local warlord, 25 years later a serious earthquake caused great damage, and during religious riots in 962CE many lost their lives. However, it was also at this time that the city was home to one of the greatest medieval scholars, renowned in the west as Avicenna and known here as Bou Ali or Bou Ali Ibn Sina (d1037). Peace and prosperity were restored under Seljuk rule in 1100, but then the Mongol armies sacked the city in 1221 and again in 1224. Hamadan was later embroiled again in political and military conflict, first suffering under Timur Leng (d1405), then from the rivalry between the Aq and Qara Qoyunlu tribal confederations, and the Safavid–Ottoman conflict. From 1724 the region was incorporated within the Ottoman Empire until Nader Shah Afshar retook it finally in 1732. Despite the English traveller Buckingham describing the city as 'a pile of ruins' in 1816, the population of Hamadan four years later stood at 40,000. This had halved by 1889. Today it stands at about 548,000, a little over one-fourth of the total population of Hamadan province, with a city plan largely laid out in 1928 by a German architect.

Its high altitude means Hamadan receives heavy snowfalls from November until mid-March. As a medieval Arab poet commented: 'Even the heat of the fire becomes frozen in Hamadan/And the cold there is a chronic evil.'

GETTING THERE AND AROUND You can reach Hamadan by intercity **bus** from Tehran, or any other large city. If coming from Qazvin, there are two buses daily and the journey takes 3½ hours and costs around 50,000 rials. There are three bus stations in Hamadan: two local minibus stations are located north of the city, while the main interprovince terminal is further north between Mellat and Enghelab Streets. It is also possible to **fly** to and from Tehran Mehrabad International Airport; flights are operated by Kish Air. The airport is located around 10km north of the city centre. Within the city, it is quickest and easiest to take a local **taxi** to get around and visit the various sights.

WHERE TO STAY AND EAT For location of listings see map, page 98.

🛏 **Baba Taher International Hotel** (135 rooms) Baba Taher Sq; 📞4227180–6517; e babataher_hotel@yahoo.com. Façade rooms overlooking the Baba Taher Tomb also have lovely views over the park, square & the mountains. The lobby is flashy, but has a comfortable seating area. Rooms are standard & come with some slightly aged furniture. While the staff are polite & friendly,

the melancholic atmosphere suggests that over the past few years tourists have laid their preferences elsewhere. **$$**

🛏 **Parsian Bou Ali** (38 rooms) Bou Ali St, up from the Avicenna tomb roundabout; 📞8252822–3, 8250788; www.buali.pih.ir. Newly refurbished, it is the best upper mid-range hotel in town. Wi-Fi in the rooms, outdoor swimming pool,

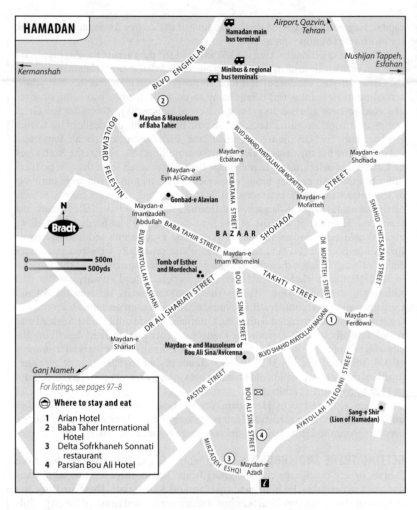

HAMADAN

Airport, Qazvin, Tehran

Hamadan main bus terminal

Nushijan Tappeh, Esfahan

Kermanshah

Minibus & regional bus terminals

BLVD ENGHELAB

BOULEVARD FELESTIN

Maydan & Mausoleum of Baba Taher

BLVD SHAHID AYATOLLAH DR MOFATTEH

Maydan-e Ecbatana

Maydan-e Eyn Al-Ghozat

Maydan-e Shohada

EKBATANA STREET

SHOHADA STREET

Gonbad-e Alavian

Maydan-e Mofatteh

Maydan-e Imamzadeh Abdullah

BABA TAHIR STREET

B A Z A A R

SHAHID CHITSAZAN STREET

N

Bradt

0   500m
0   500yds

BLVD AYATOLLAH KASHANI

DR ALI SHARIATI STREET

Tomb of Esther and Mordechai

Maydan-e Imam Khomeini

BOU ALI SINA STREET

TAKHTI STREET

DR MOFATTEH STREET

Maydan-e Ferdowsi

Maydan-e Shariati

Maydan-e and Mausoleum of Bou Ali Sina/Avicenna

BLVD SHAHID AYATOLLAH MADANI

AYATOLLAH TALEQANI STREET

Ganj Nameh

PASTOR STREET

BOU ALI SINA STREET

Sang-e Shir (Lion of Hamadan)

For listings, see pages 97–8

Where to stay and eat

1 Arian Hotel
2 Baba Taher International Hotel
3 Delta Sofrkhaneh Sonnati restaurant
4 Parsian Bou Ali Hotel

MIRZADEH ESHQI

Maydan-e Azadi

ℹ

---

shiny lobby & accommodating staff are part of the package. **$$**

🏠 **Arian Hotel** (28 rooms) Takhti St; 🕿 8261266–77. One of the newer & better options in Hamadan. Although the décor has a touch of excessive modern Rococo, the staff are sharp & professional. Rooms are clean & spacious, albeit a little overheated, & there is a reading light by the

beds, a rarity in Iranian hotels. Wi-Fi works in the lobby only, but is fast. **$**

✕ **Delta Sofrkhaneh Sonnati** 826 Mirzadeh Eshqi St; 🕿 8262640; ⏱ 09.00–16.00 & 20.00–23.00. Basement restaurant where you can lounge on day beds & enjoy traditional Iranian cuisine, in particular the wonderful local speciality *kashk-e bademjan*. **$**

WHAT TO SEE AND DO Frankly, Hamadan has more historic interest for the visitor than aesthetic architectural delights, but the surrounding area has much to offer, whether you are keen on history, archaeology or crafts. The **Tomb of Avicenna** (Ibn al-Sina or Ibn Sina) (*on the roundabout down from the Parsian Bou Ali Hotel;* ⏱ *08.00–18.00; entry 100,000 rials*) is a good example. This 10th-century Muslim scientist, who originated from Bukhara, central Asia, was mentioned in Chaucer's *Canterbury Tales* but the monument itself dates from 1952 and was clearly inspired by the early 11th-century Gonbad-e Qabus monument in northeastern Iran (see pages 149–50). The museum on the ground floor was once dull and uninformative, but it has been been completely reorganised and is now a delight. Local artefacts are located in the first room to the left on entry, while the room to the right is a library with interesting displays of historical medical instruments, such as the glass blood-letting suction 'cuppers' and manuscripts, while the main hall with the memorial to Avicenna shows the herbs, plants and seeds (with their Latin names) used in pharmacy with labelling in English and Farsi. There is a good view of Mount Alvand from outside the upper platform, and the gardens are pleasant, although one dices with death crossing to and from the roundabout. Avicenna (born c980CE) fled from his enemies at court in Bukhara (Uzbekistan), arriving in Hamadan in about 1015 to practise as a doctor for some nine years. He then moved to Rayy and Esfahan, returning to Hamadan only to die of colic in 1037. Most of his 130 or so books have been lost but fragments remain to show he wrote knowledgeably on economics, poetry, philosophy (influencing St Thomas Aquinas) and music as well as physics, mathematics and astronomy. His *Book of Healing* and *Canon of Medicine* became the standard medical textbooks in Europe until the mid 17th century; it is from Avicenna and other Muslim scientists that we get such words as algebra, alchemy, alcohol and alkaline.

Another modern tomb (1951, repaired 1970) also set in a pleasant garden commemorates **Baba Taher** (*Baba Taher Park;* ⊕ *08.00–17.30; entry 100,000 rials*), author of metaphysical works but more renowned for his passionate mystical poetic quatrains which, it was said, could melt the snows of Alvand. No-one is sure when he lived or died other than it was sometime between 900 and 1300 but his Sufi love poetry remains a favourite and is still often set to music.

Hamadan is also of historical interest because its Jewish community used to be one of the largest in Iran and it is here that lies the most important Jewish site in the county – the tomb of **Esther and Mordechai** (*off the Maydan-e Imam Khomeini roundabout, set back behind a fence, but the entrance is through the bazaar behind it;* ⊕ *09.00–13.00 & 16.00–19.00 daily except Fri afternoon/evening & Sat; entry by donation to custodian Rasad*). This small brick tomb is probably medieval in date with a (modern) devotional area below street level, but local tradition says it is much older, housing the graves of Esther and her uncle Mordechai of the Old Testament Book of Esther (despite the fact that an inscription was found naming the deceased as Elias and Samuel, sons of a certain Ismail Karlan). Another theory is that it was the tomb of Susan, the Jewish queen of the Sassanid shah Yazdegerd I (399–420CE). Entry into the tomb itself is through an old stone doorway (leaving shoes outside), which leads into various small prayer rooms and the main chamber with the two cenotaphs. The one to the right is said to be that of Esther, the Jewish consort of either Xerxes I 486–65BCE or his successor Artaxerxes I (d424BCE), but actually both are replicas of the 13th- or 14th-century cenotaphs destroyed by fire from pilgrims' candles; the actual graves are in the crypt below. You may remember the biblical story: at Susa in southern Iran a newly appointed Achaemenid court chamberlain, Haman, envious of the influence of Esther and her uncle, spread rumours that the Jewish community was conspiring against the emperor and argued for their extermination. Warned by Mordechai, Esther arranged a sumptuous royal banquet during which Haman was tricked into suggesting great rewards for Mordechai, thinking these were intended for him. At a second banquet he was denounced by Esther who then won royal permission for all the Jews to return from exile. Every Purim in the Jewish calendar, delicious pastries called 'Haman's ears' are still happily munched.

Before you leave Hamadan, visit the **Gonbad-e Alavian** (*off Maydan-e Ain al-Qozzat in Shahdad Lane;* ⊕ *08.30–18.00; entry 100,000 rials*), a glorious if dusty tomb building; the girls' school formerly here has been relocated. It is thought this was the mausoleum for members of the Alavian family, who controlled Hamadan for two centuries, but when it was built exactly is unclear. To some scholars its elaborately carved plaster of leaf and flower motifs resembles Seljuk decoration as found at Divrigi and elsewhere in Turkey – as well as on the 1148 Mausoleum Gonbad-e Surkh in Maragha (see page 171) – but others argue the almost three-dimensional, lace-like 'Baroque' quality of its motifs is early 14th-century Ilkhanid work. The original roof has gone and much of the brick and plaster strapwork exterior has been restored but don't be put off by the present monochrome colour, dust and gloom; let the plasterwork speak to you. The Quranic inscriptions inside (Q53:1–35), on the *mihrab* (Q36:1–9), outside (Q76:1–9) and over the entrance (Q5:55–6) refer to rewards and punishments, death and paradise, the importance of prayer and charity giving – all very apposite for a mausoleum and possibly the plaster leaf and plant forms symbolise the gardens of paradise. A torch is useful for the interior.

We must admit to less enthusiasm for the so-called **Lion of Hamadan** (Sang-e Shir), located in a public square in the southeast of the town. The passage of time, together with the local tradition of kissing and greasing its nose to find a husband, mean much imagination is needed to identify this battered stone sculpture as a lion, but it is agreed that this could well be a Hellenistic memorial lion to Hephaestion, the beloved general and close companion of Alexander the Great, dating to the late 4th century BCE. Nothing else of Herodotus's Ecbatana is visible to the visitor, although archaeological excavations in the 1920s uncovered two tablets naming Darius the Great (d485BCE) and Artaxerxes II. In the 1970s, 25ha were acquired for archaeological excavations and the remains of a 9m-thick defensive wall were uncovered, which was originally protected with regularly placed towers. In 1974, 15 slipper coffins, probably 1st century BCE or CE, were uncovered in a Parthian cemetery, and since 1983 two stretches of the ancient city wall, along with houses and alleys, have been located.

AROUND HAMADAN

The real reason for staying in Hamadan is its proximity to other towns and attractions in the area – aside from the Ali Sadr Caves and the Lalejin potteries (see page 96), which can be reached either by taxi or minibus. Hamadan has two minibus stations, both a few minutes from the centre of town and across the road from each other. Transport from one leaves in the direction of Kermanshah southwest and from the other towards Malayer southeast. A few kilometres further north from the minibus stations lies Hamadan's central terminal for interprovince travel. Minibuses depart as soon as they are filled and tickets are purchased on board.

About 10km west of Hamadan is **Ganj Nameh** (literally Book of Treasures). High up on a rock face, looking north, are two large panels carrying Achaemenid trilingual inscriptions recording the victories and lineage of Darius the Great and his son, Xerxes I (d465BCE), and giving thanks to the Zoroastrian deity Ahura Mazda. The area is a popular weekend and holiday spot with beautiful nature, a waterfall, restaurants and a cable car if you wish to spend half a day around here.

Going 60km in the southernly direction from Hamadan towards Malayer you arrive at **Nushijan Tappeh**, which lies about 10km south from the Jowkar crossroads, approximately 10km north of Malayer. British archaeologists worked on this small

Median site, about one-sixth the size of the main apadana platform at Persepolis, from 1967–74. Four principal buildings were found on this outcrop: two temples, a fort and a columned hall with an enclosing wall. The central temple, probably constructed before 700BCE, had a narrow entrance leading into an antechamber possessing a stepped 'Maltese cross' ground plan and a spiral ramp (like Tappeh Baba Jan, see page 108) to an upper level. It then led to a sanctuary with a triangular cella, or inner body of the temple and large blind windows with 'toothed' lintels decorating the walls. A brick fire altar (85cm high) with four steps was screened from the entrance and, perhaps to protect its sanctity from later squatters, the temple was filled with shale to a depth of 6m and carefully bricked in. This was a tremendously important find: perhaps the earliest temple with a fire altar *in situ* found in western Iran. The second temple, located just to the west, had similar rooms and a spiral ramp but with a different orientation and an asymmetrical ground plan. The fort measured 25 x 22m, approximately the size of the Gate of All Lands at Persepolis (page 197), with four long magazines and a guardroom with another spiral ramp for access to at least one other floor, while the hall with a slightly irregular ground plan was somewhat smaller with 12 columns supporting a flat roof. Very little stone was used in construction throughout the site but the bricks (especially in the vaults) were often carefully shaped. For some reason the site was then left largely unoccupied until the Parthian period (c1st century CE).

The road south takes you to **Borujerd** (population 246,000) in Lorestan province, an important military town in the 19th century when the Qajars struggled to keep control over the local tribes. More recently it was the home of the famous theologian Ayatollah Hossein Tabataba'i Borujerdi (d1962). Its Masjed-e Jame still retains its Seljuk domed prayer chamber among extensive 19th-century restoration work in the courtyard. In the past the guardian here was very suspicious of foreign visitors 'dropping in' and unless you have a spare hour to kill while he telephones for permission, it is advisable to withdraw gracefully if he objects to your presence. In the same area is the Imamzadeh Jafar with a distinctive 'sugarloaf' dome, similar to those found in southern Iran, which looks very out of place this far north. The tombstone is dated 1108 but some scholars believe the tomb building is later. About 110km to the southwest is **Khorramabad**, known for the massive Sassanid bridge spanning the River Kashkan, and the remains of its citadel in the centre of town. There is also a free-standing Seljuk minaret. Just south of here an annual horse race for women riders only is held.

The town of **Arak** (population 536,000, 214km southeast from Hamadan and 100km east from Borujerd) is the capital of Markazi province and is known today for its aluminium smelter and a huge petrochemical factory (the brainchild of Rafsanjani), but in the 19th century its fame rested on carpet production. This was at Sultanabad, where an enormous complex, 'The Qaleh' (Fort), of carpet workshops was established in 1877 by the Ziegler company of Manchester, UK; it was possibly their representatives who brought the famous twin 16th-century 'Ardabil' carpets to London in the late 1880s. They are now in London's Victoria and Albert Museum and in Los Angeles' County Museum of Art. Readers with links to the Ismaili community (see page 94) might make a short detour to **Anjedan**, 37km east of Arak. This village has long historical associations with Ismaili Shi'ism; even when the Assassins were thrown out of Alamut and lost any regional control, there was an active community here until the early 18th century. In the late 1970s it possessed two recorded historical monuments, both recently heavily restored: the 1480 tomb of Ismaili shah Qalandar and the tomb of Ismaili shah Garib, built eight years later.

Some 100km southeast towards Esfahan, passing the small town of **Khomeyn** (60km from Arak), closely associated with Ayatollah Khomeini ('of Khomeyn'), is the town of **Golpaygan**, perhaps established by the Sassanids after the famous victory over the Parthians here in 224CE. Its Masjed-e Jame has a fine domed prayer hall dating from 1105–18, constructed on the order of the son of the Seljuk sultan, Malik Shah. The rest of the courtyard buildings are 19th-century additions, paid for by one of Fath Ali Shah's wives when her son was governor here. The brickwork inside this chamber is admittedly not the finest, nor are the proportions of the chamber, especially the narrow 'squeezed' corner squinches and the heavy piers, which led one writer to comment that it was 'a masterpiece of pessimism' but it is definitely well worth a few minutes' investigation. Leaving the chamber and the mosque by the right-hand portal, walk down (southeast) into the small friendly bazaar by the main road. Almost directly opposite is a fine minaret, dated 1100, whose balconies were reached by two separate spiral staircases. At its base stand two later stone lions; the heads of their victims protrude from their mouths.

Back on the road again, the next pleasant stop is on the far southern outskirts of **Khonsar**. If you have the luxury of time, take a walk in the shady streets of Khonsar, edged with magnificent chenar trees. If you don't, be content with looking at the early 20th-century house across the stream, before leaving the town and heading towards Esfahan. The house has seen better days and presently is occupied by a number of families struggling to make ends meet, but it is still splendid with a clock (not working) over the main entrance, low reliefs of lions and also Qajar soldiers, and slowly disintegrating balconies. The tiled spandrels give details of its 1910 construction and original owner, a local wealthy merchant who had made the pilgrimage to Mecca. If you can gain entry, the servants' quarters, storerooms and cistern are off the main vestibule. Steep steps lead into the courtyard with a fine Qajar pool in the centre; today this court is occasionally used for the local Moharram ceremonies. The owner's quarters were located on the upper veranda level, as the remains of stained glass in intricate patterning over the doorways suggest.

EAST OF HAMADAN TO KERMANSHAH PROVINCE

The road east (Route 48 or A-2 although marked simply as to Kermanshah) from Hamadan towards Kermanshah (on some early post-revolutionary maps, marked as Bakhtaran) passes some interesting sights. Unfortunately, there is no easy way to move about here. It is best to come here from Tehran with a rented car or alternatively allow extra time and move around by *savari* taxi or minibus from one town to another. Do remember, however, that there is barely any English spoken in provincial areas.

Anahita Temple (*entry 100,000 rials or free of charge through the back gate in the small alley right before the mosque*) is in the town of Kangovar (population 53,000), some 95km from Hamadan and set back on the right (north) of the main road. The motorway passes through the town and if you are coming here by Kermanshah minibus from Hamadan (there are no minibuses solely to Kangovar), you can get a local taxi (around 10,000 rials) to bring you to the temple. Alternatively, you could ask locals for directions, but it is a couple of kilometres' walk from where the minibus drops you off.

This was the ancient Concobar of the 1st century CE, known for its temple to Artemis (the Greek version of the Zoroastrian Anahita) and later for the palace of the Sassanid shah Khosrow II. By medieval times its reputation among travelling merchants had sunk to being that of a place full of muggers and thieves. Many 19th-century European visitors suggested archaeological investigation around the standing columns and the immense stone platform, but extensive excavation was only undertaken from 1968 until 1977, with the final report published (in Farsi) in 1996 (and unfortunately unavailable). From brief reports of the 1970s, the first excavations revealed a plan similar to that of Persepolis, with double staircases up to the main terrace where a columned temple once stood; everything seemed to suggest an Achaemenid construction. However, as work progressed, the finds pointed instead to late Seleucid/early Parthian times, or even to Sassanid occupation with later Islamic buildings and workshops.

Today the site is largely overgrown, and there are no signs or a site map at the ticket office. The path from the ticket office leads to the remains of the double staircases fronted by some re-erected column shafts. Scrambling up the mound and looking back, you might make out the fired-brick walls of the Islamic workshops below. A little further up, to the extreme left, is a good view down on to more recent excavations, which uncovered yet more columns and bases, while high up by the road fence a mosque rests on the original stone platform.

KHOSROW AND SHIRIN

Hearing of the great beauty of Shirin, the Armenian princess, a young Sassanid prince (later Khosrow II) sent an artist bearing his portrait, mounted on his own wondrous horse, Shabdiz, to try to bring her to the Sassanid court. Falling in love with the picture, Shirin secretly stole away on Shabdiz, unaware that Khosrow was riding towards Armenia having quarrelled with his father. Their paths crossed (Khosrow even caught sight of Shirin bathing in a pool) but, neither recognising each other, they returned to their homes: Khosrow to succeed to the throne, and Shirin with her unrequited love. A rebellion then caused Khosrow to flee to Armenia where the two finally met and fell passionately in love. But the course of true love never runs smooth. Determined to regain his throne, Khosrow asked for help from the Byzantine emperor, cementing the agreement by marrying a Byzantine princess. Restored to power, he then begged Shirin to join him despite his recent marriage.

But Shirin, now queen in her own right and angry at his duplicity, sent a message of rejection from her palace, Qasr-e Shirin. Dejected and depressed, she yearned for fresh milk from her mountain pastures and commissioned a young engineer and mason, Ferhad, who had the strength of two elephants, to carve a channel through the mountains. Head over heels in love with her, Ferhad achieved this feat in weeks, but jealous Khosrow schemed to prevent any further liaison and to profit from Ferhad's skills. Persuading Ferhad to excavate a pass between the mountains at Bisotun, and carve a sculpture of Khosrow on Shabdiz at Taq-e Bostan, he promised Shirin would be Ferhad's once these impossible tasks were achieved. Hearing this, Shirin visited Ferhad who became so reinvigorated in his work that the king feared he would have to keep his promise; he lied to the engineer announcing that Shirin had suddenly died. Ferhad killed himself and a shocked Shirin was at last persuaded to visit Khosrow's palace to hear his explanation. After many recriminations, the two lovers were reunited but only briefly. Khosrow, the story goes, was stabbed to death by a stepson maddened by the beauty and devotion of Queen Shirin and she, rejecting his advances, killed herself over Khosrow's body.

4

If archaeological sites are of interest, **Godin Tappeh** lies about 13km southeast of Kangovar (coming from Hamadan turn south just before Kangovar to the signposted township of Godin, which is located just south of the *tappeh*) and as remains of certain mud-brick buildings have been consolidated, visitors can get a better understanding of the site. Canadian excavation work from 1965 onwards revealed buildings dating to 2600–1600BCE, which included an eight-columned hall largely destroyed by earthquakes, and a later Median citadel (level II) with a 30-columned audience hall, towers and magazines. Most of the residences had a raised square hearth in the main room with an elevated seat and footstool for the owner at one end and seating for guests along the side walls. Remnants of staircases showed houses had at least one upper floor, but for an idea of their external appearance, perhaps the Assyrian reliefs (at the British Museum, London) hold the key. The last season, in 1973, produced even more sensational dating evidence, pushing occupation of the site back to c4500BCE (level X), with striking artefacts uncovered from level V (3200–3000BCE).

From Kangovar, the road from Hamadan leads towards Bisotun and Taq-e Bostan; keep a telephoto lens or binoculars to hand if you have them. All of this countryside is associated with Persian legend, and in late medieval book illustrations with the star-crossed royal lovers, Khosrow II and Shirin (see box, page 103).

Among archaeologists, the region is famous for the exquisite (but frequently forged) Loristan bronzes, some of which are displayed in the National Museum and the Reza Abbasi Museum, Tehran. Used to embellish horse equipment, as standard finials, etc, these cast bronzes with their powerful stylised animal forms were manufactured in this region from the 1st millennium until c600BCE, and some perhaps even date from the 3rd millennium BCE.

As you come towards **Bisotun** (which is now on the UNESCO World Heritage List), the immense rock face recording the victories of Darius the Great dominates the skyline. You might consider, however, visiting Bisotun from Kermanshah (41km apart) as a half-day excursion. Private taxi hire for half a day to take you here and to Taq-e Bostan (below) costs around 150,000 rials. In 2013 the Bisotun relief was hidden behind a massive scaffolding platform and the site itself was open to the public free of charge. Just before the town, there is a Safavid bridge on the right, but drive on to the large layby on the left. At (modern) road level on your right there is a small reclining statue concealed under a rusting canopy. Although recently emasculated, he has now been provided with a new head. On close inspection you can just make out a club in the background and the lion skin under the figure: this is Herakles (Hercules) complete with a Greek inscription stating it was carved for Hyakin in 148BCE in honour of a local governor. But the most important set of inscriptions are about 10m to the left and very high up.

The modern road is on a much higher level than the original Royal Achaemenid road that ran from western Turkey across the Zagros Mountains to Hamadan and then south to Susa. Alexander the Great must have passed this way and presumably the significance of this enormous 18 x 7m carved panel was explained to him. However, later travellers variously described the panel as showing Shalmenezer and the ten captive tribes of Israel, Esther leading her community away, Jesus and his 12 disciples, a Sufi mystic with his followers, or a schoolmaster reprimanding his pupils. It actually depicts the Achaemenid emperor Darius the Great with his generals behind him, standing victorious on the rebel Gaumata who refused to accept the succession of Darius. Above, a winged figure, generally identified as Ahura Mazda of Zoroastrian belief, witnesses the submission of eight provincial governors who supported Gaumata's claim to the Achaemenid throne; the ninth figure of a Scythian chief with its inscription was added a few years after the main section was begun in 521BCE (see page 196).

The panel inscriptions were first copied by Sir Henry Rawlinson in 1836, then advisor to the local governor, using ropes and ladders ('the interest of the occupation entirely did away with any sense of danger'). Like reading Egyptian hieroglyphs by means of the Rosetta Stone, their decipherment was fundamentally important to our understanding of the ancient languages of Babylonian, Old Persian and Elamite. Recording that Gaumata was killed near here at the Battle of Kundurush on 29 September 522BCE, Darius had carved: 'This is what I did by the favour of Ahura Mazda in one and the same year after that I became king [521BCE]. Nineteen battles I fought, by the favour of Ahura Mazda I smote them and took prisoner nine kings. One was Gaumata by name a Magian; he lied thus he said "I am Smerdis the son of Cyrus"; he made Persia rebellious.' Darius's right to rule was emphasised: 'Eight of my family were kings before me. I am the ninth. We inherit kingship on both sides'. And promised: 'The man who co-operated with my house, him I rewarded well; who so did injury, him I punished well.' Its purpose is obvious but where did the idea of carving such a relief come from? Archaeologists point to Urartian rock carvings in Turkey and further east, but the nearest source of inspiration is the rock relief at Sar-e Pol-e Zahab, 150km west (see page 107).

Later rulers left their mark below Darius's proclamation, but to see these you have to get closer; just above the first set of steps is a worn low relief depicting the Parthian shah, Mithridates II, receiving the homage of four provincial governors while on the right his descendant, Shah Gotarzes II (c38–50CE), on his battle horse is lancing an enemy while a Roman-style Nike (Victory) flies overhead. Both have been damaged by a 17th-century panel inscription describing the endowment of a nearby caravanserai.

Further on from Bisotun, 33km away, is the Sassanid *paradeisos* (hunting garden) of **Taq-e Bostan** (⊕ *08.00–18.00; entry 100,000 rials*). As one passes a huge military base on the left of the main road, on the opposite hillside is a huge (undecorated) rock-cut surface that marks the remains of an immense platform. Legend has it that near here was an enormous reception area where the Sassanid rulers received envoys from the Chinese and Roman empires in great splendour.

A right turn leads to the two small '**grottoes**' of Taq-e Bostan. This is a popular lunch spot for local families and for pilgrims making the road journey to Karbala in Iraq. The entrance to the site is past the *chelo-kebab* cafés, at the far end of the pool; from here, it's a short walk to the first 'grotto', among elaborately carved column capitals, some showing a Sassanid shah holding the diadem or Ring of Authority, brought here from the Bisotun locale. The surrounding area was renovated in spring 2013 and is pleasant to walk around. The word 'grotto' is inaccurate although there is an air of fantasy about this place. The exact function of these two manmade caves is unclear but the hunting scenes depicted on the two side walls suggest this was part of a favourite Sassanid royal hunting park or *paradeisos*. A stylised Tree of Life, perhaps symbolising the Zoroastrian Tree of All Seeds, from which all known plants apparently germinate, is carved either side of the main 'grotto' with Rubensesque victory angels above. At the back of the cave a huge, almost free-standing figure of rider and horse has been carved from the rock, while above stand (left to right) the Zoroastrian goddess Anahita pouring a libation, a kingly figure in the centre and Ahura Mazda. But which Sassanid shah is depicted here and below as the warrior-hero? The particular crown suggests it is Peroz I (r457–84CE) but this shah had a disastrous military career, culminating in his capture and ransom in central Asia after ordering a cavalry charge right into a concealed staked ditch: scarcely a record

4

one would wish to have commemorated. The most likely candidate is Khosrow II (r590–628CE) with his legendary horse Shabdiz, who brought Byzantine Syria and Egypt under Sassanid control before his murder (see page 103). It is said he went hunting with 300 horses, 1,160 slaves with javelins, 1,040 slaves with swords and staves, 700 falconers, 300 riders with hunting panthers, 70 leopards, 700 hounds and 200 minstrels, and such scenes are beautifully depicted on both side walls. A railing infuriatingly restricts viewing, and a longer chain along each wall would simply and effectively solve the perceived threat of damage; one sometimes despairs of officialdom. High up on the far left is a low relief of Mohammed Ali Mirza, son of Fath Ali Shah, recording his governorship of the region, dating from 1822.

The next 'grotto' contains the figure of Shapur III (r383–8CE) with his grandfather Shapur II (d378CE) on the right. The inscription just visible is in the Pahlavi script, largely abandoned after the Arab conquest in the 7th century. A little further along is a low relief of the investiture of Ardashir II (r379–83CE) with Ahura Mazda on the right, while Mithra, the Zoroastrian 'Lord of Contract' or 'Justice', stands on a lotus dais, carrying a *barsom* of twigs for the sacred fire (see box, page 173). In Zoroastrian belief this manifestation of Ahura Mazda crossed the heavens daily in his sun-chariot (thus, his halo of sunrays) to check that all were keeping their word, but when he was adopted as a deity in his own right by Roman soldiery, his rituals were followed in secrecy in underground or windowless temples. Under the feet of Ardashir II lies a defeated enemy, probably a Roman emperor. It has been suggested that his beard identifies him as Julian the Apostate (responsible for reintroducing temple worship in the place of Christianity across the empire) who invaded Sassanid territory as far as Ctesiphon before being defeated and dying in 363CE. But this was 16 years before Ardashir came to the throne and furthermore Ardashir II led no campaigns against Rome during his reign; contemporary Roman rulers who might fit the bill in what was a period of turmoil are hard to establish. Just to the right of this panel is the natural spring that probably made this spot so appealing to the Sassanid shahs and explains the depiction of Anahita in the first 'grotto'.

Kermanshah (some early 1990s maps may show Bakhtaran, population 857,000) is just 11km away from Taq-e Bostan. The city, originally founded by the Sassanids in the 4th century CE, has little of historic or architectural interest, especially after constant Iraqi bombardment during the 1980s. There is, however, the early 20th-century **Takiyeh of Muavin al-Molk** (*Hadad Abil St;* ⊕ *10.00–12.00 & 16.00–19.30; entry 100,000 rials*) with interesting tiled panels in the three performance areas. Those of the first courtyard reveal the function of the small complex with a large panel, to the right just after the entry, depicting a preacher reciting one of the Ashur eulogies about Hossein while veiled ladies sit at his feet, and men dressed in white flagellate themselves in the commemorative parades along the bottom section. In the main covered hall each panel shows an episode of the Karbala story (see box, page 58); look for the one depicting Zaynab, Hossein's sister, berating the Umayyad ruler in Damascus after the battle. Close by the throne, as if they were actively involved in 7th-century Umayyad politics, are European envoys in 19th-century dress, a reflection of Iranian Europhobia a century ago. The final open courtyard has a large panel showing a Sufi mystic with the ritual vessels and dress elements, while the back of the 'stage' is covered with moulded tiles alluding to Iranian archaeological monuments and historic or legendary figures: a visual delight for tired eyes. If you are staying here overnight, the best choice is **Parsian Kermanshah Hotel** (*100 rooms; Shahid Keshvari Bd;* \ *0831 4219151-60; www.kermanshah.pih. ir;* **$$**)

A little to the southeast are the villages of **Deh Nau** and **Ishaqvand** (sometimes spelt as Sakavand). On the cliffs above the two settlements are three rock-cut tombs (another is near Sorka-deh village) associated locally with legendary Ferhad, the engineer who loved Queen Shirin (see box, page 136). Judging by the low-relief depicting a priest with uplifted hands in prayer, these Zoroastrian tombs, about 2m wide and 1.75m deep, date from the 4th or 3rd century BCE.

Rather than travelling north from Kermanshah to Sanadaj and then Takht-e Soleyman (see page 170), one could continue eastwards to Islamabad (70km) and Qasr-e Shirin, the centre of old Loristan. If taking this road, don't pack away the binoculars or telephoto lens, but remember the proximity of the Iraqi border. A number of archaeological teams worked on various sites in this region down towards Ilam (Chavar, Tappeh Var Kabud and Bani Surmah) where remains of ancient palaces and extensive cemeteries were discovered, mostly dating from the 3rd millennium BCE. Three kinds of burial were uncovered: individual interment under the family house (as often found in Anatolia), mass interment in pits just outside the settlement, and thirdly, burial in large stone vaults constructed from beautifully dressed stone with luxurious grave goods to match.

Another 50km or so brings you to Qaleh Yazdegerd, badly damaged in the Iran–Iraq war, but before this there is **Dukkan-e Da'ud**, investigated by Rawlinson in 1836. The locals then said this tomb chamber carved high up out of the living rock housed the remains of a Jewish blacksmith who became a local ruler, but today some archaeologists argue it is Median or early Achaemenid in date, while others associate it with the Seleucid low-relief (1.5 x 0.9m) carved below the tomb, depicting a Zoroastrian priest holding a *barsom*. The tomb itself has two sections: the first functioned as a columned antechamber, 9.6m wide, with a door leading into the second, a narrower tomb chamber with a small ossuary pit dug out of the rock floor.

Less than 5km away is another rock carving of great interest to archaeologists and which probably inspired the Achaemenid stonemasons working for Darius the Great at Bisotun. Slightly to the east of the village of **Sar-e Pol-e Zahab** is the famous relief, possibly carved c2200–1900BCE. A local ruler, probably King Anubanini of Lullubi, is shown standing on a platform supported by captives, with his foot firmly on the chest of a fallen enemy. Facing him is the goddess Ishtar or Inana, identified by her starred totem, presenting him with a ring or diadem while holding two roped prisoners. The similarity to the later Bisotun relief is striking. (There are four other Bisotun reliefs relating to Lullubi rulers nearby but they are much less accessible.) Below the main relief you can just make out a Parthian carving commemorating the victory of Shah Vologazes (II or III) over his rival Shah Mithdrates IV, c147CE.

The extensive site of **Qaleh Yazdegerd** was excavated by the Royal Ontario Museum, Toronto, in 1975–78. The citadel's square towers were clearly 3rd-century Parthian in date but occupation of this hill citadel continued for another thousand years. Remains of fine wall-plaster decoration, carved, moulded and colourfully painted, were found. Some were patterned with stylised floral motifs, while other schemes contained scantily clad men and women, possibly entertainers, and cupid forms.

About 30km away is **Qasr-e Shirin** (population 18,000), or 'Castle of Shirin', (see box, page 103), and just before the city centre mounds of earth concealed the remains of a large Sassanid complex just visible before the 1980–88 Iran–Iraq war. Opinions were divided as to its form and function, some identifying it as an enormous, domed fire temple over 16m² set in gardens, while others argued it was a massive audience hall for Khosrow II. Nearby, another Sassanid complex known as Imaret-e Khosrow ('Refectory') was entered by a double staircase at the eastern end, and stables, storerooms and ten courtyards were identified mainly from drawings made in the 1930s; recently these drawings, and therefore these conclusions, have been questioned. What is clear is that the complex and the town of Qasr-e Shirin were severely damaged by the Byzantine emperor, Heraclius, in 628CE, and then Arab armies some ten years later. Because of the proximity of the Iraqi border, travel to these sites is currently inadvisable.

The drive south from Kermanshah passes through lovely countryside. At Nurabad ask directions for the village of Morabad and **Tappeh Baba Jan**, excavated by a British team in 1966–69. You pass Harsin, and in this area at **Ganj Dareh** Canadian archaeologists found evidence of early Neolithic occupation with a suggested carbon-14 dating of c8450BCE. A severe fire around 7300BCE actually helped conserve certain artefacts and the mud-brick architecture, vitrifying the clay. The pottery was crude with no signs of imported trade goods but the walls, sometimes surviving up to 2m high, were carefully plastered. Some 30km further on, the main mound **Tappeh Baba Jan** revealed settlement from the 4th millennium BCE but the most important finds emerged from later levels, especially those from c900–700BCE. The ground plan and architectural details (such as blind niches, the arrow-slit forms) of these later buildings were similar to those found at Nushijan Tappeh (see pages 100–1) to the east and Hasanlu further north, incorporating defences to safeguard both the property and the inhabitants. The large columned hall had side rooms and a portico under which a horse skeleton with harness and vessels was found. This burial probably dated from a destructive fire that swept the site, perhaps caused by invading Scythian tribesmen in the 7th century BCE. On the eastern *tappeh* nearby another fortified building with a central chamber (10.4 x 12.5m) was excavated. A spiral ramp led to a second storey, but what was striking was the rich painted plaster decorating the walls of the central chamber, and shards of painted ceiling tiles, decorated with squares or diamond forms. After the fire the site was not abandoned as there was some evidence of Achaemenid occupation, but for some reason everyone left before the Seleucids took control of the region.

5

From Kashan to Esfahan

KASHAN   *Telephone code 0361*

Kashan (232km from Tehran, 210km from Esfahan, population 294,000) will always be associated in Islamic art for its high-quality ceramics (*kashi*) production, which dates from the 12th century, even enduring the Mongol campaigns. It is also renowned for its manufacture of costly silks and carpets for the Safavid court. The 17th-century English merchant, Thomas Herbert, estimated there were then approximately 4,000 families in the town mainly involved in textiles, which would mean that the community was then 'in compass not less than York or Norwich … The houses are fairly built, many of which are pargeted and painted; the mosques and *hamams* are in their cupolas curiously ceruleated with a feigned turquoise.' Undoubtedly he would also have heard that Kashan was the place from which the Three Wise Men set out for Bethlehem. Almost 250 years later, other English travellers reported that Kashan boasted 24 caravanserais, 35 hotels for foreign merchants, 34 *hamams*, 18 large mosques, and 90 small shrines but in such a bad state that Lord Curzon commented, 'A more funereal place I had not yet seen.' Matters were made no better by its reputation for poisonous scorpions.

Kashan's most recent political history has been primarily associated with the nuclear installation in Natanz, 89km southeast from the city. The details of the facility for enriching uranium were leaked in 2002 and subsequently confirmed by the President Khatami's administration. While the carpet industry here is one of the best in the country, lack of shops selling them makes it next to impossible to find a good carpet (see page 127). It is the old merchant houses, however, that make this city special.

GETTING THERE   The easiest way to reach Kashan is by intercity **bus**, although the Tehran–Esfahan/Yazd–Kerman **train** service stops in the town. A one-way bus ticket from Tehran or Esfahan costs around 70,000 rials, with the train fare double that. There is a new multi-lane toll road (not used by intercity buses) that passes behind the Bagh-e Fin gardens (see page 114), from Tehran (3½ hours) and on to Yazd (four/five hours).

WHERE TO STAY AND EAT   Two or three days could happily be spent exploring Kashan with its beautiful merchant houses and the locale. Accommodation in the city itself is rather scarce, but do try to reserve a place in the Ehsan Historical Guesthouse below. Manouchehri House is a great place to relax and eat but the next best alternative would be one of the numerous kebab restaurants along the main road outside the Bagh-e Fin. For location of listings see map, page 112.

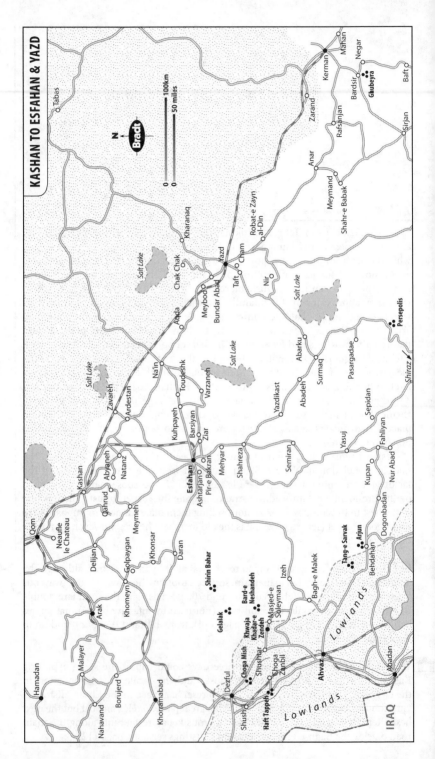

🏠 **Ehsan Historic Guesthouse** (16 rooms) Off Kamal al-Molk Sq, across from the Agha Bozorg Madrasa; ☏4446833; e info@ehsanhouse.com; www.ehsanhouse.com. The 1st historical house in Kashan to have been turned into a hotel & well converted it was indeed. Utterly charming with a beautiful inner courtyard it offers a variety of rooms, including dorms. Staff are friendly & accommodating, Wi-Fi is good & there is a traditional restaurant (dinner only) too. It is by far the best place to stay & excellent value for money. **$$**

🏠 **Hotel Amir Kabir** (102 rooms) Amir Kabir Rd; ☏5304091–5. Situated near to the Bagh-e Fin, 7km from the centre, & roughly the same distance from the quality of service & staff courteousness. Rooms are standard, but come with small balconies. The main lobby is a grand open space, but always bustling with large tour groups. **$$**

🏠 **Sayyah Hotel** (45 rooms) Abazar St; ☏4444535–6; www.sayyahhotel.ir. Simple with no particular features to highlight, this is the only budget place in town & do consider staying here if you have to stop over. Staff are polite & helpful, but Wi-Fi works in the tiny lobby only (fuller coverage is promised). **$**

✗ **Manouchehri House** 49 7th Emarat Alley, off Mohtasham St, follow green arrows on the houses; ☏2422617–5531; www.manouchehrihouse.com. This beautifully restored old merchant house (see the pre-restoration state on the poster to your left when you enter) has an airy traditional restaurant. Indoor seating area is air conditioned & a little too modern, but the courtyard is an idyllic escape from busy streets & heat. Menu is small, but the food is delicious, in particular *khoresht* dishes. **$**

WHAT TO SEE AND DO The Safavid family obviously had a soft spot for Kashan, as Shah Abbas I requested that he should be buried here in preference to Ardabil, Qom or Mashhad. His body is thought to lie in the 13th-century tomb of **Habib Ibn Musa**, understood to be a descendant of seventh imam Musa Ibn Qasem. The tomb is now incorporated into a large mosque complex decorated in 19th-century Qajar times. You will be told his cenotaph is the black marble one to the right as you enter the crypt.

It is a short walk west from here into the extensive **bazaar** complex, which contains a number of interesting historical *hamams*, mosques and *khans*. As for the shops, it seems that one in ten is somehow connected with carpetmaking, whether selling woollen yarn, renting design cartoons, selling swifts (a kind of reel of adjustable diameter on which a skein of silk is put for winding off) or dealing in carpets. The **Mosque of Mir Emad** (also known as Masjed-e Maydan, Masjed-e Maydan-e Sang, after the former name of the Maydan-e Mir Emad, or even Masjed-e Maydan-e Fayz) replaced the original Seljuk-period mosque built around 1218 and subsequently destroyed during the Mongol invasion. The mosque was then rebuilt in 1461 for Jahanshah, the leader of the Qara Qoyunlu tribal confederation. In its present state, however, it is mostly 19th-century in date, when the local Qajar governor undertook large-scale restoration work. It is justly famous for its multi-layered plaster *muqarnas* decoration and its superb tiled *mihrab*, dating from 1226, which was in place until the beginning of the 20th century and is now in the Museum für Islamische Kunst, in Berlin. On the same side of the street, with a 19th century tiled entrance, is the **Hamam Khan**, which has been converted into a wonderful local tea house, a popular spot for bazaar dwellers to have a rest with a cup of tea. It retains the basic original plan although there are some careless repairs and alterations. A short amble on the same side is the 19th-century **Khan Amin al-Dawlah Timcheh** with its soaring dome painted with original decoration, and further on the **Madrasa Imam Khomeini** (formerly sultan), built with 52 student cells during the reign of Fath Ali Shah, and which is still functioning as a theological school. A few Seljuk monuments remain in the city. Continue walking through the bazaar until the main road is reached and turn right for the **Masjed-e Jame**, extensively repaired in the 18th century, but still with its 1073 minaret. In

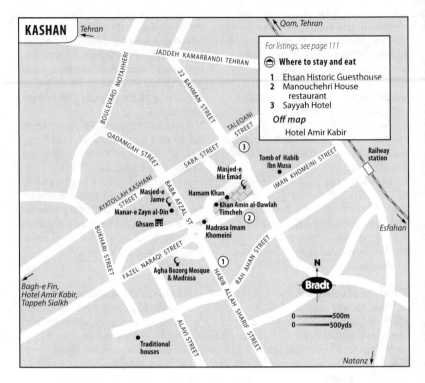

KASHAN Tehran

Qom, Tehran

For listings, see page 111

Where to stay and eat
1 Ehsan Historic Guesthouse
2 Manouchehri House
   restaurant
3 Sayyah Hotel

Off map
   Hotel Amir Kabir

JADDEH KAMARBANDI TEHRAN

BOULEVARD MOTAHHERI

22 BAHMAN STREET

QADAMGAH STREET

TALEQANI STREET

SABA STREET

SABA STREET

Railway station

AYATOLLAH KASHANI STREET

Masjed-e Mir Emad

Tomb of Habib Ibn Musa

IMAN KHOMEINI STREET

Masjed-e Jame

Hamam Khan

BABA AFZAL ST

Khan Amin al-Dawlah Timcheh

Manar-e Zayn al-Din

Ghsam

Madrasa Imam Khomeini

Esfahan

BUKHARI STREET

FAZEL NARAQI STREET

Agha Bozorg Mosque & Madrasa

HABIB ALLAH SHARIF STREET

RAH AHAN STREET

N

Bagh-e Fin,
Hotel Amir Kabir,
Tappeh Sialkh

Bradt

0 ————— 500m
0 ————— 500yds

Traditional houses

ALAVI STREET

Natanz

August 2013 restoration and repairs had also begun in the mosque's courtyard and the basement. About 500m southeast from the mosque, the 12th-century **Manar-e Zayn al-Din** (Baba Afzal St) is also worth a visit.

By retracing your steps to the bazaar entrance, this main road leads to the **Mosque and Madrasa of Agha Bozorg**, named after a famous theologian and jurist who was born in a neighbouring village and who was also known as Mehdi Naraqi (d1829). This 19th-century complex incorporates a deep sunken courtyard with a central ablution pool. The basement under the prayer hall acts as a winter assembly hall. Two wind towers, cunningly disguised as minarets, flank the main prayer *ivan*, dramatically accentuating the dome.

Three 19th-century residences are nearby, all off Alavi Street: the **Khaneh Borujerdiyeh** (⊕ *08.30–17.00; entry 100,000 rials*), **Khaneh Tabatabiyeh** (⊕ *08.30–17.00; entry 100,000 rials*) and the more recently opened **Khaneh Abbasian** (⊕ *08.30–17.00; entry 100,000 rials*). The Borujerdiyeh, formerly the house of a Kashani tea dealer, is perhaps the best known as its distinctive dome over the main audience *talar* appears on postcards and posters. The Tabatabiyeh house of 1881, to the left as you exit, is somewhat larger, with a clear division between the private family *anderun* apartments by the main entrance, the servants' quarters (extreme right) and the public *birun* rooms across the main court. The ornate plaster decoration is bichrome grey and white augmented with lively landscape paintings in the two side chambers of the *talar* (veranda). But the real delight is the more recently opened Khaneh Abbasian, down the street opposite the Borujerdiyeh. This enormous complex, completed in 1893 was built to provide an equally ornate house for Tabatabiyeh's daughter. With several levels, it is so extensive with numerous staircases, *talars*, courtyards and chambers that one can become quickly disorientated. The richly carved plaster decoration is in high relief on a Wedgewood blue or pale terracotta ground, often complemented with coloured window glass set in highly patterned pierced screens: deliciously over the top. All three residences bring home to the visitor how rich and influential late 19th-century merchants were, so if you are thinking of buying a modern Kashan carpet, just remember that the Abbasian and Tabatabiyeh families made their fortunes in carpet dealing. These restored houses have been joined by an even older one newly renovated in 2013 – the **Khan-e Ameriha** (*Alavi St; ⊕ 08.30–17.00; entry 100,000 rials*), a late 18th-century house built by an arms dealer to the Safavid court who was one of Kashan's wealthiest men and who also became its governor.

Half way along the 8km route southwest of the centre, towards the gardens established by the Safavid shahs to break their occasional royal progresses, is the tiled pyramidic dome to the south side marking the **Tomb of Abu Lulu**, honoured here in Iran for 'liquidating' Caliph Umar (d644CE), selected as caliph in preference to the Prophet's son-in-law, Ali, an insult to all Shi'is. As the tilework shows, it

AMIR KABIR (1807–52)

This 'Grand Commander' had lowly beginnings: his father was a cook in the royal palace when he himself started as a stable groom to the court. However, his abilities were quickly recognised and he was soon appointed a finance minister to the military in Iranian Azerbaijan. Aged 22, he joined the diplomatic team sent to St Petersburg and the Russian Caucasus, during which time he visited schools, factories, chambers of commerce and theatres. Only a handful of court officials had been sent abroad and these visits evidently had a lasting impact on him. He returned to the Caucasus in 1837, and spent four years in Erzincan (eastern Turkey) as an official negotiator, drawing up the Iranian–Ottoman frontier. These were the heady years of the Tanzimat period in Ottoman Turkey when the sultanate was yielding to constititutional demands, and undertaking reorganisation programmes affecting every aspect of economic and social life. On his return to Tehran in 1847 Amir Kabir was quickly promoted to tutor of the crown prince, then promoted again to chief army minister, and finally chief minister in 1848.

Iran was teetering on the edge of bankruptcy after paying a huge war indemnity to Russia (Treaty of Turkomanchay, 1828), and he moved immediately to fill the state coffers by cutting civil service pay and pensions and ordering tax to be paid direct to Tehran instead of through court tax agents; palace officials were not amused. But the public loved him as he ordered investigations into government corruption and bribery and gave the go-ahead for the construction of bazaars, canals and factories, sending craftsmen to Russia and Ottoman Turkey for training. To stem the flood of imports, customs duties were increased while domestic manufacture and agriculture production were assisted. He was involved in everything, even actively sponsoring private citizens for small-scale contracts, instituting national prizes for art and design, and establishing the first state college organised on Western lines. But, with each project, the anger of his enemies at court intensified. On 16 November 1851 he was dismissed and exiled to Kashan, but that was not enough for his foes, who engineered his assassination in January 1852. With his removal, the reorganisation programme came to a shuddering halt for many decades.

was extensively repaired in Safavid and then Qajar times. A little further, on the opposite side behind some houses, two mounds are visible, the larger being **Tappeh Sialkh**, excavated by the French during 1933–37. The elegant long-spouted pottery vessels, shaped like stylised sandpiper birds, now in the National Museum, Tehran, were found here during archaeological work. The earliest level (Sialkh I), which revealed stained red human remains buried underneath houses, has been dated to the 5th millennium BCE, or perhaps earlier. The pottery finds from level II, c4000BCE, showed indisputable use of the potter's wheel, but for some unknown reason the residents then abandoned this site for the smaller mound. This second settlement was probably destroyed by fire around 3000BCE, and there was then a gap of about 2,000 years before both sites were reinhabited. The new residents had other customs, employing stone foundations for their mud and wood buildings and burying their dead away from the town with the distinctive 'sandpiper' vessels as grave goods, along with trade items from the Gulf. During the 9th and 8th centuries BCE, a military attack caused the residents to flee, never to return. All the archaeological finds have been removed from the site, but the outlines of buildings are just visible.

The **Bagh-e Fin** (*Amir Kabir Rd;* ◷ *08.30–17.00; entry 150,000 rials*) is at the end of the street (the toll road runs immediately behind) and is by far the most visually impressive Persian garden in Iran today. It still retains much of its Safavid layout, with a central pavilion placed over the artesian water channels, though repair and rebuilding work was carried out by Karim Khan Zand of Shiraz, then by Fath Ali Shah of the Qajar dynasty and again in early 2000. A number of 19th-century foreign dignitaries, including the English envoy, Sir John Malcolm, broke their journeys here *en route* from Bushehr to the Tehran court. But there was a darker side to its history: in 1852 the forward-looking Iranian chief minister 'Amir Kabir' (see box, page 113) was assassinated here in the small *hamam* (*entry 50,000 rials*) to the left. Banished from the Tehran court, he was told the shah planned to restore him to favour and, in preparing for the ceremony, he visited this *hamam*, ignorant that it was a royal plot to kill him. There is a small museum, which has some of the finds from Tappeh Sialkh.

ON THE ROAD

On the old caravan road south to Esfahan is **Qahrud**, about 45km away on the Meymeh road, with its Masjed-e Jame (formerly Masjed-e Ali). The mosque will be locked when you visit, as its lovely Kashan tiles produced in 1307 were stolen in the 1960s, even though they were subsequently recovered and reset in the *mihrab*. It also possesses a fine carved door dedicated to 'The Crown of the Community and Religion ... the Seal of the Age', the work of an Esfahani woodworker.

Make every effort to visit **Abyaneh** (altitude 2,500m) in the hills, some 70km southeast of Kashan, close to Natanz. A small 13th-century fortress safeguarded this picturesque Zoroastrian village until Safavid sectarian intolerance drove many of the community to India; even today the official tourist pamphlet omits any reference to Zoroastrianism. A ruined but extensive fire temple built in three stages, perhaps dating from the 3rd century CE, lies in the centre of the village, and nearby is the Masjed-e Jame with a Safavid entry portal and vestibule, with a Seljuk *minbar* and a 14th-century *mihrab* inside the prayer hall. However, the real joy is the vernacular architecture of red mud-brick houses with wooden balconies and decorated doors, in narrow alleyways. There are no buses going this way and you will need to hire a taxi from Kashan. The return journey costs approximately

700,000 rials. Alternatively, you can visit the village by taxi from Natanz as intercity Esfahan–Kashan buses should stop here (but do enquire at the bus station in advance). You can also stay overnight in Abyaneh if you wish to explore the area a little bit more. **Hotel Abyaneh** (*30 rooms;* \ *036 243 62223; www.hotelabyaneh.com;* **$$**) is a little pricey, but is the best choice available.

Or you could travel to Esfahan, taking the new Kashan–Yazd road southeast and turning west at Na'in; this route allows you to see some beautiful monuments *en route*, see below. A short diversion west on this road at Bad leads to **Natanz** past numerous visible anti-aircraft military installations to protect the neaby Natanz nuclear facility. The town itself is nestling in the foothills in a beautiful setting, with the remains of the pre-Islamic castle **Qaleh Vashaq** just to the north. A beautiful portal, decorated with turquoise and cobalt glazed inserts, dated 1317, is the first thing one sees at the **Masjed-e Jame** complex, which dates mainly from post-Mongol times; this led into the *khanaqeh*, here to accommodate visiting sufis. A much smaller, insignificant doorway takes visitors into the four-*ivan* mosque, built 12 years before, incorporating an earlier Seljuk octagonal structure. The Mausoleum of the Sufi Sheikh Abd al-Samad al-Esfahani with its tiled tent dome was constructed some two years after. The *muqarnas* vaulting inside is beautiful as is the plasterwork throughout in the complex. Not far away in the northwest is the **Masjed-e Koucheh Mir**, which reportedly still retains a splendid carved plaster *mihrab* (Q11:114–5) dating to the 11th–12th centuries.

ALONG THE KASHAN–YAZD ROAD

Moving from Natanz southeast in the direction of Yazd, there are several interesting towns on the Kashan–Yazd road. Ardestan and, some 15km to the northeast, **Zavareh** (branching off in the centre of Ardestan) are two of the best. Zavareh was an important centre on the trade routes from Sassanid times until the late 11th century, which explains the number of important monuments here. The way to the **Masjed-e Jame** is through the covered bazaar, now largely empty. Turn immediately left on entry, passing at the far end a large Hosseiniyeh hall with great metal *'alams* and drapes. This takes you very close to the Masjed-e Jame, which scholars consider to be one of the earliest known mosques in Iran, built on the four-*ivan* courtyard plan in 1135, according to the Kufic inscription (Q9:18) running unusually around the court façade – such detail is generally placed inside the prayer chamber. Unfortunately, its gentle slide into decline noted in the late 1970s has accelerated, but enough remains of the prayer hall chamber and the occasional column decoration. It has a beautifully carved plaster *mihrab* with Quranic verses (Q7:52) in the angular Kufic script, and in cursive *naskhi* (Q9:18), while the dome, supported by trilobed squinches, was decorated with another inscription (Q3:187–8). Slightly to the southeast is the **Masjed-e Pa Minar** of 1069, according to the minaret inscription; this makes it one of the earliest firmly dated monuments to survive in Iran, although most of the mosque's plasterwork is 300 years later.

Ardestan was a strongly fortified town in the 10th century. Its **Masjed-e Imam Hassan** was founded during Seljuk times as a *madrasa*, perhaps the first in Iran built with a portal flanked by two minarets, although only one minaret has survived. But the purpose of the visit is the **Masjed-e Jame** whose domed prayer chamber was built, possibly on top of a fire temple, during the reign of Malik Shah (d1092; see page 94). Its main brick inscription concerns further building in 1158, and another in the prayer *ivan* of 1160 perhaps denotes the year when the present four-*ivan* layout was established. The plasterwork here is some of the best surviving in Iran, whether you look at the remains of the delicate trefoil and split palmettes once covering the prayer *ivan*, the deeply cut elegant inscription of the arch-soffits, or the richly carved *mihrab*, and well worth a visit. In the courtyard, there is access down two staircases to the winter prayer hall below which light is diffused through alabaster sheets incorporated in the courtyard pavement above.

NA'IN

Na'in (population 29,000), some 95km southeast of Ardestan and 145km east from Esfahan, is a pleasant old town with clay houses typical of the region that has managed to preserve some of its traditional charm. There are frequent buses here from both Yazd and Esfahan (*Jay Terminal; 30,000 rials one way*), but it is advisable to book tickets in advance, especially if travelling from Yazd in the afternoon.

If you are staying overnight here and wish to explore the surrounding area in detail (which might not be a bad idea as most sites here are scattered around) contact local guide Mahmood Mohammadipur (m *093 98636090*), who also happens to be the owner of the Green Memory (Hafezeh Sabz) internet café and the author of the Wikitravel internet page on Na'in. For location of Na'in see map, page 110.

⌂ WHERE TO STAY AND EAT

⌂ **Na'in Tourist Inn** (9 rooms) Shahid Rajaie St; ☏ 0323 2253081–8; f 0322 2253665. Traditional house with attractive large rooms, 2 inner courtyards & a good restaurant, but regrettably no Wi-Fi. **$$**

⌂ **Gholami Guesthouse** (11 rooms) Imam Khomeini St & Pirnia St crossroads; ☏ 0323 2252441;

m 091 32234667; e guesthousegholami@yahoo. com. Run by Vahid Gholami, the guesthouse offers simple but clean dormitories & en-suite rooms; ideal for a budget traveller. Green Memory internet café is 20m down the street. **$**

WHAT TO SEE AND DO Most books on Islamic architecture refer to the **Masjed-e Jame** (*off Shohada St; entry 50,000 rials*) here, because something of its original 10th-century 'Arab' plan remains. This 'Arab' concept of positioning arcades running parallel to the enclosing walls quickly fell out of favour as more patrons plumped for an open court dominated by two or four tall *ivans*, and a domed prayer chamber. As well as the (much-restored) brick patterning of the courtyard piers, some lovely mid 10th-century plasterwork remains in the prayer chamber, but unfortunately a high wooden railing really limits access and viewing. In the arch, soffits' and spandrels' large rosettes and have been carved deeply, while some pillars are covered with plaster strapwork framing clusters of small mulberry-like fruits. If only one could get closer. Here and there a few 14th-century tiles enliven the brickwork. To the extreme left as you exit is the **Hosseiniyeh** with a real stage for the performance of the Moharram play, and from its far doorway the remains of the town's citadel are visible.

Just across the small square is the local **Ethnographic Museum** in a traditional house (*entry 50,000 rials*). Mention an ethnographic display and we usually experience a sinking feeling, but this one is housed in a superb Safavid house of 1560. One enters to find a central sunken courtyard with rooms on both levels. Do persuade the knowledgeable curator, who speaks very good English, to take you round; his wife is a noted carpetmaker in the area. He has persuaded the townspeople to lend him interesting archival material, such as marriage contracts, as well as metalwork and ceramic objects. One display contains the *shalvar ve qamis* (trousers and tunic) as worn by Zoroastrian women in the 19th century, which are comparable in quality to items in the Victoria and Albert Museum, London;

those tiny motifs are not printed but hand embroidered. The best is yet to come: the rooms on the right of entry are stunning with their mid 16th-century plaster decoration intact. The depictions on the *talar* walls and ceiling tell of the Prophet Yusuf (biblical Joseph) whose beauty was such that the pharaoh's female slaves cut their hands in amazement, and the Egyptian queen, Zulaykha, resorted to covering her bedroom walls with erotic paintings in an attempt to seduce him. Yusuf took to his heels and lived to tell the tale. The small sitting room next door is just as beautifully decorated. There is a striking correlation between this work and designs and compositions on famous Safavid court carpets in major Western museums, and of course Persian paintings of the same date. Behind the museum and visible from the small square in front are the remains of **Narin Castle**, worth a picture, but there's nothing else to see.

Some 3km away in a northeasterly direction is **Mohammediyeh**, now virtually absorbed into Na'in. It is known for its wind towers (*badgirs*), some of which serve to ventilate small underground weaving shops producing camel-hair and pure woollen fabrics, used mainly for religious clothing, exported to Syria and Lebanon. The doors are always open and you are welcome to have a look or even purchase. The whole suburb seems to be actively engaged in some form of textile manufacture and Na'in is well known for its weavers. Near Mohammedyeh there is also an old **Rigareh Watermill** that consists of numerous underground *qanats*, but it can only be visited with a guide.

If you are here with time to spare, visit **Masjed-e Sar-e Kucha** (ask for directions). The Sar-e Kucha is (now) a small mosque that looks like a shrine because it has no courtyard, which is unusual for Iran. Both it and the alleyway may date from the 10th–11th century, because entry is through a side chamber into a tiny prayer room, with another side chamber on the other side. Its real claim to fame is the fine Kufic inscription painted along the interior walls and the base of the dome. Some of the inscription, especially around the *mihrab*, has now disappeared, but it has a specifically Sunni rather than Shi'a emphasis. This supports a late 11th-century dating, given that the Seljuks, the champions of Sunni Islam, were then in control. The inscription may look battered, but closer inspection reveals beautifully proportioned letters with elegantly curved 'swan-neck' hypostyles.

AROUND NA'IN

The road from Na'in west to Esfahan is dotted with a number of well-preserved caravanserais and the first town it passes through is **Toudeshk** (from Persian *tou dasht* meaning 'in the desert'), a small desert town with traditional clay houses. In its older part, known as Toudeshk Cho, there is **Tak Taku Homestay ($)**, a very well-run guesthouse with dormitory-style rooms, Wi-Fi and parking. If you have your own sleeping bag, you are welcome to sleep on the roof or in the courtyard for free. The man in charge is **Mohammed Jalali** (✆ *0312 6372586*; m *091 33654420*; e *crazyboyindesert@gmail.com; www.deserthome.ir*), one of the most experienced and knowledgeable guides in Iran, who can arrange overnight stays in the desert, cycling or pretty much any other tour around the province.

The next town along the road is **Kuhpayeh**, where the **Masjed-e Jame** has one of the handful of tiled *minbars* still surviving, probably made in 1528 when the tiling scheme in the prayer chamber was installed (although some scholars consider the tiling to be from c1335).

From here one could continue south for approximately 33km, and then 25km east to visit **Varzaneh** (100km east of Esfahan). In fact as Barsiyan is also worth a visit, we suggest a half-day trip from Esfahan to visit Aziran, Varzaneh, returning to Esfahan by way of Barsiyan and viewing, if only from afar, the minarets of Ziar and Gar as well as the many pigeon houses in the fields on the Ezhiyeh road. You should arrive at Varzaneh's **Masjed-e Jame** in time for midday prayer (approximately 11.50 but seasonably variable) though this means there could be a problem finding a place for lunch. There is a restaurant close by in the main square, almost opposite a wind tower, but it closes after delivering lunch to a nearby factory; so if you are a solo traveller or in a very small group, take some food/drink with you. The reason you should aim for this timing is that the women of this township attend the midday prayer enveloped in white *chadors*; the image is one of fluttering doves, going into and leaving the mosque. Everyone is very friendly and delighted that you have come to visit. And the *masjed* itself is worth seeing. With a 20m high minaret, it was built c1100 – although the mosque was largely rebuilt in the Timurid 15th century. The tilework of the *ivan* leading to the prayer chamber incorporating the name of Shah Rukh (the son of Timur Leng who took Esfahan in 1417; see box, page 254), on the *minbar* and the *mihrab* is splendid. It is on the *mihrab* that the date 1444 is recorded, after the Quranic inscription (Q3:38–9). The different appearance of the north *ivan* results from 17th-century Safavid repairs. The guardian will suggest you walk behind the mosque, leaving by the left-hand door, facing the prayer chamber, so that you can see the exterior profile of the dome which still retains just a little of two bands of ceramic decoration around the zone of transition. Varzaneh has another treat for those interested in language because most of the residents, formerly a long-surviving Zoroastrian community, still speak a form of Pahlavi in the home.

There are three other Seljuk minarets closer to Esfahan which may be approached from Varzaneh travelling west or from Kuhpayeh for 45km in the direction of Esfahan, turning south to see those at Barsiyan, Ziar and, a few kilometres before Esfahan, Gar (also spelt Jar). The one at **Barsiyan**, about 45km southeast of Esfahan on the old caravan road to Yazd, was built in 1097, probably then a little taller than its present 35m. Its cylindrical base has a diameter of 5.75m but it tapers to 4.2m at the top, where there is a brick inscription (Q22:76–7) along with five bands of very fine brick patterning. The main road now runs directly behind the domed prayer chamber of the mosque below, so the entry for visitors is now straight into this architectural space. Admittedly the caretaker is rather grumpy but all his elderly chums sitting outside will chivvy him into action for you. This section of the mosque dates from the first half of the 12th century, the dome resting on four well-proportioned trilobed squinches and engaged colonettes, with a cut-brick inscription (now damaged); the actual dome, however, had to be rebuilt in 1421. The *mihrab* is from the 16th century with lovely patterned plaster star decoration. Little else remains standing of this structure, but go next door to the Abbasi caravanserai and walk up one or other of the two staircases off the main entrance to the roof and from there look down onto the mosque. It looks as if originally it was a two-*ivan* ground plan including the long vaulted hall, with remains of two glorious 16th-century tile panels, leading into the domed prayer chamber. That tilework presumably dates from courtyard alterations carried out in the reign of Shah Tahmasp I (1524–76).

Across the river is **Ziar**, whose Safavid caravanserai was repaired in Qajar times; the amazing minaret here has provoked much discussion but for the past few years it is another monument that has been smothered in scaffolding with little sign of any building or repair activity. Two very different dates, 1155 and 1289, have been given for this highly decorated shaft, some 50m high with its balcony intact, rising from a square plinth. Turquoise-glazed brick elements were used to pick out the Quranic inscription (Q41:33); these favour the later date. A similar wide dating span has been accorded to another minaret, the Manar-e Saraban in Esfahan (see page 134) similarly decorated and with an identical Quranic verse. Here the names of the four caliphs after the death of the Prophet Mohammed are included, so this must be a Sunni, not a Shi'a, monument which strongly suggests it was built during the Seljuk period (ie: around 1155) and this Ziar minaret is now thought to be mid to late 12th century. To round off this collection, the **Gar** minaret on its octagonal base was built in 1122, according to its inscription, to serve the mosque endowed by Sayyid Reza Abu al-Qasem. Fields now surround it. Reportedly it has a double staircase, but the firmly padlocked door meant checking was impossible.

Some 25km closer to Esfahan on the road from Ziar (and some 75km from Varzaneh), passing through a countryside of wheat, rice and maize, just off the road to the west is **Aziran** where there is a domed mausoleum. It is now free-standing but it was clearly once part of a huge complex judging from the remains of mud- and fired-brick piers around. The dome rests on four lobed squinches similar to those 11th-century domes in the Masjed-e Jame in Esfahan, leading into a zone of transition composed of 16 blind niches, further decorated with lozenges of squared Kufic, but these are probably dated to the 19th-century restoration work. There are remains of an elegant cursive *naskhi* inscription in the *mihrab*.

About 65km southeast of Na'in (towards Yazd) is **Aqda** (pronounced Aghda), once known as a strong Zoroastrian centre. There are no magnificent historic buildings here, but the village is well worth walking around. Its **Masjed-e Jame** is thought to date from the 14th century, but only the winter prayer chamber retains an echo of those Timurid proportions, while outside is a large *hosseiniyeh* (1875) for the Moharram ceremonies. A number of Aqda's other monuments have either been extensively rebuilt (eg: Masjed-e Shams 1679) or closed (*hamam* 1645 and cistern 1618). The police have at last vacated the 1846 caravanserai built by the merchant Hajji Abu al-Qasim Rashti, but no-one knows what will happen to the building now. Despite this, the village has a pleasing atmosphere and the locals are very happy but curious that visitors want to walk around exploring the narrow alleys, houses, city gate and so on.

ESFAHAN *Telephone code 0311*

Esfahan (421km from Tehran) is the most complete, so to speak, city in Iran, and can only be compared, according to André Malraux, French novelist and former minister for cultural affairs, to Florence and Beijing. It is simply remarkable; nowhere else in the country exists such a harmonious mix of modernity and history. Esfahan is truly 'half the world', as an Iranian proverb suggests, and it is impossible to do full justice to all of its historic monuments, but the most famous buildings and some of special interest have been included below.

HISTORY Bisected by the Zayandeh River – the name comes from *sipahi*: soldier – Esfahan (altitude 1,585m; population 1.7 million; third-largest Iranian city after Tehran and Mashhad) has been an important trading centre since Parthian times, and possibly both the **Pol-e Sharestan** bridge and the **Ateshgah** (fire temple) just on the outskirts are early Sassanid in construction, built when the city already had separate Jewish and Christian quarters. The city initially was predominantly Jewish with small Zoroastrian and Christian communities. It fell to the Arab Muslims in 643CE and quickly gained a reputation for its textiles, becoming the capital of the Seljuk sultan Toghrol Beg (d1063CE). Bitter quarrels broke out among local Shi'as and Sunnis, so its prosperity suffered and then plummeted as the Mongols invaded. Then it was the onslaught of Timur Leng's army, which slew at least 70,000 (and possibly 200,000) Esfahanis. The rivalry between the Aq Qoyunlu and Qara Qoyunlu tribal confederations in the 15th century prevented any sustained revival, but with the Safavid court's move from battle-threatened Tabriz and Qazvin to Esfahan in 1598, the city's fortunes changed.

Town planning began in earnest immediately with the Chahar Bagh gardens, and then the main square with its royal buildings was constructed. According to the French jeweller, Jean Chardin, by the 1660s Esfahan had 162 mosques, 1,802 caravanserais, 48 colleges and 273 public baths to serve a population the size of London's, then about 600,000. The sheer scale and the beauty of its buildings amazed most foreign visitors who marvelled at the turquoise domes and the dramatic minarets. But the Safavid regime was beginning to crack at the seams and in 1722 the capital was besieged for six months by Afghan rebels. Plague outbreaks and famine followed. Nader Qolif (later Nader Shah Afshar)) ousted the Afghans but transferred the administration to Mashhad (see page 253). By 1800 the population of Esfahan was probably only 120,000.

GETTING THERE There are daily **flights** from the major cities (seasonal twice-weekly services to/from Kuwait and from spring 2013 regular twice-weekly from Istanbul), and numerous intercity **buses**. Esfahan has four bus terminals: Kaveh (North); Sofeh (South); Zayandeh Rud (West) and Jey (East). Check in advance

THE ZUKHANEH

The sport of wrestling has always been popular in Iran. Wealthy merchants and court officials traditionally sponsored wrestling teams and patronised the gymnasia (*zurkhanehs*) where the athletes practised calisthenic exercises. Traditionally, a young man has to be at least 16 years old, with a beard growth thick enough to support a comb, before being accepted for training. There are some 50 holds to learn and two tests to pass before being recognised as a junior athlete, and progress is shown in the ways the wrap is worn around the hips. Only a select few have ever been acknowledged as champion, or *pahlavan* (one reason why Reza Khan chose this title as his dynastic name in 1925).

The exercise and wrestling place is one and the same: a sunken area, often octagonal in shape, large enough to hold 12 to 18 men during their exercising. One English visitor in 1833 described it with 'seats for the spectators ... the roof, which was plastered, was painted all over with fierce figures of *pahlavans* performing their various feats of strength'. Today the *zurkhaneh* walls are usually decorated with photographs of past and present wrestlers, and objects strongly identified with Sufi and dervish fraternities, like begging bowls, axes, a sheepskin mat and posters of Imam Ali, the shrines of Karbala and Mashhad. This association with Ali and his descendants is stressed as the *morshid* (leader) beats out the rhythm for each exercise while shouting out Shi'a sayings. Each calisthenic exercise builds up the muscles: a wooden board to strengthen the shield arm, 'Indian' clubs weighing anything from 4 to 40kg substituting for heavy warclubs, and an iron bow to exercise shoulder muscles. The gymnasts' strength is publicly recognised every year when they are asked to carry the heavy *'alam* standards in the Moharram parades, but in the 1960s–70s many *zurkhanehs* were closed down as the late shah grew nervous about their members' loyalty to the crown.

with the bus driver as some buses arriving in Esfahan go to both Kaveh and Sofeh terminals. You can reach the city by **train** from Tehran; there is also a railway line between Esfahan and Shiraz. Esfahan train station is a few kilometres further along the road after Sofeh bus terminal. You can also arrive here by **taxi** directly from IK Airport in Tehran for around US$54.

GETTING AROUND Once in the city, the major Safavid buildings are located within **walking** distance of the Maydan-e Imam (also known as Maydan-e Naqsh-e Jahan, 'half the world' in Persian), but for less-frequented monuments, it is best to hire a **taxi** especially for Pir-e Bakran and Ashtarjan (see pages 137–8), or Varzaneh, Barsiyan, Ziar and Gar (see page 118). The main taxi rank, where you can hire a taxi for longer journeys, is at the top of Imam Square near Sepah Street.

In the city itself a single-line **metro** system is being built running north–south, passing very close to the University of Esfahan at Azadi Square, presently all dug up, but nearing completion.

Esfahan **Europcar** office is located near Imam Square (*Telefonkhaneh Alley; contact Amir Soleiman;* ✆ *2218013;* m *091 31143787;* e *isfahan@europcar.ir*); look for the Europcar sign.

It is also possible (for men only) to rent a **bicycle** from one of the bicycle stands around town. The first three hours are free of charge (thanks to Esfahan City Council) and the hourly rate after that is 2,500 rials. Make sure to bring a copy of your passport.

The central **Tourist Police Office** (✆ *218302, 2225593*) is the small glass building right next to the taxi rank.

TOURIST INFORMATION A tourist information office (✆ *2216832, 2213840; www. isfahancht.ir;* ⊙ *08.30–17.00, longer hours during Nou Rouz & in summer*) is next to the entrance of the Ali Qapu Palace where it is possible to arrange for an English-speaking guide for city sightseeing.

WHERE TO STAY For location of listings see map, page 123.

Luxury

Hotel Abbasi (formerly Shah Abbasi) (220 rooms) Shahid Medani St; ✆2226010–19; e abbasihotel@yahoo.com; www.abbasihotel. com. Full of character & grandeur, this is the best hotel in Iran. Rooms overlooking the inner courtyard come with small balconies & a large price tag. Cheaper options are substantially smaller. Staff wear traditional clothes & are exceptionally courteous. The abundant b/fast is served in the spectacular 1st-floor hall painted in traditional Persian style. In addition to an indoor swimming pool there are various souvenir & carpet shops & the tea house serves delicious tea with *gooshfil* sweets & the best in Esfahan *ash-e reshte* winter noodle soup. **$$$$**

Hotel Kowsar International (formerly Sheraton) (132 rooms) Bd Mellat; ✆6240230–9; e info@hotelkowsar.com; www.hotelkowsar.

com. Located by the Se-o-Se Pol bridge, this is a fine 4-star hotel with good service & excellent facilities. Rooms with a view of the river come with small balconies & the traditional tea house here is popular among Esfahani socialites. This is also the 2nd best place after Abbasi Hotel to eat *ash-e reshte*. Check out the large Khomeini & Khamenei graffiti on the hotel's outer sidewalk. **$$$$**

Above average

Hotel Ali Qapu (104 rooms) Chahar Bagh St; ✆2227929; e info@aliqapuhotel.com; www. aliqapuhotel.com. Centrally located for the sights & bazaar, this modern hotel is about a block away from the river. A little retro with a rather flashy lobby; rooms overlooking the street may be a little noisy. The location is excellent, but slightly overpriced for the service & facilities on offer. The souvenir shop sells good postcards, though. **$$$**

🛏 **Sepahan Hotel** (42 rooms) Farshadi St; ☎ 2221235; e sepahanhotel@gmail.com; www. sepahanhotel.com. Named after Esfahan, which used to be called Sepahan, it is traditionally decorated & in good taste. The inner atrium gives the hotel an airy meringue feel. Rooms are lovely & come with Wi-Fi. The Sepahan highlight, however, is the top-floor 70-seat restaurant with spectacular views over the rooftops of Imam Square & adjoining markets. The staff are pleasant & courteous & the walk here lies through the old market, if approaching from Imam Square. **$$$**

Mid-range

🛏 **Hotel Azadi** (38 rooms) Off Masjed-e Sayyed St, Takhti crossroads; ☎ 2204056; f 2203713. A very clean & quiet central hotel with modern lobby & smallish tiny rooms. Double-pricing system – with prices for foreign tourists stated in US dollars – is in place, but payment can be made in rials. **$$**

🛏 **Partikan Hotel** (11 apts) Saadi St, leading to the square; ☎ 2214247; e info@partikanhotel.com; www.partikanhotel.com. Modern, comfortable apt-style rooms, each at least 30m² in size. Traditional ground-floor restaurant serves delicious

Iranian food & the overall hotel atmosphere is welcoming & the staff are attentive. **$$**

Basic

🛏 **Amir Kabir Hostel** (32 rooms) Takhti St, next door to the stadium; ☎ 2227273. Located in the sports-bustling part of Esfahan, this cool central hostel is always full of travelling international youth. It offers very clean dormitory-style accommodation, but rooms are not en suite. The staff are caring & helpful & the heavenly calm inner courtyard is a great place to relax after a day of sightseeing. **$**

🛏 **Jolfa Hotel** (60 rooms) Next to Vank Cathedral; ☎ 6244441–2; f 6249446. Good value & excellent location, but service is a little scatty. There is a bar-style ground floor café & a shop. Wi-Fi is not the best in town, but it works. **$**

🛏 **Tourist Hotel** (30 rooms) Abbas Abad St, off Chahar Bagh St; ☎ 2204437–79; e info@ esfahantouristhotel.com. A jolly good hotel with Wi-Fi & pleasant staff. The location is superb & the value for money is even better. Book ahead; it is always full. **$**

✕ **WHERE TO EAT AND DRINK** The restaurants listed below are recommended, but for modern cafés, visit the Jolfa quarter, in particular the main square, where young Esfahanis come to hang out in the evenings. The two best cafés here are **Firuz** (*opposite Jolfa Hotel;* ☎ *6268009; also serves b/fast from 07.00–11.00*) where you absolutely must order *bahar-e narenj* tea from bitter orange flowers, and the much-liked **Ani** around the corner from the Vank Cathedral. For location of listings see map opposite.

✕ **Setareh Restaurant** (Aseman Hotel) Motahari St; ☎ 2354141; ⏰ 12.30–15.30 & 19.30–23.00. This 11th-floor modern restaurant is located on the rooftop of the Aseman Hotel & offers splendid views over the city, & traditional Iranian cuisine. **$$**

✕ **Shahrzad Restaurant** Abbas Abad St; ☎ 2204490; ⏰ 12.00–15.00 & 19.00–23.00. The food is excellent, in particular the lamb shank *mahicheh* is highly recommended. Large groups of tourists are a little too noisy. One of the few places in Iran where leaving a tip would be expected. **$$**

✕ **Beryani Golestan** Tefonkhaneh Alley, off Sepah St; ☎ 2225223; ⏰ 12.00–15.00 & 19.00–23.00. Very basic, local restaurant & you are unlikely to see any tourists here. Serves the best *beryani* in town. **$**

✕ **Traditional Banquet Hall** Imam Sq, though a small alley past a tiny shopping yard & up the 1st

floor; ☎ 2219068/3345; f 2200729; ⏰ 12.00–15.00 & 19.00–22.30. A delight of a place & Iranian cuisine experience; has indoor & outdoor seating area overlooking the yard. Try traditional Esfahani dish minced lamb *beryani* or *kofteh*, traditional meatballs. A little touristy though. **$**

☕ **Azad-e Gan Traditional Teahouse** Through the narrow alley at the top of Imam Sq, past Hakim St intersection. This basement, alternative tea house is popular among Esfahani youth, which keeps the place afloat. Authorities have closed it down in the past for allowing *qalian* smoking for both men & women. Serves delicious *abgoosht* & tea with *gooshfil*. Full of character & antique clocks, lamps & pictures suspended from the ceiling. Be discreet & avoid coming in large groups. Recommended. **$**

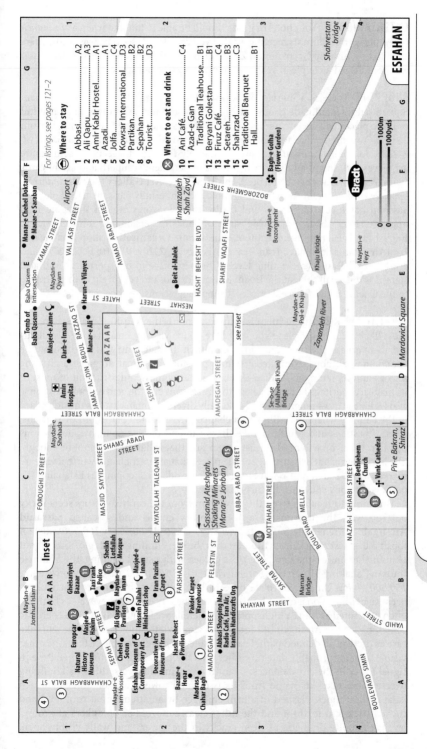

ESFAHAN

For listings, see pages 121–2

Where to stay
1 Abbasi..................A2
2 Ali Qapu...............A3
3 Amir Kabir Hostel....A1
4 Azadi...................A1
5 Jolfa...................C4
6 Kowsar International...D3
7 Partikan...............B2
8 Sepahan...............B2
9 Tourist................D3

Where to eat and drink
10 Ani Café...............C4
11 Azad-e Gan
      Traditional Teahouse....B1
12 Beryani Golestan........B1
13 Firuz Café..............C4
14 Setareh................B3
15 Shahrzad...............C3
16 Traditional Banquet
      Hall...................B1

ENTERTAINMENT Your hotel or guide should be able to find out when a *zurkhaneh* (wrestling gymnasium) is meeting, so that you can attend (see box, page 120). There used to be a historic Qajar-period Zurkhaneh Kamal near Sabzeh-e Maydan, but it was demolished a couple of years ago to give way to retail space.

SHOPPING There is a myriad of workshops and small stores all around Imam Square selling handmade goods, silverware, etc, but for cash only. Only a handful of these places will accept credit cards and always at an extra charge ranging from 2–15%. You might like to visit **Hossein Fallahi Miniaturist Shop** (*5 Saadi St;* \ *2226733;* e *info@miniatureart.org*) with easily the largest selection of miniature art pieces. Althought a little expensive, the variety here is superb and credit cards (with 6% extra charge) are accepted. **Hasht Behesht Art Gallery** (*149 Ostandari St, opposite Hasht Behesht St;* \ *2217754*) run by a wonderfully pleasant artist Soleiman Sassoon has lovely old prints and cards. The two-storey Abbasi shopping mall opposite Hotel Abbasi has a wide range of books in Persian and some classics in English, and also houses the **Iranian Handicrafts Organisation shop** (road level), **IranAir** main sales office, **Iran Travel Agency** (\ *2220990/3010;* f *2228576*) and a lovely café **Radio** (mezzanine level). The best place to buy postcards and also stamps is the small shop at the Imam Mosque or kiosk to your right at the entrance to the Chehel Sotun Palace. For carpet shop suggestions, see box, page 127.

WHAT TO SEE AND DO Esfahan is simply splendid. The Naqsh-e Jahan Square will most likely be the first place you visit here and is visually breathtaking. Esfahanis are also perhaps the most craft-minded bunch in the country, as certified by the abundant workshops, exquisite Persian carpet stores and small art galleries. It is the history and its remnants, unlike Shiraz that has witnessed destruction of most of its historical heritage in earthquakes, that make this city the gem of Iran. Esfahan is also by far the most religiously and culturally diverse Iranian city. It is the only place in the country where you will have a chance to visit sacred places of Zoroastrians, Jews, Christians and Muslims alike. If you intend to visit as many sites here as possible, then you will need at least a week and that will most likely not be enough. The list below is not exhaustive, but the places that are particularly worth a visit are marked as ✳. You may also want to leave a day aside for shopping, as Esfahan is the best place to buy souvenirs or carpets.

Driving into Esfahan from the west, 7km from the centre, visitors see a rocky outcrop with the remains of a 13th-century citadel and so-called **Sassanid Ateshgah** or fire temple (*off Saremiyeh St;* ⊕ *08.30–17.00; entry 100,000 rials*) on top. It is best visited at sunset; the view over the surrounding area is glorious. About 1km further on (on the same side), is a garden with a small building, the **Manar-e Jonban** ('Shaking Minarets') (*Saremiyeh St;* ⊕ *08.30–17.00, closed for lunch; entry 150,000 rials*). Unless you have time to kill, both can be ignored particularly because neither is on a direct bus route from the city centre. However, as both are often promoted as tourist highspots, a few details are included here. The energetic can climb up the Ateshgah hill for a panoramic view, smog permitting, but take care as there is no defined path. Leaving aside the huge concrete cistern, the other visible remains probably date no earlier than the 13th/14th century, when it was a signal tower in the city defences. As for the shaking minarets, this small building over a tomb takes its name from its two small towers, one or other of which is, at certain times, clasped in a firm embrace by an attendant at roof level and rocked back and forth; it and the other clearly move. For onlookers at ground level, it is quite dramatic as deep cracks in the towers and walls visibly open.

Lord Curzon wryly reported in 1892 that many travellers 'have exhausted their ingenuity' trying to explain this phenomenon: an underground chain linking the two minarets; an inner vertical beam in each tower resting in a socle; or a horizontal beam within the arch brickwork on which the minarets are 'balanced'. We prefer the theory that it is the Sufi sheikh Amu Abdallah in his 1317 grave beneath the building, shaking with fury at being disturbed yet again.

Believe us, a **pigeon tower** (*borj-e kabutar*) is far, far more interesting and spectacular. There are plenty of them scattered around the province. There is a Sassanid example dating back to 16th or 17th century right in the centre of Esfahan on Mardovich Square. It is well preserved with pigeons still nesting inside. A very kind guardian will let you climb up to the rooftop, but do leave a small donation before leaving. There are also marvellous examples of pigeon towers near Pir-e Bakran (see page 137) so you could combine visits to this, Pir-e Bakran itself and also Ashtarjan by hiring a taxi for half a day.

Esfahan's Maydan-e Imam ✳

As for Esfahan itself, a minimum of four hours is needed in and around the enormous public square now known as the Maydan-e Imam (formerly Maydan-e Shah or Maydan-e Naqsh-e Jahan), laid out by the Safavid Shah Abbas I (d1628), and an evening walk around is recommended as the square and the monuments are often floodlit. Said to be three times the size of St Mark's Square in Venice, this immense open space (500 x 160m) now has lawns and fountains but was once the royal parade ground, where the shahs watched military equestrian exercises, wrestling bouts and polo matches (stone goalposts are still visible at the south end). At the north end is the main entry into the bazaar, facing the Masjed-e Imam, with the coffee-coloured dome of Masjed-e Sheikh Lotfallah to the east, and opposite the Ali Qapu, the 17th-century ceremonial entrance into the royal palace compound; each is described below.

Shah Abbas I ordered the building of **Masjed-e Imam** ✳ (formerly Masjed-e Shah) (☉ *08.30–17.00, closed 11.00–13.00 Fri; entry 100,000 rials, free daily in the evenings during the prayer*) in memory of his ancestor Shah Tahmasp I (d1576). Work began in 1612 and finished in 1638, ten years after his death. Growing impatient at the length of building time, so we are told, Abbas I demanded that the labour-intensive technique of 'mosaic' tilework used for the main entrance be abandoned for the time-saving underglazed painted tile squares seen elsewhere in the mosque. The best tilework, with a purity of glaze, colour and motif design, is indeed present on the majestically tall entrance portal flanked by soaring minarets, facing on to the *maydan*. Incidentally, it has been suggested that the two peacock motifs below the central grille window were a Safavid dynastic device as they also feature at the Ardabil and Mashhad shrines. Through the great silver doors of 1636, you'll see the courtyard is set at a 45° angle necessary for the correct direction towards Mecca, so clearly Shah Abbas I was primarily concerned that the *maydan* had a north–south orientation. The call to prayer was never made from the mosque's tall minarets because, according to Lord Curzon writing in the 1890s, the shahs were fearful that the *muezzins* would have a clear uncensored view into the royal gardens. Instead the call was made from the little roof-pavilion over the *ivan* to the right of the central courtyard.

Walking slowly around the mosque allows the visitor to see the vistas as they open out, and the astonishing range in the tile colouring and pattern on the walls, vaults and side domes become apparent. Sadly, modern tiles of inferior quality are increasingly replacing original ones. Either side of the main prayer hall, set back in a small courtyard, is a small *madrasa* where students were taught until the late 19th century. But before entering the main prayer hall, do look at the bulbous shape and decoration of its exterior dome (54m high) because, inside, the dome has a different shape. This is a splendid example of a double dome, the inner one absorbing and distributing the structural load so allowing the outer dome to have a more eye-catching outline. At the apex there is a 14m gap between the two, the outer shell being supported on huge spars embedded into the inner dome. Peace and calm rarely prevail in this hall as visitors stand on a central floor slab and clap to hear the resounding echo. Perhaps Bradt travellers could establish a quieter tradition – just as effective – of tearing a piece of paper. If you have a camera which has a slow shutter release and a non-automatic flash, switch the latter off, alter the shutter speed to ½ or 1 second (check the light meter), and place the camera on the floor and you should achieve a good shot.

The Masjed-e Imam's angled entrance is best photographed from the **Ali Qapu Palace** ✳ (☉ *08.00–17.00; entry 150,000 rials*), constructed around 1600. Described disparagingly as a brick boot-box by Robert Byron (and even Della Valle in the 17th century called it 'pretty rather than magnificent'), the Ali Qapu is often called the Safavid palace, but it was actually the High Door (*qapu*: door) into the royal compound, from where the shah and his court viewed parades and celebrations in the *maydan*. The staircase with steep steps rising to the four floors is to the left of the small ticket office and lead up to the viewing area, or *talar*, added around 1644. Since late 2007 it has become another victim of scaffolding but more than enough of the beautiful decoration remains, including delicately carved, pink plaster friezes, although their original gilded top layer has been largely lost over the centuries.

After enjoying both the breeze and view from the *talar,* continue up to the so-called music rooms. The floors of these rooms appear uneven but this is a result of inserting H-girders during the extensive repair programme; similarly the *talar* columns now have metal cores. The intricate plaster ceilings were devised to assist acoustics for court musicans, or to display *objets d'art* as in the Ardabil shrine (see page 159) and certain Moghal and Rajput palaces in northern India. Use the other staircase to descend.

Across the *maydan* demurely stands the portal of the **Masjed-e Sheikh Lotfallah**, named after a famous preacher (☉ *09.00–17.00; entry 100,000 rials*). Rather than being a 'public' mosque, it possibly functioned as the mosque for the women of the royal harem; the portal dedication certainly emphasises the explicit Shi'a role of the shah as 'reviver of the virtues of his pure ancestors, and propagator of the doctrine of the pure Imams'. It also records that the decoration was started in 1603 but finished about 15 years later, the extra time needed to complete the amazing ceramic tilework throughout the building. A narrow corridor, angled to attain the correct orientation, leads into the prayer hall, where the simple square ground plan is forgotten as the impact of the decoration kicks in. The surface patterns of ceramic shapes, sometimes set into unglazed brick, disguise massively thick walls which support the single-shell dome (diameter 13m) while giant turquoise barley-twist cables outlining the full-length squinches lead the eye into the dome. We always wonder how the pattern designer calculated for the diminishing size of the motifs on the dome's concave surface. No wonder geometry, algebra and mathematics developed in the Islamic world. By employing the same technique as suggested with the Masjed-e Imam above, very successful photographs of the dome pattern can be taken, but to see the winter prayer hall below, with its *mihrab* of 1602, you must descend by the staircase near the main entrance.

Gheisariyeh Bazaar Since 1998 many more shops, including one or two selling the famous Esfahani *gaz* or nougat, have reopened in the covered arcade running all around the square. Before walking through the main 17th-century door of the bazaar, look up and you'll see a Sagittarius figure and Shah Abbas victorious over the Uzbek enemy, as described by Jean Chardin in the late 17th century. The recent cleaning has also revealed a depiction of Europeans playing chess high up on the

BUYING A CARPET

If you decided to buy a Persian carpet, Esfahan is perhaps the best place to do it. Prices in Kashan are fairer, but the choice is far smaller, especially if you are after a silk carpet, and shops in Yazd are few and unjustifiably expensive. Generally speaking there are two types of carpets: city carpets (Esfahan, Qom, etc) with often similar reproduced designs but nonetheless more expensive due to the weaver's higher fees; and nomadic carpets (Sarakhs, Qashqai, etc) without a pre-defined design.

Carpet shops in Esfahan accept Visa or MasterCard and you will need it. The credit card charge is usually 4% (it may, however, vary from 2% to 15%, though more likely to be on the lower scale for expensive carpet purchases), but sellers do prefer cash or bank transfer from abroad. They will give you all the details you need and will trust you enough to leave Iran with a carpet. There is no bargaining as such, but expect to get up to US$100 off a carpet worth around US$1,000.

The most expensive carpets and also the most manageable to bring back home are 100% silk carpets, which cost approximately US$2,000 apiece (1m wide x 1.30m long). Sarakhs, Ferdowsi and Qom regions are well-known centres. Do make sure, however, that the silk is 100% Iranian and not imported. This affects the price and most importantly the value of your purchase. The next two points to bear in mind are whether the carpet is two-sided and whether the pattern is geometric. When looking from different angles silk carpets change slightly in colour; so have a careful look from all sides and do see more than one sample. The choice is harder to make than you think.

If you are lucky and a friend or a guide happens to know a local weaver, you can purchase more cheaply directly from him or her. Carpets from Na'in, for example, are well known and Mohammed Jalali (see page 117) will happily arrange for you to visit a local weaver, if you prefer to take this route.

Finally, customs is not a problem: 100% silk carpets when folded fit into a standard luggage bag and you are allowed up to 12m² of customs-free goods. If your carpet is too big or you still cannot bring it with you, the seller will gladly take care of all the customs formalities and ship the carpet to you free of charge.

Some carpet shop suggestions:

Iran Pazirik Carpet 195 Ostandari St; ☎2201408–9; e info@iranpazirik.com; www.iranpazirik.com
Pakdel Carpet Warehouse Amadegah, Pezeshgan Bldg basement, near Abbasi Hotel; ☎2231823–4; e mahmod_pakdel@yahoo.com
Sara Carpet Gallery Ground floor of the Abbasi shopping mall opposite Abbasi Hotel; ☎2200655; e sara_carpet@yahoo.com; www.saracarpetgallery.com

right. Above, there was a gallery where musicians banged and trumpeted every sunset, causing foreign merchants to suffer violent headaches, and a Portuguese bronze bell marking the Safavid conquest of Hormuz (see page 226). Just inside the door, immediately on the right, a narrow alley leads into a small courtyard of **cotton block-printing workshops**. There is an endless variety of printed cottons; prices depend on size, quality of the fabric and the colour complexity of the design. Dealers now greatly outnumber the makers and just one or two of them are retained to show tourists the basic technique.

The bazaar runs northwards and eastwards intermittently. The main **carpet quarter** is situated to the far left (west) away from the main street; a short walk through here will raise serious doubts in your mind whether there are enough homes worldwide to house all these carpets.

West of the bazaar From the carpet quarter, or walking (west) down the tarmac road parallel to the main bazaar street and then along the Masjed Hakim alley, ask for Jurjir portal (sardar-e Jurjir), the only part of the Jurjir mosque that remains now that the Jurjir mosque has been replaced by **Masjed-e Hakim**. Discovered during 1955 repair work, this patterned (Q3:16–18) doorway is all that remains of the late 10th-century mosque of Sahib al-Kufa, a vizier (d995CE) known for his writings on theology, history and poetry. Everything else, which included a dervish centre, library, colleges, accommodation and assembly rooms and a tall minaret, was destroyed to make way for this Safavid Mosque of al-Hakim (built 1660–63), named after Shah Safi's physician Da'ud. After leaving the Esfahani court under a cloud, Da'ud made his fortune in India attending the Mughal emperor, Aurangzeb (d1707). Perhaps it is no coincidence that some of the Quranic verses used in the Taj Mahal are also included here on the 1660 *mihrab*. The prayer *ivan* has a calligraphic frieze (Q2:256) suggesting Da'ud was a (possibly Jewish) convert to Islam, while another quotation (Q62:9) around the base of the dome tells people (perhaps like today's carpet dealers) to forget business and attend the Friday prayer. The architect of the mosque is believed to be Mohammed Ali Ibn Ostad Ali Beg Esfahani.

Walking back and turning right at the Masjed Hakim alley, at the point where Sepah Street turns into Ostandari Street, set inside railings a large white building with a tall vaulted entrance originates from the 15th century, but was converted into an officers' club in Pahlavi times. It now functions as the **Natural History Museum** (*Ostandari St;* ☉ *09.00–18.00; entry 20,000 rials*) which explains the rather incongruous dinosaur and aged lion sculptures on the front steps.

West of Ali Qapu, is the most important surviving Safavid pavilion, **Chehel Sotun** ✳ (40 columns) (*Ostandari St, next door to the Natural History Museum;* ☉ *08.00–17.00; entry 150,000 rials; no flash photography*), taking its name from the reflection of its 20 columns in the algae-rich pond in front of the main *talar.* As suggested by the wall paintings all around the outside of the pavilion, this was where the Safavid rulers received foreign envoys and where Shah Soleyman was invested in 1668, some 20 years after its construction. The 16m-high columns, once painted and gilded, used to be hung with curtains sprayed with rose water to perfume the air, and the *talar* walls still retain some mirror work, originally imported from Venice at great expense.

The rooms either side of the *talar* have small, minimally labelled displays of Safavid (and later) ceramics, metalwork and textiles, but most visitors go straight into the main hall. On entry, immediately facing you is a huge 19th-century painting of Shah Ismail I attacking the Ottoman Janissaries (note the different headgear and dress details) during the famous 1514 Battle of Chaldiran, eastern Turkey; actually this battle was a resounding defeat for the Safavid army, although here Ismail looks victorious. Either side are 17th-century paintings: on the left, the royal reception held c1543 by Shah Tahmasp for the exiled Moghal ruler Humayun, and on the right, Shah Abbas I entertaining the ruler of Bukhara, Vali Mohammed Khan; both guests seem ill at ease with their surroundings. Over the main door another 19th-century picture portrays Nader Shah, the Afghan general who seized control in 1735, in typical battle mode, this time in India. To the left there's a Safavid painting of Shah Abbas II receiving another central Asian ruler, and on the other side, Isma'il II on a hennaed horse fighting Uzbeks; the sense of perspective suggests a European artist at work.

The exit by the small door to the far right leads into a gallery reopened in 1998. Despite the depiction of a scantily clad female looking somewhat flirtatious among flames, the wall-painting on the right continues the theme of battles; it perhaps records the 1649 capture of Qandahar, Afghanistan, or more exactly the wife of the city commander, killed in action, about to immolate herself on his funeral pyre.

On leaving the pavilion, take the trouble to walk round the building to view the exterior murals, painted by both court painters and, it is thought, the 17th-century artists who accompanied the various European and Russian trade delegations, eager to purchase Persian silk. There's a tiny *chaykhaneh* with toilets to the far left side as you leave the main building.

To the right of the **Chehel Sotun** palace you will take delight in visiting the **Esfahan Museum of Contemporary Art** ✹ (⏲ *08.00–17.00; entry 25,000 rials*) housing wonderful examples of contemporary Iranian art and photography. Right next to it is the **Decorative Arts Museum of Iran** (⏲ *08.00–17.00; entry 100,000 rials*).

North to the river Those lacking the strength or inclination to tackle the bazaar and carpet merchants could walk back to the **Abbasi Hotel** ✹ and sit in its main courtyard; its ice creams are very good. This was an early 18th-century caravanserai built, along with a small bazaar behind, to finance the *madrasa* next door before being converted into a hotel in 1955. It was one of the late shah's favourite hotels and several tour groups in the 1970s returned after a day's sightseeing to find their luggage in reception, as the royal retinue had unexpectedly commandeered their rooms. Guests have the evening meal on the ground floor amid painted 'Safavid' beauties, or in the garden, while breakfast is always served in the upper restaurant section decorated in a 'Qajar' style. The **Madrasa Chahar Bagh** (1706–14) (⏲ *to the public only during Nou Rouz when pupils are on holiday*) is next door. It is on the corner with the main street, the **Chahar Bagh** ('four gardens') where centuries ago with 'Night drawing on, all the pride of Esfahan was met … and the Grandees were airing themselves, prancing about with their numerous trains, striving to outvie each other in Pomp and Generosity' (Fryer, c1680). Before the revolution it was possible to enter the *madrasa* (formerly Madrasa Madar-e Shah). Built in honour of Shah Hossein's mother (as its original name suggests), its sun-yellow, patterned-tiled vaults, 160 rooms and a peaceful 'Persian' garden disguise a violent history, for Hossein was decapitated here in 1722 by the Afghan rebels. It is now a fully operational theological college once more.

On the far side of this *madrasa*, passing behind the hotel, is the single-aisled 18th-century **Bazaar-e Honar** (⏲ *08.00–13.30 & 17.00–21.30 Sat–Thu*) whose shop rents once provided an endowment to the *madrasa* to cover salaries, repairs, etc; it now houses mainly jewellery shops. In the early evening, after 16.00, it's a pleasantly cool stroll, which can take you to a small public park and the intimate Safavid **Hasht Behesht** ✹ ('Eight Paradises') pavilion (⏲ *08.00–17.00; entry 100,000 rials*), built

1669 and recently reopened. In the 17th century an English traveller described how the court was entertained in its gardens by the re-enactment of naval battles in the water channels, while Jean Chardin a few years later waxed lyrical over the place 'expressly made for love … one's heart is melted … one always leaves with a very ill grace'; many young couples today share the sentiment. The pavilion has 17th-century tiled panels decorating the external arches, a main domed ceiling set with mirror work, and remnants of wall paintings, the best-preserved surfaces being in the small rooms in each corner.

A walk down the main street towards the river takes you to the **Allahverdi Khan Bridge**, built in 1603, so named after its patron (d1613), a famous king-maker, provincial governor and Georgian commander in the Safavid army; the bridge is also known as the **Se-o-se Pol** (which stands for number 33 in Persian, referring to its 33 arches) from its multiple arches. This walk is especially recommended in the evening, when it and the Khaju Bridge are also illuminated, but during the day it is a pleasure seeing young people enjoying themselves in pedalos on the river. In times of severe drought (as in 2000–02 and 2013) the river was dammed upstream to provide water for Yazd province. The 360m long x 14m wide Allahverdi Khan Bridge, on piers some 4m thick, with its two levels and high walls to protect camel trains from wind buffeting, connected the Chahar Bagh with the Armenian Christian quarter across the river. Greatly admired in the 17th century – 'truly a very neat piece of architecture if I may say the neatest in all Persia' (Tavernier) – it is still a favourite place to walk and take tea. Further down is the **Khaju Bridge**, built in the 1660s by Shah Abbas II to join up with the old Shiraz road, with 24 arches and a central, two-storey, octagonal kiosk. Described by Engelbert Kaempfer (a late 17th-century German physician who visited Persia attached to a Swedish mission before joining the Dutch East India Company) as 'more superb [when] compared with other buildings', it probably functioned as a toll bridge and also provided a spectacular water cascade when its channels were blocked by angled wooden boards. On the south side, 36m away, a stone lion stands looking at the river. The carved symbols on its chest and side show it was a gravestone or tomb marker of a local champion wrestler, as the same types of exercise equipment are still used in today's *zurkhanehs* (see box, page 120). From behind the next bridge, Pol-e Bozorgmehr, opens up the **Bagh-e Golha** (Flower Garden) (⊕ *07.00–20.00; entry 12,000 rials*) with some of the most beautiful flowers and garden arrangements in Iran. It has a tea shop and peaceful gazebo to take a pause in.

To see the third historic and the oldest bridge in Esfahan will entail a taxi ride to **Shahrestan Bridge** (by the Esfahan International Fair), which dates from the Sassanid period but with pre-Islamic era foundations. Rebuilt by the Seljuks, and with a toll station added in the 17th century, it too acted as a weir, but the river has long been diverted.

Masjed-e Jame ✳ (*Allameh Majlisi St;* ⊕ *08.00–11.00 & 13.00 –17.00; entry 100,000 rials*) is located on the north side of the river, further into the working class district. No visit to Esfahan would be complete without a visit to the UNESCO-listed Masjed-e Jame, an architectural treasure in its own right. Just beyond the ticket office is a small room displaying a scale model of the complex and photographs of the 1970s Italian archaeological finds. The rather dusty, insignificant-looking pillars with decorated brick-plugs to one side date back to the 10th century when a small 'Arab'-style mosque was built here on the remains of a fire temple. Then, between 1072 and 1092, work began in earnest: two huge domed chambers were constructed, one inside the complex, the other just outside. After a serious attack

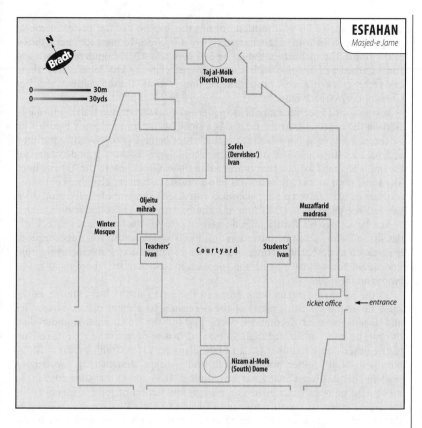

N

0 ——— 30m
0 ——— 30yds

Taj al-Molk
(North) Dome

Sofeh
(Dervishes')
Ivan

Oljeitu
mihrab

Muzaffarid
madrasa

Winter
Mosque

Teachers'
Ivan

Courtyard

Students'
Ivan

ticket office ◄— entrance

Nizam al-Molk
(South) Dome

by the Assassins (see box, page 94) in 1122, as recorded on the northeast door, the mosque was reorganised according to a four-*ivan* plan, and then two centuries later extensively redecorated and repaired by the Mongol Ilkhanids. Some 50 years later the local Muzaffarid rulers extended the mosque, bringing the second Seljuk domed chamber into the enclosure. Thereafter, work in the mosque was more or less confined to replacing tile and plasterwork.

Until January 2000, visitors were free to walk as and where they wished but 'student misbehaviour' (marijuana smoking) resulted in numerous metal fences and gates being installed. If these are locked, visitors will be accompanied by a patient guardian, who unobtrusively opens and locks gates; since October 2000, however, the gates have been usually unlocked. From the main entrance, rather than continuing down to the central courtyard, cross over and walk through the arcades in a clockwise direction and you'll soon realise how beautiful (and subtly coloured) brickwork can be, and how quickly your film is disappearing or your memory card being filled up. A yellow tile panel, far left, describes repair work after Iraqi bomb damage in the 1980s. This is the way to the first of two magnificent, 11th-century **'true' domes**, covering the south chamber, constructed on the order of the Seljuk vizier and scholar Nizam al-Molk (d1092) around 1087, judging from the titles used in the dome inscription. Let your eyes become accustomed to the darkness; what remains of the 10th-century plasterwork was probably once richly painted like the interior of Southwark Cathedral, London. Huge brick pillars support this glorious dome (diameter c17m), the four massive trilobed squinches and the 16-sided zone of transition. Ideally, the thickness of the 'perfect dome' at its apex should be $\frac{1}{45}$th of the diameter; here it is $\frac{1}{42}$nd. To meet the lateral thrust of the dome, the inclination should be 5:1; here it is 4.5:1. Compare this with St Paul's Cathedral, London, which is some 600 years later and its dome is conical. As one architectural historian wrote: 'The Seljuqs ... solved the difficulties which [Sir Christopher] Wren avoided.'

If you want to see yet more brick-patterned vaults, continue walking through, skirting the courtyard. At the far end is a small 'shrine', until recently boarded up by the authorities as 'un-Islamic'; the thick soot betrays years of candle burning. Moving into the courtyard, you pass the second large 'teachers' *ivan* decorated on the order of Shah Hossein, later murdered in the *madrasa* near to the Abbasi Hotel. The small door to its right takes you into a mid 15th-century chamber containing the famous 1310 carved plaster *mihrab*, constructed in honour of the Ilkhanid ruler, Oljeitu (see pages 173–4). Its long inscription surprisingly contains no Quranic verses, but eulogises Oljeitu alongside references to Ali, the first imam – so it clearly dates from before Oljeitu's conversion to Sunni Islam. From this room another door leads down to the Safavid **winter mosque** with transverse vaulting springing from floor level. You will have to ask the guardian to unlock it and, more importantly, switch on the lights.

In the courtyard again, walk down to the next (north) *ivan*, known as the *sofeh* ('meeting or sitting area') of the dervishes. Its elegant plaster cartouches and lozenge-shaped decorations were part of the 1682 repairs undertaken during the reign of Safavid shah Soleyman. A new door to the right takes you to the other dome chamber (c22m high, diameter c11m), built by Taj al-Molk, Nizam al-Molk's bitter political rival, and perhaps designed by the famous poet-mathematician, Omar Khayyam. Built in 1089 and at that time *outside* the mosque, it perhaps functioned as a robing, meditation or judicial chamber for the Seljuk ruler. Its proportions are so pleasing to the Western eye, relating as they do to the golden mean (the ratio of the shorter side to the longer in the golden rectangle – 1:1.6180339887 – usually called by the Greek letter phi (f)) used by architects of Renaissance Europe. The dome inscription (Q7:52, 54), describing the creation of the world in six days ends with 'Is it not His to create and govern?' before immediately giving the Seljuk vizier's Persian titles and date; the implication is undeniable. The 32 blind niches in the zone of transition have short inscriptions, each specifying a name or quality of the Almighty, while those across the large niche panels are Quranic (Q17:79–81).

After taking photographs of the courtyard, most visitors leave, but if time allows, look at the small *madrasa* behind the 'students' *ivan*' with its fine mid 14th-century mosaic tile decoration. Because the Muzaffarid ruler who paid for the work was Sunni, the star motifs in the vault include references to the first three caliphs (after the death of the Prophet) recognised by the Sunnis but not Shi'as. Returning to the courtyard *ivan*, on the far back wall, a grille protects other Sunni formulae. As you leave the complex, a little before the ticket office, tucked back on the right in deep shadow, is another elaborate plaster *mihrab*, presumably dating from the early 14th century.

We should say a word about the mosque gates. The present main (southeast) entrance was repaired in 1804 according to its inscription, while the southwest one is dated 1591. The north gate, usually locked, carries a lengthy Quranic inscription (Q76:1–27) describing the delights and rewards in paradise, while that (Q2:114) on the northeastern entrance clearly refers to repairs after the Assassins' attack in 1121: 'Who is more wicked than the men who seek to destroy the mosques of Allah?'

From the Masjed-e Jame Leaving by the main entrance, the main roundabout to your right offers two opportunities. First, the road to the right (west), the Jamal al-Din Abdulrazzaq, goes past a lovely but dilapidated **19th-century house** which lost its garden in the road-widening scheme. It was purchased by the government and now serves as a 'clubhouse' for Esfahani calligraphers. It is not open to the public, but it is sometimes possible to see inside another lovely house of this period, the **Beit al-Malek**, in Malek Street off the main roundabout. However, as it is the venue for international Quranic reading competitions, access cannot be guaranteed and refurbishment has meant much of the original decoration has been replaced. The original garden has also been ripped up to install new pools and paving, but the original entrance doorway and four porch columns have escaped unscathed. Leaving shoes in the passage, you enter the first room, with its Bohemian chandeliers and Qajar sash windows opening on to the garden, while a screened upper gallery allowed the women of the household to view visitors in secret. This room leads into a chamber, now rapidly disappearing under new highly varnished wood panelling. At its far end is a small room decorated with early 20th-century plasterwork and mirrored glass, which contains the grave of Mohammed Ibrahim Malek (d1922), the former owner. Theological permission for interment within the home is rarely given, but this Esfahani merchant was so renowned for his good works, feeding the poor and finding work for the unemployed, that an exception was made.

The second opportunity, a short walk down the minor road (southwest) off the roundabout past the carpet-loom shops, brings you to the shrine and mausoleum of **Harun-e Vilayet** built in 1513 and restored in 1656. Before the revolution, a stone lion thought to possess powers to cure sterility stood in the courtyard; today he has been banished to the exterior and a birth control clinic operates in his place. A small door leads into the public part of the shrine; leave your shoes at the door. Inside, 17th-century or later wall paintings of Ali, Fatima, and their two sons, Hassan and Hossein, introduce the main tomb chamber honouring Harun, whose life and attributes are cloaked in mystery; perhaps he was a son of one of the 12 Imams. Outside, the two enormous paintings of modern-day theologians have been replaced since 2006 with ceramic tiles depicting the faces of Khomeini and the present spiritual leader of Iran, Ayatollah Khamenei. Also represented is Dr Beheshti, formerly of Esfahan, who was the head of the judiciary and lost his life in 1981 in the bomb attack on the Tehran headquarters of the Islamic Revolutionary Party. In all about 100 were killed but here a clear reference is made to the 72 people who died with Hossein at Karbala. As you leave the shrine courtyard, turn right and you'll soon find the lion looking into the shrine and also visual proof that the tiled plaster *muqarnas* decorating the semi-dome were literally suspended from the main brick structure.

Nearby can be seen the tall **Manar-e Ali**, now about 48m high but probably originally 2m taller. Built around 1200 (or perhaps 1235), the minaret has three main bands of brick decoration with blue glazed elements, although only two can be seen from street level, with inscriptions declaring that there is no God but Allah and that all power belongs to Him, along with a Quranic verse (Q3:16). Masjed-e Ali, housing the minaret, was repaired extensively in the Safavid period according to the inscriptions, and its portal was constructed around 1522.

Another cluster of interesting monuments is in the vicinity of the Amin Hospital for Leukaemia (Saratan-e Khoon), between Masjed-e Jame and Chahar Bagh Street or to be more precise off the Maydan-e Shohada. Incidentally, the crowds around the hospital gate are waiting to collect their blood test results, legally required for marriage ceremonies. Most people around here know where the **Imamzadeh Darb-e Imam** (also referred to as the Darb-e Islam, Abdulrazzaq St, Bazzarcheh Hajj Mohammed Jafar) is, but there are no road signs. Much of this building, including the two domes, was restored in the 17th and 18th centuries, but the *ivan* portal, with its fine mosaic tile decoration guarded by yet another stone lion, the vestibule and mausoleum dates from 1453, the year when Constantinople fell to the Ottoman Turks. Constructed on the order of Jahan Shah of the Black Sheep confederation two years after taking Esfahan, the building houses his mother, but was dedicated to two imams, Ibrahim Tabataba'i (or Batha) and Zayn al-Abidin, the fourth imam; in time so many were buried here that the original door was closed by a grille. Lines of Sufi poetry frame the portal telling the visitor:

From the roof of this house of the world [ie: heaven] seek not the image of faithfulness
At its coming be not glad, nor grieve at its going
See with the eye of understanding, how that building whose *ivan* Passed above the
    seventh heaven [Saturn] fell to earth.

An inscription to the far left records that the man in charge of its construction suddenly disappeared, never to return. A large second courtyard gives access to the shrine itself, a series of rooms, some evidently restored, and a storeroom for some magnificent *'alam* standards used in the Moharram parades.

Across the Majlesi Street from Masjed-e Jame, in the Soroush quarter, north of Joubareh (originally Jewish) quarter, is the **Manar-e Saraban** (camel-driver's minaret), a fine minaret, possibly Sejluk mid 12th century, amid small houses whose front doors often have two knockers, each with a distinctive shape and sound so those inside could know if a male or female visitor was calling. This phenomenon may also be observed in traditional quarters elsewhere in Iran. The mosque has long gone, but the doorway (through which you can see the spiral staircase) some 5m up probably marked the connection with the mosque roof. Standing about 30m high, it still possesses after seven centuries good brick patterns and glazed inserts, although its balcony has gone. From here you can see the **Manar-e Chehel Dokhtaran** (*off Maydan-e Quds (formerly Tughchi) Soroush St*), which has also lost its mosque, but the staircase doorway remains. There are no coloured glazed inserts, but just look at the richness of the brickwork. Up the cylindrical shaft (24m high) there are more than seven pattern zones of rhomboids, lozenges, octagons and six-pointed stars, picked out in recessed and relief brick. Near its base, a six-line Kufic inscription panel gives the construction date (1108), making this one of the earliest minarets to survive in Iran.

Just off the Baba Qasem Intersection nearby is the 1880 tiled tent-roof of the small, rather neglected **tomb of Baba Qasem** (pronounced as Ghasem), built by a certain Soleyman Abu'l Hassan Tahit al-Damghani in 1341 'with the intention of honouring the theologian who has departed for Paradise'. The key is held by the man in the shop next door to a very new shrine which itself lies in a former shop. This visit brings home how just 20-odd years can affect a building which previously survived over six centuries with comparatively little damage. There is now no sign of its tiled portal inscription, noted in the mid 1970s, recording that Baba Qasem of Esfahan had been a devout Sunni. The original door has recently been blocked up and now entry is directly into the second chamber. In here there should be a *mihrab* decorated with Quranic verses (Q9:18–22) which emphasised the difference between devout Muslims and those who pay lip service to Islam, and

above   The Hall of Mirrors in Tehran's Golestan Palace complex was inspired by Naser al-Din Shah's visit to Versailles in 1873 (SS) pages 81–2

below   Reaching towards the Alborz Mountains, the sprawl of modern Tehran can be seen from Milad Tower (MO) page 79

above While Zoroastrians no longer use Towers of Silence as vessels for placing dead bodies instead of burying them, a few towers still remain around Yazd province (S/MK) pages 236–7

left & below Persepolis, with some of its remains dating back to 515BCE, can easily be the principle reason for visiting Iran (S/AT and S/MR) pages 195–200

top   The massive brick stepped construction of Choga Zanbil is nearly 3,500 years old (MO) pages 212–14

above left   Iranian citadels and fortresses are spectacular examples of earthen architecture, enclosing small worlds within their walls (S/MK)

above right   Naqsh-e Rostam necropolis, with tomb façades carved out of the rock, is one of the most impressive rock relief series to be found in Iran (S/MK) pages 200–2

above left The artistic metalworking technique of *ghalam-zani* is several thousand years old and is still one of the most widespread crafts in Iran (AB)

above right Iranians are keen on spices, in particular *advieh*, a mixture frequently used in Persian cuisine (SS) page 59

left Iranian bazaars offer a rich selection of traditional crafts, exquisite *qalamdan* (pen boxes) or Persian miniature paintings (SS) pages 58–60

below A Qashqai woman spins wool in a traditional dwelling in the area north of Shiraz (AB) page 175

above Breathtaking display of Persian carpets at a local store. Drop in for a cup of tea and be tempted to buy (SS) page 127

right Carpets have been made in Persia for hundreds, perhaps thousands, of years (SS)

below A family visits the mausoleum of Hafez, one of Iran's most popular poets (MO) pages 181–2

above   In the 11th century, the heavily fortified valley of the River Alamut was known as the Valley of the Assassins (MO) page 94

left   The attractive mountain village of Masouleh is more than a thousand years old (I/I/FLPA) page 142

below   Winter-morning sunshine warms the rock houses of Kandovan, an almost 1,000 year-old village in northern Iran (MO) page 165

top The Zagros Mountains run down the west of Iran, forming the border with Iraq (SS) page 3

above left The reconstructed Robate-e Zayn al-Din *caravanserai* near Yazd offers comfortable accommodation to travellers, just like in the old days (S/MK) page 238

above right Groups of nomadic pastoralists still cross the Fars province to find fresh pasture for their livestock in April and October (SS)

below Damavand, the roof of Iran and the highest peak in the Middle East, is a statuesque and proud symbol of Iranian spirit and character (SS) page 85

above   The unique ecosystem of
the Caspian Sea, the largest
body of inland water in the
world, helped to create rich
woodlands in northern Iran
(SS) pages 139–55

left   **An** Iranian *dhow* moored at
Qeshm Island in the Persian
Gulf (SS) page 225

below   A catch of sturgeon off the
coast of Iran (SS) page 145

indeed local tradition had it that liars and perjurers met horrid deaths at this shrine. The *mihrab* has gone, however, as has the mosaic tilework (Q17:1–6) embellishing the dome base; two cenotaphs, one commemorating a local wrestler hero (d1577), remain, though, but are shoved against the walls. Nearby was Baba Qasem's four-portal *madrasa*, built in 1325.

Mosques in Iran can be empty places except on Fridays. One Esfahani shrine, however, is always crowded on account of its association with Imam Hossein and the establishment of Shi'i Islam as the official religion under the Safavids but its diminutive size makes it totally unsuitable for tour groups. It will mean a taxi drive to the eastern part of the city, off the Hasht Behesht Street; take a camera in (the unlikely) case it is deserted, but don't attempt to use it otherwise. Esfahanis call it the **Imamzadeh Shah Zayd** (*Hasht Behesht St, walking south along Pozorgmehr St from Soroush quarter*), but happily admit the actual name is Zayn al-Din. A small courtyard precedes the entry portal (women enter to the right; men to the left). Its tiled frieze records repairs to the shrine in 1686, so perhaps this was when the paintings inside, depicting the harrowing tale of Hossein's last moments at Karbala, were executed, but they are probably later, dating from the late 19th century. Protected by (grubby) glass screens, the scenes are arranged in an approximate sequence, showing Abbas bringing life-restoring water to the imam, his family and supporters (he lost both hands in the process); the womenfolk are clearly depicted, including Rukayya, whose popular tomb-shrine is in Cairo. Look for a horse wounded by so many arrows that it looks like a pincushion; this is Hossein's steed and he is shown veiled with a halo. The lion underneath recalls the miracle of a certain Sultan Qays who, attacked by a lion in India, invoked the help of Hossein just as the imam was fighting for his own life in Iraq. Miraculously, Hossein was momentarily transported to India, causing the lion to cower in submission, while the imam reappeared at Karbala only to be slain himself.

Armenian quarter Do not leave Esfahan without visiting the Armenian quarter in the Nazar Street/Kelisa Street area south of the river, known as **(New) Jolfa**, and its churches, in particular the **All Saviours' (or Vank) Cathedral** (*Kelisa St; ☉ 08.30–17.30 Sat–Thu, 08.00–12.30 Fri; Nou Rouz 09.00–20.15 daily; entry including museum 100,000 rials*). Authorisation to visit the Armenian cemetery (see page 136) is obtained here.

Around 1603 the Safavid shah ordered the resettlement of some 10,000 Armenian families from the Caucasus into this quarter and nearby villages, probably to ensure their skills in silk trading remained in Safavid hands, and to thwart any Armenian schemes of siding with the Ottomans to get autonomy. The community was allowed freedom of worship, and Abbas I himself, we are told, attended Epiphany celebrations and commanded important Christian relics – such as the arm of St Gregory the Illuminator, who converted Armenia in 301CE – to be brought here; it was returned to Echtmiadzin, Armenia, in 1637. By 1701 this quarter boasted about 30 churches but now only about 13 survive, and the community has shrunk considerably from 100,000 in the mid 1960s to approximately 7,000 in 1995 and it has not changed since. Several of the 18th-century **merchants' houses** with interesting painted decoration were open in the 1970s but as many now function as government offices, official permission is required. The Jani house close to All Saviours' Cathedral, for example, is now the art college.

Construction of All Saviours' began in 1606 but it was largely rebuilt during the years 1650–63, with the bell tower added in 1764. The decorative plaster and paintings covering the interior date from 1660–70, the gift of an Armenian merchant, Avandich, but the tiles are somewhat later. In the east dome, the story of the Creation, the Expulsion and the Killing of Abel are depicted, but elsewhere the painted decoration is arranged to show episodes from the Old Testament, with related New Testament themes below. So Abraham and the Angels is paired with the Annunciation, Hagar and Ismail with the Nativity, and almost opposite the entrance, Moses and the Tablets above the Transfiguration. Over the door itself a huge Last Judgement fills the space; centuries' worth of candle soot and incense accumulation has now been removed to reveal the vibrant colours of the original. It is not known whether the artists were Esfahani Armenians or Europeans attached to the various East India companies resident in this quarter, but clearly they had seen engravings by the contemporary Dutch artist, Van Sichem. At shoulder level, small panels gruesomely retell the tortures faced by the early Armenian Christians, the costume and textile details proving that these too are 17th century. One near the main door depicts St Gregory the Illuminator curing the Armenian king who had been transformed into a pig (or wolf according to some traditions) as a punishment for lusting after and torturing Christian maidens (or nuns). The murals go on to show the conversion of the king and the people in 301CE, and the honouring of the saint. On the left side of the small west door you see that St Gregory went through a particularly nasty form of colonic irrigation as part of his torture cycle.

Behind the west wall in the courtyard lie a few gravestones of British missionaries, their families and soldiers who died in the Esfahani and Yazdikast areas. Underneath the canopy another 19th-century grave is decorated with the famous bathing episode of Shirin, the Armenian princess, watched by Shah Khosrow II who bites the 'finger of astonishment' (see box, page 103). Directly opposite is a striking monument, erected in 1975, marking the early 20th-century Ottoman atrocities. Further down is the museum building with displays (labelling in English) on two floors of rich liturgical vestments and objects, illuminated and illustrated manuscripts, oil paintings, the first (1636) printing press in Iran, historic documents, etc. The small museum shop at the main entrance usually has pamphlets and books.

If All Saviours' Cathedral is crowded, a short walk takes you to **Bethlehem Church** (*Nazar St;* ⊕ *08.30–12.30 & 14.30–17.30; entry 100,000 rials*), which lies immediately to the northeast behind the cathedral. The decorative scheme is very similar to All Saviours', but perhaps some 30 years earlier in date and in a strange sequence. The donor's picture is on the north wall, and horrific scenes on the west wall illustrate the tortures inflicted on St Gregory the Illuminator, St Sergius, St Mercurius and St Theodore. In the narrow alley behind Bethlehem Church there are two more churches: **Saint Mary's**, built in 1613, which has fine 17th-century tiles, and some paintings, including the Beheading of John the Baptist, with a figure of the donor in the bottom left; and **Saint Hagop**, built in 1607. Both are closed to the general public and can only be visited on Sundays 09.00–11.30 during service.

The main **Armenian cemetery** is located off Sepahan Road near to al-Zahra Hospital (Shiraz direction), but visiting permission is needed from the cathedral authorities (see page 135). Here are the graves of Rodolph Stadler (d1637), the Swiss watchmaker to Shah Safi I, and Claudius James Rich, the British Resident (Consul) in the early 19th century, among many others. Sadly, there have been reports that this cemetery, as with some other non-Muslim burial places, has been vandalised.

Further afield About 30km south of Esfahan, off the Sohan (Steel Factory) Highway, is the town of **Pir-e Bakran**, in an area once strongly associated with the Jewish community and, in early medieval times, overshadowed by several Assassin castles from where attacks on Esfahan (see page 94) were conducted. Around here is grown the famous small-grained Linjan rice, with its distinctive flavour. Set aside half a day (and around 500,000 rials for taxi hire) for a visit to Pir-e Bakran and the surrounding area.

There is no direct access from the main road to the early 14th-century building which gives the township its name, so walk past with the enclosing wall on the left and then double back along the alley below. Many of the houses along here have the characteristic two doorknockers, one for female, the other for male visitors. The children are helpful and will fetch the guardian to unlock the gate. Walk straight through, into the small tomb chamber at the back, pushing away a grimy curtain into a small domed chamber with faint depictions of cypresses or minarets on the walls. This was probably the actual teaching room of the famous Sufi sheikh Mohammed Ibn Bakran known as *pir* namely 'revealer of the secrets of the Truth, venerated Master of the Way', as the inscriptions here repeatedly describe him. Shortly after his death in 1304, the small tomb chamber with its massive cenotaph was constructed and decorated in turquoise and cobalt blue tilework, but sticky fingers since World War II have removed most of the tiles. A steep slope behind the teaching room precluded any further building at that end, so in 1312 a lofty prayer hall was constructed in front of the tomb. It too was once covered in early 14th-century moulded tiles in two shades of blue and a few dusty ones remain, too high up to be stolen. But fortunately most of the marvellously carved plasterwork is intact, whether calligraphic Kufic 'seal-squares' resembling Chinese chop marks, 'Baroque' leaf forms carved through several levels, once all highly coloured, or the beautifully patterned brick end plugs. The *mihrab* is splendid. Look for the rock jutting out from floor level; this is where the horse of the prophet Elijah set down his hoof before he rode into the heavens. This *ivan* extension of 1312 meant a new entry passage which didn't interfere with the *qibla* orientation and a *mihrab* had to be constructed; as you leave, take time to look at its decoration, somewhat damaged but still fine.

In the township itself there is an old **Jewish synagogue** and **cemetery**, known locally as Esther Khatun (Lady Esther). You need permission from the Jewish authorities in Esfahan to visit both. Enquire at the tourist information office (page 121). The complex bears signs of vandalism but pilgrims still come here, leaving mint leaves on the gravestones. The synagogue has rooms for pilgrims, but it is doubtful whether these are now much used. The main room, a domed chamber with the Torah stand, is at ground level, while above there are small prayer rooms with stone panels carved with Hebrew texts. In a small garden behind is a free-standing domed chamber where Esther (or Sarah, who has also been mentioned) disappeared into the walls. (The Jewish community in Esfahan, which was once the largest in Iran, is now mainly based around the Junbare Street of the Sabz-e Maydan quarter of the city.)

Along the road to **Ashtarjan** about 5km away in agricultural land are two fine **pigeon towers**. Just as the towers come into view, turn down a narrow road to the right, and then left, which takes you up to the larger tower. Hover, and hopefully a key will materialise to allow you in, but even if it doesn't this is a splendid building even when viewed from the outside.

You will be just as awestruck by these immense edifices as the 17th-century traveller Jean Chardin was, amazed that they were 'six times as big as the biggest we have: they are built with Brick overlaid with Plaister and Lime'. Looking like giant chess pieces, they provide multi-storeyed nesting boxes inside for pigeons, not for breeding and eating (the birds have traditional sacred connotations) but for the guano used to fertilise the local melon fields; a cynic would argue that the pigeons destroyed more crops with their voracious appetites than they helped grow. To prevent snakes from getting in, there are no windows and only one door opened once a year to collect the guano. Nothing prepares you for the size of these towers, and the simple grandeur of their interiors. Even without a torch, the impact is sensational, almost as good as any Gothic cathedral. Stairs go up to the roof but some of the steps are damaged.

Proceeding onwards you could complete this half-day trip with **Ashtarjan** (signposted as Oshtarjan), 35km southwest of Esfahan, for the little **Masjed-e Jame**, gifted by a local man in 1305, and there is the *imamzadeh* of Rabia Khatun close by, dated 1308. While waiting for the mosque guardian, as perhaps the famous Arab geographer Ibn Battuta did during his visit in 1327, have a look at the exterior doorways. This small two-*ivan* mosque is quiet and serene, with exquisite decoration with numerous chinoiserie motifs. It has seen better days, but remains of painting show the detailed plasterwork and the dome interior was once brilliantly coloured, complementing the plain brick and coloured tilework (the work of Hajji Mohammed of Tabriz) and a lovely *mihrab*. The *qibla ivan* is dominated with a large lozenge motif giving the names of the 12 imams, edged with Kufic inscription (Q36:1–9) on one side, and on the other wall another containing the 99 names of God, edged with more calligraphy (Q59:23–4). Around the dome inside, more Quranic verses (Q48:1–6) ask for forgiveness of past faults, and the reward of paradise in richly plaited Kufic, while the *mihrab* records the date of completion as 1316. A carved stone panel on one of the courtyard piers states: 'In the time of the caliphate of his majesty, the Emperor of Islam, the greatest Sultan, Lord over the necks of the peoples … Uzun Hassan [of the Aq Qoyunlu 1453–78] … the repair of this Masjed-e Jame [was undertaken by a local Sufi master] at his own personal expense.'

The road from Esfahan to Shiraz or to Yazd via Abadeh and Abarku runs through interesting scenery scattered with the remains of walled villages and caravanserais. Some 80km south of Esfahan is **Shahreza** with its *imamzadeh*, built in Safavid times and then greatly reworked in the 19th century; there are clean toilets here in the new small hotel set back from the row of shops just below the shrine. Just before **Yazdikast** (also spelt Izad Khast) 60km further on, there is a dirt spur road to the right (notionally west), which leads directly to the old fortress that controlled the main caravan route to the southeast. Built on Sassanid foundations, judging from the substructure, this fort is splendid despite its ruined appearance; even the remains of the old drawbridge are still visible. Sometimes the guardian can be found, who will unlock the drawbridge door. Inside is a jumble of rooms and as usual with a castle, the function of most is unclear except for the well house with the bathhouse opposite, and the bread ovens. If the guardian is not available, never mind; backtrack a little from the drawbridge and turn left along the narrow alley which will lead to a vantage place for a superb view across the old river valley and the Safavid caravanserai on the other side. Below are the ruins of houses. In the 19th century the regional governor ordered the killing of all the menfolk (by throwing them down into the valley) as punishment for non-payment of taxes, and it was here that two young army officers buried in the All Saviours' courtyard, Esfahan, lost their lives. Yazdikast traditionally had another claim to fame as a 17th-century French traveller recorded: 'That to live happy, a man must have a wife of Yazd, eat the bread of Yazdikast, and drink the wine of Shiraz.'

6

The Caspian Region

The road from Tehran to the shores of the Caspian is surely one of the most beautiful in Iran, with lush greenery, tree-covered mountains and valleys. The Caspian region has been a favourite royal hunting ground over the centuries, while from the 15th century onwards foreign visitors knew it for the breeding and usage of silkworms, with all the associated processing. This was the source of the silk eagerly snapped up by Western and Russian merchant adventurers until the mid 19th century when pebrine, a disease of silkworms, struck. Attempts to revive the industry were made but by 1870 the Suez Canal was bringing cheaper Japanese, Chinese and Indian silk to the West. Another Caspian luxury product has since fared badly: caviar. And again the fault did not lie at Iran's door, but this time with inadequate Soviet and post-Soviet control of water pollution and poaching, which have largely killed off the sturgeon.

The severe earthquake of 1991, which killed some 40,000 in the Caspian region, and the comparatively few foreign visitors to this area have meant development priorities have lain elsewhere, such as with building holiday apartments and villas for Tehranis eager to escape the capital. The region, however, has a wonderful hospitality tradition and you can be sure that hotel staff are most welcoming here. Finding accommodation, especially during the Nou Rouz holiday, can be a problem. For details, look under the relevant towns below.

The Caspian region comprises three provinces: Gilan (stretching towards the border with Azerbaijan), Golestan (at the border with Turkmenistan) and Mazandaran in between the two and to the north of Tehran.

GETTING THERE

Apart from daily one-hour **flights** to Rasht from Tehran, there are 'express' **rail** services from Tehran, especially towards Mashhad, that pass via Shahrud in the province of Semnan. Road transport, however, offers the greatest opportunity to enjoy the scenery and some of the sites. Daily intercity **buses** and *savari* services run north from Tehran to Bandar-e Anzali (368km northeast) via Qazvin and, subsequently, Rasht and Chalus (174km north) from the Western Bus Terminal at Azadi Square. Be prepared to pay around 100,000 rials for a *savari* ride to Bandar-e Anzali. Buses are about half this price, but operate less regularly.

Comparatively few non-Iranians come this way, as historic monuments are few and far between, but do go to this region before its distinctive village character is completely swamped in holiday apartment complexes, which are taking over the shoreline. The roads are good and well engineered, but the hundreds of Tehrani families travelling to and from the region to these holiday homes mean the driving can be as mindless and dangerous as in the capital itself. The coastal road running along

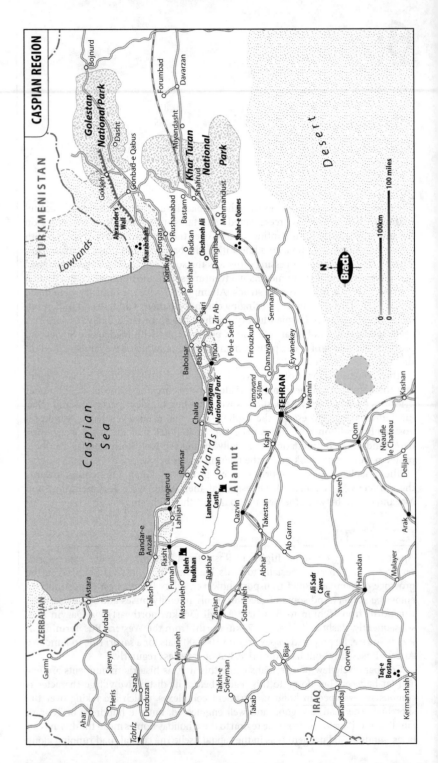

the Caspian Sea all the way from Astara to Chalus will not leave you disappointed. Here it is also reasonably easy to hitch a *savari* taxi passing by at great speed.

If there is no time to explore the whole of this region, there are three choices from Tehran: due north to Chalus; northwest to Gilan (this route runs through Qazvin, which is the best stopover if visiting Alamut; see pages 94–5), or east and subsequently northeast to Mazandaran and Golestan provinces.

TOWARDS GILAN

The motorway towards Gilan curves in the northeasterly direction after Qazvin and stretches a further 114km to the town of **Rudbar** (65km before reaching Rasht) which lies to the northwest and is famous locally for its olives. It is here that the tree-lined hillsides and the distinctive high-gabled roofs of Gilan houses begin. The whole area is associated with the marvellous finds from the Marlik royal necropolis, locally known as Cheragh Ali Tappeh, excavated during 1961–66 by the Iranian authorities and already overgrown by the mid 1970s. Although most of the 53 stone-slab tombs excavated had been looted by grave robbers (probably a major source of the so-called Amlash artefacts sold in the West in the 1950s) enough survives to show that this site continued to be used for burials over two or three centuries from about the 1st millennium BCE. The grave goods, some on display at Tehran's Reza Abbasi Museum, fell into three groupings: bronze weapons and ornament, belonging to 'warrior kings'; jewellery and figurines associated with their womenfolk; and more domestic artefacts, which the archaeologists associated with servants. For those interested in the transmission of beliefs about the afterlife, it is fascinating to note that tombs with horse skeletons were also uncovered, which immediately recalls burial traditions found across Asia from northern Cyprus to China and southern Siberia. Noting similarities in the finds with those from the Sialkh, Ziwiyeh and Hasanlu excavations and the striking parallels with Assyrian motifs, the Iranian archaeologists suggest that the population for some reason moved from Marlik to resettle at Sialkh (level VI) around 900BCE. A number of other archaeological settlements similarly dated have been identified in the region, for example Rostamabad, some 15km north of Rudbar. In this region were the valley strongholds associated with the medieval Assassins, the scourge of Crusader and Muslim leaders alike, but it is best to approach the so-called Valley of the Assassins from Qazvin (see page 95), and also overnight there (see page 92).

RASHT The regional capital (current population 698,000) since Safavid times, Rasht in the 19th century was renowned for its high-quality patchwork (Rasht work) used for wall-hangings, saddlecloths, floor coverings and for the gloriously coloured tents used in court circles when hunting. Like the Ottoman tents currently displayed in the Military Museum, Istanbul, these Qajar tents bore no resemblance to the canvas tents of early 20th-century Europe but were glorious architectural statements in rainbow colours with eye-catching designs composed of patchwork decorated with chain-stitch embroidery. Today, Rasht is known only for its reputation as perhaps the wettest place in Iran, its good food (one well-known restaurant is Moharram, close to the new Masjed-e Jame) and a more relaxed attitude to the separation of the genders. It is also the birthplace of Mirza Kuchek Khan, founder of the revolutionary, early 20th-century Nehzat-e Jangal (Forest Movement) and who is considered a national hero in Iran. His tomb is at the **Soleiman Darab cemetery** in Rasht. The city boasts no historic buildings, as Russian forces ran amok in 1668 slaughtering the population and destroying everything that stood on their way, even sinking the Persian Navy on the Caspian Sea before ransacking Rasht. Further occupation during World War I caused more damage, with the total destruction of the bazaar by the Bolsheviks in 1920. The 1991 earthquake brought down anything that had survived, including the former Masjed-e Jame, now rebuilt to a new design, an unhappy mixture of 'classical Safavid' and Gilani vernacular styles. For location of Rasht see map, page 140.

🏠 Where to stay and eat

🏠 **Rasht Grand Kadus Hotel** (100+ rooms) Azadi Bd; ☏ 0131 3223075; f 0131 3220050. A self-proclaimed 4-star option located at the edge of the city centre. Comes with many amenities such as tennis court & outdoor pool, but the décor is standard & rather lacking in flair, albeit rooms facing the street come with small balconies. **$$$**

🏠 **Pardis Hotel** (40 rooms) Emam Bd; ☏ 0131 3221101–5, 3221177–88; www.rashtpardishotel. com. Founded in 1985 & located just a few blocks down the road from Grand Kadus Hotel this is a pleasant place with an inviting lobby & reception area. The staff are helpful & polite. Smallish rooms are pristine & come with little balconies, but unfortunately not all have Western-style toilets. **$$**

🏠 **Hotel Ordibehesht** (30 rooms) Shahrdari Sq; ☏ 0131 2229210–11; f 0131 2229276–8. Charming, central & a little old-fashioned, the hotel has large rooms & equally large bathrooms. Reception has a cosy velvety seating area where you can have a cup of tea & use the Wi-Fi, which is not available in rooms. It is perhaps the only hotel in Iran where b/fast is not included in the room rate. **$**

✕ **Restaurant Moharram** Emam Bd, near Pardis Hotel; ☏ 0131 6661493, 6666090. The décor is more suitable to a fast-food restaurant, but the smallish local specialities menu is really good & well served with a small starter of Gilan olives. Fried Caspian white fish, easily the best fish dish in Iran, is recommended. **$**

MASOULEH In this region is the attractive hill village of Masouleh, over 1,000 years old and 56km west of Rasht via Fuman, which is always cut off by snow during the winter months. When in Fuman, make sure to try the traditional freshly baked and still warm *koluche* biscuit filled with soft walnut paste. It is also sold in shops around Rasht and even Tehran, but is really the best in Fuman. Some 25km southwest from Fuman up in the mountain forests you find the visually impressive Islamili fort **Qaleh Rudkhan**, which was rebuilt during Sejluk times. It boasts 65 well-preserved towers and its outer walls stretch 1,500m. You can combine a visit here as part of a one-day trip to Masouleh. Masouleh has managed to retain its charm, thanks to its welcoming residents and stunning nature, despite crowds of young tourists coming here in groups to smoke *qalian* and relax in one of the local cafés. Go up to the cemetery on the opposite hill for better views of the village.

Getting there Take a *savari* from Rasht to Fuman 30km away (about 30,000 rials) and another one from there to Masouleh, around 32km or 45 minutes from Fuman (another 30,000 rials). Alternatively, *darbaz* **taxi** from Rasht to Masouleh costs around 400,000 rials.

🏠 Where to stay and eat

🏠 **Mehran Hotel** (10 rooms) There is no specific address, arrange for a hotel staff member to come & fetch you; ☏ 0132 7572096. Towards the back of the village, rooms come with kitchenette & terraces with beautiful views. Excellent & clean mountain accommodation. Recommended. **$**

🏠 **Monfared Hotel** (26 rooms) There is no specific address, the hotel is located at the edge of the village; ☏ 0132 7573250, 7572374. Simple but clean budget hotel, albeit with a little less character than the option above. English is spoken. **$**

✕ **Khaneh Moallem Restaurant** Located behind the Monfared Hotel. Has excellent local dishes. **$**

BANDAR-E ANZALI The road to Bandar-e Anzali, the main commercial port of the Iranian Caspian (40km away from Rasht), celebrated in its former name, Bandar-e Pahlavi, passes through more green hills spotted with sharply angled thatched farm buildings. Development began as early as the 15th century, but major improvements were made to the port facilities during the 1920s and 30s. By all reports the Saturday market is very good. The town itself is divided by an inlet: the easterly section is the commercial port area, while the west is less developed.

Where to stay and eat You may prefer staying in Bandar-e Anzali, as Rasht hotels are a little more expensive. Most hotels here are located in buildings more than 80 years old and do not lack a certain charm. For location of Bandar-e Anzali see map, page 140.

Gol-e Sang Hotel (19 rooms) Imam Sq; ☎0181 4245404; m 091 19827639. Very central & charming, the hotel is located in an early 20th-century Russian building with high ceilings & matching wooden doors. Has a traditional restaurant. **$**

Hotel Hemmat (16 rooms) Imam Sq, next to Gol-e Sang Hotel; ☎0181 4243844, 4246956;

f 0181 4240584. Very basic & clean accommodation. The cheapest option in town. **$**
Hotel Iran (40 rooms) Motahhari St; ☎0181 4242524, 4247896, 4248006; f 0181 4248060. A pleasant old-fashioned hotel right by the port & a park. Rooms come with seaview & antique furniture. Staff are chatty & knowledgeable about the area. **$**

WEST AND SOUTHWEST OF BANDAR-E ANZALI

TALESH From Bandar-e Anzali it is an attractive drive among conifers, beeches and rice fields along a good road westwards following the coastline. Some 15km on, and again 7km before Talesh (also called Hashtpar) and 65km from Bandar-e Anzali, there are roadside displays of colourful *ghelims* made in the hill villages, adding yet more colour to the vibrant greens of the rice fields. Keep an eye open for the low, long, thatched **silkworm sheds** set within mulberry plantations, and the steeply dipping storage roofs supported by chunky stone pillars. Accommodation in Talesh is very basic, but if you do decide to stay here, there is an excellent beachside hotel/camping site offering ten wooden cabins (**$**) and 20 suites (**$$**) to rent right by the sea. For details, contact its manager, Esrafil Mirzai (☎ *0182 4292163;* m *0911 3823985*) for directions. Local taxis know the site quite well.

This road leads on to **Astara**, the frontier with the Republic of Azerbaijan. A kilometre or so beyond Astara is the **Espinas International Hotel** (*160 rooms;* ☎*0182 5252700;* e *info@espinashotel.ir; www.espinashotel.ir;* **$$**), a luxury resort on the shore of Lake Estil with stunning views of the lake and mountains. A turn-off west into the mountains leads to the famous shrine of **Ardabil** (see pages 158–60) strongly linked with the Safavid dynasty.

EAST OF BANDAR-E ANZALI

LAHIJAN The road eastwards from Anzali similarly follows the coastline. Many of the Qajar kings and princes built retreats here as bases for hunting expeditions but, with the exception of Lahijan, one needs to travel further east if historic monuments are of interest. Lahijan, 79km from Bandar-e Anzali, was where the young Ismail (r1501–24) of the Safavid family was brought up secretly for five years, to protect him from further imprisonment and possible assassination by the Aq Qoyunlu. Today it is known for tea growing and processing. In its thriving western bazaar area, just off the *maydan* bearing the same local name, is the **Masjed-e Chahar Padishah** (Four Kings), more correctly called Chahar Oleyeh and better described as a mausoleum. Despite the name, only three cenotaphs of the family Sadat-e Keyeh are housed here in two main rooms under a low gabled roof. It has been suggested that the mausoleum dates from early Mongol times but nothing about the building indicates that. The exterior wall paintings, depicting Abu Fazl Abbas riding off to find water for Hossein's supporters and their families at Karbala, are late 19th century, as are the colourful dado tiles; both schemes bear 1920s–30s repair dates. The beautiful wooden doors that once graced its main entrance from the bazaar have been removed to the new Islamic section of the Tehran Archaeological Museum. In the opposite (east) direction, about 3km outside the town, set up on the hillside from the main coast road, is the **Bogheh Sheikh Zahid Gilani**, a square mausoleum honouring the spiritual advisor to Sheikh Safi, founder of the Safavid dynasty. A carved inscription gives a construction date of 1419 but there is nothing 15th century about the present building and its unusual tiered, pyramidal tent roof tiled in turquoise and yellow. Not unlike many other towns along the Caspian coast Lahijan has a telecabin (*130,000–160,000 rials return trip*) up to the **Bam-e Sabz**, where you can have a cup of tea and *qalian* while enjoying the spectacular views.

LANGERUD AND RAMSAR Some 10km further east by the coast is **Langerud**, famous for its late 19th- to early 20th-century wall paintings decorating the Mahalla shrine of Agha Sayyid Hossein and Ibrahim, largely rebuilt in the 18th

STURGEON FISH FARMING IN IRAN

The Caspian Sea is the source of 90% of caviar produced in the world and it is home to the greatest variety (six out of 27 species worldwide) and number of sturgeon. Iran is considered to be one of the leading producers of caviar and the decline in species, caused by poaching, overfishing and pollution, is of serious cultural and economic concern to the Islamic Republic. Scientists broadly agree that fish hatcheries represent the only viable way to restore depleted stocks.

In 2013, the International Sturgeon Research Institute (*www.sturgeon.ir*), based in Bandar-e Anzali, confirmed that after 18 years of research it had successfully applied biotechnology in fish farming and achieved artificial reproduction of all sturgeon species from the Caspian Sea.

Around one tonne of farmed sturgeon caviar was produced in Iran in 2013 and more than 50% of it was exported to Europe and the rest of the world. The Institute anticipates that the produce will rise to three tonnes in 2014. Furthermore, in 2012 and equally in 2013, the Iranian Fisheries Organisation, Shilat, in charge of production and distribution of Iranian caviar, has released more than five million sturgeon fry into the Caspian Sea.

Sturgeon fish-farming potential in Iran, with its 900km of coastline, remains, however, underdeveloped. Sturgeon can be farmed in 16 out of 31 provinces. The Gomishan area of Golestan Province, with its numerous shrimp farms, offers some of the best conditions for sturgeon farming. Iran is considered as the most proactive of the five Caspian Sea bordering countries (Azerbaijan, Kazakhstan, Russia and Turkmenistan) in controlling poaching in the sea.

century. About 60km on, continuing eastwards, is **Ramsar**, formerly a favourite haunt of the two Pahlavi rulers. Mazandaran province starts here, at the Ramsar telecabin (*160,000 rials return trip*). In 1971, the Ramsar Convention was signed here by 21 nations (see page 4). The number of signatory parties today stands at 168. For more details see www.ramsar.org. Next to the Ramsar hotels, two exquisite **villas** will catch your eye. Formerly Reza Shah's property, these are now completely in abandon. Ramsar itself is thriving thanks to the Tehran holiday trade, with many shops now catering for their custom; **market days** are Saturday and Tuesday. For location of Ramsar see map, page 140.

Where to stay

New Ramsar Parsian Azadi Hotel
(121 rooms) Rajaie St, Ramsar; 0192 5223593–5; e info@ramsarhotel.ir; www.ramsarparsianhotels. ir. Commissioned by Reza Shah in the 1930s & echoing the furnishings of Istanbul's Khedive Palace on the Bosphorus. At the foothill of the Alborz Mountains & next door to the current Ramsar Grand & administered by it, the hotel is a treat. **$$$**

Ramsar Parsian Azadi Grand Hotel
(30 rooms) Rejai St, Ramsar; 0192 5223593–5; f 0192 5225174/0730. Built by the late Shah, this is a barn of a place with good-humoured staff. The underworked barmen love to concoct cocktails (alcohol-free, of course). **$$$**

Moving on From Ramsar via Tonekabon, 10km further along the coast, you can get a *savari* for **Chalus**. Leaving Gilan province behind you will possibly, not unlike Tehranis, wish to retreat here for fresh air, forests and the best fish in Iran. While Mazandaran province is similar to Gilan geographically, it is a little more traditional in terms of dresscode and the further east you move in the direction of Mashhad, the more noticeable the differences between the two will appear.

AMOL AND AROUND

With the fast road linking Tehran with Chalus, passing through pleasant mountain scenery, new holiday complexes have largely taken over the shoreline, but a number of large national parks and woods still offer refuge. From **Chalus**, the more southerly road leads to Amol (population 222,000), once the capital of medieval Tabaristan province and famous for a certain kind of 13th-century pottery that was, perhaps, produced here. The settlement was destroyed by Mongol forces, so its monuments post-date their ravages. The easiest to find is the **Imamzadeh Ibrahim** set within a cemetery enclosure on the northern outskirts. Locals understand this 'Ibrahim' to be the son of Imam Musa, but the 1519 wooden cenotaph – now totally cloth-covered – suggests another (unidentified) Ibrahim was interred here along with his brother Yahya and their mother. A large modern ambulatory has been constructed around the square tomb tower (c1426), but modern repairs and decoration have cheerfully ignored the historic architecture. Inside the actual tomb tower a riot of rainbow gloss paint overshadows remnants of 15th-century wall painting, while flat mirror glass and highly varnished wooden pillars confidently detract any merit from the new construction. In the same cemetery is another 15th-century mausoleum, built to honour **Hajji Namdar**, who reportedly travelled from eastern Iran to repair his friend Ibrahim's tomb but died before completion. Judging from the exterior, more remains of the original building, but it now serves as the local headquarters for the Revolutionary Guard and is totally inaccessible.

In the bazaar, off Mostafa Khomeini Street and Bahanor, is a modern complex, **Mashhad Mir Bozorg**, which includes a 17th-century building, possibly a *khanaqeh*, with some external tiling in place. No-one knew the whereabouts of its door key when we visited and unless you're into checklists of monuments you may decide to save your energy. Having read about the early 15th-century **Imamzadeh Qasem** 'located behind the main bazaar … adjoining a modern mosque', whose octagonal exterior was described as having rich plasterwork, we tried to find it. Finally we were directed 3km west outside the town, to a clump of trees shielding a sad cemetery with many unmarked graves, the final resting place of local *mujahedins* killed during the early years of the revolution. Only recently have relatives been allowed to place some gravestones, but dried rose petals and burnt candles show they are remembered as family rather than for any political activity. As for the *imamzadeh*, nothing about the small building there accorded with the published description. A case of mistaken identity? Or is the 'original' Qasem now known by a different name? Three more 15th-century **tomb towers** survive in Amol, all near to each other: that of **Naser al-Haqq** (also known as Gonbad-e Sayyid Sadaf) has a square plan inside and out with an eight-sided tent-dome, as does the **Gonbad-e Gabri** (or Shams-e Rasul), but the **Imamzadeh Seh Tan** ('three bodies') is octagonal in plan.

About 50km further east is **Babol**, which in the last 70 or so years has lost many of its architectural treasures and now just two 15th-century *imamzadehs* remain. One is set just back on the main Amol–Sari road, built to honour the dervish, Fakhr al-Din, in 1430. Its basic circular form and tent roof, separated by two rows of blind niches with light and dark blue tiles in the drum, is reminiscent of the Galata Tower, Istanbul, though of course it is much smaller. The other tomb tower stands some

SILKWORMS AND THE CASPIAN

Chinese histories record how central Asia finally managed to learn the secrets of silkworm rearing and how to acquire the eggs. About 1,600 years ago a central Asian ruler was cunning enough to warn his Chinese princess bride-to-be that as silkworms were unknown in his country, she could never have new silk robes to wear unless she brought her own supply. Knowing that imperial customs officials would search her luggage but never her person, she smuggled silkworm eggs out of the country in her headdress to her wedding. By the early 9th century the shores of the Caspian were famous for the quantity and quality of their raw silk, and plantations of mulberries were being harvested to feed the silkworms. There are no medieval descriptions of the 'nursery' huts but very probably they were essentially the same as they are today: long, low-lying huts with thatched roofs to maintain a shaded, warm but humid atmosphere to ensure that the eggs hatch in the large flat trays in which they are kept. The worms feed greedily and very noisily on white mulberry leaves, growing noticeably in size over the course of six weeks before beginning their cocoon spinning over the next ten days. Some are kept aside to complete the full cycle, turning into the moth and producing eggs, but for most of the cocoons the end comes quickly. They are subjected to full sunlight or hot water, which kills the pupa before it breaks out of its silk protection (which damages the length of silk filament to be harvested). The natural gumminess of the cocoon is water soluble so a stick or fingers are used to gather up the fine filament, which is then reeled off, each up to a kilometre long.

4km to the north of the Amol road. It was built in 1471 to commemorate **Sultan Mohammed Tahir Ibn Musa Qasem** by his two sons, using the architect Shams al-Din Ibn Nasrallah Motahhari according to the cenotaph inscription. One set of doors records another date 20 years after, which perhaps was the completion date.

A quick glance at the map and one could confuse Babol with the town of **Babolsar**, some 30km north, by the Caspian coast. This too has a couple of 15th-century octagonal **tomb towers**, which have seen better years. One was built to honour Ibrahim Abu Javeh – or rather his head, which is all that is buried here; he was a son of Imam Musa and the brother of Imam Reza (see box, page 260), and some 300m away is another *imamzadeh* marking the burial place of Bibi Sakineh, a sister of Imam Reza.

WHERE TO STAY
You may stay in Chalus, or in Babol. Better hotels are all located along the Caspian coast. For location of Amol see map, page 140.

Marjan Hotel (60 rooms) Keshvari Sq, Babol; \0111 2252186–9; f 0111 2250433/1483. Very basic, but clean, conveniently located across the road from the *savari* terminal for Sari & beyond. **$**

SARI

With a population of around 300,000, a **Saturday market** day in Sari buzzes, with money and people coming from the many rice and tea plantations in the area. It was one of the last important Iranian towns to fall to the Muslim Arabs in the 7th century, and a strong Zoroastrian community lasted here until the 19th century. Like many towns in this area, Sari, 72km east from Amol, suffered badly from both the Mongol and then Timurid campaigns sweeping through the eastern provinces. So, although the small local **museum** houses some Sassanid gold and silver artefacts found locally, its three historic buildings date from the Timurid period and once again they are tomb towers. The **Imamzadeh Yahya** is situated in the bazaar southwest of the Maydan-e Saat (Clock Square). The shrine has at its hub a cylindrical tower with a 12-sided tent roof, built in 1442–46 to house the remains of a descendant of Imam Musa, but is now faced by a modern brick portico and its beautiful pair of doors has been removed for safe keeping to Tehran. Just behind it is a slightly later square tower with an eight-sided tent-like dome, the **Imamzadeh Sayyid Zaynolabeddin** (though Jamal and Kamal are also named in the tile inscription); in some publications the monument is given as Sayyid Mohammed Reza. Originally constructed in 1448–50, the tomb retains some of its 15th-century *cuerda seca* tiling inside, and on the exterior some turquoise brick inserts survive in the zone of transition. Just off Enghelab Street down from the Maydan-e Saat, you will find Qajar-period **Kolbadi House** (*Emarat-e Kolbadi; entry 5,000 rials*) presently a museum and formerly private house of Manuchehr Khan Kolbadi, member of the parliament of Iran. Walk past it and you will come across an old, possibly Qajar-period, *ab-e anbar*.

Some 3km from the centre, off Imam Reza Boulevard, stands the **Imamzadeh Abbas** in a small garden. Its beautifully carved cenotaph dates the octagonal tomb tower with its eight-sided tent roof to 1492, stating that it was constructed after Imam Abbas, a son of Imam Musa, appeared here in a vision in 1424; an inverted Safavid blue and white bowl marks the apex of the inner hemispherical dome. A low-lying brick building has recently been added to the front; a young guardian who takes great pride in keeping the place immaculate sprinkles rose water on the paving and rugs. For the location of Sari see map, page 140.

WHERE TO STAY

Asram Hotel (60 rooms) ☎ 0151 3255090–2; m 091 21013273; www.asramco.com. Very reasonable & clean central hotel. Rooms are spacious & come with small balconies. There is also a travel agency, run by the hotel, which can organise tours around Sari. **$**

EXCURSIONS FROM SARI If time allows, it is worth making a detour from Sari, dropping south via Qaem Shahr, formerly Shahi (or alternatively, a longer drive north from Semnan via Firouzkuh), to **Zir Ab** for the tomb tower at **Lajim** 29km further east, and another at **Resget**, near Pol-e Sefid. Locally known as the **Imamzadeh Abdullah**, the Lajim tower was probably erected in 1023 and – although Iran had then been under Muslim rule for almost four centuries – the patron had the brick inscription for her beloved son, Shahriyar Ibn al-Abbas Ibn Shahriyar, written in pre-Islamic Pahlavi script as well as Arabic. So it's interesting on two counts: firstly, the Pahlavi script and, secondly, this is the earliest known building commissioned by a female patron in this part of Iran; she was possibly related through marriage to the famous tomb-tower builder Qabus Ibn Wushmgir (see page 150). To see the tomb tower at Resget, it is probably best to backtrack and continue to the village of Duab, just before Pol-e Sefid, although some prefer to walk the 2km or more cross-country. It is now thought the Resget tomb tower dates from c1106, during the first years of rule by the Seljuk sultan, Sanjar (r1097–1157), and once again Pahlavi script occurs even at this late date, this time in the names of the two brothers interred here, Hormuzd and Hdyer. Yet at the same time there is the *shahada* ('There is no God but God. Mohammed is the messenger of God.') recorded in the plaster door-plaque, and Quranic floriated Kufic inscriptions relating to death (Q1:36) running around the cylindrical exterior, below the dome and the elaborate decoration.

From Sari, the road continues northeastwards through woodlands, orange groves and rice fields towards **Behshahr**. Archaeological investigation carried out in the 1950s by a Pennsylvanian team in the limestone cliff caves to the south, at **Turujan Tappeh**, between Gelin and Fars Abad, proved the place had been settled around 9500BCE. Besides pottery shards and evidence of seal fishing, the Neolithic skeleton of a teenage girl was found, whose bones had been ritually painted red after removal of the flesh. Signs of even earlier settlements were found in other caves, just south of Behshahr itself, by Cambridge (UK) archaeologists in 1964, pushing the date back another millennium. Behshahr, earlier known as Ashraf, has a royal pavilion and gardens, established in Safavid times, which were heavily restored in the 1930s by Reza Shah, high in the hills overlooking the town. For many years it was used for official purposes, but now what remains of the garden may be visited from dawn to dusk.

Some 40km further east, past Gaz, is **Kharabshahr** ('ruined city'), the 9th-century city of Tammisha, excavated in the mid 1960s by a London University team. In the Sassanid period, probably around the 550s CE, thick defence walls were constructed to protect the townspeople from tribal raids launched from the central Asian steppes. It became the administrative centre for a local warlord with a Friday mosque and citadel, until destroyed by the first Mongol wave in 1220. From here, stretching eastwards along the minor road to Gokjeh and passing **Hajji Qushan** (on some maps, Hajehlar) are the remains of the huge brick walls – originally over 170km long with some 33 fortresses – known locally as **Alexander the Great's Wall** (Divar-e Iskandar), although it probably dates from Parthian times (ie: late 2nd century BCE). Thirteenth-century Iranian chroniclers and artists understood that it had been built to hold back those great enemies of civilisation, Gog and Magog. Stretching east from Gumishan to Mount Pishkamer and perhaps continuing into present-day Turkmenistan, it consisted of a ditch, some 3m wide, before the wall, defended by towers and forts. On the Iranian side, field cultivation came up to the wall line so the contrast between the wild steppe and settled agriculture would have been obvious.

Fifteen kilometres south of Kordkuy near the village of **Radkan** is an 11th-century cylindrical tomb tower 35m high, referred to as 'Radkan West' in academic publications. The two inscriptions, one above the door and the other just below the dome, in Arabic, plaited Kufic and also in Pahlavi, identify that a certain Abu Jafar Mohammed Ibn Wandarin was a local warlord whose Bawanid family had controlled the eastern Caspian region from around 665CE until it fragmented in 1349, having converted to Islam in 854CE. He ordered its construction in 1016, to house his remains after death.

Rushanabad is located 18km west of Gorgan, and within its main cemetery is the *imamzadeh* of Abdullah and Fazlullah, constructed in 1460 according to the doors, although some scholars have suggested 1420. A long prayer hall introduces the tomb tower, which is described as possessing an 'extraordinary use of glazed tiles' and 'unique painting' on the interior depicting buildings, perhaps symbolising the Ardabil shrine, Mecca or Medina.

Gorgan The main road continues to **Gorgan** (population 344,000), where the occasional Turkoman woman still wears her distinctive colourful shawl with a floral dress. The medieval town was famous for its amazing lustre-decorated pottery vessels; excavation work 4km west of the modern city between 1970–77 found superb examples. Today most visitors come to visit the tomb tower **Gonbad-e Qabus** (also pronounced *qavus*), located some 80km away on the outskirts of Gonbad town. But Gorgan itself is worth a couple of hours' exploration, if only to look out for late 19th-century shops and houses which retain their traditional brick, wood and terracotta tiling, despite a severe earthquake in 1928. Buried in the vegetable and fruit section of the bazaar, near to Maydan Wahdat, there is the two-*ivan* **Masjed-e Jame**, with the remains of a Seljuk minaret over the main entrance, but the courtyard tilework dates from the 20th century. The helpful guardian will unlock the *ivan* to the far left of the main entrance which contains some exuberant Qajar plasterwork as well as the original mosque doors, moved here some years ago for their preservation. The lower carving has been worn away by the worshippers kissing and stroking the panels, but in the upper section the exquisite 15th-century work is clearly visible despite the thick modern varnish. Also here is a walnut *minbar*, gloriously unvarnished and decorated with the names of the 12 Imams; across the front section is a date corresponding to 1609. A five-minute walk behind this mosque and straight through the bazaar, passing some lovely traditional houses with deep overhanging eaves, leads to the **Imamzadeh Nur** (or Ishaq Ibn Musa Ibn Jafar). Although this 12-sided tomb tower has lost its original roof, its brick patterning is still attractive, and inside a little of the original, deeply carved plaster decoration remains, especially in the *mihrab*. Although the original wooden doors have now vanished, one had a date corresponding to 1453 carved into it. If you decide to stay here, 9km south of Gorgan town there is a **Tourist Inn** (*67 rooms; 0171 5543278, 7278, 0034; $$*) located in a lovely foresty area.

GONBAD-E QABUS

This UNESCO World Heritage monument (⊕ *08.00–20.00; entry 100,000 rials; the actual tower is closed, but ask a soldier on duty to let you have a quick look inside*) is always mentioned in books on Iranian Islamic architecture. Its staggering size and strength of form look very out of place in the fragile, pretty garden now surrounding it. Two weary *kibitka*s or domed trellis tents stand by its side. We know something of the man who had it built in 1006 as a suitable family mausoleum. This was before he was deposed in 1012 and deliberately left to freeze to death in the Gorgan winter snows. He was the military commander, Amir Qabus Ibn Wushmgir, a famous calligrapher, known scholar (the famous medieval polymath al-Biruni dedicated his multi-volume *Chronology of Ancient Nations* to him), patron of the arts and renowned, bloodthirsty warlord. An artificial mound conceals the formidable foundations (late 19th-century Russian archaeologists gave up digging down after 10m) for this 51m-high tower of coffee-coloured brick. The basic circular plan, 17m in diameter, is quickly broken by ten soaring angular flanges and one small door. Two brick inscriptions run around the shaft in between the angled buttresses, one low down and the other high up, under the superbly 'tailored' conical dome which was once in grey-green brick, though what you see now is a modern replacement; both refer to the promise of paradise awaiting the true believer. There is just one small window in the roof, positioned to catch the rising sun which would illuminate, according to local legend, a suspended rock-crystal coffin holding the body of Qabus (not quite the cheap wooden coffin recommended in Islamic law).

South of here, Cambridge (UK) archaeologists excavating caves found evidence that people had inhabited the region from at least 40,000BCE and possibly much earlier (65,000BCE), hunting, working flint and living off bears, rhinoceros and also horses. This last point is interesting; the Caspian and Turkoman regions were once known for two special types of horse (see box, below).

AROUND GONBAD-E QABUS Just as intriguing, but very different, is a cemetery about 70km northeast of Gonbad-e Qabus, named after a tomb to a certain **Halat (Khaled) Nabi**, near to the mountain called Gokjeh Dagh; up a steep, largely unmetalled road. No-one knows who Halat Nabi was, let alone if he was Muslim, but the real mystery is the 600-odd standing stones. Some are cylindrical and

CASPIAN AND TURKOMAN HORSES

The Caspian horse is similar but far from identical to the stocky Turkoman horse, the sturdy mount of the 12th-century Seljuk Turks and later Turkoman tribesmen. The Caspian stands about 11 or 13 hands high, but is narrower in width across the back, with a pronounced forehead and small ears, a distinctive oval hoof, which needs infrequent shoeing, and a unique haemoglobin structure. A small stud was established in 1965 near Shiraz, and later in Tehran, and immediately after the Islamic Revolution this section of the then-royal stables came under the Ministry of Jihad, but it is not known whether that stud still exists. The breed continues in the USA, Australia and also in the UK, as a mare and stallion were presented to Philip, Duke of Edinburgh, in 1971.

The Turkoman horse continues today in the modern breed known as Akhal Teke, often pale gold or possibly grey or bay in colour. It stands taller than the Caspian, at about 15 hands with a narrow chest, flat ribs and long back. The tail is comparatively short and the mane even more so. Its well-known stamina and ability to go without water for over 300km in desert conditions are put down to a distinct, constructed diet, low in bulk and high in protein, often made with animal fat and eggs mixed with barley.

anything from 1–5m high, while others are rectangular with two upper lobes. There are no dating inscriptions, but a conservative guess is that these date from the 17th or 18th century and may mark a traditional Turkoman tribal burial site.

MOVING ON From Gorgan, most travellers continue towards Mashhad, or indeed to the Irano–Turkmenistan frontier (see page 255), but if you have to return to Tehran there is no need to backtrack – go by the 'southern' road via Shahrud and Semnan, as detailed below.

SHAHRUD Shahrud (population 166,000) is on the main road from Mashhad to Tehran. Train and daily bus services to and from Mashhad stop here. If you want to visit the Masjed-e Jame and famous shrine at Bastam, 12km to the north, you can stay in Bastam itself in the conveniently located Tourist Inn (see page 149), just a few metres up from the site. But do note that there is nothing else of historical interest around here and you might prefer to continue on to Damghan instead. There are numerous *savari* taxis and the journey between the two towns takes around one hour. But if you are indeed staying here and completely bored, around 15km past Bastam in the small village of Qaleh Mirza Soleyman there is a mausoleum of Sheikh Abolhassan Kharaghani, a prominent 10th-century Iranian Sufi mystic

BASTAM AND AROUND

BAYAZID HISTORICAL COMPLEX Like many other pilgrims, Oljeitu, then the local governor, came to pay homage to the grave of the famous Sufi charismatic mystic, Sheikh Bayazid al-Bastami (d874), and was initiated as a Sufi here in 1300. He later undertook a massive programme of rebuilding, enlarging the **shrine complex** and became Ilkhanid ruler of Iran (d1317). Today one enters into a large court and to the immediate right (north) is a **tomb tower**, often referred to as that of Sheikh Bayazid, although his actual grave is in the courtyard immediately in front of the main shrine building alongside a later one of Azam Khan Afghani; it now functions as an office. Rather than walking ahead, bear left and walk through an east-facing portal, beautifully embellished with turquoise strapwork and moulded brick-plugs, leading into a long hall. Constructed in 1313 perhaps as the main entrance, it now has an almost central position in the extended enclosure. High on the inside walls is a lengthy, elegant plaster inscription, the work of a Damghani master craftsman, naming Oljeitu and his brother, Ghazan Khan 'Sultan of the land of the East and China, king of the servants of the horizons' (r1295–1304) as patrons. At the end, not only does Bayazid's tower come into view but also another lofty *ivan* for teaching, also decorated with turquoise blue tile inserts. On the left, a small locked door – peek through the side window – gives entry into one of two small 'hermitages' which served as a *chehelkhaneh*, both richly decorated with soot-blackened, early 14th-century plasterwork.

In the main building, there is an *imamzadeh* shrine immediately to the right with a grilled cenotaph commemorating Mohammed Ibn Jafar; women have to don a *chador*. The hexagonal, tiled dado is much earlier in date than the painted decoration of the walls and dome, restored in 1894. Viewed from the outside, this shrine is underneath a tiled tent roof with a brick-patterned minaret of 1120, its lower section incorporated into the hall further into the building. This vaulted hall was constructed after the decorative brick wall of the little mosque, with two intricately carved 14th-century doors now behind glass. In the late 15th century the roof of this mosque fell in and a wooden roof was installed but the carved plaster *mihrab*, dated 1314, the work of Mohammed Ibn Hossein Abi Talib al-Mohandis, was saved. Some beautiful plasterwork also remains in the winter prayer hall next door but its *mihrab* has been removed.

To get to the **Masjed-e Jame**, leave the complex by the main gate and walk southwest, keeping the shrine on the left. The mosque is down a side road nearby. At its back is a large 13.6m circular tomb tower of 1313, again the work of Mohammed al-Damghani, with some 26 vertical flanges and remains of glazed inserts in the two inscription bands under the roof. Inside, it is 12-sided (possibly to symbolise the 12 Imams) with blind niches in three zones accentuating the height. Its door, firmly locked, is located within the mosque at the end of a small vestibule decorated with 14th-century carved plaster and well hidden behind a curtain. Very little of the original Masjed-e Jame remains but do wait for the guardian to let you into the *mihrab* area as it still retains some wonderful plasterwork, exquisitely carved in 1306 with unusually shaped arch profiles, akin to upturned pagoda eaves. This decoration was clearly applied on to an earlier structure, and above the *mihrab* the Qajar ruler Fath Ali Shah recorded his own 1809 repairs to the building.

WEST OF BASTAM AND SHAHRUD About 55km west from Shahrud is **Mehmandust**, the Safavids finally defeated the Afghan rebels in 1729. In a cemetery on the southern outskirts stands another lovely tomb tower, popularly known as Imamzadeh Qasem, a son of the seventh imam, despite the fact that its Kufic inscription above the bird-like frieze clearly stated it was made for a commander, Abu Jafar Mohammed, 'the hospitable *mehmandust*' (thus the name of the township), before modern restoration messed up the reading. Built in 1097, the tower (external diameter c10m) was about 21m high but its original conical roof has not survived. The number of flanges, 12 in all, was probably deliberate symbolism (12 Imams) as the verse (Q41:31) in the inscription has strong Shi'a connotations.

Nearer Damghan (altitude 1,120m) **Qaleh Gerdkuh** comes into view. Known for its Ismaili connections as early as the 10th century, this is where the Assassins (see box, page 94) constructed a fortress so well defended that Hulagu, the grandson of Genghis Khan, laid siege for many months before finally taking it in 1256. By all reports, sections of the enclosing walls, the gatehouse and cisterns remain; as yet no archaeological survey has been undertaken. Access is through the village of Qaleh Gerdkuh, and may still be difficult.

Where to stay

Tourist Inn (25 rooms) Shahid Motahhari Park; Shahid Beheshti Bd; 0274 5222262/3811/4596/4597; www.ittic.com. Rooms are standard, clean & with Western toilet facilities. Has a lovely outdoor garden & seating area, but the staff are a little uninterested. Wi-Fi, although it exists, is unreliable. **$**

DAMGHAN

It is thought Damghan (population 65,000) was originally known as Deh-e Magi (Village of the Magi/Zoroastrian Priests), and in the past some scholars wondered if it was Hecatompylos (also known as Sad Darvazeh or 'The City of 100 Gates'), the ancient Parthian capital under the Arsacid Dynasty (248BCE–224CE). However, finds from the Shahr-e Qomes excavations in the 1970s have established that Hecatompylos was indeed located in the area (see page 154). Damghan was a prosperous walled city in Sassanid times as confirmed by American archaeological excavations in the early 1930s (Philadelphia Museum of Art, USA, has decorative plaster from the Sassanid palace at Tappeh Hesar, southeast of the present town) and possibly its importance then was linked to certain Zoroastrian sacred fires in the region, although there had been occupation from at least 2,000 years before. The earthquake of 856CE destroyed the Sassanid defensive walls, killing about 45,000 people by some reports, so there was massive rebuilding in the 920s. As local warlords and governors battled for control, real authority rested in the Assassins' fortress above and Hassan al-Sabbah (see box, page 94) felt safe enough to enter the city itself. With the Mongol conquest, the power struggle continued with the rulers of Khwarizm (present-day Turkmenistan) also intervening. The city was taken by Timur Leng in 1381 but raids and massacres continued for the next 50 years. In 1528 the Safavid regime brought a measure of stability to the region, ended by Afghan incursions in the 1720s. By the time Nader Shah finished bombarding the town in 1729, its population had shrunk to 3,000. Prosperity slowly returned with the Qajar dynasty (Fath Ali Shah was born here in 1772) but the town was torn apart in 1911 when pro-constitutionalist activists met their opponents head-on; hundreds were left dead. In 1929 the town had a population of 5,000 and today it is over 50,000.

If you are approaching Damghan from the Sari direction, you are likely to drive past **Cheshmeh Ali** (Spring Water of Ali), 35km north of Damghan, but do not confuse it with Cheshmeh Ali in Rayy (see pages 86–7). This is one of the permanent springs in the area, collecting water from the mountains in the north. For location of Damghan see map, page 140.

WHERE TO STAY

⌂ **ITTIC Damghan Inn** (14 rooms) Azadi Bd; ☏0232 5242070; damghan_ittic@yahoo.com; www.ittic.com. Recently renovated, & central, this 1-storey inn offers spacious rooms with high vaulted ceilings & large bathrooms. B/fast is a little poor, but the whole place is comfortable enough & there is Wi-Fi. **$**

WHAT TO SEE AND DO Despite its turbulent history, the city boasts some important historic buildings. About 500m southeast of the main square, Maydan-e Imam Khomeini, is the **Masjed-e Tarik Khaneh** (also known as Masjed-e Chehel Sotun) (*Motahari St;* ◷ *08.30–13.00 & 15.00–17.00 Sat–Thu; entry 100,000 rials*) thought to be the second-oldest mosque surviving in Iran. A very helpful Persian-speaking guardian, Emadi Bozorghe, holds the key to Pir-e Alamdar (see page 154) and can direct you to Tappeh Hesar. He can also arrange for you to visit the underground section of the Masjed-e Jame. This is a 'majestically simple' mosque, retaining something of its 8th-century 'Arab' plan, a design that quickly fell out of favour with Iranian patrons. The arrangement of arches running parallel to the enclosing walls and some of the fat, stumpy brick piers are from the original 760CE construction, but the remains of the brick and plaster patterning are from an 11th-century Seljuk restoration. Its **minaret**, just outside the mosque, 25m high, was erected in 1028, making it the earliest Iranian minaret still standing. Its inscription among the six bands of brick set in relief and recess records that the mason was the man who built the Semnan minaret (see page 155) while the costs were met by the governor who before his appointment also paid for the Pir-e Alamdar tomb tower nearby.

From here it takes about eight minutes to walk to the **Masjed-e Jame** (also called Masjed-e Imam Hossein), crossing the main road and going northeast. You've come here just for the **Seljuk minaret**, constructed sometime between 1031–35, which has ten lovely brick-pattern zones still retaining some glazed inserts, including the Quranic verse (Q24:35) which talks of the message of Islam burning brightly in a glass lamp, very apposite for Imam Hossein, often represented by a lighted candle.

6

Presently it is about 27m high but the upper section was destroyed in 1933. Check out the handles on the old door leading up to the mosque courtyard. The one with the circle is for women and the other is for men to knock. Each makes a different sound thus signalling to the person inside the mosque whom to expect. About 100m away is the 16m-high **tomb tower of Pir-e Alamdar** (*remember to get the keyholder to come from the Masjed-e Tarik Khaneh*) of 1027. It no longer has its original exterior tent roof, but the brickwork with the main inscription below the dome is still lovely, recording that it was built for the then governor of Damghan, Abu Jafar Mohammed Ibn Ibrahim, by his son who was also responsible for the Tarik Khaneh minaret described above. But the best work is inside: a splendidly ornate plaited Kufic band running around the interior (Q39:53–4) in blue, and justly described as 'a tour de force', speaks of God's forgiveness.

Also near the Maydan-e Imam Khomeini there is the historical complex of **Khanaqeh of Shah Rukh**, but locals are unlikely to be familiar with this name. The site is commonly known as Imamzadeh Jafar. The first building is a much-restored tomb presently known as **Imamzadeh Mohammed Ibn Musa Kazem** but the Sufi meeting place, which gives the complex its name, is a small square building with a 15th-century Timurid tile panel high over the door, recording that Shah Rukh, Timur Leng's son (see box, page 254), paid for extensive repairs. Today in its crypt it houses another Shah Rukh, a relative of Nader Shah Afshar killed by the first Qajar ruler in 1796. Adjoining it is the large **Imamzadeh Jafar**, still retaining its Seljuk inner dome, probably the reason for establishing a *khanaqeh* here. It commemorates Jafar Ibn Ali (d901), a descendant of the third imam. Just behind is a cylindrical tomb tower standing 14.8m high called the **Chehel Dokhtaran** (40 Maidens) but, as its two inscriptions used to record before modern restoration, it was built in 1055, by and for the military commander Abu Shuja 'Asfar Beg 'preparing for his sleep a tomb for himself and his sons'. Resembling the Pir-e Alamdar above, it is the second-earliest dated tomb tower surviving in Iran.

Just 5km southeast of Damghan, close to the railway line, archaeological work at **Tappeh Hesar** uncovered not only the remains of a 6th-century Sassanid palace, but also evidence of settlement from at least the early 2nd millennium BCE with charred remains of skeletons and weapons. The main excavations were undertaken during the two world wars when splendid conical bowls bearing fine black-painted motifs (now in the National Museum, Tehran; see pages 80–1) were uncovered alongside finely modelled rams' heads in gold foil for textile decoration. Road widening in 1995 has presumably put paid to further discoveries.

Again south of the main road from Damghan to Semnan another interesting archaeological site was found, **Shahr-e Qomes**. Excavation work here in 1967 revealed rich Parthian finds from mud-brick vaulted tombs (c70BCE), and evidence of a Parthian fortified encampment. Part of the 28km² site was then inhabited into Seljuk times, before its destruction by the Mongols in the early 13th century. But, importantly, the archaeologists left the excavation convinced that indeed they had found Hecatompylos or 'The City of a Hundred Gates' where Alexander the Great broke the news to his soldiers that they were not returning home, but carrying on into India.

SEMNAN

The next major city on the road back towards Tehran is Senman, 232km east from the capital, population 163,000. Centuries ago its wealth came from the trade caravans passing to and from central Asia and Afghanistan via Mashhad going west, but now it is a centre for light industry and serves as the provincial capital; it lies on the main railway from Tehran to Mashhad and several of the trains stop there.

WHAT TO SEE AND DO Famous for its pistachios, it also has a couple of interesting buildings as well as the remains of the mud-brick **citadel** which once defended the city. Its **Masjed-e Jame**, on the western outskirts off the Maydan Motahhari, was established in the 8th century but the only visual evidence of this is the restored fat brick pillars and a boarded-up *mihrab* in the arcade opposite the excessively tall prayer *ivan*. That main *ivan* is part of the major Timurid rebuilding programme undertaken by Shah Rukh around 1424, and the large underground winter prayer hall may also date from this period or later, though locals think it is Seljuk work. What is clearly Seljuk is the prayer chamber itself. At first sight its proportions – height of walls to dome, squinches and zone of transition, etc – seem illogical and the only explanation is that for some reason the later Timurid repairs involved raising the original ground level of this chamber considerably. The **minaret**, standing over 28m high, is also Seljuk, constructed in 1031–35 by the same man responsible for the minaret at Tarik Khaneh, Damghan. It has at least eight pattern zones, including two bands of inscription (including Q41:33) and an attractive wooden balcony. Within easy walking distance through the bazaar, about 200m northeast, is the 19th-century **Masjed-e Imam Khomeini** (formerly Masjed-e Shah), proof of the city's prosperity in the Qajar period. Somewhat understated for Qajar religious buildings, the exuberant tiling and colouring dating from the reign of Fath Ali Shah are delicious. Another Qajar monument, the **Arg-e Darwazir** dated 1884, once marked an entrance gate into the town but is now transformed into a busy roundabout. Its tile panels feature armed soldiers and a cannon. For location of Semnan, see map, page 140.

WHERE TO STAY
Tourist Inn (36 rooms) Basij Blvd, after Amir Kabir bridge; 0231 4441433. Provides a more than adequate stay, albeit booking might prove to be a problem as the staff are unwilling to make a reservation in advance. **$$**

SEMNAN TO TEHRAN

From Semnan, there are two routes to Tehran: the more southerly route goes through Garmsar, while the other heads off via Firouzkuh and passes close to the town of **Damavand**, named after the mountain standing 5,610m high to the north. The area is dotted with the ruins of numerous fortresses, strongholds of the Assassins in the late medieval period. Close to Damavand's Masjed-e Jame is a tomb tower known locally as the **tomb of Sheikh Shibli**, a Sunni mystic and former local deputy governor before his death in Baghdad in 945CE. His actual tomb still survives there, though it was probably built for someone completely different as its style suggests the late 11th century. It has an octagonal exterior with a rounded buttress at each corner, decorated in brick patterns with octagons, lozenges, eight-pointed stars and an octagonal flanged tent roof.

The road from **Eyvanekey**, 25km west of Garmsar, into Tehran goes through marvellous scenery with spectacularly coloured rocks. But this route, known locally as 'Alexander's [the Great] Gate', still has some sharp hairpin bends (despite improvements) which Tehrani drivers acknowledge only at the last moment.

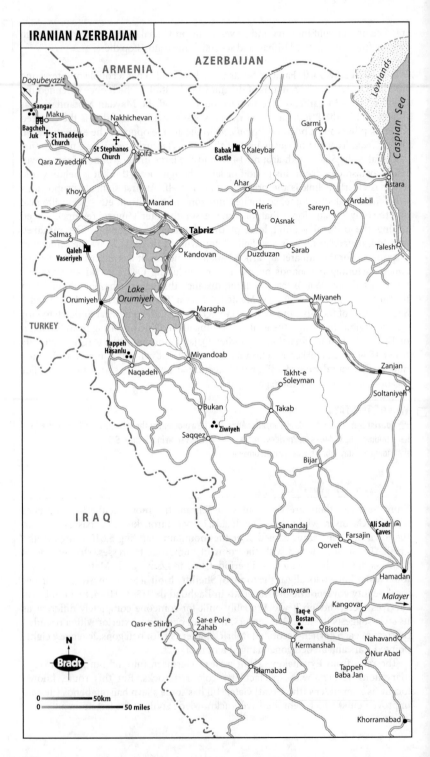

IRANIAN AZERBAIJAN

ARMENIA

AZERBAIJAN

Lowlands

Caspian Sea

Doğubeyazit

Sangar
Maku
Bagcheh
Juk
St Thaddeus
Church

Nakhichevan

Garmi

St Stephanos
Church

Jolfa

Babak
Castle
Kaleybar

Astara

Qara Ziyaeddin

Ahar

Khoy

Marand

Heris

Sareyn

Ardabil

Salmas

Tabriz

Asnak

Qaleh
Vaseriyeh

Kandovan

Duzduzan
Sarab

Talesh

Lake
Orumiyeh

Maragha

Miyaneh

Orumiyeh

TURKEY

Tappeh
Hasanlu

Miyandoab

Zanjan

Naqadeh

Takht-e
Soleyman

Soltaniyeh

Bukan

Takab

Saqqez
Ziwiyeh

Bijar

IRAQ

Sanandaj

Ali Sadr
Caves

Qorveh
Farsajin

Hamadan

Kamyaran

Malayer

Kangovar

Qasr-e Shirin

Sar-e Pol-e
Zahab

Taq-e
Bostan
Bisotun

Nahavand

Nur Abad

Kermanshah

Islamabad

Tappeh
Baba Jan

N

Bradt

Khorramabad

0 _____ 50km
0 _____ 50 miles

7

Iranian Azerbaijan

For centuries this region formed a major gateway into both Europe and Asia, with merchants and armies travelling the trade routes along the foothills of the Caucasus separating modern-day Turkey and Iran from the modern republics of Georgia, Armenia and Azerbaijan, and through the Zagros Mountains dividing Iraq and Iran. Today's political frontiers are less than a century old, so unsuprisingly excavations in this region of Iran frequently reveal archaeological proof of strong cultural links with ancient civilisations associated with Anatolia, Mesopotamia and across the Caucasus. Because of its location, surrounded on two sides by mountains and with the Caspian Sea to the east, the region was a battle arena in more recent times: some 400 centuries of conflict against the Ottoman armies and then Russian (and Bolshevik/Soviet) campaigns in the 19th and 20th centuries. In Iran the area is known as Eastern Azerbaijan, while in Azerbaijan it is referred to as Southern Azerbaijan.

The region was always known for its Christian communities, which before World War I made up over 30% of the total local population. This was where Western missionaries came in the 19th and early 20th centuries, establishing medical centres and schools, and fired with the wish to 'convert' the Nestorians and Armenian Gregorians, to join various Protestant denominations. Although tolerated by the central administration as long as there was no evidence of Muslim conversions, such activity caused problems to all layers of Iranian society and fuelled xenophobic anxieties. The region, however, has retained some of the most beautiful and well-preserved churches in Iran, in particular in the vicinity of Maku and Jolfa.

Eastern Azerbaijan is ideal for hill walking and mountain trekking. There is good budget accommodation in smaller towns and **Alp Tour Iran** (\ *0411 3310340;* e *info@alptouriran.com, alptouriran@yahoo.com; www.alptouriran.com*), run by Hossein Mohammed, can arrange all kinds of travel activities in the area.

GETTING THERE

The main highway northwest from Tehran to the provincial capital Tabriz (about 215km; altitude 1,340m) is good but not spectacularly scenic, taking about 12 hours by express **bus**. If you wish to visit places such as Soltaniyeh and Zanjan, the slower 'old' road will have to be used in part. To avoid returning on the same route, why not travel from Tehran to Bandar-e Anzali (see page 143), staying there for the night and then continue up the western shores of the Caspian to visit Ardabil? There are regular bus services from there to Tabriz, the provincial capital (270km away). After visiting various sites to the north, one could then make one's way back to Tehran.

Do note that the winters in this region are very long and harsh. Snowfalls are heavy and the temperature plummets, so visits are best made from early May to mid-October.

ARDABIL AND AROUND

With the establishment of the Safavid regime (1501–c1735), Ardabil (altitude 1,300m) became increasingly important. Five centuries earlier it had been a walled town, but in such a ruinous, filthy state that the Arab geographer al-Muqaddasi (flourished 967–85ce) described it as 'one of the latrines of the world'. Local campaigns against the Georgian princes in 1208, which resulted in the sacking of Ani (eastern Turkey) and the deaths of 12,000 Christians, led to swift and violent retribution in 1209 when over 12,000 Ardabil citizens were slain. Later, the conflict between the two great tribal confederations – the Qara and Aq Qoyunlu – had repercussions on the local economy. But once the Safavid leader Ismail I took control in 1501, the town's future became more secure, for this was the burial place of the Sufi teacher considered to be the founder of the dynastic family, Sheikh Safi al-Din (1251–1334). It also benefited from its proximity to the new Safavid capital, Tabriz, until the court moved south to Qazvin and later Esfahan. Time and money were lavished on Ardabil, especially on the tomb of Safi al-Din, as the shahs sought to emphasise their lineage and championship of the Ithna 'Ashari branch of Shi'a Islam. By 1656 the shrine and town were crown domain, endowed with superb costly carpets like the Ardabil carpet (now in the Victoria and Albert Museum, London) and its twin (Los Angeles County Museum of Art, USA), and a magnificent collection of Chinese porcelain including celadon (as in the Ardabil Shrine, and the Islamic section of the Archaeological Museum, Tehran). It also had a vast library, but this was ransacked during the Irano-Russian wars of 1826–28 when Ardabil was occupied by Russian troops, and anything valuable was taken back to St Petersburg.

In 1993 the now former Iranian president Mahmoud Ahmadinejad was sent to Ardabil to be governor of the province and he stayed there until 1997. Ardabil is now a large city of 485,000 people and as with many other cities in the region, in particular Tabriz, it has, in recent years, seen a rise in the number of Azerbaijanis coming from across the border for medial treatment. The city itself has few historical sites and the main tourist attraction here is the UNESCO World Heritage Site Sheikh Safi Mausoleum. Among Iranians, however, the area is known for its clean air, beautiful surroundings and natural springs.

GETTING THERE There are several **flights** a day from Tehran with a journey time of just over an hour, and there are a few flights each week to and from Mashhad. The city is also well served by long-distance **buses** connecting to destinations near and far.

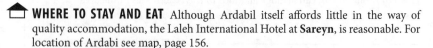 **WHERE TO STAY AND EAT** Although Ardabil itself affords little in the way of quality accommodation, the Laleh International Hotel at **Sareyn**, is reasonable. For location of Ardabi see map, page 156.

🏠 **Laleh International Hotel** (97 rooms) Opposite Sabalan Centre, Sareyn; \0452 2222750–6; f 0452 2222322. Close to the town centre & the sights. Among other facilities, this large holiday resort has a traditional *sofreh khaneh* restaurant, coffee shop & Wi-Fi. **$$**

🏠 **Hotel Mahdi** (21 rooms) Besat St; \0451 6614011–12; f 0451 6623237. Very basic & standard hotel, & more central than Hotel Shorabil. **$**

🏠 **Hotel Shorabil** (40 rooms) On banks of Lake Shorabil, 4km southeast of the centre; \0451 5513096; f 0451 5513097. The soothing natural setting of Hotel Shorabil makes it the best of a poor bunch. Rooms are basic with oldish furniture. The décor is suggestive of initial grander ambitions, but at present it's a simple budget-style accommodation with exceptionally friendly & caring staff. Do not expect Wi-Fi. Reserve in advance as it is quite popular with Azerbaijanis coming to Iran for medical treatment. **$**

WHAT TO SEE AND DO

Sheikh Safi Mausoleum (*Sheikh Safi Al-Din Ardabili St;*⊕ *08.00–18.00; entry 150,000 rials*) It was Sheikh Safi himself who established a *khanaqeh* in the 13th century, perhaps on the site of the present Chini-khaneh (Porcelain Room). After his death, his followers built a tomb to honour him and thereafter over the centuries buildings were added, torn down or converted. The main entrance into the shrine complex dates from 1926 when the four or so shops either side were built, their rents going towards the upkeep of the shrine. This leads directly into a garden laid out in c1834, which today is a favourite meeting place for elderly gentlemen. At the other end a porch from 1629 (heavily restored), leads into a courtyard with 'very fair and spacious vault[s] arched above, paved without with green and blue [tile] stones', as seen by one European traveller in 1637. The domed structure immediately on the left, hidden by a large wooden grille, was originally constructed on the orders of Shah Tahmasp I around 1540, perhaps as another *khanaqeh,* and it is possible that the two Ardabil carpets (if they were ever here; see opposite) were made for this octagonal building. By 1843 it was in a sorry state, having lost its dome, and it was perhaps at this point it was turned into a mosque, the Jannat Sura; major repairs were undertaken from 1935 onwards to this building and in fact to all the tiled façades in this courtyard.

A small door takes the visitor into the main building and a long prayer hall known as **qandilkhaneh** (Lantern Hall); the endowments paid for teams of Quran readers to sit and intone before the tombs. The portal inscription stresses the importance of reading the Holy Book, and it has long been assumed the door and hall were part of Tahmasp's building programme. However, recent research suggests perhaps both were constructed two centuries earlier. For a number of years it housed a huge vertical loom, as the authorities decided a copy of the Ardabil carpet should be made but, like many projects in the new republic, resources were diverted elsewhere and progress was painfully slow. The massive silver doors were a royal gift in 1602–03, and then ten years later Shah Abbas ordered the hall to be painted and gilded, and silver grilles erected.

A doorway immediately on the left leads into the **chinikhaneh**, a large octagonal room with plasterwork niches, which once held some of the fine Chinese porcelain pieces from the Safavid court. It is here that the finished copy of the Ardabil carpet is now displayed. In all, over 1,160 pieces of costly, rare Chinese blue and white porcelain and celadon vessels were given by the Safavid shahs, some probably taken as battle spoils from the defeated Uzun Hasan, leader of the Aq Qoyunlu (d1478). In the 1930s about half of these were moved to Tehran for safe keeping. A number of dishes are displayed alongside manuscripts and other historical artefacts. Most of the structure dates from the Safavid rebuilding programme of 1607–11 but, as you will spot, the domed roof is new, dating from 1971.

Returning to the qandilkhaneh, you can explore the other small rooms off to the left housing numerous cenotaphs marking interments in the crypts below. Thick but fine-quality 'inlaid' patterned felts cover the floors, getting dirtier and more moth-eaten every year. Important members of the Safavid court, military generals and the royal ladies rest here, including Shah Ismail's mother and the shah himself with a magnificent cenotaph (see below), presented, so the locals say, by the Indian Moghul emperor, Humayun, in about 1530, in gratitude for giving him refuge during his exile from India.

The **haramkhaneh** should, as the name suggests, contain the cenotaphs of the royal ladies but as one scholar has noted, at least one of the deceased was the eldest son of Sheikh Safi, who died in 1324 when the room was probably constructed and not, as first thought, the wife of Safi. The tomb chamber nearest that of the Sheikh himself contains Ismail's large cenotaph and little else, other than deep cobalt blue tiles with stencilled fired gold patterns and smoke-damaged wall decoration. Next door, at the end of the prayer hall, once decorated with costly rugs and gold lamps but ransacked over a century ago, is the circular tomb chamber of Sheikh Safi himself, constructed in 1334 and extensively repaired (on the outside) in 1949. Before you leave the courtyard outside, don't forget to walk round to see the exteriors of these tomb chambers with their tile decoration.

WEST OF ARDABIL There is an interesting mosque about 75km to the west, on either the Ahar (north) road or that going through Sarab. Near the village of Mehraban (south of Heris, north of Duzduzan, west of Sarab) is **Asnak**, whose **Masjed-e Jame** is remarkably fashioned of red stone. It was built around 1333 on the so-called 'Arab' hypostyle plan with wooden columns inside and a flat wooden roof. Very unusual for this pre-Safavid date, the foundation inscription under the left window of the entrance portal is in Persian, written in the Arabic script, recording that 'Malikshah … made all its decoration with the point of an adze, may his hand be steady and may Allah preserve him.'

About 70km north of Ahar is **Kaleybar**, which can also be approached directly from Tabriz further west. There are three daily buses and the journey takes up to three hours and costs 30,000 rials. The town is known for its well-preserved **Babak Castle** (Qaleh Babak) at an altitude of 2,300m, some 3km from the town. This Sassanid castle, named after Babak the warlord, managed to resist the Arab armies until 839CE. In the ruins of the rooms and corridors, pottery and coins dating from the 13th century have been found by Iranian archaeologists and restoration teams, working here since 1998. Access is difficult, but the scenery is stunning, involving an arduous uphill walk from the base of what used to be Babak Hotel (may reopen in the future) taking over an hour each way. Do, however, arrange for a guide to accompany you (contact Alp Tour Iran, see page 157, or enquire with Rahim Bolandi from Kollywood Hotel, see below), as there is an alternative route accessible to 4x4 vehicles only and check the weather in advance; access to the castle will most likely be blocked by winter snow until early May. For location of Kaleybar see map, page 156.

Where to stay and eat

Anza Hotel (14 rooms) Off Farmandari St, Kaleybar; ☎ 0427 4224202–10; e anza. hotel@yahoo.com, anza.hotel@gmail.com. An unexpectedly glitzy & modern hotel with spacious rooms & bathrooms. The staff, however, seem a little unsure as to their purpose there; be patient. **$$**

Kollywood Hotel (12 rooms) Farmandari St, Kaleybar; ☎ 0427 4224200, 4223838; e info@ kollywood.ir; www.kollywood.ir. A family-run hotel with simple, pristine dormitory-style accommodation & restaurant. You absolutely have to stay here, if simply to spend some time in the company of charismatic Rahim Bolandi, locally well-known film director (thus the hotel's name) & his wife Hamida, who will make you feel welcome in no time. Try their homemade tea from mountain herbs. Website in Persian only. Recommended. **$**

TABRIZ *Telephone code 0411*

Tabriz, said to have been founded by Khosrow Arshakid (Arsacid) of Armenia in c220, has been hit by earthquakes many times during its history, with those in 858CE and 1042 wiping out any structure from the pre-Islamic period. By the end of the 10th century it was such a prosperous trading centre that it was selected as the venue for the marriage celebrations of the Seljuk sultan Tughril Beg (d1063) and a daughter of the Baghdad caliph. It achieved the status of a 'royal' capital first with the Mongol Ilkhanid ruler Abaqa (r1265–81) and even then it had a reputation for business acumen as the city's traders rioted over the introduction of paper money to replace coinage. Abaqa's descendant Ghazan Khan (r1295–1304) kept Tabriz as his capital and ordered the building of the city walls and defences, the bazaars and an enormous mausoleum, spending a vast amount, but sadly nothing of this has remained. Moreover, Ghazan's conversion to Islam was marked by persecution of all non-Muslims in the region and within Tabriz itself all churches, synagogues and fire temples were razed to the ground.

From the mid 14th century, the city and the surrounding area came under the control of various warlords, until the Qara Qoyunlu tribal chiefs made Tabriz their capital from 1436–67, after which it came into the Aq Qoyunlu domain. For the early years of the Safavid regime it again had capital status, until hostilities with the Ottoman Empire became too close for comfort. (Tabriz was first occupied by Ottoman forces in 1514 and again in 1585.) A year after the 1721 earthquake, Russian forces invaded the region and attacked Tabriz, occupying the city 1826–28 until, under the terms of the 1828 Peace of Turkomanchay and the payment of a crippling war indemnity, it was returned to Qajar control. No wonder a distinct Russian influence still lingers in the city's architecture. In 1916 the Russian Tbilisi–Jolfa–Tabriz railway was completed, but any idea of re-taking Tabriz was postponed with the advent of the Bolshevik Revolution. As the Russians moved out, so Ottoman forces moved in until the frontiers with Turkey were finally settled. The city was reoccupied by Soviet forces in 1941, after Reza Shah was forced to abdicate by the Allies, and four years later the short-lived autonomous regime of the Democratic Party in Azerbaijan was set up by the Bolsheviks. In December 1946 the army of Mohammed Reza Shah, assisted by American personnel, took the city and all Bolshevik and communist elements were purged.

Tabrizi businessmen and manufacturers are still known throughout Iran for their commercial acumen, and the city has mainly (light) industry, specialising in food production.

Tabriz has historically been known as the cornerstone of the Constitutional Revolution and the most progressive city in Iran. It is also the birthplace of Grand Ayatollah Mohammed Kazem Shariatmadari, one of the strongest rivals to Khomeini and strong opponent of the post-revolutionary constitution that Khomeini had set to bring forward in the early 1980s. The city now has more than 1.5 million residents and is a major transit point on the movement of goods between Turkey and Iran. In fact, the motorway from Tabriz to Tehran is easily the busiest in the country.

GETTING THERE AND AROUND The **airport** in Tabriz is classed as international and there are services from Istanbul in Turkey as well as the Gulf States; there are also domestic services from Tehran and Mashhad with a number of different airlines depending on the day of the week. There are daily flight connections for a return fare of around £520 from London with Turkish Airlines. There are also regular **bus** and **train** services for Ankara, Istanbul, Armenia, Azerbaijan and Georgia. The Tehran–Tabriz railine was one of the first to be completed in Iran. Both rail (west of the city) and bus (south of the city) terminals are located outside the city centre, at least a ten-minute taxi ride from the bazaar area.

Tabriz is a vast city with hilly streets and you are strongly recommended to hire a taxi to move around. The historical part is relatively small and walkable, but the main park – El Goli – is not reachable on foot. Most sites are quite a distance apart and walking around may prove to be more of an inconvenience rather than a pleasure. Do consider taking **taxis** that charge around 50,000 rials for a single ride.

🏠 **WHERE TO STAY AND EAT** Tabriz hotels enjoy high season all year round thanks to Azerbaijanis coming here for medical treatment. Accommodation is thus priced accordingly. For location of listings see map opposite.

🏠 **El-Goli Pars Hotel** (180 rooms) El Goli St, in a park around 8km away from city centre; ☎3807820; www.pars-hotels.com. The best hotel available in Tabriz & the best of the Pars chain. Spacious rooms are decorated in good taste & come with excellent views, but you need to pay an extra 300,000 rials to have windows overlooking the park. Service is good & staff are polite & well-mannered. **$$$$**

🏠 **Shahryar International Hotel** (200 rooms) El Goli St; ☎3337812–18, 3291420–9; www. shahryar-hotel.com. This hotel – named after a renowned 20th-century poet – has a good range of facilities & several restaurants, as well as Turkish Airlines office on the ground floor. A little more central than El-Goli, but staff regrettably lack finesse. **$$$**

🏠 **Hotel Gostaresh** (130 rooms) Imam St, intersection with Azadi Bd; ☎3345021–4, 3366590–9; e info@gostaresh-hotel.com; www. gostaresh-hotel.com. Standard rooms with kitchenette are a little pricey. The building is a little run-down & the staff are slightly disparaging in their manner. **$$**

🏠 **Tabriz International** (130 rooms) Imam St; ☎3341081–9; f 3341080. Central with good-size clean & bright rooms & accommodating personnel. The lobby is a little crowded & has a somewhat disorientating layout, but the rest of the building is tranquil. **$$**

🏠 **Hotel Darya** (100 rooms) Rahahan St; ☎f 4459501–8. Very basic, near the railway station. Not all rooms are en suite & it is only recommended staying here if you are travelling on a tight budget & by train. **$**

🏠 **Iran Hotel** (54 rooms) Rahahan St, in front of Haft Tir Hospital & next to Darya Hotel; ☎4459515–16. Very similar to Hotel Darya in what it has to offer in terms of accommodation, albeit the staff are more friendly & considerate. **$**

✖ **Shahryar Traditional Restaurant** Saat Sq, Imam St; ☎5540057; ⏰ 12.00–15.00 & 19.00–24.00. Located in a restored bathhouse, it serves regional dishes. *Kofte tabrizi* traditional meatballs are recommended. $

WHAT TO SEE AND DO The extensive UNESCO World Heritage-listed bazaar, parts of which date from the 15th century, is arranged very compactly across two main roads, but otherwise Tabriz has a few historic monuments.

Arguably, the most famous monument in town is the **Arg** (Citadel) (*entrance from Imam St*) as it is locally known. In fact, only the massive walls remain of what was not a fort but the enormous four-*ivan* **Masjed-e Shah** (or Masjed-e Ali Shah), once smothered with tile panels. This structure of 1312–22 was the brainchild of a 14th-century vizier serving in Oljeitu's court (see page 173) who obviously wanted to build bigger and better than anyone else. Judging from the surviving height (26m) and thickness (10.5m) of the walls, it is thought the *ivan* leading to the prayer chamber stood about 66m high, with the vault springing starting around 24.5m, across a staggering span of almost 31m (wider than anything attempted in 14th-century Europe). Chronicles described the mosque as having a huge 285 x 228m marble-paved courtyard, surrounded by an alabaster-columned arcade and with an ablution pool so large that, two centuries later, Shah Ismail I would sail across it in a beautiful barge. Its minarets, probably soaring over 60m high, were said to have so impressed envoys from the Mamluk Court of Cairo that they influenced the design of those built in 1330 at the no longer extant Mosque of Amir Qarasunqur in Cairo.

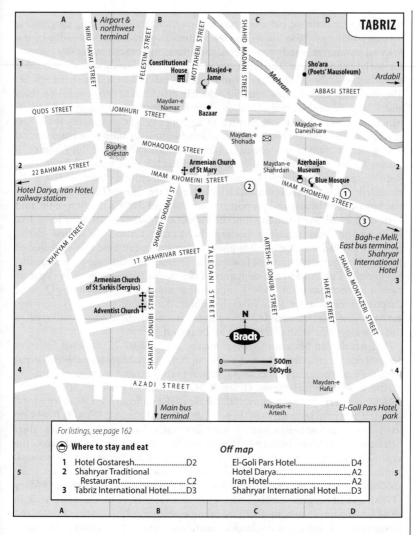

TABRIZ

Airport &
northwest
terminal

Ardabil

Hotel Darya, Iran Hotel,
railway station

Bagh-e Melli,
East bus terminal,
Shahryar
International
Hotel

Main bus
terminal

El-Goli Pars Hotel,
park

For listings, see page 162

Where to stay and eat

1 Hotel Gostaresh............................D2
2 Shahryar Traditional
   Restaurant...................................C2
3 Tabriz International Hotel.........D3

Off map

El-Goli Pars Hotel............................D4
Hotel Darya...A2
Iran Hotel..A2
Shahryar International Hotel.......D3

By the 17th century the mosque was in ruins, although there was enough cover for the Friday prayer still to be conducted. In 1809 the Qajar governor took over the building, turning it into a citadel (an earlier Arg built elsewhere under Ottoman occupation had been destroyed in 1603), with a defensive ditch. Even so, some original mosque tilework was seen *in situ* by the English envoy, Ker Porter, ten years later but shortly afterwards Tabriz fell to the Russians. The Arg's defences were finally dismantled in the late 19th century and by then not one tile panel remained.

Well worth the effort of a taxi drive and a short walk from the main road is the so-called **Blue Mosque** (Masjed-e Kabud) (*Imam Khomeini St; ⊕ 08.00–20.00, closed Fri afternoon; entry 100,000 rials*), known in Iran for centuries as the 'Turquoise of Islam' because of its tilework. This mosque was built on the orders of Saliha Khanum, the daughter of Jahan Shah, chief of the Qara Qoyunlu, or of his wife, Khatun Jan. It was finished in 1465, two years before Jahan Shah was killed in an Aq Qoyunlu ambush in 1467. A severe earthquake in 1776 caused some of the building to collapse, but an extensive and sympathetic rebuilding programme between 1950 and 1966 allows today's visitors to gain an accurate idea of the original layout, scale and proportions, and also to inspect the incredible 'mosaic' tilework inside and out. The main entrance portal still stands with its rich cable moulding and tiling, but otherwise much of the exterior façade has been rebuilt. This leads into a five-domed 'corridor' which in turn leads to two domed side aisles and a large central domed chamber (diameter 16m) supported by eight piers, which had internal staircases that led to an upper gallery. Essentially it is a fine example of the 'covered mosque' plan of nine domes, including the main central one, which is more usually found in early Ottoman architecture, for instance in Bursa, Turkey. But there's something else: behind the *qibla* wall and down a few steps there is another domed chamber, so the actual ground plan is similar to the so-called 'T-shaped' mosques of 15th-century Bursa (eg: 1414–20 Yeşil Cami), but function, emphasis and proportions are different. Only a fraction of the mid 15th-century tilework remains, but the impact is sensational, with the jewel-like intensity and depth of colour modern glazes rarely match. The second domed chamber behind was also at some point covered in cobalt blue tiles embellished with a gilded pattern, but only a few remain. The impact must have been dramatic, but perhaps lightened by the calm grey of the marble panelling with its elegantly carved inscriptions (Q26, 36, 48), some still *in situ*. The selection of the Quranic chapters is interesting: aside from describing the joys of paradise (suggesting, perhaps, that this was intended to be a tomb chamber), there is a clear allusion to the then large Christian community in the region.

The **Azerbaijan Museum** (*Imam Khomeini St;* ⊕ *08.00–17.00, closed Fri; entry 100,000 rials*) is located nearby with an ethnographic collection and archival material from the Constitutional period, for Tabriz was in the forefront of the movement.

The **Constitutional House** (Khaneh Mashrouteh) (*Motahhari St;* ⊕ *08.00– 17.00, closed Fri afternoon; entry 100,000 rials*), dating from 1868, built by a local architect and used by so many of the activists, is near the bazaar. Walking from here to the bazaar, at Saat Square look up at the distinctive clock tower. This is the Tabriz Municipality building, built in 1934 under supervision of German architects. The central **bazaar area** is interesting to walk around because, apart from the shops, some sections are 18th and 19th century and some even earlier. There are some six churches still in the locale, the oldest being the Armenian **Church of St Mary** (1785), and **St Sergius** (Sarkis), extensively renovated in 1845. Do take a walk in this central part of town, for there are innumerable early 20th-century houses and businesses with patterned brickwork decoration around the windows and doors, especially around Maydan-e Shahrdari, Tarbiat and Mahabeh streets. Not on a par with the Kharraqan tomb towers (see page 96) or the brick vaults of the Masjed-e Jame, Esfahan (see pages 130–3), maybe, but still worth a look.

Of interest to lovers of Persian poetry is the **Poets' Mausoleum** (Sho'ara) (*Said Hamzeh St, next to Imamzadeh Sayed Hamzeh;* ⊕ *08.00–20.00 except holidays; entry free*) where 400 famous Iranian poets are buried. Built in 1971, it is located in the Sorkhab historical district of Tabris in a park. Take a stroll down Seqqet Islam Street to look at some of the oldest houses in Tabriz.

In fine weather many Tabrizi families will spend the day in the central **Golestan Gardens National Park** (also known as Bagh-e Fajr), established in the 1930s, which incorporates over 53,000m², or they'll go 8km south of the city to the slightly larger **Bagh-e Melli Park** (known locally as El Goli, previously called Shah Goli) with its artificial lake, perhaps first constructed in the 15th century but definitely extended in the Safavid period.

SOUTH OF TABRIZ The historic troglodyte village of **Kandovan** is located 62km from Tabriz and 22km southeast from Osku, and offers a unique insight into traditional rock-house living in Iran. The geology of the area is similar to Cappadocia in Turkey and some of the houses here are more than 800 years old and are still inhabited. The village has a natural spring and pleasant rest areas by the river, as well as one of the most luxurious and expensive hotels in Iran. For location of Kandovan see map, page 156.

Where to stay

Laleh Kandovan International Rock Hotel (10 rooms) \0412 3230191–7; f 0412 3230190. The cave hotel is the only one of its kind in Iran & is designed & decorated to international standards, with luxurious spa bathrooms, underfloor heating & simple rooms with tribal rugs & Persian carpets. **$$$$**

NORTH OF TABRIZ

Travelling north takes one into the region once heavily populated by Armenian Christians. It was from here that Shah Abbas I took tens of thousands of Armenians to Esfahan in the 17th century to exploit their expertise in silk trading with European and Russian merchants, and it was to here that many 19th-century European and American missionaries came, hoping to introduce such Monophysite Christians into the Baptist, Methodist or other Protestant churches. In 1946–47 most of the Armenians were 'repatriated' into Soviet Armenia.

There are still some beautiful but austere Armenian churches surviving in this mountainous area, the most famous being St Stephanos in Jolfa, close to the Azerbaijan frontier, and the Qara Kelisa ('Black Church'), near Maku and the Turkish border.

The road to Jolfa goes through **Marand**, 70km from Tabriz, whose **Masjed-e Jame** (*Kashani St;* ⊕ *11.00–17.00*) was established in Seljuk times and then rebuilt in the 14th century; it has a splendid plaster *mihrab*. Some 10km further north is a caravanserai built around 1330 but badly damaged in the mid 19th century. It is another 55km or so to **Jolfa**. If you are going to explore the Armenian heritage of this area, you may contemplate staying here, but don't expect it to be overly comfortable. Try the **Jolfa Tourist Inn** (*23 rooms; Behesti Sq, Imam Khomeini St;* \ *0492 3022220, 3022824;* f *0492 3024825;* **$**) but be warned: not all rooms have private facilities.

From Jolfa, a further 16km west and 3km from Aras River, brings you to the UNESCO World Heritage Site of **St Stephanos** (⊕ *opening hours vary with the season, but best to arrive here between 10.00–15.00; at the approach to the church there is also an area with restaurants & cafés, but these are closed in winter & early spring; entry 100,000 rials*) named after the first Christian martyr (locally known as **Kelisa Darre Sham** after the name of the village formerly located here). A few years ago foreign visitors needed to obtain a letter from the Armenian cathedral authorities in Esfahan, or a gendermerie permit from Shah Abbasi, west of Jolfa, but this authorisation is no longer required. The monastery church is said to have been founded by St Bartholomew around 62CE, with the late 9th-century king of Armenia, Ashot, ordering its construction, but most of the present structure dates from the 16th century. The large church faces east with a long cloister along the north side, but surprisingly it does not possess the usual large *gavit* (where the congregation stood) seen in most medieval churches in the Armenian Republic. Instead, the layout bears a closer resemblance to 10th-century Armenian churches in present-day Turkey (eg: Ani and Akdamar), of a single nave form, with a tall belfry in the south wall. The exterior 'prismatic' tent-like dome (and the interior hemispherical one) in red and white stone, along with the *muqarnas* portal, date from the 16th century and the numerous stone carvings of saints and patriachs, especially on the drum, remind one of churches at Akdamar, which were decorated some 600 years earlier.

A few kilometres further west down by the Aras River, your eyes will catch the sight of **Nana Maryam Church**. It is not accessible, unfortunately, and you can only see it from the road. As it lies by the Aras free trade zone there is military presence in the area; be careful what you take pictures of.

A visit to another UNESCO World Heritage Site, **St Thaddeus** (Qara Kelisa) (⊕ *no set opening hours, your taxi driver will help you find the man with the key in the nearby village; entry 150,000 rials*), 45km from Maku, deep in the hills is also recommended, but take some refreshments with you as there is no tea house (or toilets) here. As with Jolfa, you could overnight at **Maku**, in a very pleasant and clean hotel with large rooms, **Maku Tourist Inn** (*30 rooms; Imam Khomeini St;* \ *0462 3223212;* f *0462 3223184;* **$**). However, most visitors make a day trip from Tabriz.

Nothing seems to have survived from the first church built here to fulfil the dream of St Gregory the Illuminator (see page 136) to commemorate the martyrdom of St Thaddeus, whose death (c68CE) was ordered by King Abgar of Edessa on revoking his brief conversion to Christianity. Part of the 10th-century church remains specifically in the area around the altar, to the right of which the saint is said to be interred, and the dome. The rest was destroyed by earthquakes in 1329 and in 1689, so most of the fortified church seen today dates from the rebuilding, with the exterior decoration added about two centuries later. Very few visitors come here except in the summer to celebrate the movable Feast of St Thaddeus (usually July) when pilgrims come and camp out. The guardian kindly allows people to explore the buildings (formerly refectory, kitchens, flour mill, stores and dormitories) around the huge courtyard, and to climb up to roof level to take photographs of the church façade. Why it is called the Black Church is a mystery. It is indeed very gloomy inside, with the austere walls covered in soot from the thousands of candles lit over the centuries, and the 10th-century eastern section is clad in dark tuff, but the exterior church walls are a wonderful creamy-yellow limestone, decorated with a lively narrow frieze running around the building, depicting scenes from the *Shahnameh* (see page 262) among which are musket-bearing hunters taking potshots at wild animals. There is a similarity to the highly carved exterior of the 10th-century church of Akdamar on Lake Van, Turkey, perhaps because of early close links to that diocese, and to the deeply worked decoration of the Ishak Pasha palace, Dogubayazit, eastern Turkey, which throughout the 18th century controlled the trade routes west to east. The Akdamar architectural details resemble Georgian church decoration, but the sombre interior of St Thaddeus is totally in the manner of the massive stone churches across the Caucasus in the Armenian Republic.

There are three other little churches nearby, all probably dating to the same period. The villages around here are mainly Kurdish, so the women dress in brightly coloured clothes rather than wearing dark *chadors* or *manteaux*.

Between Maku and the Turkish border crossing at Bazargan and just off the main road you will find the fine Qajar-period palace, **Baghcheh Juk** (⊕ *09.00–17.00 Tue–Sun; entry 100,000 rials*). It was built for a commander of Shah Mozafereddin (r1896–1907) and is surrounded with 11ha of gardens. The building exhibits a mixture of European and local styles and is embellished with plaster decoration, mirror work and painting.

In this region close to the frontiers with Turkey and the Caucasian republics, archaeologists have identified over 50 Urartian settlements, such as the 8th-century BCE citadel of **Sangar**, northwest of Maku, with its rock-cut chambers and steps cut from the bedrock. Perhaps you have visited Cavus Tappeh, east of Lake Van, Turkey; the stoneworking in that palace-citadel site and the presence of bichrome, recessed 'blind' windows have prompted more than one archaeologist to suggest an Urartian influence at Pasargadae and Naqsh-e Rostam (see pages 202–4 and 200–2).

The main road **south from Maku** passes many other Urartian sites, including the important **Bastam**, near Qara Ziyaeddin. This excavation site, 70km southeast from Maku and not far from Qara Kelisa on the old road, should not be confused with Bastam to the east of the Caspian (see pages 151–2). This one was the Urartian 'town' of Ruzu-Urutur, associated in the histories with the famous king, Rusa II (685–645BCE). The German archaeological team that worked here from 1968 until the late 1970s found the site extended over an area 850 x 400m, and something of the huge stone walls, once topped by mud-brick galleries and ramparts, may still

URARTU

Today, Mount Ararat forms the frontier between Turkey and the Republic of Armenia, but the kingdom of Urartu, or Ararat, is mentioned in Assyrian texts dating from 1275BCE and also in the Bible (Jeremiah 51:27; II Kings 19). European scholars became very interested in this civilisation after the decipherment of a lengthy cuneiform inscription from the citadel of Van, Turkey, in the 1840s, but it was almost a century later before serious archaeological investigations started in (then) Soviet Armenia, followed by British work around Van in the 1950s and in northwest Iran by German scholars in the late 1960s.

Urartian power grew during the reign of Sarduri (also spelt Sardusi) II, c760–735BCE, whose successful military expeditions were recorded in the Van text; from just one campaign his armies captured over 21,000 people, 1,600 horses, 16,500 cattle and nearly 40,000 sheep. Urartian merchants came to control the major trade routes across Anatolia and the Caucasus into the Mediterranean, as shown by finds of huge Urartian bronze cauldrons in excavations in France, Greece and Italy. Although increasingly threatened by the Assyrian Empire to the south, Rusa I (735–714BCE) undertook such major irrigation schemes that even Sargon II of Assyria grudgingly admitted he 'changed the entire surface of its unproductive region into meadowland and the fresh green grass of spring'. Much time and effort went into the construction of palace-citadels, carving down into the bedrock, and working ashlar stone blocks so accurately that a sheet of paper cannot be inserted between them. Attention was given to temple buildings to honour the Urartian pantheon of some 50 gods, dominated by three deities with their consorts, each requiring a daily sacrifice of at least six bulls and sheep: Khaldi the warrior 'father' god often depicted standing on a bull; the rain god Tesheba; and Shivini of the sun, always shown holding a winged disc.

After fending off Assyrian attacks, Urartu negotiated peace in 650BCE, which should have guaranteed its survival, but the 605BCE Battle of Carcemish marked the end of the great Assyrian Empire. Without this ally, the days of the Urartian kingdom were numbered. A Scythian attack from the north c590BCE and the rise of the Medians in the south dealt the final blows.

be seen. A citadel was constructed by the north gate from the 8th century BCE but then, possibly due to political instability after Rusa's death in 645BCE, it was dismantled in preference for a new defensive structure near the south gate, with stables, barracks and storerooms. Above was the palace area with the remains of a 14m² tower temple (somewhat like those at Pasargadae and Naqsh-e Rostam) dedicated to the god Khaldi, and a large audience hall with 14 column bases. Banqueting was obviously important in court life and one chamber served as a meat store judging from the cuneiform tablets listing the stock found there. The site continued to be occupied in Median and Achaemenid times until the 13th century when, recognising its strategic importance on the trade routes, an Armenian warlord built a fortress here. The Mongol invasion put paid to his activities and the site was abandoned to the nasty local black spiders.

Khoy, 136km north of Orumiyeh, is probably the best place for restaurants if you are continuing your journey southwest towards Orumiyeh. A Safavid gateway, an unusual Armenian church and the Shams Tabrizi minaret are the only reminders of Khoy's turbulent past, when it was a walled town belonging to local warlords. Shams Tabrizi (d1248) was a Sufi mystic who intoduced Mawlana Jalal ud-Din, otherwise known as Rumi, to Islamic mysticism. After some years with Rumi, Shams left him and came to Khoy where he died and was buried; the minaret, with its protruding rams horns, is associated with the tomb. On the southern outskirts of Salmas (also given as Shahpur), a Manchester University (UK) archaeological team undertook excavations from 1968–78 at Butan Tappeh, near **Haftavan**. Apart from signs of settlement since the 4th century BCE and buildings and artefacts from around 2000BCE, remains of an Urartian citadel were found. Occupation continued during Median and Achaemenid periods, continuing up to Sassanid times when the settlement was walled. Some 30km south on the main road, those with sharp eyesight might see a **Sassanid relief** of Ardashir and his son, later Shapur I, recording his victories in this region. Above are the remains of the Urartian fort of **Qaleh Vaseriyeh**.

ORUMIYEH AND BEYOND (TO THE SOUTH AND SOUTHEAST)

ORUMIYEH Formerly known as Rezaiyeh, Orumiyeh or Urmia (altitude 1,330m; population 670,000) was a city of Christians in the 19th century, mainly Nestorian and Armenian Monophysite Orthodox along with Western missionaries. However, its ancient history bears a tradition that it was the birthplace of Zarathustra, founder of Zoroastrianism. Its geographical position led later to its being contested territory, passing at various times between Kurdish and Turkish tribes before being controlled by the Safavids in the 17th century. The first Qajar ruler of Iran, Agha Mohammed Khan, was crowned there in 1795.

Getting there There are a few daily direct **flights** from/to Tehran with journey time 1½ hours, and daily long-distance **buses** to and from Esfahan (one-way bus journey, leaving Esfahan at 16.00 and arriving in Orumiyeh at around 10.00 the following morning, costs around 140,000 rials; double that for VIP buses). The university in Orumiyeh is popular with students from Esfahan and you are advised to book your ticket in advance as buses depart full most of the time.

Where to stay and eat Hotel accommodation is limited as so few foreign visitors stay here – apart from Turkish truck drivers – and so advance reservation is strongly advised. For location of listings see map opposite.

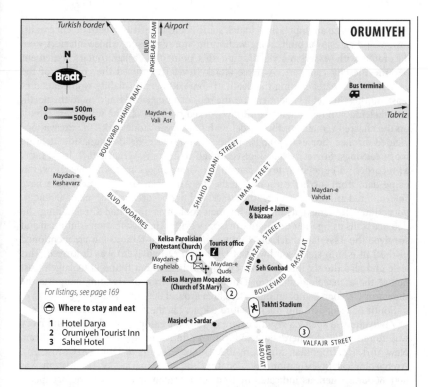

🏠 **Orumiyeh Tourist Inn** (74 rooms) Kashani St; ☎0441 2223080; f 0441 2223202. Clean & acceptable, althought a little old-fashioned in décor & furniture. The lobby is spacious, but the choice of colour in the coffee shop is somewhat surprising. **$$**

🏠 **Sahel Hotel** (66 rooms) Valfajr St, opposite the TV station; ☎0441 3369970; f 0441 3363261.

Slightly away from the centre, but by the river & parks, offers reasonable accommodation and a restaurant, albeit a little overpriced for this small town. **$$**

🏠 **Hotel Darya** (60 rooms) Tarzi St/Imam St; ☎0441 2229945, 2229564; f 0441 2223451. Central & quiet, this pleasant hotel is friendly & not too shabby. **$**

What to see and do The **Masjed-e Jame**, perhaps built in the Seljuk period with a domed prayer chamber over the remains of a Zoroastrian fire temple, has a beautiful plaster *mihrab* dated to 1277, one of the earliest post-Mongol architectural remains. On the southwestern outskirts is the **Seh Gonbad** tomb tower, standing 9m high; built in 1184, it has some fine plasterwork and *muqarnas* details. In the centre, a modern church (1960s) of **St Mary** (**Kelisa Maryam Moqaddas**), replacing a much older shrine, marks, according to local belief, the burial place of one of the Three Wise Men. Not unlike the nearby **Protestant church** churches here do not have regular opening hours and remain closed to members outside the local community.

SOUTH OF ORUMIYEH The road south from Orumiyeh passes several important archaeological sites such as **Tappeh Hasanlu** (probably Manaai in the Assyrian texts) about 5km north of **Naqadeh**. The main excavations carried out during 1956–74 by Pennsylvania University (US) and then the Metropolitan Museum of Art showed that Hasanlu was settled from the 6th millennium BCE. Carbon-14 tests in the 1980s suggested that the main period of occupation was c1350–1150BCE.

Around 1000BCE an impressive citadel, some 200m in diameter with defence walls, towers and gates, was built, along with multi-storey housing whose interiors were decorated with Assyrian-style tiles. At this point the earlier (outer) settlement became the city cemetery. A fierce attack (level III) caused the collapse of the eastern citadel gate, causing the death of some 40 people, mainly women, and at least another 30 met a violent end on the roof of a porticoed building to the north, one skeleton still holding a beautifully worked gold vessel. The walls were rebuilt on the charred remains of the citadel with Cyclopean stonework. The excavations yielded bronze horse trappings, helmets and mace heads alongside delicate ivory carvings. Soviet archaeologists argued that the Assyrian attack in 714BCE, as recorded in cuneiform texts, caused the Urartian occupants to flee. However, using data from further carbon-14 tests, the American archaeological team have since offered another sequence: the attack and fire occured earlier (c850–800BCE), perpetrated by Urartian forces, who then took over the citadel, rebuilding the defence walls using their distinctive masonry skills. This occupation continued and survived the Assyrian attack of 714BCE, when the then-famous temple mentioned in the Kul-e Shin stele (southwest of Ushnuyeh/Oshnaviyeh) was destroyed. This stele and also the six-line Urartian cuneiform inscription found at Qalatgeh (just before the archaeological site of Dinkh Tappeh), west of Hasanlu, supports the theory of Urartian campaigning in this area around 800BCE.

South of Naqadeh and 40km before Saqqez, is the famous archaeological site of **Ziwiyeh** (also spelt Zawiyeh), where in 1947 a treasure of gold, silver and ivory was found by a shepherd boy; today these finds are divided between Tehran, New York (Metropolitan Museum of Art) and Cincinnati, Ohio (Art Museum). Archaeological investigation revealed that the main period of occupation was 800–600BCE when, as indicated by finds of Scythian arrowheads, the occupants fled their citadel. Illicit digging has since destroyed much of the site, but an Iranian archaeological team restarted work in 1994.

SOUTHEAST OF ORUMIYEH Much more is visible at the World Heritage Site of **Takht-e Soleyman** (🕐 *no opening hours, but best visited early in the morning; entry 150,000 rials*), which can be approached from Miyanoab by travelling around 200km southeast to Takab (pronounced as Tekab). The road twists and turns, but the surface is good and there is little traffic along this route. You can overnight in Takab in the simple but clean **Hotel Ranji** (*27 rooms; Enghelab St; ☎ 0482 522 3179; $*) and take a taxi to Takht-e Soleyman 40km away in the morning. A return taxi trip will cost around 350,000 rials. Alternatively you could drive from Zanjan (see page 172). Its location is dramatic, up in the mountains at over 2,600m with a large volcanic lake in the centre. The depth of the lake remains unknown. Exercise caution: a couple of years ago a young man drowned here. The asphalt road leads right up to the north entrance. The enclosing walls, built in early Sassanid (or possibly Parthian) times to honour this place, is home to one of the four important sacred fires of Zoroastrianism, the Adur Gushnasp or Royal Warrior Fire (see box, page 173). Its reputation may even date from the Achaemenid period, as there is evidence of occupation around the small dead volcano rising 100m, 3km northwest of the walled site. You can easily climb it for beautiful views over the area and the Takht-e Soleyman complex. It is thought that the Sassanid shahs always came here after their investiture at Ctesiphon, Iraq, to pay their respects to this fire, and there are the remains of at least two fire temples along the processional way from the north gate to the lakeshore: the Hasht Taq with its eight arches of fine stonework to the east, and the main temple marked by four huge brick piers facing the lake.

A small shrine lies behind a columned hall, 'Khosrow's Palace', immediately to the west of the main temple.

The German archaeologists working here 1959–77 discovered that, during the last quarter of the 13th century, the largely abandoned site measuring some 550m x 400m was reoccupied as a summer palace by the Ilkhanid ruler, Abaqa, when the main temple building was used for a royal reception hall and the columned hall for private rooms. At this time certain alterations (eg: blind niche forms) were made to the structure of the large west *ivan*. A south gate was also constructed and arcading erected all around the lake. A 12-sided hall, perhaps inspired by the nomadic felt domed tent, is located just south of the two western octagonal buildings on the northwest corner of the arcading. This, it is suggested, possibly functioned as a storehouse where the wife of Abaqa kept the royal treasures for her grandson, the later Ghazan Khan. Numerous splendid examples of 13th-century tiles (which must have decorated the walls), remains of marble flooring and – an important find for Islamic architectural history – a carved stone slab detailing a *muqarnas* pattern composition were all found. Here finally was proof of how medieval masons calculated and devised the intricate arrangements of various three-dimensional architectural elements. Remains of kilns and a pottery workshop were unearthed behind the main north palace hall, to the northeast.

If time allows, a short diversion to the southeastern corner of Lake Orumiyeh should be made. This is where you'll find **Maragha**, famous in the late medieval histories for its 'state-of-the-art' astronomical observatory, constructed on the order of Hulagu (r1256–65), grandson of Genghis Khan, the scourge of all Asia. Nothing remains of this Star House, as it was called, but it was from here that the scientist Naser al-Din Tusi (d1274) solved the seeming incompatibility between Ptolemy's planetary model and Aristotelian theory about planetary movement, which was then taken up and developed by Copernicus. The city still possesses three fine tomb towers. The **Gonbad-e Surkh** (also known as Gonbad-e Qermez), built in 1148 for a local prince, a certain Abd al-Aziz, has been described by one scholar as 'the most beautiful example of brickwork known'. We are not convinced. The square brick mausoleum rises from a stone base and then the brick patterns begin, 'contained' within two blind niche frames on three of the four external sides, including the foliated Kufic inscription over the door and over the blind niche frames. Twelve sizes of interlocking brick units were used, with some glazed strips inserted for highlights. The original, eight-sided tent-like roof has gone, but the octagonal drum and the inner dome remain, though much restored.

Slightly to the north is the 12-sided blue **Gonbad-e Kabud** of 1197. Standing 14.5m high, it has long been associated with Hulagu as local people thought the tomb was built to honour either his mother or his daughter, though there is nothing to prove this assumption. It has lost its original roof but retains much of its very ornate exterior decoration consisting of intersecting turquoise blue 'strap' brickwork of hexagons and six-pointed stars. Just under the exterior cornice is an inscription band (Q2:255) while inside around the dome is another (Q67:1): 'Blessed be He to whom all sovereignty belongs; He has power over all things', while downstairs in the crypt there is another inscription (Q55:26–7) alluding to death and paradise. Nearby is an anonymous tomb tower, circular in plan, built around 1330 and known locally as **Koyburj**, looking more like a defence tower than a mausoleum. Also in the northern outskirts is a 14th-century tomb tower known as the **Gonbad-e Ghaffariyeh**, which in its decorative scheme includes a heraldic device of two polo sticks, indicating the bearer was Master of the Royal Polo; he was Amir Qara Sunghur, who worked for both the Egyptian Mamluk regime and then the Ilkhanids, as a local governor at a time when Maragha was known as 'Little Damascus'.

It is known that Hulagu built a palace (or at least reception rooms) on the largest island in **Lake Orumiyeh**, Jazir-e Kabudi (formerly Shah's island), and indeed he and his successor are said to have been buried here. Like the water of Takht-e Soleyman, this lake, over 120km long and 25km wide, has a high mineral content which, although good for rheumatism, means fish and other wildlife are limited. The whole region was made a conservation area before the Islamic Revolution in order to protect the thousands of migratory birds, such as pelicans, flamingos and wild duck but the Department of Environment, which is responsible for such matters, is publicly acknowledged to be one of the most underfunded government sections.

ZANJAN Capital (population 389,000) of the province of the same name, the town was allegedly founded in Sassanid times. Its main claims to fame are its close associations with the Baha'i faith in 1851 and today its proximity to the World Heritage Site of Soltaniyeh. Its handicraft traditions are unfortunately in decline but it is still known for its distinctive, colourful, animal-covered *sumak* (warp-wrapped) rugs and its thriving bazaar. Zanjan is just off the motorway that runs between Tehran and Tabriz and is only 340km from the Iranian capital. Admittedly not a town known for historic monuments, it still has the richly tiled **Khanum Mosque** built in 1905 on the order of Jamileh Khanum, the daughter of a local tribal chief.

Getting there The best connections are by the long-distance **bus** network, but **trains** *en route* to Tabriz and places beyond also call here although the timetables may not always be very convenient. If you are travelling here from Takab, around 226km away, the picturesque route lies through Bijar and takes around four hours by bus. There are two daily buses from Takab to Tehran (10.00 and 14.00) that pass by Zanjan as well. The one-way ticket fare is around 50,000 rials. For location of Zanjan see map, page 156.

 **Where to stay and eat**

Zanjan Grand Hotel (48 rooms) Baseej Sq; ☏0241 7288190–5; f 0241 7288199. Facilities are quite good & there is a restaurant. Rooms have Wi-Fi, but the hotel is a distance from the centre & a little pricey. Foreign tourists are required to pay in US$. **$$**

Tourist Inn (24 rooms) 1km from the Raskhshooy historic complex & the old bazaar; ☏0241 7271910. Located in a green & quiet area. The rooms are adequate & en suite. **$**

SOLTANIYEH

Getting there and away Zanjan is without doubt the most convenient place from which to visit Soltaniyeh, but you will have to hire a taxi. Alternatively, you can arrive here by bus bound for Tehran and get off on the motoway at the turn for Soltaniyeh, 10km south. From here you would have to walk or hitch a ride towards the centre of the town, but this is not recommended. From Soltaniyeh, it is about 100km to Qazvin (see pages 91–6) to the southeast.

What to see and do If there is an opportunity to visit this 14th-century World Heritage Site, the **Mausoleum of Oljeitu** (also known as Gonbad-e Soltanieyh) (⏱ 08.00–17.00; entry 150,000 rials), take it even though you'll be met by a wall of scaffolding. Constructed in just 11 years (1306–17), this huge mausoleum proudly stands on a fertile plain on the old road to Zanjan with a backdrop of purple-blue mountains and is clearly visible from the surrounding area. Its turquoise-blue dome is the earliest existing example of the double-shelled dome in Iran. Nothing else remains of the 14th-century walled town although recent excavations have revealed foundations of a mosque, *madrasas*, *khanaqeh*, palace pavilions and other buildings, all part of Oljeitu's plan to make this small town his capital.

Oljeitu (r1304–17) was a descendant of Genghis Khan. Historical records state that after sending architect-engineers to survey the vast palace audience hall of the Sassanid shahs at Ctesiphon, Iraq, he employed 10,000 men to lay the foundations of this tomb and the surrounding structures, as well as 500 carpenters and 5,000 marble-masons. His idea, it was said, was not to build a funerary monument for himself, but rather to bring the remains of Hossein, the third imam, from Karbala to this place; he had already procured a lock of the Prophet's hair. Oljeitu had been slow to accept Islam, preferring at first Buddhism and then Christianity, the faith of his mother, before adopting Shi'a Islam; he finally (c1313) decided on Sunni Islam. It was at this point, so some argue, that he announced that the brick mausoleum was to be his own memorial.

THE SACRED FIRE

The idea that Zoroastrians are 'fire worshippers' is technically incorrect but traditionally great reverence has always been shown to this, surely the most important 'gift' to humanity. Prayer, for instance, is always made towards a fire or other light source such as a lamp, the sun or the moon. To devout Zoroastrians even domestic fires should be treated with care, their embers taken to the temple every third day for cleansing of any accidental pollution by adding cold embers from the temple fires. Every ninth day fires of blacksmiths had to be cleansed nine times before those embers could be taken to the temple for such renewal.

It is held that there were four great sacred fires, each later associated with a social class. The Adur Gushnasp fire originated near or in Lake Orumiyeh in the lands of the Medes. In around 400CE it was transported to Takht-e Soleyman where it became firmly associated with royalty and warriors. The second, the Adur Barzea fire of the agricultural class, was known to exist in the 3rd century CE in Parthian lands, perhaps in a major temple complex between Shahrud and Sabzevar or further east on Mount Revand, near Borzinan. The Zoroastrian priests understood the third Adur Farnbag fire to be their special fire, which had been brought into southwest Iran from central Asia. To protect its survival during the Arab Muslim conquests, this fire was divided into two, one being kept in Fasa and the other transported to Sharifabad, north of Yazd. The fourth fire, Adur Karkuy, is associated with Kuh-e Khwaja, near Lake Hamun in Sistan, where the oldest known fire temple in Iran stands.

The Zoroastrian priest is the only person to attend the temple fire, during which he wears a white cotton robe and mouth-mask to prevent his breath polluting the sacred flames, which are fed five times a day. In ancient times a *barsom* bundle of pomegranate twigs was offered to the flame but today a bunch of brass or silver wire replace this. However, fires at shrines (eg: at Chak Chak, see page 237) are tended by laymen because they are used only in a minor role, such as cooking the special *dron* – unleavened cakes – used for certain Zoroastrian services.

Its size and scale are immense. The huge egg-shaped dome (interior diameter 26m) rests on eight internal piers but their massive size is disguised by their soaring, tapering height, high arches and a rhythmic arrangement of connecting galleries. Pretend that the abandoned forest of scaffolding (which largely creates the gloom) is just a figment of your imagination. From the floor to the apex of the dome is a staggering 52m. And viewing from the outside, forget the untidy brick infills and imagine continuous open galleries all around. When completed, this once turquoise-tiled dome, framed with eight slender 'minarets' around the roof, must have appeared to be magically balanced on a graceful network of arches and vaults. Indeed, certain Italian scholars are sure it influenced the work of Brunelleschi, the Renaissance architect, and in particular his Santa Maria del Fiore in Florence. Inside, two different layers of decoration are apparent here and there: glazed brick strapwork and also patterned plasterwork, perhaps visual evidence of Oljeitu's change of faith from Shi'a to Sunni Islam. Access to the crypt, housing three tombs, lies to the south.

An internal staircase near the entrance leads up to the galleries, where the 'openness' and inner proportions of the building become much more apparent. In places, the intricate decoration of these galleries still survives, but for the best work another narrow and steep staircase to the exterior galleries has to be tackled. Here you'll find the richest, most exquisitely carved and painted plasterwork on the vaulted ceilings – quite mouth-wateringly superb. There are also wonderful views over the countryside, despite the higgledy-piggledy housing at ground level.

The curse of scaffolding continues all around outside. It's as if officialdom feels its work is done once scaffolding is erected. Funding then dries up, the labour force is removed and rusting iron is left as today's contribution to Iran's architectural heritage. But a short walk around the building means you can see some of the original tilework, along with some scattered 14th-century ceramic shards found during excavating work.

In the town, around 1km away diagonally opposite the tomb, there is another historic site of interest. The blue-domed, but much smaller **Molana Hassan Kashi Tomb**, built in honour of one of the poets and gnostics of the Oljeitu court. The building of the tomb itself is closed, but the site with the mountains as a backdrop is spectacular.

8

Shiraz and Around

SHIRAZ   *Telephone code 0711*

Shiraz (altitude 1,600m, 910km south of Tehran), with its long and rich history, friendliness and the laid-back attitude of its inhabitants, is one of the nicest and most welcoming cities in Iran. As the Iranian saying goes, 'Esfahan for the head, but Shiraz for the heart'. Despite dramatic growth in the last two decades to a population of around 1.5 million and the resultant traffic nightmare, Shiraz has miraculously managed to preserve the relaxed atmosphere of a provincial town, despite the daily assault on both its infrastructure and the nerves of its inhabitants. It has an excellent university, which annually floods the city with an appealing wave of young, educated and friendly Iranians, who provide the real energy driving this fine city. Many foreign visitors are surprised that Shiraz itself has so few surviving historical monuments when there are such archaeological treasures in the neighbouring countryside, but earthquakes over the centuries have taken a heavy toll, along with the less excusable 'urban development plans' of the Pahlavis (for whom Shiraz was an unfortunate target of their dubious vision and largesse).

Shiraz is a place to stroll in fine gardens, see the Azadi Park Ferris wheel and roundabouts crowded with excited schoolgirls, *chadors* flying in the breeze. Both in the bazaar and in the major shrine, Shah Cheragh, you may glimpse the darker complexions of men and women from various tribal clans such as the Qashqai, the Qash Kuli and the Khamseh, visiting the city for provisions, clothing and jewellery. Older men often wear a beige, hemispherical felt cap with a tall upturned rim, while women cover their immense skirts and glittering lurex tabards with black *chadors*; both caps and skirts are made in the bazaar. Many of these families still retain a migratory lifestyle, travelling with goats and sheep from Hamadan to Shiraz and the south in late autumn, returning in the spring, but some are now at least partially settled in outlying villages. If you wish to see the rugs and carpets associated with such clans, the Shiraz bazaar is a good place to look, but prices are no longer low and quality is variable since such work was highly acclaimed in the West during the 1976 World of Islam exhibitions in the UK.

HISTORY Shiraz was once the route from Susa to Persepolis and there are tentative whispers in the archaeological record of an Elamite settlement on the site of modern Shiraz, with further occupation during the Achaemenid dynasty (reputedly the site of a depository of Achaemenid Imperial records), but settlement here truly prospered from the early Islamic era, burgeoning quickly into a grand walled city. Predictable rivalries between local warlords during the 11th and 12th centuries created significant problems, but Shiraz miraculously

175

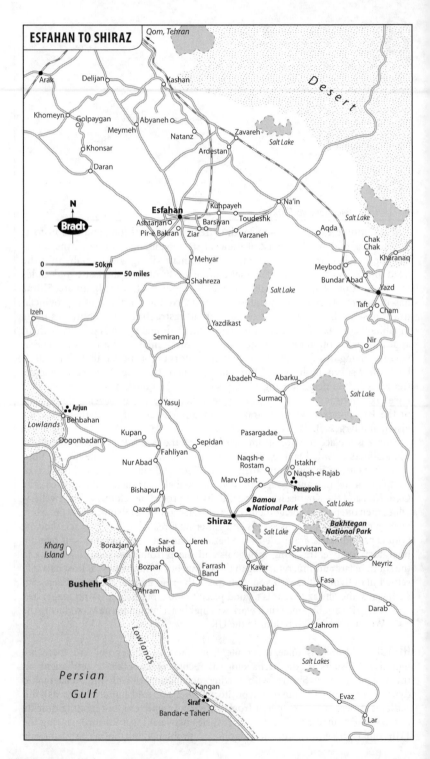

ESFAHAN TO SHIRAZ

Qom, Tehran

Desert

Arak
Delijan
Kashan

Khomeyn
Golpaygan
Abyaneh
Zavareh

Meymeh
Natanz
Salt Lake

Khonsar
Ardestan

Daran

N
Bradt

Kuhpayeh
Na'in

Esfahan
Toudeshk
Salt Lake

Ashtarjan
Barsiyan
Aqda

Pir-e Bakran
Ziar
Varzaneh
Chak Chak

0   50km
Mehyar
Meybod
Kharanaq

0   50 miles
Shahreza
Bundar Abad
Yazd

Izeh
Salt Lake
Taft
Cham

Yazdikast

Semiran
Nir

Abadeh
Abarku

Surmaq
Salt Lake

Yasuj

Arjun
Pasargadae

Behbahan
Lowlands

Kupan
Sepidan
Naqsh-e Rostam
Istakhr

Dogonbadan
Fahliyan
Naqsh-e Rajab

Nur Abad
Marv Dasht
Persepolis

Bishapur
Bamou National Park

Qazerun
Shiraz
Salt Lakes

Kharg Island
Borazjan
Sar-e Mashhad
Jereh
Salt Lake
Bakhtegan National Park

Bozpar
Sarvistan
Neyriz

Bushehr
Farrash Band
Kavar
Fasa

Ahram
Firuzabad

Darab

Jahrom

Persian Gulf
Lowlands
Salt Lakes

Kangan
Evaz

Siraf
Bandar-e Taheri
Lar

escaped severe damage from the Mongol armies by a tactical surrender. This successful tactic was again adopted when the city was confronted by the armies of Timur Leng in 1395, and such foresightedness by the city elders was rewarded with significant investment and prosperity under Leng's grandson's governorship. But good times never last forever, and in 1668 severe flooding – almost impossible to comprehend when glimpsing the almost permanently dry bed of the River Khoshk (meaning 'dry' in Persian) running through the centre of the city – brought death and outbreaks of plague. Shiraz's traumatised citizens had barely recovered from this disaster when Afghan rebels, bent on destroying the remnants of Safavid authority, set about massacring the population with gusto in 1725. However, order and stability brought to the city through the rule of Karim Khan Zand (d1779, and still remembered with great affection today) and his descendants meant that Shiraz regained its former prosperity as the Zand capital for some 20 years in the second half of the 18th century. Yet even those days of tolerance were sadly short-lived; 15% of the population were Jewish in the early 19th century, but few Jews remain today. Shiraz was also the home of Baha'ism in Iran (see page 29), but mass executions of members of the community in 1852, followed by the forced exile of the leader, sadly denuded Shiraz's rich cultural garden of one of its most intriguing blooms.

Today the city is still the best place in Iran to smell beautiful Shiraz roses, buy perfume and locally distilled rose water, but thanks to the 1979 revolution, it's no longer possible to enjoy the world-famous Shirazi wine grape, except as fruit – unless, that is, you are fortunate enough to be invited to a party by enterprising local medical students, and try a surprisingly passable home-brewed hooch.

GETTING THERE AND AROUND There are regular **flights** from major Iranian cities and abroad; Turkish Airlines have five weekly flights, although fewer regular flights out of season. A return flight from London to Shiraz with Turkish Airlines takes under four hours and another three hours to Shiraz, and costs around £500. Shiraz is connected by numerous intercity **bus** links. The six-hour bus journey from Esfahan costs 80,000 rials and double that amount for a VIP bus. Do note that **taxis** at the central bus station must be ordered and paid for at the taxi kiosk. Expect to pay up to 50,000 rials for a taxi to the city centre. The reasonably fast and reliable **railway** first linked Shiraz to Esfahan and Tehran in 2009. Train tickets are usually twice the price of bus service, and take longer. In 2013 the Iranian government signed a deal with a Portuguese construction firm to build a new railway line from Shiraz to Ahvaz as well as two new highways: Shiraz–Bushehr and Shiraz–Sadra.

You can arrange **taxi** trips around and outside the city at your hotel, from a taxi driver directly or from any of the guides listed below. Do keep in mind, however, that trips with English-speaking guides will most likely be double the price of an (honest) taxi driver.

LOCAL GUIDES An independent guide in Shiraz who can easily organise a car for the day (or even a helicopter trip costing around US$2,000 per hour) is **Aria Gojerati** (m *0917 3135938*; e *ariagojerati@yahoo.com*). A highly recommended female guide is **Azadeh Khademi** (m *0917 1052191*; e *tbs-azadehkhademi@ hotmail.com*), who is fluent in both French and English. **Hossein Soltani** (m *0917 7131517*; e *h-soltani-n@hotmail.com*) has worked with international travellers for many years and is also recommended as a knowledgeable and friendly guide to the area. **Arash Sadeghzadeh** (m *0917 3171652*; Facebook: *Trip To Persia*) has worked for French multi-national Danone and is bilingual in French and English and very knowledgeable. He can easily organise great itineraries for tours either around Iran, or around Shiraz and the surrounding region.

TOUR OPERATORS For those interested in trekking, camping and nomadic migrations, contact either **Arash Sadeghzadeh** (see page 177) or **Gasht Tour** (*Shahid Faqihi St;* \ *0711 2301900;* e *info@gashttour.com; or via Dr Harry McQuillan in New Zealand:* e *zagros@ts.co.nz*). With prior notice the Gasht Tour can also organise tours by English-speaking wildlife and birdwatching specialists. Another friendly, professional and splendidly organised local travel agency (with their own horses and ski lodge) specialising in all manner of outdoor activities, including skiing, mountain biking, horse treks, hiking, mountain and rock climbing are **Iran Sightseeing Tours** (*2nd Flr, 3rd Alley, Shahid Faqihi St, off Zand St;* \ *2355939;* e *info@iransightseeing.com; www.iransightseeing.com*), who come highly recommended. The largest local agency in Shiraz is **Pars Tours** (*Zand St;* \ *2223163; www.key2persia.com*), which, while very competitive in travel offerings and price, does have a somewhat mixed reputation for customer care.

TOURIST INFORMATION If you are simply looking for some friendly advice and information about the sites in Shiraz and around, contact the main **tourist office**, located in a small kiosk outside Arg-e Karim Khan Zand. The man behind the desk, the most helpful and courteous Sayyed Mahmoud Hamidi (e *dandelion_2004@ yahoo.com*), will willingly give you the maps you need and suggest itineraries.

 WHERE TO STAY For location of listings see map, page 180.

Luxury

🏠 **Chamran Grand Hotel** (150+ rooms) Chamran St; 6271218; e info@chamranhotel. com; www.hotelchamran.com. The Chamran is a new & glittering addition to the Shiraz hotel scene, & while the public areas are fairly grand, in a Western 5-star manner, the rooms themselves can be somewhat unkempt & the AC unpredictable. However, beds are large & comfortable. A decent top-floor restaurant with spectacular views across the city, & a very good gym & spa almost make up for the distance from Shiraz's city centre. **$$$$**

Above average

🏠 **Hotel Homa** (200+ rooms) Meshkinfam St, nr Azadi Park; \ 2288000–12; e shiraz@ homahotels.com; www.homahotels.com. The Homa (in its pre-revolutionary incarnation as the Hilton) was *the* hotel to stay in when visiting Shiraz, under the Pahlavis. Beautiful gardens, which double as an alfresco dining area during good weather, are to the rear of the hotel, overlooking Azadi Park. Hotel-wide Wi-Fi is both fast & works on every floor. Also coffee shops, a sauna, tennis courts (with lessons available: check

out Shiraz's 'ladies who lunch' popping in for their lunchtime lessons), a barber shop & 3 restaurants. **$$$**

🏠 **Niayesh Boutique Hotel** (18 rooms) 10 Shahzadeh Jamaili Lane; \ 2233622; www. key2persia.com. The Niayesh is part owned by the Pars Tourist Agency & is Shiraz's only traditional-style hotel. Developed from a converted house in the old quarter, the original dwelling has been expanded with a purpose-built annex, & offers both backpacker-style dormitories & individual rooms. The hotel can be tricky to locate, but is signposted from Imamzadeh Bibi Dokhtar. Make sure to book well in advance as it has increasingly grown in popularity. **$$$**

🏠 **Pars International Hotel** (150+ rooms) Zand St; \ 2332255; e info@ parsinternationalhotel.com; www.pars-international-hotel.com. Rooms here are bland but comfortable, & unlike the Homa, the management are politically conservative, so BBC is not available in the rooms. However, hotel staff are both efficient & friendly, & the Pars makes a good 2nd-best choice to the Homa. **$$$**

Mid-range

🏠 **Hotel Aryo Barzan** (50+ rooms) Roudaki St; ☎2247182–4; e info@aryohotel.com; www. aryohotel.com. Rooms are kept pristine, & the Aryo Barzan is a popular choice with businessmen from the Gulf States & group tours, so it is recommended to book ahead. Some rooms are let down by tiny bathrooms. **$$**

🏠 **Hotel Eram** (100+ rooms) Zand St; ☎2300814; e info@eramhotel.com; www. eramhotel.com. With friendly staff & solid service, the Eram is a reliably good-value choice: just be sure to ask for rooms in the 'new' wing. **$$**

🏠 **Park Saadi Hotel** (50 rooms) Hafez St, across from the Jahan Nama Gdn; ☎2274901, 2285881; e info@parksaadihotel.com; www.parksaadihotel. com. A laid-back modern hotel with large clean rooms; suites come with spacious balconies facing the Jahan Nama Garden. The location is excellent & staff are friendly. **$**

🏠 **Parsian Hotel** (61 rooms) Roudaki St, 2 blocks down & across the road from Hotel Aryo Barzan; ☎2330000, 2331000; e shiraz@ parsianhotel.com. Very central with a somewhat 1980s feel. The rooms are pristine & the savvy staff will willingly offer a discount. Regrettably, Wi-Fi is in the lobby only & not reliable. **$$**

Basic

🏠 **Kakh Apartment Hotel** (24 apts of differing sizes) 36 Alley, opposite Anvari St; ☎2340763–6; e www.hotelkakh.com. Built during the last 5 years, this apt hotel offers AC, satellite TV, decent kitchens, big bathrooms (with Western-style toilets) & Wi-Fi available in the lobby. **$$–$**

🏠 **Anvari Hotel** (20+ rooms) Anvari St; ☎2337591, 2300970. One of the few & perhaps the best budget option in town offering a variety of rooms with different kinds of facilities. Enquire in advance if you have a preference. Popular with budget travellers & backpackers. The rooms are standard & simple, but you get value for money here. Very central. **$**

WHERE TO EAT Below are a few good suggestions, but you may also want to consider **Sufi One** (*Afif Abad Bd;* ☎6263877, 6275881; **$$**), **Sufi Two** (*Zargar Bd/ Motahhari Bd;* ☎6261573; **$$**) and **Shatar Abbas One** (*Khahshenasi St;* ☎2271612, 2270914; **$$**). For location of listings see map, page 180.

✖ **Haft Khan Restaurant Complex** 17th Alley, Jomhuri Bd, nr the Quran Gate; ☎2270000, 2280000; e info@haftkhanco.com; www. haftkhanco.com; ⊕ all day, except for the traditional Iranian restaurant in the basement, which is open for dinner from 19.00. Opened in 2011, this Persian & international cuisine 5-storey complex is popular with the Shirazian middle class. The décor is fancy & modern. Tables by the window or in the outdoor seating area have great views. Food is excellent & so is the service. **$$**

✖ **Saray-e Mehr Restaurant** Saray-e Moushir Bazaar, signposted at the entrance to Rouhollah Bazaar, when exiting the south wing of the Vakil Bazaar; ⊕ Vakil Bazaar opening hours. Lovely traditional restaurant serving good *dizzi*. **$**

✖ **Shapouri Restaurant** Shapouri Mansion, Anvari St; ⊕ ground floor tea house: all day, restaurant: 12:00–15.00 & 19.00–24.00. Wonderful traditional restaurant on the 1st floor of this protected mansion (up until 2008 used as a private home) surrounded by a garden (*entry to garden 10,000 rials*). **$**

✖ **Sharzeh Traditional Restaurant** Vakil St, in the basement of the shopping centre across the square from the Vakil Bazaar entrance; ⊕ 12.00– 15.00 & 19.00–24.00. Popular Shirazi restaurant, serving excellent local *kalam polo* (cabbage with rice) & famous Shirazi salad, which you must try. There is often live traditional music. **$**

🍵 **Foroug Café** Hafez St, across from Jahan Nama Gdn; ☎2278585. Modern & hip coffee shop, full of young Shirazis chatting away. **$**

🍵 **Old Bazaar Tea house** To the right when leaving Vakil Bazaar in the direction of the Baba Khan *madrasa*. This old & nameless tea house with outdoor tables is a popular local meeting place & serves tea with *qalian* for both men & women alike. **$**

WHAT TO SEE AND DO Entering Shiraz from the north (Esfahan) or northeast (Persepolis), the first visible monument is the **Quran Gate** (Darvazeh-e Quran),

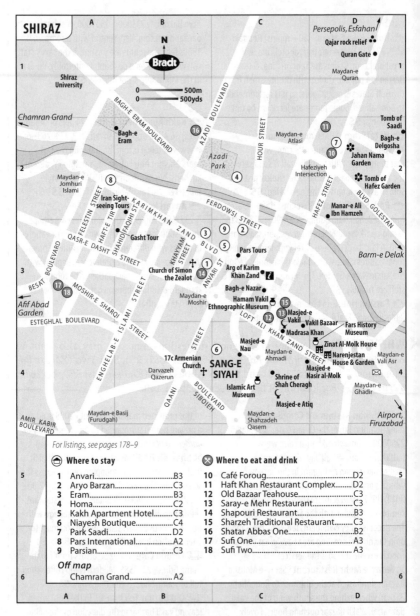

SHIRAZ

Persepolis, Esfahan
Qajar rock relief ••
Quran Gate •

N

Bradt

0 ————— 500m
0 ————— 500yds

Shiraz University

Chamran Grand

Bagh-e Eram

BAGH-E ERAM BOULEVARD

AZADI BOULEVARD

HOUR STREET

Maydan-e Quran

Maydan-e Atlasi

Tomb of Saadi

Bagh-e Delgosha

Jahan Nama Garden

Azadi Park

Hafeziyeh Intersection

Tomb of Hafez Garden

HAFEZ STREET

BLVD GOLESTAN

Maydan-e Jomhuri Islami

Iran Sight-seeing Tours

KARIMKHAN ZAND BLVD

FERDOWSI STREET

Manar-e Ali Ibn Hamzeh

FELESTIN STREET

HAFT-E TIR

SHAHID FAQIHI ST

Gasht Tour

QASR-E DASHT STREET

KHAYYAM STREET

Pars Tours

Barm-e Delak

BESAT BOULEVARD

MOSHIR-E SHARQI STREET

Church of Simon the Zealot

ANVARI ST

Arg of Karim Khan Zand

Afif Abad Garden

ESTEGHLAL BOULEVARD

ENGHELAB-E ISLAMI STREET

Maydan-e Moshir

Bagh-e Nazar

Hamam Vakil
Ethnographic Museum

LOFT ALI KHAN ZAND STREET

Masjed-e Vakil

Vakil Bazaar

Fars History Museum

Madrasa Khan

Zinat Al-Molk House

Masjed-e Nau

17c Armenian Church

SANG-E SIYAH

Darvazeh Qazerun

QAANI STREET

BOULEVARD SIBOIEN

Maydan-e Ahmadi

Masjed-e Nasir al-Molk

Narenjestan House & Garden

Maydan-e Vali Asr

Islamic Art Museum

Shrine of Shah Cheragh

Maydan-e Ghadir

AMIR KABIR BOULEVARD

Maydan-e Basij (Furudgah)

Masjed-e Atiq

Maydan-e Shahzadeh Qasem

Airport, Firuzabad

For listings, see pages 178–9

🛏 **Where to stay**

1	Anvari	B3
2	Aryo Barzan	C3
3	Eram	B3
4	Homa	C2
5	Kakh Apartment Hotel	C3
6	Niayesh Boutique	C4
7	Park Saadi	D2
8	Pars International	A2
9	Parsian	C3

Off map
Chamran Grand A2

✕ **Where to eat and drink**

10	Café Foroug	D2
11	Haft Khan Restaurant Complex	D2
12	Old Bazaar Teahouse	C3
13	Saray-e Mehr Restaurant	C3
14	Shapouri Restaurant	B3
15	Sharzeh Traditional Restaurant	C3
16	Shatar Abbas One	B2
17	Sufi One	A3
18	Sufi Two	A3

originally built in the 10th century in the city walls. It was a benign Karim Khan Zand who ordered a Quran to be placed in the gatehouse so that travellers would be blessed as they left for the open road. In the 1950s increased traffic dictated a new road and the demolition of the original gate, whereupon a pious Shirazi citizen paid for it to be rebuilt in its present location.

Halfway up the hillside, above the gate, is the tomb of one of Shiraz's famous poets, Khvaju Kermani (d1352), and one of the eight known **Qajar rock-reliefs**, c1824, showing Fath Ali Shah on a throne dais supported by two angels, with two of his numerous sons in attendance. The hillsides have been landscaped with terraces, water cascades, the odd kiosk and a tea house, 'the Khajou', while many Iranian families camp out here, in *Tardis*-like tiny tents. While offering unparalleled views of the city lights at night, the traffic noise and pollution can be overwhelming and the views are not enhanced by the *Thunderbirds*-style 'Shiraz Grand Hotel 5 Star', which clings to the upper rock face and has been due to open 'soon', for the last five years.

Nearby, down from an 18th-century bridge, is the **Manar-e Ali Ibn Hamzeh** (⊕ *dawn to dusk*), probably constructed in the 9th century BCE to honour one of the innumerable relatives of the fourth imam. Its two minarets, exterior dome, entrance vestibule and courtyard rooms, however, date from the late 18th and 19th centuries. If (as is sadly likely) a visit to the Shah Cheragh shrine (see page 186) is not possible during your stay, this shrine possesses similar extensive Qajar mirror work on its interior walls and vaults. There is one entrance into the shrine sanctuary (women are asked to don a *chador*) and as the *qibla* wall is immediately to the right on entry, one should move quickly to one or other side to minimise disruption to anyone praying (although you will see many worshippers happily chatting to family and friends on their mobile phones).

One of Shiraz's jewels is the beautiful **Bagh-e Eram** (*Eram Bd;* ⊕ *08.00–17.00; entry 150,000 rials*), a garden named after one of the four gardens of paradise described in the Quran. The garden and grand house were originally created by a chief of the Qashqai clan around 1823, with the house later rebuilt by Hajji Mohammed Hasan Mi'mar, following his successful pilgrimage to Mecca, to include fine reception rooms, an orangery, stables and pavilion. Both garden and buildings were confiscated in 1953 and given to the late shah for his private use; this was when the original mud-brick enclosing walls were torn down and replaced by metal fencing. Later, Shiraz University was permitted to establish a botanical garden. After the fall of the Pahlavi regime it was returned to the Qashqai family, but then handed over in its entirety to the university, and today houses the **Law Faculty**. Some small areas of the lower garden are out of bounds, as the garden doubles as the Shiraz municipal nursery (where all those ornamental cabbages, decorating roundabouts, are propagated), but otherwise visitors have freedom to range and explore the rock gardens, traditional Chahar Bagh (primary four-quarter garden) and rose garden, which was entirely replanted in 2010. Almost all the specimens of plants and trees are labelled with their Farsi, Latin and common English names, and this is a popular location for parties of young schoolchildren larking about on day trips, older university students quietly flirting away from prying eyes and Shirazis simply escaping the noise and traffic of the city.

Entry into the main rooms of the actual house itself is sadly not permitted (except for the bathrooms and a small tea house, which is usually closed anyway), but the exterior is photogenic enough, with stunning late 19th-century tiling under the roof. The central main panel shows the legendary Sassanid king, Khosrow II, coming across the Armenian princess Shirin bathing (see box, page 103) while to the right is the Quranic/biblical story describing how the beauty of the prophet Yusuf (Joseph) caused the ladies in Pharaoh's court to gasp in thrilled delight and cut their fingers, distracted, while peeling fruit. Above is depicted the famous meeting of King Soleyman (Solomon) and the Queen of Sheba, Bilqis, with all of the protagonists depicted in a curious melange of 'traditional' and 19th-century clothing.

There are three other major gardens in Shiraz although two are 20th-century constructions, owing little to the classic Persian garden layout, but pleasant places to visit nonetheless, and perfect for trying to envision the Shiraz that so entranced 18th-century European visitors. One garden surrounds the **Tomb of Hafeziah**

(Aramgah-e Hafeziah) (*Golestan Bd;* ⏰ *08.00–19.00; entry 150,000 rials*), the great Shirazi poet (1326–c1390) who wrote lyrical poems about love and the beloved, which are understood to be imbued with deep Sufi mystical meaning; his epithet 'Hafez' is an honorific bestowed because of his memorising of the Quran by heart as a small child. Because of Hafez's Sufi associations, one or two dervishes still come here on Wednesdays and Thursdays, while families and visitors enjoy the small garden and take tea in the ugly modern tea house in the far right corner (sadly the lovely 18th-century *chaykhaneh* closed in a 2008 dispute with the government over taxation and smoking, and hasn't yet reopened). Karim Khan Zand ordered a suitable tomb to be built in 1773 to honour this most famous son of Shiraz, but that was torn down in 1938 to erect the present octagonal kiosk. Further embellishments were made for the 1971 Pahlavi extravaganza. The bookshop at the far end of the terrace often has a good selection of history and art books in English, as well as maps and postcards, but the English translations of Hafez on sale mostly render the beauty of Hafez's poetry into something opaque and incomprehensible. Before leaving, why not have your fortune told? For a small sum, a copy of Hafez's best-known anthology, the *Divan*, will be opened randomly by a canary or budgerigar, which plucks out a card inscribed with couplets; the proffered verses offer a portent to the future.

In an easterly direction, some 10km further on, is **Barm-e Delak**, where there are two battered Sassanid rock reliefs 6m above ground level. The larger one depicts a shah offering a flower to a lady, perhaps the divine Anahita, although some scholars think this portrays Shah Narseh (d301) making a peace offering to the consort of either Bahram II or III. The other panel definitely shows Bahram II raising his hand, with the (infamous) high priest Kartir lurking off to one side.

The **Tomb of Saadi** (*Bustan Bd;* ⏰ *07.30–20.00; entry 150,000 rials*) is set in similar grounds near to the Hafez garden. Born around 1185 or 1208 (or possibly 1215) and dying around 1292, Saadi fled the Mongol invasions, travelling on to Baghdad and then Syria, where he was imprisoned by Crusaders. Ransomed by an Aleppan man, he felt duty-bound to marry the man's daughter, a deeply unhappy decision he later commemorated in a couplet: 'A bad wife comes with a good man to dwell / She soon converts his earthly heaven to hell.'

Saadi's two major poetic works are the *Golestan*, a series of anecdotes composed in 1257, and the *Bustan* (1258) in which he wittily and humorously expounded his thoughts on justice and government. One of his most famous verses – a version of which adorns the United Nations building in New York – has prompted comparisons with the 16th–17th-century English poet, John Donne:

> The sons of man are limbs of one another,
> Created of the same stuff, and none other.
> One limb by turn of time and fate distressed,
> The others feel its pain and cannot rest.
> Who unperturbed another's grief can scan
> Is no more worthy of the name of man.

Again, like the tomb of Hafez, the mausoleum of Saadi is quite an elegant product of 1950s modernist architecture, replacing an earlier 18th-century Zand structure. To the left of the tomb is an intriguing underground structure, which now contains a *chaykhaneh* and is often packed with visitors. The main attractions are the deep, subterranean spring, into which visitors throw coins for good luck, and the strange, grey fish that haunt the depths, coming up to nibble on crumbs. The spring also provides water to the garden surrounding the tomb and, traditionally, the surrounding houses too. The most interesting element of this structure is that when the spring and *qanat* (underground water channel) were dredged during the 1950s, Sassanian pottery and coins were discovered, hinting at its use as a possible cultic site, probably dedicated to Anahita. As with early Christian sites in Europe, often constructed over pagan religious sites, many pre-Islamic sites in Iran show a similar and shadowy continuity with earlier traditions, here in the modern visitor 'dedicating' coins to the well and the fish (both associated with Anahita herself.)

Also suggested is a visit to the **Bagh-e Delgosha** (Garden of Heart's Ease) (*entry 150,000*) nearby. The extensive grounds broadly retain their 1820 layout (actually originally set out in 1790), although the water channels have been relined with tacky modern turquoise tiles and the original mud-brick walls were destroyed in 2000 for new railings. In the centre stands a pavilion from late Zand or early Qajar times, in a dramatic setting, with surrounding hills and tall cypresses. Together with the Bagh-e Eram, this garden and a small one within the Arg of Karim Khan Zand (see pages 183–4) are the best examples of the 'classical' Persian garden outside Mahan (see pages 245–6) and Kashan (see pages 109–14).

The city centre The citadel, **Arg-e Karim Khan Zand** (*Shohada Sq;* ⊕ *08.00– 17.00; entry 150,000 rials*), was constructed around 1767 and is perhaps the best-preserved 18th-century example of urban fortification in Iran. Used from the

THE PERSIAN GARDEN

From Achaemenid and Sassanid times, rulers and princes established formal gardens with stone watercourses feeding pools, shaded terraces and pavilions. This was the essential plan which spread across the Muslim world to Spain and north Africa and eastwards to north India, for this is the image of the heavenly paradise as described in the Quran (Q55:45ff). In the 'classical' Persian garden, mud-brick walls kept the desert out while providing support for climbing plants and shade from the fierce midday sun. The English visitor, Thomas Herbert, in 1628 described the Shirazi gardens as:

Safeguarded with walls fourteen feet high and four feet thick; and which from their spaciousness and plenty of trees resemble groves or wildernesses ... they abound in lofty pyramidic cypresses, broad-spreading chenars, tough elm, straight ash, knotty pines, fragrant mastics, kingly oaks, sweet myrtles, useful maples ... also flowers rare to the eye, sweet to the smell, and useful in physic.

To Persian poets the cypress was like a young Muslim man, evergreen and enduring in his faith, while the chenar tree with its open five-fingered leaves was the prayer leader for all plants in the garden. Around the wall were planted climbing roses, whose very fragrance came from a bead of perspiration falling from the Prophet Mohammad's brow, jasmine and pomegranates. Fruit trees such as cherries (whose scented blossom was as short-lived as a woman's beauty), oranges, limes, apples and quinces were also placed by the walls or in raised beds divided by straight water channels in which fish, ducks and swans swam. Or the beds were planted with sweet-smelling herbs, or spring bulbs such as hyacinths, whose heavy scent reminded the poets of the beloved's hair, narcissi ('red-eyed' like a weeping lover) and red tulips (willingly shedding blood for the beloved). All would lower their heads in worship on hearing the nightingale's song (Quranic verses) on the evening breeze.

1930s as a police station and prison, access was long impossible, but in autumn 1999 the primary courtyard and surrounding rooms were opened to visitors and now regularly house temporary art and photographic exhibitions, such as a display of early 20th-century photographs of Shiraz in 2011. Four 15m round towers with good brick patterning mark the corners of the enclosure joined by 12m-high walls which, in Zand times, surrounded an audience hall, barracks, bathhouse and a garden with two pools. When a Qajar prince used the Arg as his official governor's residence, further building and decoration were undertaken. Over the main entrance is a huge tiled panel depicting an episode from the *Shahnameh* in which the famous Persian warrior, Rostam, fights the white Deev (demon or devil).

The entry vestibule leads into the main Zand court. A notice in charming, broken English lures you on, and it's a very pleasant walk around the central, four-garden layout (note the original stone water channels in the paving.) Restoration work means it takes but little effort to imagine colourful 18th-century public audiences held under the painted *talar* verandas, with waterpipes and tea prepared with hot coals from the numerous fireplaces. A suite of rooms that once housed the Cultural Heritage Organisation is now a museum of daily life of the period, complete with atrocious waxwork dummies. Restorers from the organisation still regularly bring work from their offices at the rear of the Arg into the garden itself, and are very happy to chat with visitors.

Outside, across the street is the small octagonal reception pavilion of Karim Khan Zand, **Bagh-e Nazar** (*entry 100,000 rials, inclusive of a visit to Pars Museum, see below*). Set in a small garden gloriously smothered in bougainvillea and roses, it offers another peaceful haven away from Shiraz's traffic and crowds. At its centre is an octagonal pavilion, home to the small **Pars Museum** (⊕ *08.00–12.00 & 14.00–17.30*), which houses a small collection of mainly 18th- and 19th-century items. Most of its original interior is intact and the tiled panels outside are mainly contemporary with the building. Karim Khan must have loved this place, as it was chosen as his mausoleum. However, he was not allowed to rest in peace: Agha Mohammed Qajar (not particularly renowned for his generosity of spirit) ordered the remains to be exhumed and sent to Tehran, where they were reburied in the Golestan Palace, so that every time the Qajar shah and his ministers crossed the threshold they trod on Karim Khan. Reza Shah Pahlavi stopped this practice in 1925, allowing the Zand family to reinter his unfortunate remains.

Bazaar-e Vakil (⊕ *usually 08.00–20.00 Sat–Thu*) is within walking distance of the Arg and within five minutes' walk of the entrance to Bagh-e Nazar. As the name suggests, its construction formed part of the extensive building programme undertaken by Karim Khan, so-called *vakil* (regent) to the last Safavids. The bazaar maintains much of its late 18th-century character with a northeast–southwest orientation (the direction of Mecca) laid out about a century earlier. Originally, it was one long street with four large caravanserais to accommodate merchants, but in the 20th century a main road was constructed across the street and two of the four caravanserais were demolished in an unfortunate Pahlavi city modernising scheme. Rents from the bazaar and its *hamam* endowed the **Masjed-e Vakil** (⊕ *08.00–12.00 & 14.00–17.00; entry 15,000 rials*), constructed around 1773 and for many years out of bounds to foreign tourists. It retains a sense of intimacy despite its large size and is organised on the two-*ivan* plan. Forty-eight stumpy stone columns, each carved in a barley-sugar spiral, mark the sanctuary area, producing a space vaguely reminiscent of Durham Cathedral. The original *mihrab* of 1634, which suggested that an earlier mosque had been demolished, is no longer in place, but the 18th-century, 14-stepped *minbar* cut from one huge block of marble, is still standing.

Some idea of the tile decoration inside can be imagined from the exterior panels. Purists may raise eyebrows at the flamboyant flower motifs and the colourful pastel palette but our spirits soar at such cheerful ornateness. Not all the tiles are original, as some restoration was carried out in 1828 and later years.

Next door towards the main road is the bathhouse, converted in 2001 into a tea house and restaurant but then closed again by the authorities. It now functions as the **Hamam Vakil Ethnographic Museum** (⊕ *08.00–20.00; entry 100,000 rials*).

Exiting the bazaar by the carpet quarter, turning right and then right again, leads to a truly charming mosque, the **Masjed-e Nasir al-Molk** (⊕ *08.00–14.00 & 15.30–19.00; entry 30,000 rials*), which feels like a personal and secret discovery when chanced upon. It's a two-*ivan* mosque built 1876–87 by Mohammed Hassan, with a covered arcade on the left (facing the sanctuary) and the winter mosque on the right. The entry vestibule is smothered in painted tiles (not *cuerda seca* as sometimes described) of floral ornaments framing small pictures of landscapes clearly inspired by Russian sketches. The winter prayer hall is interesting as it has stone cable-spiral columns very similar to those of the Vakil Mosque, and most of the vividly coloured window glass dates from the 19th century. Morning is the best time for photography.

To the right before reaching the main street stands what was **Nasir al-Molk's house** (⊕ *08.00–18.00; entry 100,000 rials*). The mirror work on the ground-floor reception rooms is pure 19th century, as are the painted ceilings upstairs, decorated with an assortment of coyly smiling ladies, all deliciously camp and over the top. The house is often closed to the public, but a good local guide such as Azadeh Khademi or Arash Sadeghzadeh (see page 177) can easily arrange access.

Back to the main road, and nearby on the other side and set back a little, is the **Madrasa Khan**. The four-*ivan* theological college is still a teaching institute, training young men, including many Shi'a Afghan Hazara, to become imams and jurists. The building was originally a warehouse, as the name suggests, built in 1615 by Allahverdi Khan and his son Imam Kholi Khan, although most of its extensive tiling scheme dates from an 1833 restoration.

If you enjoyed the excesses of the Nasir al-Molk house (or if it was closed), return to the main street (Lotf Ali Khan Zand) and continue (to the left, if coming from the *madrasa*, or right from the house) away from the main bazaar. On the *madrasa* side of the road there are two large 19th-century houses behind massive brick walls.

The second is the **Orangery** (Narenjestan) (*Lotf Ali Khan Zand St;* ⊕ *07.30–18.00; entry 150,000 rials*), home of the famous Asia Institute, organised by the American Iranologist Arthur Upham Pope during the 1960s and '70s. The house was built in the late 1870s by Mohammed Reza and Ibrahim Qavam al-Molk, a former mayor and tax agent of Shiraz, as their public reception rooms, connected by a tunnel to the house next door, which functioned as the *anderun* or private quarters. A vestibule leads into a small walled garden, essentially 19th century in character, with tiled panels of attendants bearing platters of fruits. The house itself is sparsely furnished but the mirrors and floor tiles, the latter decorated to look like ikat fabrics, especially on the ground floor and *talar*, are decoration enough, with crude imitations of Persepolis reliefs decorating the lower exterior wall. A small Museum of Antique Objects has been opened in the basement.

The first, which has only recently opened to the public, is the **Zinat al-Molk House** (⊕ *07.30–18.00; entry 200,000 rials*) (which some people would swear was the Nasir al-Molk House and guide you accordingly). It was used as a home for Qavam al-Molk's close family only and was connected to the orangery by an underground passageway. Walking along the same alley brings you to the **Fars**

History Museum (*entry 100,000 rials*), **Fars Coins Museum** and **Fars Textile Museum**; all signposted.

Most strangers to the city, whatever their nationality, aspire to visit the **Mausoleum of Shah Cheragh** (*due to construction work the site entrance lies through the Shah Cheragh Bazaar (King of the Lamp); ⊕ 24hrs; entry 10,000 rials + 50,000 rials deposit + 10,000 rials rental fee for essential* chador *hire from one of the sellers at the entrance; no photography inside*). From early October 2002, after a noisy and disruptive visit by a foreign group, non-Muslims were not allowed entry even into the courtyard, but at the time of writing foreigners are occasionally admitted to the courtyard, although not to the shrine itself. The most popular shrine is the large one to the right after entering the courtyard, which commemorates the brother of the eighth Imam Reza, Sayyid Amir Ahmad, while the tomb of another brother, Sayyid Mir Mohammed, is situated further down on the left. Sayyid Amir Ahmad came to Shiraz in 808CE and died here in 835CE. Only a *mihrab* remains from the mausoleum and *madrasa* built to honour him in the 1340s by the mother of the then local ruler, as the shrine was largely rebuilt in 1506, then extensively repaired after an earthquake in 1588. Its local reputation was such that Nader Shah Afshar, despite being a Sunni Muslim, ordered further repair work in 1729, and Karim Khan Zand added further repairs in 1765. What is seen today is essentially 19th century, especially the mirror work smothering the interior, the silver doors and tilework, but the exterior dome is a 1959 fantasy, and the minaret dates from around 1970. If entry is possible, note that men enter the shrine from the far left while women access on the right.

Across the courtyard to the left is the mausoleum to Shah Cheragh's brother, which has retained more of its 16th-century structure, but the decoration is again predominately Qajar in date. For some undefined reason, this tomb always has fewer visitors, as does the mausoleum of a third brother, Sayyid Ala al-Din, situated in the southwest of the city. This is also a 16th-century structure on an earlier 14th-century building, but extensively repaired and covered with mirror work in the 19th century.

The gate to its far right leads into the Qashqai bazaar or to the Masjed-e Nasir al-Molk. Nearby are two mosques, much repaired after the 1852 earthquake. The **Masjed-e Nau** (meaning 'new mosque', referring to its status as the new Jame mosque) is also known as the Atabak Mosque after its patron, the military governor (*atabeg*) of Shiraz, Sa'd Ibn Zangi. To mark his sick child's miraculous recovery, he had this mosque, possibly with the largest courtyard (220 x 100m) in Iran, built on the site of his palace in 1201. The mosque was extensively repaired in Safavid times and then practically reconstructed after 1852. It now acts as the Friday mosque, so entry on Fridays is restricted from noon. Masjed-e Nau is considered to be the second historically most important mosque in Shiraz, after Masjed-e Atiq (see below). Masjed-e Vakil is the third most important historically (see page 184).

Some 300m southeast is the **Masjed-e Atiq** (⊕ *irregularly*), which functioned as the Masjed-e Jame until the Islamic Revolution. Nothing remains of the original structure of 894CE, and recently the little free-standing building in the courtyard, thought to date from 1351, has been reassessed. This is the Beit al-Mashaf (or the Khodakhaneh (God's house), echoing the shape of the Ka'ba in Mecca, and which once housed the mosque's Qurans and other manuscripts. Its tiled portico inscription gives the 1351 foundation date, but recent conservation work has revealed that its present appearance is largely a result of an extensive post-1935 repair programme. Originally the complex had a *madrasa*, two hostels for visiting scholars, a reading room and hospital, but its dilapidated state persuaded Shah Abbas I in 1567 to rebuild in this present four-*ivan* layout, with large sections of the west and north sides reconstructed 50 years later. This was also when the main avenue of the bazaar was constructed along the processional way used by the Safavid and then Zand rulers riding from their residences for the Friday prayer. Such occasions offered one of the few regular times when the public were certain of seeing the ruler, and Islamic history is dotted by assassination attempts during the Friday procession: two 20th-century victims were King Feisal of Iraq and King Abdullah I of Jordan.

The **Islamic Art Museum** (*Hazrati St;* ⊕ *08.30–13.30 & 16.30–19.30; entry 10,000 rials*), cosily housed in a Qajar-period residence, is right across the road from the old Sang-e Siyah (Black Stone) district, named after the large 600-year-old black stone in the courtyard of the **Scientist Sibuvey House**, located herein. The gate to the district lies opposite the bus stop and the first site you walk past is **Imamzadeh Bibi Khadija** (known as Bibi Dokhtar, b760–786AH), then old **Saadat House** and **Masjed-e Moushir**, across the road from the Armenian church.

There are still Christians, Jews and Zoroastrians living in Shiraz but community numbers have shrunk dramatically during the last three decades. Access to the **Armenian church**, built and decorated in the reign of the Safavid shah, Abbas II (d1666), in the eastern section of Qaani Street, in the Sare Jouye Aramaneh district of the city, is permitted only with prior authorisation from the local Ershad (guidance) office in Shiraz through one of the guides listed at the start of the chapter (see page 177). But the new **Church of Simon the Zealot** (Kelisa-e Moghaddas-e Shamun-e Qaur) in Nou Baher Lane, off Zand Street, is open to all-comers on Sundays; according to a local tradition, Simon was martyred in Iran. Close by is one of several **synagogues** in the city, and Shiraz also has a **fire temple** (permission to visit must again be obtained from the local Ershad office). Few will admit to knowing the whereabouts of the original house of the Bab, the founder of the Baha'i movement (see page 29), but Canadian sources say it is located near Beit al-Mahdi, Shahid Dastgheyb Street, 100m from Shah Cheragh shrine. Please exercise great care in who you ask for directions, especially in the currently febrile political atmosphere.

Slightly less central is the **Afif Abad Garden** (*Afif Abad;* ⊕ *08.00–18.00; entry 100,000 rials*) with a military museum inside. The garden itself is lovely and is less touristy than other places in town, but it is the guns displayed here that you really come to see.

AROUND SHIRAZ

Most visitors stay in Shiraz in order to visit Sassanid Bishapur and Firuzabad, and most importantly the Achaemenid palace complex of Persepolis – situated in the west, south and northeast respectively, some way from the city. To visit all three will entail a minimum three-night stay, and even then this leaves little time for exploring Shiraz itself. Furthermore, there are some skiing opportunities around Shiraz and located 80km northeast is Sepidan, home to **Pooladkaf Ski Resort**, where you can stay overnight (☏ *6353243–4, hotel reservation 2247182;* m *091 74111197–8;* **$$**).

A taxi to go to either Bishapur or Firuzabad and return to Shiraz will cost US$40, and slightly more in the 'tourist' season. Alternatively, you will need to use public transport, which will take longer.

BISHAPUR The historical city of Bishapur (*125km west of Shiraz;* ⊕ *07.30–19.30; entry 150,000 rials*) lies off the Qazerun road, which passes through some dramatic scenery, climbing up to and then through the 'Old Woman' Gorge. Other than Qazerun there is no place to buy lunch in this area, so take the bulk of a picnic with you, and buy fresh bread *en route*. With a very early start it should be possible to incorporate a short visit to the bird sanctuary at Lake Parisan (formerly Famur), if you are there during the spring or autumn migrating seasons. The road is asphalted but there is little shade. This diversion takes you past a small bridge, Pol-e Abgineh, and a Qajar rock-relief of 1829, depicting the prince-governor conquering a lion. This commemorated the reopening of the road in 1824, after a severe earthquake. The prince, a grandson of Shah Fath Ali Shah, had to flee to England in 1834 after his father's unsuccessful attempt to seize the throne on the shah's death. Also in this area is the Safavid caravanserai of Mian Kotal, for many years a police post but now open for general exploration and scrambling around.

Getting there There is no direct bus service from Shiraz. If travelling by public transport, take a bus (*40,000 rials*) from Amir Kabir bus station to Qazerun and from there take a taxi to Bishapur, 20km away. A one-way taxi journey will cost around 100,000 rials, but you should negotiate a return fare as the historical site is on the outskirts of the town and taxis here are few.

What to see and do Bishapur was a **palace-town complex**, built in 266CE (according to dedicatory column inscriptions) on a Hellenistic–Roman grid system rather than the circular plan traditionally favoured by the Parthians and early Sassanids. The city was the creation of Shapur I, using Roman prisoners of war. There was a decade of archaeological work here before World War II, carried out by the French, and then from 1968 by the Iranian Archaeological Service, but these excavations involved only 3% of a site that probably housed over 50,000 townspeople. It is best to visit these ruins first, remembering to take a torch. Then have a picnic by the river, looking at the low reliefs either side of the gorge.

On entering the site, there are Sassanid walls surviving up to about 3m high with solid round towers, but at some point one in three was demolished, perhaps contributing to its capture by the Arab armies around 637CE. The place has a rather desolate air as it was stripped bare of all its sculptures, mosaics, decorative plaster and other treasures; most went to the Louvre, Paris, with a few pieces going to Tehran's National Museum. Before visiting the main buildings of the excavated site, head towards the museum building (closed at present) from where you'll see in the distance, straight ahead, a votive column; this marks the centre of the original city. None of that vast area in front of you has been excavated.

Returning to the excavated area, the main building, some 20m² with its stepped cruciform plan and four huge *ivans* or portals, probably functioned as the **royal audience chamber**. Opinions are much divided as to whether it was covered by a huge dome or left open to the skies, but there is no evidence of springing high on the walls. Thick wall plaster remains in places, but you have to imagine the deeply carved, moulded and painted decoration. Behind, and close to the walls, is a stone-lined chamber below the ground level; several masons' marks are still visible on the ashlar blocks. This chamber was 'identified' by the French archaeologist as the prison of Valerian.

Retracing your steps to the audience hall, west of this on the same ground level is another chamber entered through a triple-arched doorway. This was where most of the 'mosaic' work was found, depicting entertainers and courtiers, and some small tesserae can be seen close by the doorways. The way the walls meet the ground level strongly suggests that radical alterations were made at sometime. This is just one reason why modern archaeologists question the early conclusions, which were reached after digging in such a small sector of the whole site.

There is an intriguing building to the north with high-quality, honey-coloured ashlar stonework. The staircase down is restored but 15m of the original walls remain, forming four faces of a central courtyard, with a covered ambulatory behind. This was in fact a huge shallow pool, as inside the interior ambulatory (the reason for bringing a torch) there are narrow water channels with blocking or damming devices. This was probably a **temple to Anahita**, the Zoroastrian deity associated with battle, fertility and water, an identification further supported by the two (damaged) bull capitals found nearby and now incorporated high on the wall opposite the stairs, for bull sacrifices were regular offerings at various other Anahita shrines. As the Sassanid shahs traced their lineage back to a high priest at the Istakhr Temple of Anahita, near Persepolis (see page 202), what could be more logical than Shapur I, victorious over Rome, honouring this goddess by constructing a temple in his new city by the river?

A short walk away are the remains of a small **mosque** built, possibly, over a small fire temple, as a fire altar was found incorporated into the structure. French archaeologists believed the entire site was abandoned in the 10th century, but with so little of the site excavated it is impossible to be certain.

Leaving the site, look up into the hills on the immediate right: all that rubble was originally **defence walls** and towers guarding the approach to the city of Bishapur. The minor tarmac road on the right-hand riverbank brings you to the first of the **rock-reliefs** (*open site; entry free*). It is badly damaged, but enough survives to identify the characters as the Zoroastrian uncreated god, Ahura Mazda, on the left, investing Shah Shapur I (c240–272) on the right; note that in a motif possibly drawn from the West, the *farshang* (ring of authority) is carried by a putto. Both are on horseback, but there is a prone figure under Shapur's mount, probably the Roman emperor, Gordianus III, killed by his own men after their defeat on the Euphrates in 243CE. The kneeling Roman is thought to be Philip the Arab (r244–49CE), who paid 500,000 gold denarii to secure peace terms a year later. His monumental buildings, with their exquisite mosaics (sadly looted in 2011 in the chaos of the Syrian conflict), still standing in his birthplace Philippopolis (today's Shahba) south of Damascus, Syria, reveal nothing of this ignominious submission. Further along this road, but set up high, is another panel in better condition, once plastered and painted. In billowing drapery, Shapur grips the wrist of a Roman emperor, probably Valerian (r253–60CE) who was captured by the Sassanid army in Edessa (today's Sanliurfa, southeast Turkey), an event that drew the opportunistic Queen Zenoubia of Palmyra into the conflict. Shapur's horse tramples on a fallen enemy, thought to represent the unfortunate Gordianus III again, while the kneeling figure is Philip the Arab; this panel therefore records royal victories over a span of 20 years and was probably a commemoration panel for Shapur's funeral. Behind the shah are courtiers and generals, while figures behind Philip may represent the Roman governor of Syria and a court archivist witnessing the submission. To the right are two rows of figures, one set carrying the sacred *barsom* to feed the fire, the others, perhaps builders of Bishapur, carrying swords and spades.

On the left bank in the open area called **Tang-e Chogan** (🕐 *07.30–17.30; entry 100,000 rials; picnic area crowded with locals on Fri*) are several further rock-reliefs in better condition, also once plastered and painted. The first **low relief** again depicts Shapur I with his three sons victorious over the same three Roman emperors, with five splendidly depicted rows of soldiers, elephants, lions and chariots, in all numbering over 200 figures. It probably dates from 260–73CE. All of the figures are badly stained by water seepage. The next panel shows Bahram II (r274–91CE) receiving the submission of rebellious Arab tribesmen whose thumbs have been removed to prevent them drawing bows again; this may commemorate his famous victory at Mesene (in modern-day Iraq), around 282CE. Further on there's a low relief of Ahura

Mazda, on the left, handing over the ring of authority to Bahram I (r271–74CE). However, Bahram's brother Narseh (r292–301CE) later had his own name inscribed in Pahlavi, top right, presumably still smarting that Bahram I selected his son and not him as successor. In removing the water conduit in 1975, a figure lying under the horse's hooves was revealed, possibly representing the troublesome Bahram (later III) or his advisor Wahnam, who persuaded him to seize power after his father's death (Bahram II); both caused Narseh several sleepless nights.

The last relief, with two rows of figures, looks very crude, but perhaps was never finished. Who the centrally placed shah is, is unclear; eight 'possibles' have been suggested. Probably it is either Shapur I accepting the submission of central Asian rebels or Shapur II (309–79CE), the grandson of Narseh, celebrating his victories in eastern Iran over certain Indian tribes. There are altogether over 200 human figures, along with elephants, carved into the rocks, some carrying decapitated heads.

From the path on the right bank of the stream, look up across the Bishapur River to the far hills. Close to the top ridge you will spot a large cave, the **Gar-e Shapur** *(entry free)*, so named because a free-standing statue over 7m high of Shapur I was carved from the living rock, perhaps to mark his (as yet unlocated) tomb. The statue collapsed some years ago but has been re-erected. In order to visit, keep on this river road past the Qashqai village of Abdallah Khan. Turn left (following handwritten signs in Persian) and drive over the bridge and then walk for about another hour. There are 329 steps up to the cave and it is advisable to climb these in the afternoon.

In all, the trip to the Bishapur archaeological site takes four hours there and back, so such an expedition may mean spending more than one day in the Bishapur area. There is a small **Bishapur Hotel** (*25 rooms; Qadamgah St;* \ *0721 2218200–2;* **$**) where you might consider staying overnight.

NORTH OF BISHAPUR Some 10km north of Bishapur is **Naqsh-e Qandil** (45km south of Nur Abad, to the left of the main road). After the village, the road is unpaved. Bear right at the water cistern and follow the dirt track by the dry riverbed for 400m; the boulder bearing the carving is in the river bed. The relief depicts Shahpur I giving flowers to his wife in the presence of Anahita. Also in this area, once on the Achaemenid royal road from Persepolis to Susa, is another Sassanid relief panel known as **Sarab-e** (or Tang-e) **Bahram**. It is easier to access on the right, about 29km after the Qazerun junction on the Ahvaz–Shiraz road. Measuring 2.75m wide by 2.10m high, scholars cannot agree who is represented here, but Western archaeologists generally identify the king as Bahram II being offered a lotus flower by his queen, with the crown prince, later Bahram III, holding the ring of authority. A Sassanid rock panel, known locally as Naqsh-e Bahram, depicts Bahram II with an attendant on either side; the one at the shah's right is clearly Kartir, as his cap carries the distinctive 'scissor' motif.

Some 20km further on, the remains of a possible Achaemanid stone tower, resembling those at Naqsh-e Rostam and Pasargadae (see pages 200–2 and 202–4), were found and about 10km further on (5km northwest of **Fahliyan**) Sir Aurel Stein, famous for his archaeological discoveries along the Chinese Silk Road, discovered column bases of an Achaemenid palace. About 10km north of Fahliyan are the Elamite rock-reliefs of **Kurangun**, located high up the hillside (you will need a local guide to find them), close to Seh Talu, and, to the east, **Tel-e Sepid**, an Elamite settlement dating from c1500 to 1000BCE. It was a local route across the mountains that took Alexander the Great behind Achaemenid defence lines to capture Persepolis. The main Kurangun panel shows two divine – or perhaps regal – figures, one sitting on a throne like a coiled serpent pouring a libation. Their date is disputed, some scholars arguing for c2400BCE, while others prefer 16th–15th century BCE. Most agree, however, that the second section, depicting three rows of worshippers returning from the libation ceremony, was carved much later, probably during the 8th century BCE. Nearby and off the main road to the right stop briefly to view the vast and impressive Sasanian bridge at **Basht** where there are also the remains of an ancient fire temple on the escarpment from where one may look down on the bridge.

West of here is **Dai-e Dokhtar** (Nurse of the Daughter) 3km from Kupan, between Fahliyan and Dogonbadan. This is a rock-cut tomb now thought to date from the Seleucid or possibly early Parthian period because there are visual similarities in the carved columns 'supporting' a crenellated frieze to those of the rock tombs at Naqsh-e Rostam, although they remind the author of the Nabatean tombs at Maidan Salah, Saudi Arabia, and Petra, Jordan. The tomb was comprehensively identified as an Achaemenid construction when first recorded during the late 1920s.

SOUTH OF BISHAPUR A dirt track leads southwest of Jereh (55km south of Qazerun) via Hassan Abad to **Sar-e Mashhad** (otherwise, from Firuzabad, turn northwest at Farrash Band) to a rock panel depicting the Sassanid Bahram II (r274–91CE) protecting his wife and son from a lion attack, with a lengthy Pahlavi inscription detailing Zoroastrian religious teachings and rituals; four figures, one of whom may represent Anahita, witness the actions of the 'Hero King'. Some 12km further south along another dirt track (which may require a 4x4 vehicle) is **Bozpar**, famous among archaeologists for one small building, the **Gur-e Dokhtar** (Daughter's Cave), first noted by Western scholars just after World War II. A small limestone tomb with a gabled roof stands on a three-tiered platform, bearing remarkable similarity to Cyrus the Great's tomb at Pasargadae (see page 203), northeast of Shiraz. This is smaller, being 4.45m high, 5.10m long and 4.40m wide (Cyrus's tomb at Pasargadae is 10.6 x 13.2 x 12.2m). It was first thought that this was the resting place of Cyrus's grandfather, but the metal clamps holding the stone blocks suggest not a 7th-century BCE date after all but a 5th-century one, so perhaps it was the final resting place of Cyrus the Younger (d401BCE) killed in battle nearby.

FIRUZABAD About 110km south of Shiraz, Firuzabad makes for an enjoyable day trip through striking and dramatic scenery, passing the large salt lake of **Maharlu** with its salt pans, some 20km after leaving Shiraz. Emerging from the second road tunnel, about 15km before reaching Firuzabad, look for the well-preserved Sassanid fortress on the cliff top on your left. This is the palace complex known as **Qaleh Dokhtar** (Daughter's Castle) (*entry 100,000 rials*), from the local legend that a girl continually carried a young heifer from birth to maturity up to the castle and down to the river (the *Shahnameh* contains a related story linked with the Sassanid shah Bahram V). Access is possible but entails about 40 minutes' hard walking, the path snaking upwards opposite (and just past) the new roadside rest stop (with bathrooms) on the bend of the road. A German archaeological survey in the late 1960s identified a three-terraced complex, with a large circular tower, visible from the road, and a central square chamber dominated by a barrel-vaulted hall and series of chambers, all originally set within a garden. Given the neighbouring rock reliefs depicting Shah Ardashir (d240CE), it seems likely the palace was constructed for him, but Shapur I (d272CE) has also been suggested. There is a parking place just past the rest stop, and a short walk down below the road allows you to see the remains of a Sassanid bridge, which presumably once connected a small fort on the other bank with the palace. Continue walking to see an eroded Sassanid **rock-relief** on the far bank, showing Ardashir standing before a fire altar with three sons and a page, all facing Ahura Mazda on the left. About 1km further on, but very difficult to spot, is another relief (18m wide x 4m high), depicting Ardashir unseating the last Parthian ruler, Artabanus V, from his horse in 224CE, while his son Shapur tackles the Parthian vizier and a Sassanid courtier dispatches another opponent.

From this road, the remains of a huge **Sassanid palace** (approximately 105 x 55m) soon come into view on the right, but to visit it one has to drive down into Firuzabad and approach by a parallel road, so you can also visit the remains of the Sassanid city of Ardashir Khurreh (The Glory of Ardashir), known as **Gur**. In Gur turn right at the roundabout bearing a gas flame, taking the left fork at the cemetery. On the town outskirts, opposite a small cluster of light industrial buildings, is a dirt track leading through what remains of the massive circular defence walls of Gur, to the far right of the solitary ruined tower. Follow until it threatens to take you into a farmhouse, then swing on to the left, over a pot-holed track which leads closer to the ruined tower. The last 1km or so must be walked. Even in its overgrown state, visitors can make out the ruins of city walls, buildings, wells and water channels, and Sassanid pot shards litter the track. Archaeologists think this circular city, over 2km in diameter, was originally a Parthian settlement, but tradition says that Ardashir I built it to mark his victory over the Parthian regime. A deep ditch and huge ramparts with four gates protected it. The centrally placed solitary tower, with traces of an external spiral staircase, was probably a huge fire altar standing some 30m high and 10m square. To one side in the near distance a 25m² stone terrace is visible, on which stood a cruciform domed chamber with side rooms, perhaps functioning as the main temple compound.

Retrace the rough drive to get to the huge **Sassanid palace** that lours conspicuously over the flat plain. Continue past the light industrial building, keeping the tower of Gur on the right, and eventually the road leads right up to the site. The present-day entrance is not the original one, so walk from the small car park to view the little lake and the huge *ivan* opening on to it, once the official palace entry. The thick stone walls, relieved by groups of three engaged columns, look unprepossessing without their top layer of plaster, once painted and decorated. The modern entrance leads immediately into a series of huge domed chambers with early examples of squinches; tall blind niches decorated with Pharaonic-looking cornices elegantly spaced along the walls accentuate the vast space. The doorways go either to the audience *ivan*, once decorated like the royal 'coronation' *ivan* at the Sassanid capital of Ctesiphon (near Baghdad), Iraq, which had a huge jewelled crown suspended from the apex and a rich bejewelled, gold and silver floor carpet; or, in the opposite direction, to a courtyard surrounded by rooms and passageways. A spiral staircase connects with the upper floor and roof, and this can usually be accessed with a polite word to the site guardian. The local Cultural Heritage Organisation staff have always been very generous, and although eating within the boundaries of the site is not officially allowed, with a polite word it is often possible to get permission to enjoy a picnic by the pool at the front of the palace, which marked the original entrance. Few experiences make history as pleasurable as a languid alfresco lunch at this site: a watermelon cooling in the water, mongooses scurrying around in the underbrush, and birds and frogs chattering as the sun climbs high over the palace allow the lucky visitor to picture the Sassanid court at play and marvel at the fact that they are among the few guests at this remarkable site.

Where to stay and eat In modern Firuzabad, a well-known trading centre until the 11th century, there's a simple but clean **Tourist Inn** (*20 rooms; Gas Sq;* \ *0712 6223699;* **$$**) set in a small garden to one side of the gas flame roundabout. It has basic accommodation and good food, but be sure to make advance reservations as the rooms are often occupied by local factory personnel.

SARVISTAN AND BEYOND From Shiraz, a main road leads southeast to Sarvistan (80km). The small town has a mausoleum, the **Imamzadeh Pol** (known also as Mazar-e Sheikh Yusuf Sarvastani), with a 1282 dating inscription that seems at odds with its form, which resembles a Zoroastrian fire temple. But the real reason for stopping is the restored **Sassanid palace** complex just outside the town. A triple-arched portico formed the entrance, the two smaller arches leading into a series of halls with interesting vaulted systems, which connected to other smaller rooms. The central arch opens directly into the main brick-domed chamber, a large central courtyard and then other rooms, each architecturally different from the other. Perhaps built for Bahram V (r421–39CE), it might have functioned as a royal hunting lodge and surrounding walled *paradeisos*. Surface pottery shards litter the ground everywhere and the palace is splendidly illuminated by night.

From Sarvistan, it is approximately 140km due east to **Neyriz** (and eventually **Sirjan**) with its **Masjed-e Jame**, important for its single-barrel-vaulted *ivan*, which is thought to be the oldest to survive in Iran. This section of the present building could well date from 951CE when the mosque was constructed over the remains of a fire temple, or perhaps 20 years later, as its Seljuk plaster *mihrab* refers to further work here begun in 972CE. The south *ivan* and side arcades were added during the Seljuk period. The small gardens and sleepy atmosphere make this an excellent picnic lunch stop if travelling to Shiraz from Yazd.

Fasa is no longer the sleepy village seen by Sylvia Matheson in the late 1970s but a thriving township with the municipality busily landscaping its historic mounds into leisure areas. The road continues to **Darab** (275km from Shiraz) and neighbouring **Darabgerd**, 8km southwest, known for its Sassanid remains. Before being abandoned in the 12th or early 13th century, the circular fortress Qaleh Dahyeh measured 1,850m in diameter with a 55m-wide defensive ditch, and walls at least 12m high with four gates. On the hillside nearby is the rock-relief known locally as **Naqsh-e Rostam Darab**. It depicts a Sassanid shah on horseback, with rows of courtiers behind receiving the submission of two important men, while a third lies on the ground and rows of Roman captives line up to the right. Opinions are divided over who is depicted: the shah's crown suggests it is Ardashir I, once regional governor here, recording his victory in 230CE over the Roman emperors, Severus Alexander and Maximinus Thrax, before overthrowing the Parthians, but the depiction could as easily be Shapur I giving Valerian and Philip the Arab another good kicking. Be aware that this site is not easy to find and was sadly sprayed with graffiti in 2008. About 5km further to the southeast is a rock-cut chamber. Although it has a *mihrab* dating from 1254 and is known locally as **Masjed-e Sangi**, the presence of a narthex and a cruciform chamber has led some archaeologists to associate it with the 3rd-century Nestorian bishopric in the locale.

Where to stay and eat For location of Sirjan see map, page 176.

⌂ **Tourist Inn** (9 rooms) Khayyam St, Sirjan; ✆0345 3227878. Situated in a pine grove. Simple & clean accommodation with good, simple food available by arrangement. **$$**

PERSEPOLIS The Achaemenid palace complex of Persepolis is covered in the following chapter.

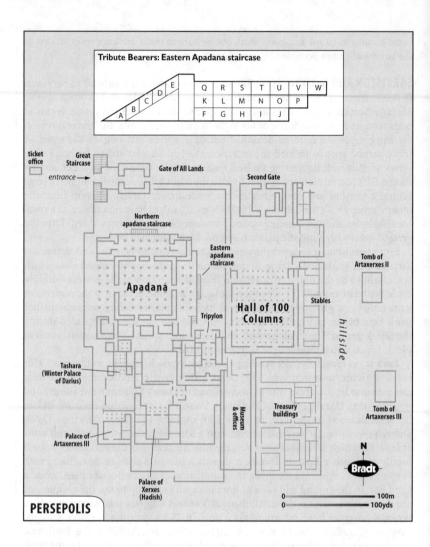

Tribute Bearers: Eastern Apadana staircase

PERSEPOLIS

9

Persepolis and the Surrounding Area

PERSEPOLIS

More than any other ancient site in Iran, Persepolis (Takht-e Jamshid in Persian) embodies all the glory – and the demise – of the Persian Empire. It was here that the Achaemenid kings received their subjects, celebrated the new year and ran their empire before Alexander the Great burnt the whole thing to the ground as he conquered the world.

GETTING THERE Transport to Persepolis and nearby sites is a problem. There is a scheduled **bus** service between Shiraz and Marv Dasht but not to and from Persepolis itself, so the easiest solution is to hire (and retain for the return trip) a **taxi**, if not from Shiraz (50km southwest) then from Marv Dasht about 15km away. It is also possible to arrange a taxi from Shiraz to Yazd or Kerman, stopping at Persepolis and other sites in this chapter. This one-way trip takes a full day and costs US$60–80.

WHERE TO STAY AND EAT

🏠 **Apadana Hotel** (17 rooms) Opposite the site; ✆ 0728 4432636; f 0728 4432638. Expensive, because it can cash in on its favourable position. Has a certain charm, but overall rather standard both in service & facilities on offer. Has its own Facebook page if you decide to have a look at some pictures of the interior (*www.facebook.com/Apadana.Hotel*). **$$$**

🏠 **Persepolis Tourist Complex (Mojtameh Touristi Takht-e Jamshid)** (22 rooms) Takht-e Jamshid St; ✆ 0728 4474001; f 0728 4474000. Just a few mins' walk from the site; has a very nice alfresco tea house. **$$**

✖ **Parsian Restaurant** Takht-e Jamshid St; ✆ 0728 4473555. Cave-like interior & reliable meals. **$**

WHAT TO SEE AND DO

The site of Persepolis (🕐 *site 07.30–17.00, museum 08.00–17.00; entry site 150,000 rials, museum 100,000 rials*) Archaeological excavations began here in earnest in 1931 and have continued on and off ever since. The immense scale and grandeur of this site (over 13ha) has long been recognised and in 1979 it was awarded the status of UNESCO World Heritage Site. Locals thought it could only be the throne dais (*takht*) of Jamshid, a legendary figure in the *Shahnameh* (see box, page 262), while in the 14th century it was known as Chehel Manar (40 Minarets), from the standing columns seen from a distance. In the early 1980s hysterical reports in the Western media announced that revolutionary zeal had destroyed much of this pre-Islamic site. Nonsense. Admittedly few visitors appreciate the recently installed new 'protection measures', such as covering the stone stairs with wooden ones and roping off access to parts of the complex as well as 'guiding' visitors along prescribed paths, but there has been no gratuitous damage.

It was Darius the Great who began construction around 515BCE, with his successors adding buildings, but it was still unfinished when, in early 330BCE, Alexander the Great burnt it to the ground after looting the city, seven years before his death. It took him, according to Plutarch, 10,000 mules and 5,000 camels to carry away the booty from this revenge attack for the Achaemenid firing of Athens. The stone came from nearby quarries but the labourers came from all over the Achaemenid Empire including Greece, as the marks of the Greek toothed chisel testifies. Gold and silver foundation tablets (now in Tehran's National Museum) were found on the site but more fascinating, for their wealth of detailed information, were the 30,000-odd clay tablets that were uncovered. The complex consisted of military quarters, treasury stores, small private rooms and huge reception areas, but the exact function of the complex remains an intriguing mystery. Susa was the Achaemenid winter capital and Hamadan the summer residence, while Pasagarda was perhaps built to commemorate Cyrus the Great's victory over the Medians.

KEY TO EASTERN APADANA STAIRCASE RELIEFS

FIRST RISE UPWARDS
A   Ethiopians or Nubians bringing a giraffe or okapi
B   'People of the Punt', probably Libyans, with an antelope and chariot
C   People of the eastern regions, possibly the so-called Carians, with a bull
D   Arabs leading a dromedary camel
E   Unidentified, but possibly Greeks, wearing pointed caps and offering a horse

PANELS AT GROUND LEVEL, LEFT TO RIGHT
F   Indians from Sind wearing skirt wraps, bringing an ass
G   Parthians leading a Bactrian camel and carrying metal objects
H   Ionians holding cloth and honeycombs or balls of yarn
I   Cappadocians carrying garments and leading horses
J   Lydians with a chariot

MIDDLE ROW, LEFT TO RIGHT
K   Soghdians (today's Samarkand region) with gifts of a horse and metalwork
L   People of Gandhara (Pakistan) with a humped bull
M   Scythians with a distinctive pointed cap, bearing clothing
N   Assyrians with sheep
O   Babylonians with a fringed cloth and a humped bull
P   Armenians, bringing a horse and double-handled ewer

TOP ROW, LEFT TO RIGHT
Q   Possibly Median people or Sagartians with a horse and textiles
R   Bactrians with a Bactrian camel
S   Egyptians (very fragmentary)
T   Drangianans (north of Afghanistan) bringing a Bactrian camel
U   Arians (Baluchistan) with a Bactrian camel and a lion skin
V   Elamite archers from Susa bringing a lioness – the only female form in Persepolis – and two cubs
W   Medians with metal objects and clothing

But Persepolis? On the evidence of low reliefs showing visitors bearing gifts, and lions attacking bulls (Leo ascendant over Taurus), many assume Persepolis was used once a year to celebrate Nou Rouz, the spring equinox, but such festivities are not mentioned in Achaemenid and later sources. There seem to have been only two occasions when the Achaemenid ruler received gifts: on the official imperial birthday, and the annual sacrifice to Mithra.

Orientation and facilities The only access to the site is at the end of the main road. A clutch of wooden 'chalets' (slightly larger than garden sheds) have been recently erected on the north side, some 150m short of the roundabout near the Achaemenid terrace wall. Cars, taxis, tourist buses, etc have to stop here and park behind this new development and visitors have to walk from here, having purchased the entry tickets from one of these 'chalets'. There are also decent toilets situated underground near the complex. The other toilets are on the site, to the right of the museum entrance, where drinks may also be purchased in the small bar with its blaring music.

Ticket in hand, walk down the street, round the roundabout and through an irritating glass-screened entrance, some ten years old. Sited in full sunlight all the information (in English and Farsi) printed on the boards has been rendered totally illegible, and the ancient stonework immediately behind silently roasts. However, essential signs (location of toilets, cafeteria, etc) are shown clearly with international symbols.

If possible, two visits should be made to the site: in early morning to explore when the light is much 'whiter', and about 90 minutes before sunset, when the stone takes on a softer, golden colour. Most of the stone now has a rough grey appearance, a result of wind-blown dust over the millennia, so do make a point of visiting the National Museum in Tehran to see the 'waxed' reliefs and column ensemble from Persepolis. This rich, dark brown stone set alongside a creamy limestone was the original colouring. If you are limited to one visit, it will take three hours or so to walk around and take photographs, especially if you plan to walk up to the Achaemenid royal tombs behind for a magnificent view over the site. Take a telephoto lens or binoculars for viewing these tombs; these will also be useful if you're going to Naqsh-e Rostam (usually included on the same day).

Guided tour of the ruins There are neither guides waiting nor audio guides; most tourists arrive with a guide from Shiraz or a driver who does not enter the site with them, so have to rely on a book such as this or the excellent local one by Dr A Shahpur Shahbazi, *The Authoritative Guide to Persepolis*, Tehran, 2004. The great double staircase with low risers, perhaps to allow horses to be ridden up, leads to the monumental **Gate of All Lands**, constructed c475BCE on the order of Xerxes I, successor to Darius the Great. Here trumpeters would have sounded a welcome as visitors walked through enormous wooden doors flanked by giant sculptures of two quadrupeds, while two huge human-headed winged bulls in the Assyrian style face into the palace area. High over the sculptures is a trilingual cuneiform inscription proclaiming:

> I am Xerxes, the great king, King of Kings, King of the lands of many people, King of this great earth far and wide … By Ahura Mazda's favour I have had made this Gate of All Lands. Much that is beautiful has been built in this [region] which I and my father have built. All that has been built and appears beautiful … we have built by the favour of Ahura Mazda.' It is one of the 110 inscriptions here, many of which reaffirm belief in the Zoroastrian creator God. Please resist the temptation to add your name to all the graffiti, which include Stanley (of Dr Livingstone fame).

Past the gate, on the left, are examples of bird-headed 'push-me-pull-you' addorsed animal capitals designed to carry ceiling crossbeams of Lebanese cedars; this *homa* bird is used as the logo of IranAir. If the light is good, you may wish to go immediately towards the right to photograph the **northern apadana staircase**. The informality of the carved figures, the Medes in their rounded caps and knee-length tunics, and the Persians with distinctive 'Victoria sponge finger' caps and long pleated robes, is charming. They slowly ascend up the left side chatting, carrying lotus buds, touching arms, holding hands. In the 19th century Lord Curzon must have felt very jaded to comment wearily, 'It is all the same, and the same again, and yet again … there is no variation in their steady, ceremonious tramp.'

Most visitors, however, continue past the sound and light seating to the second gate or doorway flanked by unfinished horse figures, once the formal entrance into the **Hall of 100 Columns** (70m²) and probably constructed c480–60BCE. These unfinished pieces show how the blocks were brought, set up and then carved *in situ*. Also note the unfinished column shafts and square bases. Having borne the brunt of Alexander the Great's arson attack, the hall no longer possesses the thick brick walls, once colourfully decorated with painted plaster or glazed tiles (as displayed in the National Museum, Tehran, and the Louvre, Paris) between the stone window and door frames. The far door-jamb reliefs, showing the enthroned Achaemenid ruler protected by his Median and Persian guards, suggest this was where the envoys presented their gifts, which were then stored in the Treasury beyond. Above, as on

DARIUS THE GREAT

When Cyrus the Great died in 529BCE, both north and south Iran had been brought together under Achaemenid rule and most of Libya, Sudan and Egypt were added by the military campaigns of his son, Cambyses II, before his own death in Egypt in 522BCE. Having just quelled an uprising against Cambyses, a small group of courtiers including Darius, a close relative, agreed that Cambyses' successor should be chosen by supernatural forces: the owner of the first horse to neigh at dawn would be crowned. Darius's groom decided to assist the gods and Darius was selected, only to be immediately faced with an Elamite revolt in southern Iran and uprisings in the northern regions (see page 8). Order was restored, and Darius then campaigned successfully in India, returning with cargo loads of booty. Four years later the Achaemenid Empire was further extended by moving into Anatolia, crossing the Bosphorus and marching into the Balkans and along the River Danube, although a Greek revolt in 500BCE regained some ground. By the time of his death in 486BCE, he had consolidated the foundations of an empire of 23 peoples that was to last for another 200 years, using an efficient administration with standardised weights and measures run from at least three major centres, Ecbatana, Susa and Persepolis. His legal code, only fragments of which have survived, was praised by Plato. Merchants and others travelled safely along the patrolled Royal Road from Sardis in modern-day Turkey to Susa, and sailors navigated through the ancient Suez Canal, started and abandoned by the Egyptian pharaoh Necho but completed by Darius. As the Persepolis apadana foundation tablet proudly recorded: 'This is the kingdom which I hold from Saka beyond Soghdia to Ethiopia, from India to Sardis, which Ahura Mazda greatest of the gods presented me.' As his name suggested, he was the 'Holder of Good'.

reliefs here and elsewhere (eg: Bisotun, Naqsh-e Rostam) a winged composition hovers over the royal canopy; it represents Ahura Mazda, the one uncreated God according to Zoroastrian scriptures, and/or the spirit of the royal ancestors holding out the *farshang* (ring of authority). The door jambs of the hall's side chambers are carved with a giant male figure, perhaps the emperor as the Perfect Hero, slaying evil spirits. Similar images are repeated on the doorways of the **Palace of Xerxes** near the museum.

To the far right is the famous main **eastern apadana staircase**, which can be glimpsed through rusting supports of an enormous canopy. Erected at the same time as the glass entrance, the canopy's purpose is likewise totally unclear. It is a badly designed, corroding eyesore, casting slanting shadows so infuriating for photographers. Furthermore, the reliefs are roped off, preventing close examination of the fine sculpted detail.

This staircase was uncovered in 1932, so it has the best-preserved reliefs. The right-hand section has lines of Medes and Persians representing the famous 10,000 Immortals, the imperial bodyguards, and attendants leading small horses, some with Elamite chariots, or carrying intricately worked furniture and textiles, etc. To the left side, the panels depict envoys from the 23 subject nations in fine detail, right down to the cuticles of their fingernails, bringing gifts. They are usually identified as in the key on page 196.

Neither this nor the northern staircase still possesses its original centre panel of the enthroned ruler *in situ*. The central panel of the northern stairs is now in Tehran's National Museum, but the one from this eastern staircase is here albeit in the Treasury building near the site museum (see page 200). But both staircases retain their dramatic depictions of a voracious lion sinking its teeth and claws into the neck of a bull, which cause some to think Persepolis was used in Nou Rouz festivities symbolically representing the astrological season.

On reaching the **apadana** level, look back at the low central section of the eastern stairs, to see various stages of stone carving in the row of shield-bearing guards. The vast platform was the floor of an enormous audience hall capable of holding 10,000 people, covered with a timber roof supported by 36 columns, each 20m high, surmounted by a huge addorsed animal capital. Tall cedars from newly conquered Lebanon permitted Achaemenid masons to space out the column bases, unlike the more closely grouped ones seen at Pasargadae (see pages 202–4).

To the south, on a terrace some 2m higher, is the **Winter Palace of Darius** (Tashara, as given in the trilingual cuneiform inscription), built around 486BCE. It is entered by a western staircase ordered by Artaxerxes III, decorated with figures of servants (or possibly priests, as some appear to wear a *padam* – a white mask used to avoid polluting the sacred fire) carrying food, vessels and lambs. As with the apadana's bell-shaped column bases with lotus designs, there are echoes of Egyptian architectural detail here with the curved mouldings over the doors. The intimate scale of this room, the polished stone, the remains of a red plaster floor and the low reliefs showing royal attendants with parasol, fly whisk, towel and perfume box have led some archaeologists to identify these rooms as royal private apartments with a bath. In the central area Darius, again as the Perfect Hero, is depicted slaying legendary animals trying to enter. The now empty spaces between window and door frames would have been filled with mud-brick walls decorated with painted plaster or glazed brick.

Across the courtyard, due south, lies the **Palace of Artaxerxes III** (c359–338BCE), entered from staircases carved with further figures of delegates and attendants. A keen eye will spot the marks on stones at ground level left by the Achaemenid masons for positioning columns and corner stones. To the left (east) is the Hadish or **Palace of Xerxes** ('Ruling over Heroes') with its 36 columns and five doorways with low reliefs showing Xerxes himself. To its northeast is the small building known as the **Tripylon** because of its three doors. This is where the polished staircase, now in the National Museum, came from. On the eastern doorway, Xerxes is shown standing behind Darius who is seated on a throne, supported by representatives of the subject nations. Down in the hollow is the small **museum** (*entry 100,000 rials*) constructed in the Achaemenid style over the foundations of a building identified on very slim evidence as the **Harem** (Queen's apartments). It houses a number of the smaller treasures found on site, including an Achaemenid trumpet, and has a small book-cum-gift shop. To the far right of the entrance (exterior) are toilets, and facing the museum door a small cafeteria selling drinks.

In front of the hillside, low walls mark the **Treasury** buildings where tens of thousands of clay tablets were unearthed, recording, among other things, the numbers, nationalities and wages of the palace labourers. Its main feature today is the **central relief panel** from the eastern apadana staircase, moved here in late Achaemenid times. This damaged panel shows an enthroned Achaemenid emperor, perhaps Darius or Xerxes, holding the royal staff and a lotus flower. Behind him are the crown prince, a court eunuch and an official, while in front a general pays homage.

If there's time (and especially if you aren't visiting nearby Naqsh-e Rostam; see below) walk up the hillside for a good panoramic view and a close-up of two of the four **royal tombs** cut into the rock. There are stairs behind the Treasury and paths to the side of the sound and light seating, the latter an easier path. The tomb above the Hall of 100 Columns is thought to have housed the bones of Artaxerxes II (d358BCE); the other further on behind the Treasury was perhaps constructed for Artaxerxes III (d338BCE) but the owners of the other two concealed from immediate view are not known. (The title Artaxerxes meant 'Ruling through Truth'.)

NAQSH-E ROSTAM

A 3km drive northwards from Persepolis across the main Shiraz to Esfahan road brings you to **Naqsh-e Rostam** (⊕ *08.00–17.00; entry 100,000 rials*). Take your binoculars or telephoto lens. The words *naqsh* (picture) and 'Rostam', a legendary Persian warrior (see Matthew Arnold's poem *Sohrab and Rostam*), were given to this place by locals seeing the Sassanid rock reliefs of jousting and investiture scenes, but the **four Achaemenid tombs** carved high into the rock face are more dramatic for today's visitors.

The first, on the left, was probably the tomb for Darius II (d405BCE); the next for Artaxerxes I (d424BCE); the third and most imposing, held the remains of Darius the Great (d486BCE); and the last, on the adjoining rock face, was carved for Xerxes I (d465BCE) or possibly Xerxes II (d423BCE). Why the rock face was worked in such a cruciform shape is unclear. Perhaps it symbolised the empire, covering the four quarters of the known world, the four cardinal points or perhaps an abstract stylisation of the Ahura Mazda figure (the head and torso, the protective wings, etc). Or perhaps the surfaces were prepared for inscription panels, as at Bisotun, which were never added.

As with the Persepolis tombs, the Achaemenid ruler is depicted as if standing above a columned portico, making an offering to the fire altar with the composite Ahura Mazda figure flying above. He stands on a platform (which, incidentally, has the same proportions as Solomon's dais, as mentioned in Chronicles II) held up by representatives of the subject nations. Their inclusion is deliberate, for the Darius tomb inscription states: 'If now you shall think: how many are the countries which King Darius held? Look at the sculptures'.

Before going over to the rock-reliefs below the tombs, walk over to the half-submerged stone cube building to appreciate the original ground level. Known locally as the **Kaba-e Zardosht** (Zoroaster's Kaba or shrine), it is a single-storey building with one entrance and no windows, standing 12.6m high. Perhaps inspired by earlier (Anatolian) Urartian architecture, it is clearly Achaemenid but its function is a mystery, although it is far better preserved than its Pasargadae cousin (see page 203). It could not have been a fire temple as there is no smoke vent. Perhaps it held royal archives or royal battle standards or served as a mortuary chamber. There is a long inscription along the bottom at the far right of the staircase, but this is Sassanid, added by the high priest Kartir recording the victories of Shapur I, including his own name wherever possible, stating that he, Kartir, was responsible for establishing fire temples in Cappadocia, Syria, Armenia and Georgia.

Clearly the Sassanid shahs wanted to associate themselves, historically and visually, with the Achaemenid monuments in this place. Apart from this inscription there are **seven Sassanid panels**. Starting on the far left by the boundary fence, they are as follows:

- Ardashir I on the left with a courtier behind is invested with the ring of authority by Ahura Mazda, holding the sacred *barsom* of twigs (for tending the sacred fire), carved near the end of his reign in c240CE. Here, as on other Sassanid reliefs, the shah sees himself as the equal, physically at least, of the deity. His horse tramples on the last Parthian king, while Ahura Mazda's steed crushes Ahriman, the evil one.
- The next relief on a convex surface shows Bahram II (d291CE) with his courtiers, each with distinctive headgear. This was carved over a much earlier panel, c9th century BCE, of which the figure of an Elamite king is clearly visible on the far right, whereas to the far left the crowned head of his queen is less distinct.
- Under the first tomb and opposite the stone building is an unidentified Sassanid jousting scene.
- Under the second tomb is another jousting scene, possibly showing Bahram V causing his opponent to fall dramatically from his horse.
- Below Darius's tomb, slightly to the left, Shapur I on horseback holds captive the Roman emperor Valerian, while a kneeling Philip the Arab sues for peace (see page 189). Behind is the bust of his vizier, the high priest Kartir, responsible for collating the remains of the Zoroastrian scriptures after Alexander the Great burnt the Achaemenid library, and who initiated official persecution of Christians and Jews in the Sassanid Empire.
- Directly under the tomb are two Sassanid equestrian battles one over the other. The shah lancing the enemy's horse is probably Hormuzd II (r302–09CE) or perhaps Bahram II.
- A relief showing Shah Narseh (d301CE) with two attendants, invested with the ring of authority by the Zoroastrian divinity, Anahita; between them the small figure is, perhaps, the crown prince. The depiction of Anahita, the goddess of fertility and also of war, indirectly supports the theory that the Kaba-e Zardosht was a depository for battle flags. One of her main temples was located at Istakhr nearby (see page 202).

If you have a free hour, walk up the hill to view the two fire altars still standing on the top. The path is situated behind the first Sassanid relief (A) but outside the perimeter fence.

Return to the main Shiraz–Esfahan road. Opposite the junction is a lay-by in front of **Naqsh-e Rajab** (Picture of Rajab) (⏲ *08.00–17.00; entry 50,000 rials*), so called after a former local café owner. Only since late 2001 has the metal fence been erected. The ticket booth is occasionally unmanned and locked, as is the gate. Exactly why these important Sassanid investiture reliefs are carved here is unclear. The first relief on the left, possibly worked in c250CE, shows Shapur I on horseback, with his distinctive crown and a bilingual inscription on his chest, while behind him are courtiers and perhaps the crown prince. On the panel almost opposite he is shown again, taking the ring of authority from Ahura Mazda on the left, so perhaps this relief commemorates Shapur's investiture in March 242CE. As at Naqsh-e Rostam, both god and shah are shown as equal in size. The last relief at the back depicts Shapur's father, Ardashir I, the first of the dynasty, with Ahura Mazda on the right handing him the *farshang* ring while holding a *barsom* for the sacred fire. The figure behind Ardashir is probably Shapur, then the crown prince, and behind him – and clearly added later – the *éminence grise* (high priest Kartir), crooking his finger in respect. Between Ardashir and his god are children, perhaps the shah's grandsons. Two female figures to the far right complete the panel: these are thought to represent the queen, or Ardashir's mother with an attendant, but it is a mystery why they are depicted apparently leaving the scene.

✗ **WHERE TO EAT** You could ponder over the mystery of the Naqshe-e Rajab reliefs in the pleasant nearby garden restaurant, **Laneh-e Tavoos** (✆ *0728 4472095;* m *091 71280058;* $) identified by a white stone porch just set back from the main road, on the same side of the road as Naqsh-e Rajab. It often caters for tour groups so service is efficient, with reliably good food. Opt for the main dish of the day with or without soup, yoghurt and salad; if there's *fasinjan* on the menu, just check the number of ducks in the pool before and after the meal. There is usually one English-speaking member of staff on duty, and the toilets are spotless.

ISTAKHR

The place perhaps most associated with the Sassanid dynasty is Istakhr, less than 3km on from Naqsh-e Rajab towards Esfahan. An ancestor served as high priest at the Temple of Anahita here and it is possible the shahs' investitures were celebrated in this place. But as only one column and a few corner blocks remain standing, the site requires a great deal of imagination. Preliminary excavation many years ago revealed a vast walled enclosure (1,400 x 650m), with stone blocks reused from Persepolis. Taken by the Arabs in 643CE, it was later totally sacked as punishment for a local rebellion, and by the 11th century only a village of 100 inhabitants remained. The site is totally overgrown but lots of Sassanid shards of the distinctive turquoise-blue glazed earthenware still lie on the surface. Foreign visitors rarely stop here, so expect any passing police or army vehicle to drive over to check you out.

PASARGADAE

About 115km further on towards Esfahan, past brick kilns, is the turn-off for Pasargadae. Some 4km from the village of Kord-e Shul, the site is not regularly served by any intercity bus. There is a **Pasargad Restaurant**, located just off the main road well before the village, which serves good lunches and dinners but why not picnic under the trees looking at Cyrus the Great's tomb? Go through the village, bearing left at the fork, until the road is barred; the **ticket office** (with toilets) is on the right.

Undoubtedly, Persepolis was a ceremonial centre fit for an emperor, but **Pasargadae's buildings** (classified as a World Heritage Site in 2004) (⏰ *08.00–17.00; entry 150,000 rials*) are on a more intimate, smaller scale, as if catering for a warlord about to emerge on the world stage – perhaps Cyrus himself commemorating his famous victory against the Medes. Excavation work started here in 1949–54 and continued with a British team in the 1960s, when the full extent of the site was realised. The first monument to be seen is the **Tomb of Cyrus the Great** (d529BCE) standing on its three-stepped platforms, the lowest one measuring 13.5 x 12.2m. Alexander the Great came here during his conquest of Persia. The tomb chamber has a simple almost square form (5.25m², 6m high) with a gabled roof. Its form has reminded scholars of Mesopotamian work, Turkish Phrygian or 7th-century BCE Urartian buildings (perhaps Cavustepe, by Lake Van in eastern Turkey). A few of the lead and iron swallow-tail clamps remain *in situ*, but the small entry doors have long gone, as have all the precious treasures they protected. Nor can one see from ground level the simple rosette form carved on top of the roof gable; such multi-petalled motifs, perhaps symbolising fertility, prosperity or the wingless disc of Ahura Mazda, are repeated throughout Persepolis. And there is no sign either of the tomb inscription recorded by Strabo: 'O man, I am Cyrus who founded the empire of the Persians and was king of Asia. Grudge me not this monument.'

Follow the road into the site. In the hills immediately in front a huge retaining wall and terrace are still visible, known locally as Takht-e Madar-e Soleyman (Throne of Solomon's Mother), and similarly Cyrus's tomb was locally attributed to her. This was the main **citadel** area, occupied until its destruction by the Seleucids in 280BCE; across from it is a platform with two stone **fire altars**. In the foreground at ground level, looking like a Hollywood film-set prop supported by scaffolding (this time essential) is all that remains of a single-storey building, known locally as the **Zendan-e Soleyman** (Solomon's Prison). It probably pre-dates its cousin at Naqsh-e Rostam (see page 201), as here there is no sign of marks left by the Greek toothed chisel, but its function is just as enigmatic.

The road to the right leads eventually to ruins of a **gatehouse**, a small chamber whose huge stone corner blocks once supported mud-brick walls. The eight large column bases are set remarkably close together, suggesting construction pre-dated the Achaemenid conquest of Lebanon and easy access to its famous cedars used for ceiling beams. The four doorways were once embellished by human-headed bull sculptures as in Persepolis, but their present whereabouts (since the late 1930s) is unknown. However, one low relief remains to fox the archaeologists. It features a standing, winged genie figure facing into the building; its headgear is Egyptian in form, its robe Elamite and its four-winged stance is Assyrian. Perhaps it symbolises the submission and offerings of these conquered peoples entering into the Achaemenid stronghold. Retracing one's steps on the road, there is the first of two **audience palaces** whose columns, except for one, were removed to build a mosque near Cyrus's tomb. Again, huge corner blocks once supported the walls, one with a trilingual cuneiform inscription recording 'I Cyrus, the king, the Achaemenid, built this.' Around the eight-columned central hall on all four sides were porticoes with stone doorways. Their carved decoration suggests to some visitors that this was a temple rather than an audience hall; only the feet and ankles have survived but one set appears to belong to a priest in a fish-like costume accompanied by standing bulls and huge bird forms. In Persepolis a similar combination, but much more confrontational, can be found (see pages 198–9).

Further on to the right are the remains of a larger **audience hall** with some 30 central column bases and two porticoes, one originally stretching the length of the building. Its flooring is worth looking at, a veritable jigsaw of limestone slabs with small repairs to imperfections. Polished, it would have served Fred Astaire and Ginger Rogers splendidly. Facing into the building from this portico, the corner block to the left carries another of the 24 trilingual inscriptions found on the site, which records 'Cyrus the Great King the Achaemenid'; the omission of the personal pronoun leads some scholars to suggest that a successor, perhaps Darius, ordered the carving. At the far end a doorway relief, to the height of 1.5m, showing a standing figure in a pleated robe inscribed with cuneiform characters, again reads 'Cyrus, the Great King'. There are small drilled holes, perhaps to carry jewels or gold plaques as at Persepolis.

Walking back to the tarmac surface, look for signs of stone water channels. In 1963 David Stronach found evidence of a garden with a pavilion, and unearthed a jar containing jewellery, beads and charms, hidden in Achaemenid times perhaps to foil Alexander's men.

10

The South Coast

For centuries this mainly Arabic-speaking region was one of the most prosperous in all Iran, handling the cargoes and supplying the ships calling in for water, food and repairs on their voyages to and from Europe and Asia. (It's such continual trade with the Arab world that accounts for many residents speaking Arabic as their first language.) The 'discovery' of the sea route around Africa by Vasco da Gama resulted in a certain loss of trade, and Shah Abbas battled endlessly to promote the advantages of shipping Persian silk and Indian chintzes from these Iranian ports on the south coast. He had limited success, possibly because European merchants and sailors found the high humidity and extreme summer temperatures very difficult, and because once the cargoes were unloaded traders were still faced by tortuous journeys into the interior. Caravans and travellers also had to contend with raids by tribesmen; even in the 1920s and '30s foreign oil companies paid protection money to the tribes to prevent damage to the oil lines and installations. The one wide river, the Karun, was not navigable until 19th-century British soldiers took matters into their own hands and blew obstructing rocks and boulders out of the water. At present it is the only navigable river in Iran.

The Iran–Iraq war set back the oil, petroleum and natural gas industrial development in this region, but now a number of projects are back on line, and the number of foreign business people visiting this area is increasing.

AHVAZ   *Telephone code 0611*

Ahvaz (altitude 17m; population 1.4 million) once witnessed Achaemenid ships unloading goods for transportation on the 'royal road' to Susa and Persepolis, and later the fleets of Alexander the Great moored here on their return from the Indian campaign. The port and town centre were developed by the early Sassanid shahs and an extensive Christian community here had its own bishop by 410CE. Its fortunes declined in the 630s CE after the Arab conquests, and uprisings against the Abbasid regime in Baghdad in the 9th century brought further retribution. Matters did not improve, with the Mongol armies blamed for the destruction of the 9th-century bridge-cum-dam, and by the 14th century Ahvaz had an unhealthy reputation for voracious mosquitoes and jaundice. The local economy revived a little in 1857 when Anglo-Indian troops were stationed there during the Anglo–Persian war; and the opening up of the lower Karun River area in 1888, which facilitated water transport, led to a new settlement, but still the population was estimated at a mere 700 people.

Then oil production started in the Masjed-e Soleyman area and Ahvaz was established as the provincial capital in 1926. In fact, the so-called Chah-e Shomare Yek (well number one, in Persian) in Masjed-e Soleyman was the first oil well dug

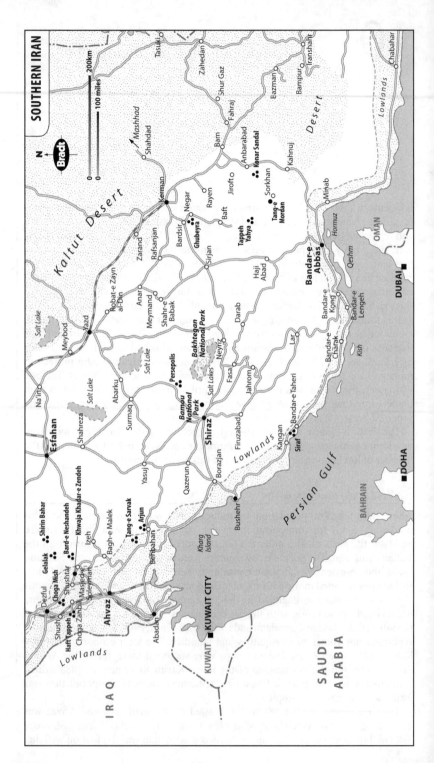

SOUTHERN IRAN

in the Middle East. It was completed in 1908 when oil exploration in the area was under the command of the Englishman George Bernard Reynolds. The discovery of oil here was reportedly the cornerstone of the formation of the Anglo-Persian Oil Company (presently known as BP). With the disruption of the late 1970s, many of the 330,000 inhabitants left and did so again in the 1980s because of the Iran–Iraq conflict. However, Ahvaz was not extensively bombed (unlike Dezful) because, it was rumoured, Saddam Hussein's mother-in-law came from Ahvaz. The 1986 census (during the war) gave the population as 580,000. The city today is arranged on the grid plan with a tortuous one-way system. Foreign visitors come to the city for business purposes, or to see the archaeological sites in the region; the city itself is very modern.

GETTING THERE The quickest and easiest way to Ahvaz is **by air** from Tehran. There are numerous daily 1½ hour flights with IranAir. The airport here is also linked by frequent flights to various other Iranian cities, such as Esfahan, Shiraz and Mashhad. Additionally there are some flights to overseas Persian Gulf destinations such as Dubai. However, the existing airport will soon be relocated 15km from the city due to the discovery of oil deposits under the present runway. The National Iranian Oil Company confirmed the purchase of the airport in 2012.

There is a daily **train** service from Tehran but the journey takes more than 15 hours and costs around 400,000 rials (prices are likely to rise, as in 2013 Iranian Railways were introducing new Chinese trains). Ahvaz is also served by frequent intercity **bus** services from the major centres, but journey times are lengthy. A one-way trip from Esfahan, for example, costs less than 100,000 rials and takes around seven hours. The main **roads** are good but the lorries and oil tankers plying between Ahvaz, Abadan or Bushehr and the interior means congestion is inevitable. An oil pipeline runs next to the motorway, and approaching Ahvaz from the south you will be welcomed to this region by numerous oil rigs with gas flares.

GETTING AROUND Once **in the city**, the best mode of transport to travel between the sites is a **taxi**, hiring one for the day to visit Shushtar, Susa and Choga Zanbil unless you have time to investigate and utilise the local bus connections. Another reason for using a taxi is the distinct lack of direction markers, both within the city and outside, at all major crossroads and roundabouts; everything seems to conspire to keep you wandering around in circles unless you have the help of a local driver. For such a trip, unless you are travelling between late October/November and February/early March when temperatures are moderate, do leave very early in the morning. Remember Strabo's words: 'Although Susa is fertile, it has a hot and scorching atmosphere', and there is little shade. A metro system is currently under construction.

Unless you have business in Ahvaz, you will probably be here because you want to explore the **surrounding area**, which in spring turns a distinctive yellow from wheat fields – it is a memorable feature of the province. From Shushtar, about one hour's drive away, you could continue to Shush (115km from Ahvaz; about 60km from Shushtar) and then visit Choga Zanbil (where there is a lovely picnic spot nearby). We would suggest this order of visits as you might well feel disappointed with the Susa excavation site.

Not to pull any punches: it takes money, time and energy to travel down to this region, and archaeology has to be a passion in order to feel the effort has been worthwhile. Single female travellers are strongly requested to avoid travelling alone here.

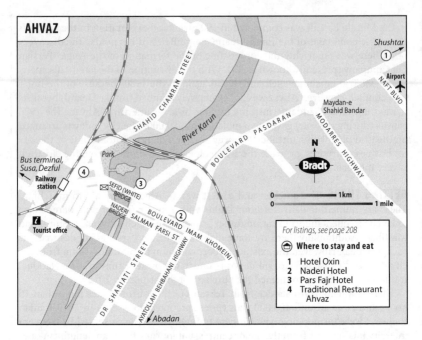

AHVAZ

Shushtar ①

Airport ✈ NAFT BLVD

Maydan-e Shahid Bandar

SHAHID CHAMRAN STREET

River Karun

BOULEVARD PASDARAN

MODARRES HIGHWAY

N

Bradt

Bus terminal, Susa, Dezful ←
Railway station

Park

④

SEFID (WHITE) BRIDGE

③

NADERI BRIDGE

BOULEVARD SALMAN FARSI ST

② BOULEVARD IMAM KHOMEINI

ℹ Tourist office

DR SHARIATI STREET

AYATOLLAH BEHBAHANI HIGHWAY

↓ *Abadan*

0 ————— 1km
0 ————— 1 mile

For listings, see page 208

⌂ **Where to stay and eat**

1 Hotel Oxin
2 Naderi Hotel
3 Pars Fajr Hotel
4 Traditional Restaurant Ahvaz

TOUR OPERATOR A very helpful English-speaking guide who could take you to, or organise tours to, the many interesting sites detailed in this chapter is **Ashkan Nezampour** (*30 Vahid St, Golestan;* m *093 57561313, 091 66114373;* e *ashkan. iran@gmail.com; www.travelguide.ir*).

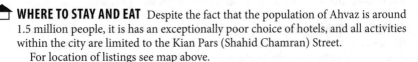 **WHERE TO STAY AND EAT** Despite the fact that the population of Ahvaz is around 1.5 million people, it is has an exceptionally poor choice of hotels, and all activities within the city are limited to the Kian Pars (Shahid Chamran) Street.

For location of listings see map above.

⌂ **Pars Fajr Hotel** (130 rooms) Abedi St, Azadegan St; ☎2220091; www.pars-hotels. com. Founded in 1968, this hotel has welcome AC, & is near the river & well-known suspension bridge, known as Sefid (white) Bridge. By far the best in town among the very poor bunch. It has 2 traditional restaurants & Wi-Fi that works. **$$$**

⌂ **Hotel Oxin** (51 rooms) Pasdaran Bd, close to Airport Rd; ☎4442133–4; f 4442135. Close to the old airport, but quite a distance away from the city centre, with modern facilities & service with a smile. **$$**

⌂ **Naderi Hotel** (90 rooms) Imam Khomeini Bd; ☎2225757; f 2222610. Centrally located in the old part of town, the hotel caters for business travellers from the Gulf States, has clean, smallish, but regrettably somewhat windowless rooms but friendly staff. The building is a little shabby & Wi-Fi is slow beyong belief. Foreign visitors are requested to pay higher rates & in US$. Serves perhaps the worst b/fast in Iran. **$$**

✗ **Traditional Restaurant Ahvaz** Kian Pars St; ☎3921811, 3921709. A locally known restaurant serving good Iranian food. Owner's son runs an Iranian restaurant in London. **$**

SHUSHTAR

Shushtar (approximately 100km north of Ahvaz) was once famous for its exquisite silks and other luxury textiles, one orator comparing the fabrics with 'every flowering plant in spring, the dewy freshness on the cheek of his mistress'. It was founded in Sassanid times and a few remains of the great dams-cum-bridges and canals, constructed by Roman POWs (prisoners of war) from the 3rd century, survive. One barrage of dressed stone and concrete (**Band-e Qaisar** or Valerian's Bridge) is seen when coming from Dezful. Also visible high up on an outcrop are the ruins of the upper citadel with 18th-century walls on Sassanid foundations, with 3rd-century, rock-cut tunnels to provide agricultural irrigation. Further along the road on an outcrop, with its white sugarloaf dome and two minarets, is the **Shrine of Khwaja Khadar-e Zendeh** (the 'Green Man'), reputedly the anonymous friend of Prophet Moses described in the Quran (Q18:59–81). Local tradition holds that Hajji Khadr took a boat to Abadan, telling the boatman to accompany him as he walked. The boatman refused but the boat followed, recognising his saintliness, and its anchor is kept as a relic in his shrine at Abadan (see page 217).

In Shushtar itself there is the mid 9th-century **Masjed-e Jame**, one of a dozen or so in Iran retaining something of its early 'Arab' plan, evident in the fat piers placed parallel to the enclosing walls. A major rebuilding scheme was completed c1125 when its *minbar* and *mihrab* were probably installed. The minaret, with its glazed bricks spelling out the word Allah, was built in 1419. The courtyard is now full of girders and this structure is covered in corrugated iron. The space is divided in two for gender separation to increase the prayer space, but the old interior is somewhat decayed and the *mihrab* has disappeared.

The town has a pleasant welcoming atmosphere but the young Baktiari men who once proudly sported their distinctive 'piano keyboard' black-and-white jackets, black pillbox *kulah* caps and wide-legged black trousers are now more likely to wear *Saturday Night Fever* attire. On the northern outskirts the road passes over a small modern dam, **Abshar** (waterfall in Persian), built on Sassanid foundations, which are part of the UNESCO World Heritage protected dam complex. A narrow staircase to one side heads down to impressive archaeological remains of the mill races, drop towers, rock-cut steps and carved rock-channels to the left and right. In the 1930s there were some 40 mills here grinding silica (for glass making), sugar cane and cereals. Only a few mills remain in private hands, and the Sassanid bridge has been destroyed, but the area is being imaginatively landscaped for a park. Some mills have been restored as museums.

Also in this region is the site of **Gelalak** (about 77km northeast of Masjed-e Soleyman, in the mountains; latitude 32.38, longitude 49.71), excavated since 1986 by the Iran Cultural Heritage Organisation. Five splendid brick tombs, one with a pottery sarcophagus decorated with vines and garlands, have reportedly been found along with burial finds thought to date from the Parthian period (1st–2nd century CE).

SHUSH (SUSA)

The town of Shush (population 87,000) is located at 197km north of Ahvaz and is reachable by regular *savari* service from the Shush/Shushtar terminal. The journey takes around two hours. The town's main claim to fame are the remains of the ancient city of Susa that it has effectively grown to incorporate. Shush suffered during the Iran–Iraq war, when at times the front line was a mere 4km away. Few scars are now visible and earlier requirements for official authorisation to visit the Susa site and nearby Choga Zanbil have been dropped.

HISTORY It was a British amateur archaeologist, William Loftus, who in the 1850s first identified Susa with the biblical Shushan and located some Achaemenid palace remains, but Sir Henry Rawlinson persuaded the British Museum that the site had little to offer. So French archaeological teams took over from 1885 and this is why such a wonderful range of artefacts from Susa is displayed in the Louvre Museum, Paris, instead of London. Arguably, the most significant find they made was the black stele containing the Code of Hammurabi, unearthed in 1901. Archaeological work is still continuing. The earliest carbon-14 dating, c4300–3500BCE, was recorded from finds mainly discovered in the Acropolis sector. It was from here too that a bronze and copper statue of Queen Napirasu, wife of Untash (r1359–1333BCE) known from Choga Zanbil, was uncovered in 1903 in the **Temple of the Goddess Ninhursag**. Weighing 1,750kg, it stands now headless 1.29m high, inscribed with a warning to anyone causing it damage that 'his name shall become extinct, that his offspring be barren'. Unlike Choga Zanbil, where construction ceased after Nebuchadnezzar's invasion, new buildings at Susa were erected, perhaps to mark the victories of the Susan ruler against the Babylonians, and to exploit a new ceramic technology in making glazed moulded bricks. Then the city declined into obscurity, only to be devastated by the Assyrian armies in c640BCE, in a sacking that continued for over 50 days.

About a century later it was rebuilt by the Achaemenid rulers as their winter capital, and it is this settlement that is associated with the story of Esther and her uncle Mordechai (see page 99), the biblical Shushan king 'Ahasuerus' being either Darius the Great's son and successor, Xerxes I, or possibly Artaxerxes I, his grandson. It was from Susa that Xerxes set out against Greece and Athens, an action that later provided Alexander the Great with a motive to destroy Persepolis (see page 196). Alexander's generals continued to reside here after his death in 323BCE, as did the Parthians, but the final battle between the Parthian, Artanbanus V, and the Sassanid leader, Ardashir, in 224CE resulted in great damage. Further destruction followed in c339CE, possibly linked to Shapur II's persecution of Christians in the town.

SUSA Soon after arriving at Susa (*Khomeini Bd;* ⊕ *08.00–17.00; entry 150,000 rials*), you'll understand why virtually every photograph of Susa shows the French château (**Château de Morgan**) constructed to house the archaeological teams. There is precious little else to see as all the excavation trenches that clearly revealed the foundations of buildings have collapsed, and once again signposting is virtually non-existent. But if archaeology is a passion, it will still be fascinating to try to identify the important locations.

To the left (actually signposted!) is where the most important Achaemenid remains were found, including the huge **apadana terrace of Darius the Great** (d486BCE), measuring 109m² with the remains of 36 column bases, column shafts and massive addorsed animal capitals which once supported the roof beams of Lebanese cedars. In 1970 two foundation tablets were located under the pavement on which Darius acknowledged divine help from Ahura Mazda and described how workers had come from all over the empire – Babylonian brickmakers, Assyrian carpenters, Egyptians and others – as indeed had the treasures, such as gold from Anatolia and Afghanistan, lapis lazuli, turquoise and cornelian from central Asia, silver from Egypt and ivory from Ethiopia and India. Your imagination will have to go into overdrive to envisage the colour and ornateness of the original decoration of the ceiling and walls. Any surviving painted plaster and glazed brick panels of pacing animals and motionless military guards and attendants were all removed to Paris, with a few examples going to Tehran.

Was it here or in the enormous Palace of Darius (246 x 155m) to the south that Esther revealed the duplicity of the minister Haman, plotting to kill all the

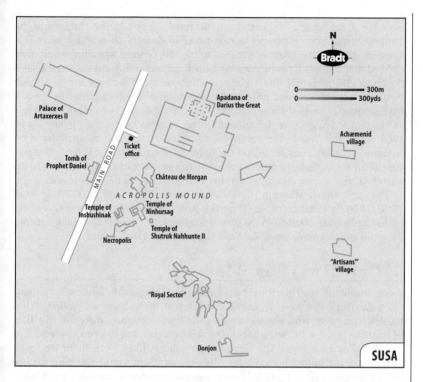

Jews, and was it here that Alexander the Great held the celebrations in 324BCE to mark the wedding of 10,000 of his soldiers to Persian women? Did either of these legendary figures enter through the monumental doorway (40 x 30m) where the fragmented granite statue of Darius, now in Tehran (see page 80), was found in 1972, its quadrilingual inscription recording his victories in Egypt?

The mounds far behind the château mark the so-called **Royal Sector**, that the site guardian is unlikely to allow you to approach, where the French found evidence of at least 15 layers of occupation, reaching from 2700BCE up to the Islamic period. Remains of the streets and buildings uncovered dated from the Elamite period, c1900BCE, but this section, especially House A, proved to be rich in Seleucid figurines so this was probably where the Seleucid military garrison was stationed after the death of Alexander the Great. Various Seleucid inscriptions suggest that, as with Dura Europos in eastern Syria, a stadium, gymnasium, archive and law court were constructed along with at least three temples: to Apollo, to the Mesopotamian goddess Nanaya and to Ma, an Anatolian deity. Later this area was occupied in the Sassanid and early Islamic periods, up to the 10th century CE. To the east in the distance is the '**Artisans' village**' where clear evidence of Seleucid and Parthian workshops, and an early Islamic mosque were discovered. Immediately south of the château was the Acropolis where a mass burial place was found and the Elamite temples uncovered. It doesn't seem possible that from such a jumble of lumps and humps, such unique and fascinating artefacts were uncovered in such a marvellous state of preservation. Make a mental note to visit the Louvre in Paris.

Across the road from the Acropolis, the white sugarloaf conical roof of the **Tomb of the Prophet Daniel** (⊕ 08.00 until late evening; women & men use separate entrances; women must wear a chador available to rent outside the tomb building) is visible at the far end of a late Qajar courtyard. Many pilgrims throughout the centuries came here, especially during times of drought to pray for rain. This association with water goes back at least to the 12th century when the Seljuk ruler decreed that Daniel's body be put into a (rock) crystal coffin and suspended from the bridge. The present shrine has been carefully restored following serious damage by Iraqi bombardment, and prior to that, as a result of floods in 1869. The interior has mirror work and a shallow dome and the current shrine is also Qajar in style.

The remains of another Achaemenid palace came to light during ploughing in 1969, across the river to the northwest. Excavation uncovered an **apadana** of 64 columns, probably constructed on the order of Artaxerxes II (d359BCE) because cuneiform inscription on certain column bases on the earlier apadana of Darius record Artaxerxes's rebuilding works after a fire there during his predecessor's reign.

The small **Shush Museum** (*Susa Park, Khomeini St, Shush;* ⊕ *07.30–13.00 & 15.30–18.00 Sat–Thu; entry 50,000 rials*) is now separate from the Susa site. Many of the displayed artefacts from the site are fragmentary in nature and come not only from this site, but some from Masjed-e Soleyman and Haft Tappeh.

NORTHWEST OF SHUSH/SUSA

From Shush the road northwest goes towards Kermanshah, Khorramabad and Hamadan (see pages 96–100). Just south of **Dezful**, itself almost obliterated during the Iran–Iraq war, which would explain the heavy presence, there are two sites of textbook interest to the archaeologist and historian, but a very knowledgeable taxi driver or, even better, the very pleasant guide Ashkan Nezampour (see page 208), is needed to find both: Choga Mish (about 25km south) and 6km further on the Sassanid site of Jondi Shapur (sometimes spelt Gundeshapur). **Choga Mish** was first excavated in the early 1960s by the University of California (US). Besides Achaemenid and Parthian remains, the real interest lay in the early Elamite defence walls, platform and private houses, with a drainage system dating from the Proto-Elamite period (c3000BCE). Subsequently the team found evidence of earlier settlement, perhaps dating back to 7000BCE. Carbon deposits showed serious fire caused damage around 4500BCE, and shortly afterwards about two-thirds of the site was abandoned, perhaps to be resettled at Choga Zanbil. The best accommodation around here is in Dezful: the **Tourist Inn** (*15th Khordad St, opposite the stadium;* \0641 6261100–1; www.dezfulhotel.com; $) offers reasonable rooms with breakfast.

Jondi Shapur was a city rebuilt to a grid plan to accommodate the many Roman captives taken by the Sassanid shah Shapur I (r240–72CE), and it was perhaps here that Emperor Valerian died, as did the founder of Manichaeism, Mani, in 276CE (see box, page 215). It was a Sassanid winter palace until the first half of the 4th century, but its real reputation came from Shapur's famous hospital, run on Hippocratic lines, which endured until 869CE when Baghdad became the centre for medical science. The city is mentioned in Syriac Christian documents, in the Talmud (eg: Beth Lapat, etc), and by the Byzantine chronicler, Procopius. The numerous surface Islamic pot shards on the site, described in the 1970s as 'indistinct clusters of low mounds', show it had been a cultural centre of some standing, with a strong Nestorian Christian community and housing the metropolitan bishop until 1318.

SOUTHEAST OF SHUSH/SUSA

CHOGA ZANBIL (⊕ *07.00–18.00; entry 150,000 rials*) From Susa/Shush a short drive (30km) due south and then east will take you to Choga Zanbil, the Elamite

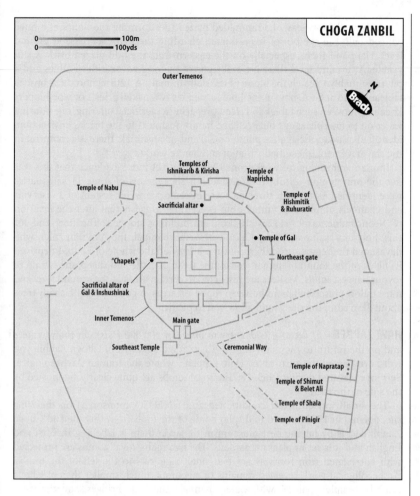

Outer Temenos

Temples of
Ishnikarib & Kirisha

Temple of
Napirisha

Temple of Nabu

Temple of
Hishmitik
& Ruhuratir

Sacrificial altar ●

● Temple of Gal

"Chapels" ●

Northeast gate

Sacrificial altar of
Gal & Inshushinak

Inner Temenos

Main gate

Southeast Temple

Ceremonial Way

Temple of Napratap

Temple of Shimut
& Belet Ali

Temple of Shala

Temple of Pinigir

0 ━━━━━ 100m
0 ━━━━━ 100yds

city of Dur-Untash, which dates from around 1340BCE and was classfied as a World Heritage Site in 1979. The site was spotted from the air by oil survey engineers in 1935 and archaeologists were quickly sent in, but the main excavation campaign was delayed until 1950, lasting 12 years and recommencing after 1965.

The visitor is immediately struck by the huge brick stepped construction nearly 3,500 years old, surrounded by remains of a vast walled precinct (1,200 x 800m) originally with seven gates. This ziggurat (105m²), originally with four, now three, terraces connected by external staircases, was surmounted by a temple dedicated to the god Inshushinak, 'Lord of Shush'; its total height was probably 53m. The similarity with ancient Mesopotamian ziggurats is striking but archaeological work has shown that this one at Choga Zanbil has a different construction, erected from the centre outwards; in other words, the highest (now vanished) section was built first and then each of the 'steps' built around to a lower height. All around the lower terrace there are, in every 11th row or so, bricks inscribed in Elamite cuneiform giving the name of Untash Napirisha (r1359–1333BCE), the king who ordered its building. The numerous remains of glazed brick, glass and ivory suggest that the exterior of the temple was richly decorated about two centuries later, and at least one wall (northeast) had moulded glazed tiles forming the figure of a huge winged bull, the symbol of Inshushinak, guarding the main staircase at ground level. Here and there, especially on the eastern wall, the odd glazed brick is still visible. At ground level there are still signs of the original sacrificial tables and a pit, presumably to catch the blood of the slain animals. A 12th-century BCE bronze tableau found at Susa, now in the Louvre, depicts two naked priests or worshippers kneeling between such tables and trees, preparing a sacrificial offering, one pouring water on to his colleague's outstretched hands. Just next to the brick construction, identified as a sacrificial altar plinth of Gal and Inshushinak, there is a footprint in the clay pavement, presumably that of an Elamite worker.

Iranian archaeological work from 1965 found yet more evidence that this was not the only temple within the precinct. In all, remains of some 11 sanctuaries were identified along with three palaces, an elaborate water system of a reservoir and channels, tombs and tunnels, but everything suggests that after the invasion of Nebuchadnezzar I (r1125–1104BCE) all building stopped. The final end for this 'holy city' came around 640BCE with Ashurbanipal, the Assyrian ruler, who devastated the region, proudly recording: 'I levelled the whole of Elam, I deprived its fields of the sound of human voices, the tread of cattle and sheep, the refrain of joyous harvest songs.' Visitors are restricted to certain areas of the ground level and must follow prescribed paths between roped-off areas. A good spot with shady trees about 2km from the site would allow you to picnic.

HAFT TAPPEH (☉ *08.00–17.00; entry to museum 100,000 rials*) On the way here and on the return to the main Shush–Ahvaz road, 30km from Choga Zanbil, you will have passed the turn-off to Haft Tappeh , where the Iranian Archaeological Service excavated during 1965–78. The royal tombs are quite clearly signposted by the side of the road.

The **small museum** (air conditioned and UNESCO sponsored) on the 30ha site, opened in 1973, is used to display some of the finds from this site and Choga Zanbil and is by far the best museum in the area; there is labelling in Farsi and English and it is set in pleasant gardens. The two main 'royal' tombs are protected with corrugated iron roofs as are two small ziggurats to the left of the tombs. Archaeological work revealed remains of ziggurats (much smaller than at Choga Zanbil), temples, palaces with water channels and little bridges, and the royal tombs. The first settlement appears to date back some 8,000 years and parts of the enclosing walls were constructed before the early 3rd millennium BCE, with numerous finds produced c1500–1300BCE, from the Proto-Elamite period according to the archaeologists. The larger of the two **tombs**, measuring about 10 x 3m, contained 21 skeletons on a raised platform, while the other adjoining it held in all 23 bodies, with nine others bundled unceremoniously in the doorway. Their brick vaulting system caused much excitement in archaeological circles as it pre-dated that at Choga Zanbil, as well as the stone vaulted passages at Bögazköy, central Turkey and at Ugarit, northern Syria, which were probably constructed a hundred or so years later.

EAST OF SHUSH/SUSA

AROUND MASJED-E SOLEYMAN If time allows, the region east in the direction of Izeh (population 120,000) around 360km away, has interesting sites, such as Bard-e Nishandeh and Sar-e Masjed detailed below. The faster motorway lies through Ahvaz, but the slower and more picturesque route passes Masjed-e Soleyman.

WHERE TO STAY There used to be no tourist hotels in the area, but now, in **Masjed-e Soleyman**, an important oil exploration region, there is one. Alternatively, you could continue on to Esfahan via Shahr-e Kord on a new fast (but long) road, or return to Ahvaz for the night. For location of Masjed-e Soleyman see map, page 206.

⌂ **Tourist Inn** (30+ rooms) Panj Bangeleh Sq; ☎ 0681 3333985; f 0681 3333224. Comfortable enough for 1 night, geared to visiting oil workers. Do not expect Wi-Fi connection, but the staff are exceptionally helpful & friendly. **$**

WHAT TO SEE AND DO Some 35km beyond Masjed-e Soleyman, in the centre of the local oilfields, is the Seleucid–Elymaian–Parthian site of **Bard-e Neshandeh**, perched dramatically above the town. Its name ('Raised Stone' in Lori language) comes from the huge stone platform or terrace, about 54 x 91m, reached by staircases to the north (the best preserved), south and east. A cult niche and crudely carved relief of a king offering a *barsom* of sacred twigs to the fire altar were found, which supported the theory that a Parthian temple once stood on this terrace, but the numerous Seleucid/Elymaian figurines, pilgrim flasks and coins found under and around this platform strongly suggest it was constructed in pre-Parthian times. In 2005 the headless statue of a Parthian 'princess' was unearthed.

MANI AND MANICHAEISM

Think of St Augustine and one thinks of an early Church father, but he was a Manichaean for at least nine years before his conversion. Mani himself was born in 216ce in southwest Iran of princely parents. Inspired by revelations when he was 12 and 24 years old, he formulated a religious philosophy that appealed to many in Iran, central Asia, China and west into Syria, north Africa, Italy and Roman Gaul. To him the essence of all religion was Truth, and that existence was a constant cosmic battle between Good and Evil, the former offering peaceful harmony and the latter constant agitation. The importance of such religious leaders as the Buddha, Zoroaster and Jesus was acknowledged, but their roles defined according to Manichaean scriptures. Believers were divided into two groups, the Elect and the Hearers. The role of the hearers was to assist the elect by performing tasks that would, if carried out by the elect themselves, pollute them, in the manner of Hinayana Buddhism. Circumcision was practised, as was vegetarianism (though hearers could eat meat), and the Sabbath kept, while in devotions St Paul was abhorred.

On his return from India, Mani converted the brother of Shapur I in 242ce and from then was greatly honoured at the Sassanid court. At this time Zoroastrianism, although influential, especially in the figure of Kartir the high priest (see page 201), was not officially the state religion and Mani gained many converts in eastern and northwest Iran. On Shapur's death Mani was still allowed to preach but succeeding shahs, probably persuaded by Kartir, were increasingly hostile. In 276ce Mani, accompanied by two disciples, was summoned before Bahram II and arrested, to die horribly in captivity. His followers were persecuted in Iran, and then across the Roman Empire by Diocletian, but pockets of Manichaeans survived in Iran and Iraq until the mid 10th century, dying out in Europe some 50 years later but continuing until the 15th century in central Asia and western China.

10

To the south of Masjed-e Soleyman, at **Ateshgah Sar-e Masjed** (Fire temple Sar-e Masjed), were found fragments of a larger-than-life-size statue of Herakles (Hercules) with a Nemean lion on a platform surrounded by remains of a porticoed temple, probably Parthian in date, although the defence walls are thought to be older. Most of the finds, including this statue and other beautifully carved heads from the first site (often clearly deliberately smashed, perhaps in post-Sassanid times), were moved in the 1960s to the Susa Museum for safe keeping. Also in this region, a new discovery of a Parthian rock carving was made in 1999 at **Shirin Bahar**. Although known by the local Bakhtiari tribespeople, it was unkown to scholars because of the area's distance from population centres. The relief (2 x 1.45m) high, shows three frontal figures: the one on the left carrying a lance sits on a throne; another appears to raise his right arm towards the seated figure; while the one on the right is depicted with his arms crossed. It may be an investiture scene but it's difficult to ascertain as the surface is very worn.

Further south lies Izeh, with its important Elamite remains, and to its north (via Peyan and Mehrenanis) is **Shami**. This is where the superb bronze Parthian king or warrior (possibly the general described by Plutarch, called Surena, of the late 1st century BCE and now in the National Museum) was found in 1934 by the famous archaeologist, Sir Aurel Stein, on an artificial terrace in a building which had been torched. The scattered fragments of stone slab tombs below suggests it was a royal Elymaian cemetery. Further on in the same direction, some 60km northeast of Masjed-e Soleyman, is **Tang-e Butan**, where rock reliefs depict four investiture scenes and a portrayal of Herakles (Hercules).

IZEH

Izeh was once the capital of the Lori people whose name is perpetuated in the nearby Lorestan province. There is no suitable accommodation in the area and you are advised to stay overnight in Masjed-e Soleyman, Dezful or Ahvaz.

What to see and do If coming from Bagh-e Malik to the south, about 25km before Izeh, keep an eye out for a **cemetery** on the left which contains three or more standing stone lions thought to mark the graves of Bakhtiari tribal chiefs. An even better collection of **lion tomb markers** is to be found on the other side of town just off the road towards Esfahan. After 2km turn right, opposite a car office and follow the road through three villages until it becomes a dirt track; some 500m further at the base of the mountain is a large cemetery with more than 33 stone lion tomb markers.

Just on the southwest outskirts of Izeh itself is the grotto of **Ishkaft-e** (or **Shikaft-e**) **Salman**. The Izeh Municipality has really made an effort here, planting trees, landscaping the hillside, and even installing toilets below the goldfish pond. Inside the shallow cave, two badly eroded **Elamite reliefs** commemorate a local 8th-century BCE ruler, Prince Hanni, and his consort. A large notice provides the full inscription in Farsi, giving Hanni's royal lineage, listing the villages and areas under his authority and dedicating the grotto to an Elamite goddess. High on the right-hand rock face is the carved figure of Hanni and his queen and another showing, according to some scholars, his chief minister and family, facing the grotto. Purists will dislike the modern plaster animals scattered around but young children adore them.

Kul-e Farah, a site with Neo-Elamite rock reliefs is straight across town from here, 7km to the northeast. It is more accessible than Tang-e Butan (see above) – but wear comfortable, tough shoes as the ground is very stony. The rock-cut reliefs clearly formed an open-air sanctuary of deep religious significance for local Elamite rulers. At the far end of the tarmac road is the village, in a hollow at the foot of the hills, now totally deserted after a new dam cut off its water supply. In a recent visit we could find only two series of Elamite rock reliefs out of the six published, but the megaron layout of the village houses, and the evident reuse of old stone columns to support roofs and floors, makes the village itself interesting to explore. As one faces the village, the reliefs are to the far right (east). One cluster is high on the limestone rock, with attendants facing into a deep crack, while on the other face a larger regal figure, Prince Hanni again, mirrors the direction. Despite severe erosion, the multiplicity of figures is amazing and some retain considerable fine details. On another surface the prince is shown seated witnessing animal sacrifices. From here, walk downwards and towards a dried-up stream. You're looking for a massive boulder carrying reliefs on all sides, carved probably in the 8th century BCE. One side depicts a religious procession featuring nearly 200 human figures and 21 other animals, with a (badly eroded) kingly figure welcoming a cult image carried by four priests. On another side the prince is attended by three rows of courtiers, priests with vessels and harpists. Their hands held at the waist presumably denote a posture of prayer or reverence. Another face of the boulder depicts the priests despatching the sacrificial animals. If the proposed dating for this and all the other carvings is accurate, this place held sacred connotations for the worship of the Elamite deities of Tepti, Tirutur, Napir and others for some 400 years.

Tang (or **Hung**)**-e Nouruzi** (some 6km north), among other villages in this area, has similar representations, but these are generally thought to have a much earlier date, c1950–1800BCE. Alongside it is a Parthian investiture scene, first attributed to Mithradites I (171–138BCE), but this is no longer accepted. Also in the locality of Izeh, some 30km east, a rock relief depicting four reclining figures was discovered in 1987, but there are no details of its exact location; it is thought to date from the Parthian or Sassanid period.

SOUTH OF AHVAZ

ABADAN Business affairs often take foreigners, but very few tourists, to Abadan (altitude a mere 3m; population 230,000), 150km south of Ahvaz. The heat here is fierce during the summer months (58°C has been recorded) and the humidity can be as high as 99%.

Since at least the 4th century CE its location at the junction of the rivers Tigris, Euphrates, Karun, and the Gulf gave Abadan a significant commercial importance, and in medieval times many came on pilgrimage to visit the **Shrine of Khadar** (the 'Green Man'; see page 209) with its relic of the anchor from the boat that faithfully followed him. The grid layout of the city dates from the early 20th century when the oil and petroleum refineries were constructed and urban expansion went hand in hand with increases in output; it has been described as the Surbiton of Iran. Needless to say it was a prime target for Iraqi bombing during the 1980–88 Iran–Iraq war, but there has since been an extensive rebuilding programme.

On 19 August 1978 a fire at Abadan's Rex Cinema killed at least 370 people and proved to be one of the turning points in the pre-revolutionary movement, as the Shah's SAVAK security service were accused of orchestrating it.

Getting there and around There are two direct IranAir **flights** per week from Tehran to Abadan, as well as flights from several other centres, such as Mashhad and Shiraz. The airport is around 12km away from the city. The **rail** network links Tehran to nearby Khorramshahr daily and there is the usual selection of long-distance **buses** connecting the area to the main population centres. Bus is perhaps the most convenient means of arriving here. Note, however, that buses coming from the south (eg: Bushehr) are not as frequent as services from Esfahan, Shiraz or Tehran.

Within the city, as always, **taxi** is probably the best option for visitor. For location of Abadan see map, page 206.

Where to stay

⌂ **Abadan Caravansarai Hotel** (95 rooms) International airport, north of the centre; ☎0631 3334002; f 0631 3332107. Built with reference to traditional architecture, though mixed with plenty of 1970s glamour – see for example the peacock-tail mosaics decorating the reception. Room rates for foreign tourists are stated in US$, but you can pay in rials. **$$**

⌂ **Azadi Hotel** (90 rooms) Abadan Rd; ☎0631 3330060; f 0631 3330068. Near the port, this hotel used to have a famous disco before the revolution. Now it has clean rooms, internet access in the lobby & charming service typical of this hospitable area. **$$**

EASTWARDS ALONG THE COAST

A slight detour along the coast road from Abadan, or on the eastern route from Ahvaz to Bushehr via Behbedan, will take you to **Tang-e Sarvak** (54km northwest of Behbehan) where boulders are carved with Elymaian or Parthian reliefs dating from c200BCE onwards. Registers of standing figures attend a figure reclining on a couch, while another rock face depicts a ruler and his family. Elsewhere the representation of a priest standing by a fire altar is carved alongside depictions of hunting activities. Some scholars believe this to be the site of the Nanaia-Artemis temple referred to by Strabo.

About 10km northeast of Behbahan is **Arjun**, where a 9th–8th-century BCE stone burial chamber was found during construction work for a dam in 1982. Inside was a U-shaped coffin and the remains of a body with grave goods including ornate gold jewellery, a bronze lamp stand, and daggers. A magnificent decoratively patterned bronze platter, over 43cm in diameter, is engraved with over a hundred human figures, 66 animals of 33 kinds, trees and rock formations in scenes of banqueting, hunting and harvesting, processions and musical performances. The deceased, according to an inscription on a beautifully worked bracelet in the grave, was the Elamite ruler Hutran, son of Korlash. All these treasures are now in the National Museum, Tehran, but unfortunately not on public display.

BUSHEHR Before holding on to its present name, the city of Bushehr used to be called Syam, Abu Shehr and Risehr. About 350km southwest of Shiraz on the coast of the Gulf, it is stiflingly hot and humid in the summer months.

Bushehr (also written Bandar-e Bushehr) first became important as a port when Nader Shah Afshar made it his principal naval station in 1734. Some 25 years later the British East India Company set up its 'factory' (headquarters) here after losing its Bandar-e Abbas base. Control then passed to an Arab family until 1857 when it came under Qajar authority.

Bushehr's current importance as a military establishment means personal exploration is somewhat restricted, and much was destroyed in the severe 1806 earthquake. The 2013 Bushehr province 6.3-magnitude earthquake that killed over 30 people and injured around 800 did not affect the city itself. With the epicentre 91km south of Bushehr and around 30km south from the Russian-built nuclear plant, the shockwaves were felt in various parts of the country, including Shiraz, and across the Persian Gulf. The plant was reportedly unaffected with the reactor working in the normal regime. In fact in late 2013 Russia and Iran were discussing construction of a second unit at the nuclear plant.

Getting there and around Bushehr is a major centre for oil development projects (on and offshore) in Iran and there are numerous daily two-hour **flights** from Tehran to Bushehr in addition to air links with Dubai (operated by Iran Aseman Airlines) and other cities in Iran. The city is also well served by long-distance **bus** services from the major cities but it can be difficult to get here from Kish by public transport.

Within the city, **taxis** are your best option. The standard rate is around 40,000 rials.

Where to stay and eat The choice of hotels here is limited, as visitors prefer so-called apartment hotels with up to five beds per room. For location of Bushehr, see map, page 206.

⌂ **Aseman Apartment Hotel** (16 rooms: 3 & 5 beds per room) Hafez Jonoubi St; ☎ 0771 2580889–90; f 0771 2534226. Old-fashioned rooms with slightly grim décor come with either Western or squat facilities. Do ask in advance in case of preference. **$$**

⌂ **Hotel Delvar** (also known as Tourist Hotel) (50 rooms) Dalrian-e Tangestan Sq; ☎ 0771 2526342–6; f 0771 2526881. The best hotel in town near the seafront & very central. It has good facilities & large rooms that come with balconies. The staff are pleasant & professional & Wi-Fi is fast. **$$**

⌂ **Pasargad Apartment Hotel** (30 rooms: 2 & 4 beds per room) Imam Khomeini St; ☎ 0771 2529251; f 0771 2524893. Very modern & clean apts but here again do enquire in advance about toilet facilities in case of preference. The lobby is tiny, but inner atrium creates a relaxed atmosphere & some space. Centally located & not too shabby. Wi-Fi in the lobby only. **$$**

⌂ **Hotel Siraf** (40 rooms) Imam Khomeini St, across from the Pasargad above; ☎ 0771 2527171; f 0771 2527173. Your last resort, even though the rooms are clean & have Western-style toilets. It is overall rather poorly maintained & the acid red colour of the restaurant furniture is quite disorientating & so are the manners of the personnel here. No towels provided. **$**

✕ **Ghavam Restaurant** Sahali St; ☎ 0771 2530700, 2521790; e ghavam.restaurant@gmail. com ⏲ 12.00–15.00 & 19.00–23.00. Fashioned from a restored water cistern this is one of the best restaurants in Iran, serving home-baked bread & delicious food. Do note, however, that local cuisine is spicey. **$$**

What to see and do There are the remains of two large merchant houses here, one of which is the Qajar-period **Emarat-e Malak** (former residency of the famous trader Mohammed Mehdi Malak the Merchant), which was built under the supervision of French engineers, and is where the first printing press in Iran was located. The other is **Emarat-e Haj Ris** and it was also built under the Qajar dynasty for Haj Abdul Rasul Talebi, known as Ris the Merchant. Both of these tradesmen made their fortunes in India and Pakistan trade. The **British Cemetery**, located 7km south of the city at Bahmani, is closed and there does not seem to be anyone removing the weeds. Nearby, the site and the building of the pre-revolutionary **British Consulate** have been converted into a museum. A few kilometres further on are the remains of the original port of **Rishehr**, which got its name either from the Elamite word meaning 'great' (*rishair*) or from a Sassanid fortress here, **Rev-Ardashir** – named after the first Sassanid ruler – which was later built over by the Portuguese and Safavid occupiers. Elamite remains have been found: there are foundations of a town near to the original port and about 14km away (4km from **Saadabad**) the site of an Elamite temple has been identified. French archaeologists concluded the main period of settlement was c2500–1200BCE, and possibly a millennium earlier.

The old quarter still has some good examples of traditional architecture with wooden doors and overhanging balconies with lattice windows that allow the women of the household to view the streets below without being seen. Do try to visit this quarter before it disappears in the zeal for modernisation. There is a beach, and swimming facilities for men. The Corniche is a popular family retreat in the evening with bands playing; all swim here but women enter the sea fully clothed.

EAST OF BUSHEHR Driving from Bushehr towards Shiraz via Qazerun gives the opportunity of seeing a series of rock-cut caves on the old medieval road which have intrigued several archaeologists, who have suggested they functioned as Christian or possibly Buddhist monastic dwellings. **Chehelkhaneh** with, as its name suggests, some 40 caves (*chehel:* 'forty'), is situated 17km northwest of Borazjan (itself 70km from Bushehr). South is **Kalat-e Haydari**, where there is another cluster of caves with intersecting passages, and rectangular and 'domed' chambers on two levels. In the early 1970s, some 5km before Chehelkhaneh, the remains of an **Achaemenid palace** (Sang-e Siah) were found. Its layout (the closeness of the column bases) and the use of black and white limestone suggested it was constructed during the reign of Cyrus the Great c529BCE, but abandoned after his death. Nearby on the large **Tappeh Mor** (also known as Tel-e Mor) traces of an Elamite fortress were located.

KHARG ISLAND About 31 nautical miles northwest off Bushehr (see pages 218–20) is Kharg Island (Jazir-e Kharg) whose oil-pumping facilities suffered such serious bomb damage during the 1980–88 war that French engineers asserted that the Kharg Fire Brigade was the most experienced in the world. It has a population of some 15,000, mostly employed in the oil industry as 90% of Iran's oil exports pass through these facilities.

In the 1950s archaeological finds of bricks with cuneiform inscriptions proved the island was under Elamite authority during the 3rd millennium BCE, but the two megalithic tombs found probably date back only to c1000BCE. Thirty years later, a marble figurine, probably of Sumerian manufacture, was uncovered suggesting the importance of the island to maritime trade. Strabo, writing in the 1st century BCE, was probably referring to this island when he reported the remains of a large temple to Apollo with an oracle, and two centuries later Pliny recorded that Kharg was 'sacred to Neptune'; the ruins of a Roman temple may relate to this. On top of this complex a Sassanid fire temple, dated by a coin find to the early 4th century, was built, and then a mosque was later constructed. Today there stands a mosque and shrine of Mir Mohammed, both surmounted with a 'sugarloaf' dome, characteristic of the region. Nearby more than 80 rock-cut tombs were found, probably carved in Sassanid times for Zoroastrian use, though Christian crosses have been carved on some doorways. Two hypogea for multiple interments were located, which the French archaeologists thought suggested Palmyran merchant occupation. To the west, extensive remains of a Nestorian monastery and a basilica church were uncovered. The 60 cells, each containing three stone-and-plaster bed-couches, suggest a community of over 150 monks.

The island's strategic position between India and Arabia resulted in occupation by the Portuguese and then the Dutch East India Company after it closed down its Basra operations in 1752. The French then moved in with the blessing of Karim Khan Zand (see page 13) but the island was returned to the Qajar dynasty in 1809, and again in 1857 after a brief British occupation. As recently as 2007 an Achaemenid cuneiform inscription praising one who brought water was discovered, but this has since been vandalised as was reported in January 2008.

Getting there There are daily round trips to Kharg Island from Bushehr, but these are for workers and residents only. Permission is necessary in order to visit. During Nou Rouz there are tours for Iranians (holding permits). For foreigners, it is necessary to apply to the governorate in Bushehr, but it is likely to be a lengthy process, which may well not result in permission. Students at the university on the island are issued with a commuting card.

There are currently no places on the island for outsiders to stay.

FURTHER ALONG THE COAST ROAD

Almost due south from Shiraz (although there is no direct road) is **Bandar-e Taheri** (220km southeast of Bushehr) where British archaeologists excavated the important medieval port of Siraf for over nine years from 1966. The fishing port of **Kangan** is 45km to the northwest.

According to the histories, **Siraf** was trading with India and China, and by 950CE its population approximated that of Shiraz. However, a severe earthquake in 977CE caused many to leave, and by 1200 most of the trade had been transferred to the eastern port of Qais. The final report describing the excavations on this enormous 250ha site and its finds was finally published in 2010 after a 30-year delay. The quantities of Chinese ceramic shards uncovered in the first season of work proved the accuracy of the medieval historians. It was discovered that the large ruined mosque noted in 1930 had been built on top of a large Sassanid fort constructed shortly after 804CE, and which was then altered some five times before the site was abandoned c1263. Nearby, a six-roomed *hamam* with hypocaust system had been in operation, along with the workshops and warehouses of a bazaar, some clearly involved in metalworking. Remains of about 30 pottery kilns were found with their shelf-support systems still largely intact. Streets with residential buildings, often incorporating a well for drinking water, were also identified, and a large cemetery with 9th- and 10th-century tombs was located.

KISH From Bandar-e Taheri there is a good road eastwards along the coast to Bandar-e Charak from where ferries leave for the island of Kish (Jazir-e Kish). In the past, like Hormuz (see pages 226–7), it had a lively trading community over ten times as large as now, and was known for its pearls and beautiful women. The late shah had a large villa with an airstrip, and desalination plants (for drinking water) constructed here, and this infrastructure remains the basis of the recent development of this free trade zone. The Kish Free Zone Organisation (KFZO), which answers only to the president, is currently targeting foreign companies for investment, promoting the island as an offshore banking centre, and a number of the official regulations (eg: partnership with an Iranian representative) were removed in spring 2000. Many Iranians come here to shop, as, reputedly, the prices are lower than in Dubai, or to visit the Kish Dolphin Park.

A visa waiver system operates for foreigners wishing to visit Kish (see page 35), but this is not valid for further mainland travel; a tourist visa for the rest of Iran can usually be issued here, however. A number of Dubai workers come here to wait for their Emirati visa renewal.

Getting there and around There are frequent international **flights** to and from Dubai and other Persian Gulf destinations; there are daily flights with Kish Air from Tehran and two flights per week on Sundays and Thursdays from Esfahan. Regular comfortable **ferries** leave from the nearby mainland ports of Bandar-e

Charak (from where the journey takes 90 minutes) and Bandar-e Lengeh further down the coast (less frequent departures and longer journey time). A one-way ferry from Bandar-e Charak costs around 100,000 rials and from Bandar-e Lengeh 220,000 rials. Make sure to have your passport with you as it will be checked when buying a ferry ticket. **Taxi** services exist on the 15km by 8km island.

🏠 **Where to stay and eat** There are no budget hotels on the island, despite the fact that some hotels have different classes of accommodation on the same site. Room prices tend to vary with the season. All the hotel complexes and shopping malls have a variety of restaurants, but for a cool evening venue try the **Payab Restaurant** (*near the underground water reservoir;* \ *0764 4423638;* $$) for fish and other specialities. For location of Kish see map, page 206.

🏠 **Dariush Grand Hotel** (163 rooms) Dariush Sq; \0764 4444900; e reservation@ dariushgrandhotel.com; www.dariushgrandhotel. com. One of Iran's most luxurious hotels with the front façade built to resemble Persepolis & the Gateway of All Lands. Completed in 2003, it simply stuns with its nonchalant flamboyance. If you are lucky, you might even be able to snatch a room with a sea view. $$$$

🏠 **Sadaf International Hotel** (54 rooms) Amir Kabir Sq; \0764 4420590; www.sadafkish.com. Friendly staff, shiny lobby, clean rooms & facilities,

which include an internet café, pool room & sauna & jacuzzi, not to mention the restaurant built into a 'mountain'. Recommended. $$$

🏠 **Shayan International Hotel** (195 rooms) Sahel Sq; \0764 4422771; f 0764 4422409. The late shah's original concrete hotel, now a homage to retro kitsch. $$$

🏠 **Kish Parsian Hotel** (90 rooms) Between Trade Centre & Zeitoon malls; \0764 4423616. A little dear for what you get. The rooms are standard & the lobby is flashy touristy. The staff are not very attentive & even somewhat indifferent. $$

What to see and do There are a couple of places of interest here, but they can all be visited in one day. All tourist groups are guided alike and if you are looking for a romantic moment to share the sunset you will be sharing it with hundreds of others. Hotel buses drive everyone around along the same route. **The Underground City of Kish** (*Kariz;* ⊕ *08.30–22.30; entry 100,000 rials*), which is made of a series of interconnected underground passageways built around subterranean water channels, is effectively a place for walking around, exploring the ancient system of canals, some light souvenir shopping and enjoying a bite to eat in its lively open-pit traditional restaurant and music venue.

The main attraction is of course still the duty-free shopping, but the beached Greek ship is also very popular. Otherwise, perhaps the turtle colony and scuba diving (for men only) may be of interest. Although it is very cheap to dive here, diving equipment is not easy to find on the island. Windsurfing, jet skis and waterskiing are also available. There is a beach for women only; enquire at your hotel for directions

In the northern corner of the island, between Saffeyn and the New Jetty, there are a few remains of the **palace and fort complex** built in the 11th–12th century when, according to the chronicler Benjamin of Tuleda, Kish was an important and prosperous trading port with large Jewish and Indian communities. In 1135 the ruler of Kish felt strong enough to attack Aden, and 15 years later it is known that his navy consisted of 50 vessels, each capable of carrying 200 men. Its wealth attracted the attention of the ruler of Hormuz who seized the island in 1229, only to divert traffic away. There was a brief period of prosperity from 1292 when Kish became a major port for the Ilkhanid regime (see page 12) but again Hormuz acted to stop trade in 1330, and the island never recovered. An archaeological survey in

1974 recorded a number of cisterns and kilns, while surface finds of 13th–14th-century Chinese pottery shards revealed a busy trade with medieval China. In the early 1990s archaeological excavations in the **Harireh** historic port uncovered evidence of workshops, a mosque and a bathhouse from Ilkhanid and Timurid periods, and plotted the coastal location of numerous manmade loading bays, with rock-cut steps to serve the trading dhows in these waters. For shows with dolphins and white whales, visit the 70ha Kish Dolphin Park (*www.kishdolphinpark.ir, in Persian only*), built in 2000. It has a lovely garden and teahouse. Your hotel will book a show ticket for you on request.

BANDAR-E ABBAS As with the rest of the south coast of Iran, the best time to visit Bandar-e Abbas (altitude 3m; population 449,000) is during the winter months, November to April. Summer temperatures often soar over 45°C, with the humidity of a Turkish bath; 18th-century English sailors used to moan that 'there was but an Inch-deal betwixt Gombroon [Bandar-e Abbas] and Hell'. The heat and humidity explains why a blind eye is turned to local women having bare feet.

Bandar-e Abbas was the name given to the medieval port of Suru in 1615 by the Safavid shah Abbas I after ejecting the Portuguese from their forts here and on Hormuz Island, ending both their occupation and their strategic and commercial control of the Straits of Hormuz. He saw the possibility of circumventing the Ottoman embargo on Persian silk passing through its empire by sending bales by sea, as well as the potential of pearl fishing, and it was probably this commercial connection which led the English in particular to refer to Bandar-e Abbas as 'Gombroon' (Turkish for 'customs house'), a name later given to the high-quality soft paste porcelain ware from Iran so avidly collected in 19th-century Europe. A preliminary archaeological survey undertaken near Tiab, southeast of the present city, shows this trade had a long history; over 2,000 sherds of fine 13th–14th-century Chinese porcelain from the site are now at the Ashmolean Museum, Oxford (UK). Like much of Iran, the area is subject to earthquakes: there was a serious one in 2005 measuring 5.6 on the Richter scale and a slightly stronger one in September 2008 which affected the island of Qeshm quite severely.

Work on port facilities in 1964–67, and then the setting up of the Iranian naval headquarters in 1973 meant increased business, and an international deep-water port was constructed in 1976–86. Now Bandar-e Abbas is the main port of Iran. The traditional *dhow* boats can still be seen in the old port, plying their trade between India, Zanzibar and Dubai, carrying tyres, oil drums, children's bicycles, spices and bales of cloth.

Bandar-e Abbas came to international attention at the end of the Iran–Iraq war when on 3 July 1988, US warship, USS *Vincennes*, the 'supership' of the Persian Gulf, shot down IranAir 655 Airbus A300 on a regular civilian flight from Bandar-e Abbas to Dubai. All 290 passengers and crew were killed. In the atmosphere of heightened tension between the two countries, the United States government never admitted responsibility, but agreed to compensate the families of the victims. The Iranian regime, in return, refused to accept that what happened was an accident.

Getting there and around There are several daily **flights** from Tehran and a daily service to Shiraz as well as flights from other cities. There are also international flight connections with Dubai and less regular services to Iraq and Saudi Arabia. As a port, daily **sailings** link Bandar-e Abbas with Hormuz and Qeshm; there is also an international service, usually twice a week, to Sharjah (UAE), costing about 1,600,000 rials one way.

Intercity **bus** connections run between the major cities, such as Shiraz and Kerman, but you must count on a minimum of eight hours' travel time even to reach Shiraz. The road from Shiraz and the north (1,050km to Tehran) is good, but as it is the main route from the coast to the interior there is a constant stream of lorries and tankers, a reminder that Iran relies heavily on imported manufactured goods and raw materials. To this tedium must be added the heat in the coastal regions. There are also daily overnight buses from Esfahan, leaving at 17.00 with arrival at Bandar-e Abbas at around 08.00.

It is also possible to reach Bandar-e Abbas by **train**; there are good connections with all the major cities but it takes a minimum of 19 hours to Tehran, for example.

Within the city **taxis** are available, though the centre is fairly compact.

Where to stay and eat
Hotels in this part of Iran are usually more expensive than anywhere else, even in low season, and there are no budget options here. For location of Bandar-e Abbas see map, page 206.

Homa Hotel (180 rooms) Meraj St, Pasdaran Bd; \0761 5553080–9; e info@homahotels.com; www.homahotels.com. Located by the sea in a lush green garden with a tennis court & a good traditional restaurant. The staff are exceptionally helpful & rooms are excellent. **$$$**

Hormoz Hotel (345 rooms) Enghelab Sq; \0761 3342201; e info@hormozhotel.com; www. hormozhotel.com. With several restaurants, indoor swimming pool & a central location, this is by far the fanciest place to stay. Some rooms come with a view of the Persian Gulf. **$$$**

Amin Hotel (50 rooms) Talaqani St, beside jetty for Qeshm & Hormuz; \0761 2244305–9; f 0761 2228138. Basic & clean, although rooms are a little dark & small. It is cheapest option in town. **$$**

Samco Restaurant \0761 4351743. A few kilometres along the coast from town, Samco is locally famous for excellent seafood. You will need to arrange a taxi to bring you here & to take you back. Enquire at your hotel. **$$**

What to see and do It has to be said, there is not a multiplicity of tourist attractions in the city; even in 1622 one Portuguese diplomat described it as 'more of an emporium than a town', while his English counterparts remarked that the town's fame rested on its *panj* ('five') or punch, made of *arak* (date alcohol), lemon juice, sugar, nutmeg and water, which 'occasions a Guddiness in the Head, Feavers and Fluxes, and is so corrosive that some, who have drunk immoderately of it, died'. The much-vaunted **Hindu temple** is a small stone and concrete building set back from the main boulevard, but as it is no longer a functioning place of worship, all the temple ornaments, statuary and images have been removed. The temple was built in 1888 to serve a large Indian community working for the British East India Company. Its 'factors' or merchants had withdrawn from Bandar-e Abbas after the fall of the Safavid dynasty c1735, but they returned in 1793 to administer the port and Hormuz on behalf of the ruler of Oman who had seized control. The temple dome is decorated with 72 small towers with lily flower carvings. And as for the little **Masjed-e Khadr** (Green Mosque) in the grounds of the Homa Hotel, it has been heavily repaired inside and outside with a new glass- and metal-frame extension. There is also a historical **Galedary Bathhouse** located behind Amin Hotel; it is presently closed, but an exception may be made for large groups. Enquire at the Amin Hotel reception for details.

The thriving, bustling **bazaars** of Bandar-e Abbas are fun, offering a very different range of goods imported mainly from the Far East; sunglasses are very good buys. Also on sale are the distinctive red cloth or leather facemasks and heavily (machine-) embroidered tight-legged trousers worn by women in the region. Offering different but just as colourful and fantastic produce is the small **fish market** at the western end of the coastal promenade. It seems a shame there is no good fish restaurant next door.

QESHM ISLAND Some 150km further east along the coast, the large island of Qeshm (pronounced Gheshm; 1,330km²), with a population of 100,000, comes into view, but the landing point is on the far eastern tip of the island, easily reached by ferry from Bandar-e Abbas less than an hour away. There's also a daily direct bus from Esfahan that takes you all the way to the island through the narrowest point between the mainland and the island at Bandar-e Pol. There is also an international airport on the island with connections to Dubai as well as daily flights to Tehran with a journey time of just over two hours. Tickets are best purchased from any Kish Air sales office located in every major city.

The vast resources of natural gas here have led the government to promote the island as an industrial free and duty-free zone since 1990. In the 1970s, preliminary archaeological surveys recorded an Achaemenid and Sassanid settlement and for centuries many cargo ships docked here for supplies and cargo, as recorded by Marco Polo.

Although the tourist potential for watersports, diving and recreation on the island has remained largely undeveloped, there is excellent birdwatching to be enjoyed on the island, justifying a day trip here.

Qeshm is a much livelier and a less glamorous island than Kish, but with more sites to attract foreign tourists looking for authentic experience. It was Kish, in fact, that was intended to become Iran's Dubai, which explains a myriad of luxurious hotels and cars on the island. All residents on Qeshm, of the other hand, have maintained their traditions and use Arabic and Persian interchangeably with older generations conversing essentially in Arabic. Due to the close cultural links to the other side of the Persian Gulf, Qeshm Iranians do not need a visa to visit Dubai if travelling by boat, but still require one for air travel. For location of Qeshm Island see map, page 206.

Where to stay and eat
🏠 **Golden Beach Resort** (54 rooms) Simin Beach Resort, South Saheli Rd beside Shah Shahid holy shrine; ✆f 0763 5342900–7. The nearest thing to a resort hotel is a few kilometres out of town, with bungalows, a restaurant & dive shop where you can hire equipment & book courses. **$$$**

🏠 **Park Hotel** (34 rooms) Azadegan St, beside the Red Crescent; ✆0763 5221459, f 0763 5226640. Popular with Iranians & offers accommodation in semi-detached houses grouped around a lovely inner courtyard. Has Alvand Restaurant where you can taste a local shark dish while looking over the town & the shimmering sea. **$$**

Getting around The town of Dargahan, 15km from the town of Qeshm, is the commercial centre of the island and is the terminal for buses arriving from the mainland. From here take a taxi to Qeshm, the actual capital and the ferry terminal for Bandar-e Abbas and Hormuz. Here you can hire a taxi for a day for approximately US$30 to explore the island and all the attractions it has to offer.

What to see and do The ruins of the **Portuguese castle** (*entry 5,000 rials*), built in the early 16th century in order to exert their control over the island, will most likely be the first site you visit. The castle remained in Portugese hands until its takeover by the Safavid army under the command of Imam Gholi Khan.

Around 15km further along the coast, passing by the Golden Beach Resort and the **Khorbas Caves** (☉ *07.00–17.00; entry 5,000 rials*), the tourist route leads towards the **Stars Valley** (Darreh Setaregan). This spectacular rock plateau formed around two million years ago as a result of wind and rain, and not by falling stars as the name suggests, is by far the most picturesque place on the island.

On the opposite shore of Qeshm and amid the oil rigs lies the famous **Mangrove Forest** (Jangal-e hara) where you can hire a boat to sail amid these amazing trees.

HORMUZ ISLAND (JAZIR-E HORMOZ) It's an enjoyable half-day trip from Bandar-e Abbas to Hormuz, about 18km from Bandar-e Abbas and 85km from Oman. Today it has a population of about 4,000 but, in times of political upheaval and military confrontation, ten times this number have sought temporary refuge on the island, despite the limited freshwater supplies; today water is piped over. If you have a torch, take it with you, as local children amuse themselves by damaging the electrical wiring in the fortress. (Finding a toilet is very difficult and there are no hotels here.)

Getting there By fibreglass **speedboat** from the main jetty in Bandar-e Abbas to the quay (Iskel-e Qadim) the journey takes approximately 45 minutes. For groups, it should be possible, with prior notice, to hire a ***dhow***, but the sailing time will be much longer. To gain access to the pier itself, entry tickets (*40,000 rials one-way*) have to be purchased from the ticket kiosk and surrendered to the officials sitting at the desk right in front.

What to see and do The best, and, in fact, the only way, to explore the whole island is to hire one of the local guides waiting on their pick-up motorcycles at the boat terminal. Such a tour is recommended and costs around 150,000 rials per person and is certainly worth it.

The driver will take you first to the **Portuguese sea fort** located on the north tip (far left) of Hormuz Island. It is clearly visible to your left from the ferry landing. If the main entry door is locked, retrace your steps to the metal gates immediately by the loading sheds to find the Iran Cultural Heritage Organisation representative, who will be delighted to show you around. The fortress was built from local pink, brown and green coral shortly after the island was taken by the Portuguese military hero, Alfonzo Albuquerque, in 1515, quickly taking advantage of the severe Safavid military defeat at Chaldiran (see pages 128–9) to maintain and extend Portuguese control of the sea trading routes from India and the East Indies to Europe. Portuguese military history tells of an eight-hour battle by a few hundred soldiers against 30,000 islanders and defence troops, but Persian records state Albuquerque took the island by bribery and treachery. The Ottoman navy tried but failed to seize the island in 1550, but after Shah Abbas I took control of Suru and renamed it Bandar-e Abbas in 1615, it was only a matter of time before the Portuguese were pushed out of Hormuz, in 1622, for in the 1580s only seven or eight soldiers defended the castle. As the English had assisted the shah in this action, the fort and all of the 40km²-odd island, along with 50% of the customs dues, were ceded to the East India Company, but the gradual collapse of Safavid authority, advancing rebel Afghan forces, and changes to the customs levies led 18th-century European merchants to move trading activities further west to Bushehr. It was not until 1868 that the Qajar shah regained authority, but it was too late, for the newly opened Suez Canal was causing most shipping companies to reroute their vessels. By 1893, life on the island was described by the British consul as 'miserable', with just 200 residents. Matters improved from the mid 1960s, when Bandar-e Abbas received development funds, and it later became the naval headquarters.

Originally the fortress was completely surrounded by water, but now the sea laps around less than half of the walls. By the main entrance are the **prison dungeons** but you need a torch to explore. A walk across the main courtyard leads to the **underground church**, whose cross-groined vaults are supported on great columns; the altar must have stood where the entry now is. From here it is a short walk to the splendid **underground cistern,** built with an inner walkway around it. It's easy to imagine off-duty Portuguese soldiers sitting, talking, smoking and drinking here in the delicious cool. There is no spring water on the island to speak of, so rainwater would have filtered through the coral stone to collect in this and other cisterns throughout the fortress. Other than the remains of a tower (now one floor) with windows and cannons, there are just the ramparts left to explore.

From the loading quays, the driver will then drive you along the sea walls past a pink stone building with a pseudo-Portuguese frontage. Until recently it served as an **army post** built as a residence for Mohammed Reza Shah, but is closed at present with no military personnel around. The exterior wall is decorated with paintings of military officers and their relatives, some of whom were killed while undertaking the hajj to Mecca in the 1980s. Further on are fishermen's houses with nets placed ready for the evening fishing, and children playing table tennis on rusting metal doors. Some archaeological excavation was undertaken in 1977 during which 14th- to 17th-century pottery kilns and also shards, including Chinese export ware, came to light. It is known that the famous 14th-century Arab geographer, Ibn Battuta, stayed in the Ziyaret-e Khadr, located in the main cemetery alongside the Ziyaret-e Mollah, but little remains. The whole island has a desolate air, having been neglected for many decades, but that said, the municipality is installing a new sewage system and constructing roads (for non-existent cars), so this investment should benefit the community.

The highlight of the island's natural beauty, however, is the multi-coloured salt **rock formations**, covering large areas of Hormuz. Your driver will willingly accompany you through the rocky landscape and show you around. Salt and associated sedimentary and igneous rocks with seawater running through have over the centuries created remarkable landscape, locally known as Kuh-e Namak (salt mountains). One of the pick-up motorcycle guides will also take you to salt mountain caves and the most beautiful beaches on the island. Swimming is allowed, but women, unfortunately, have to be fully dressed.

BACK ON THE MAINLAND The road north from Bandar-e Abbas leads directly to Kerman but this is a very busy road, especially the first 150km climbing up into the mountains, crowded with lorries and tankers. But this route does take you past **Sirjan** (see page 243) where a British team found the remains of a Sassanid palace in the 1970s. Less tortuous, and with almost as dramatic scenery, is the road east towards Minab and then north via Kahnuj and Sabzvaran. The shelters for the Baluchi migratory families in this region are very distinctive, reminiscent of **reed huts** in the Iraqi delta area. Tall reeds are bent over to form a long barrel vault and covered with palm fronds, so making a shaded but well-ventilated shelter.

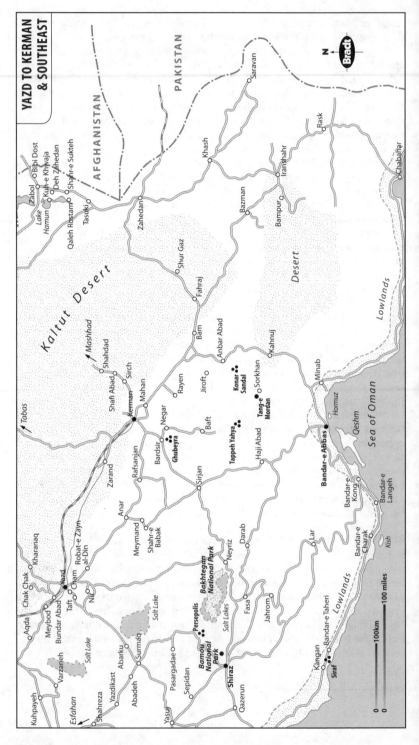

11

En Route to Yazd and Kerman

Yazd is the most historically interesting Zoroastrian city in Iran and is a must-see site for its wind towers, minarets and the nearby 'towers of silence'. However, the smaller city of Kerman, is also worth a visit – not only for its architecture that reflects 1,700 years of settlement, but also for the carpets and jewellery on sale in its sprawling bazaars. The motorway south runs from Tehran past Yazd, and continues on to Kerman and beyond.

COMING TO YAZD FROM THE SOUTHWEST

From the crossroads at Surmaq, on the south–north route from Shiraz to Esfahan, the road to the northeast goes through **Abarku** (also spelt Aburqeh, literally 'On the Mountain') 45km away. The town (population 31,000) is best visited by car or rented taxi from Shiraz or Yazd. Buses from Esfahan depart inconveniently at 16.00 daily and the journey takes up to four hours. (The Abarku Tourist Inn is unfortunately no longer open for foreign tourists.)

Abarku had been a famous textile and trading centre in medieval times, but it never recovered from being devastated by rebel Afghan troops in the early 18th century. In the centre of town is the Masjed-e Jame with a classic four-*ivan* ground plan, probably established in the 14th century when its 'Baroque' plaster *mihrab* (1338) was installed in the left (on entering) *ivan*, although the domed prayer chamber could be from 12th-century Seljuk times. The town still has a very run-down air, though 50 years ago architectural historians began clamouring that urgent repairs to the sun dried and fired bricks should be made at a number of once-beautiful 14th-century tombs here before it was too late to save them. In particular, archaeologists pointed to tombs such as the Mausoleum of Pir-e Hamza Sabz Push, with its lovely Ilkhanid *mihrab*, and the 1315 **Tomb of Hassan Ibn Kaikhosrow** (also known as Mazar-e Tavus) with its decorated interior. One mausoleum, one of the earliest tomb towers surviving in Iran, is on the hillside just to the south as you leave Abarku for Yazd. Small, austere and (over) restored, this octagonal Gonbad-e Ali was built for a local warlord, 'the illustrious, the pure, the happy … Amid al-Din Shams al-Dawla' and his wife, by their son in 1057, according to the brick inscription around the exterior. The area is often litter-strewn, but there is a superb view across the plateau from which the local ice houses can easily be spotted.

If you are keen on good vernacular architecture, do examine the layout and arrangement of an **ice house** (*yakhchal*) while in this region. There is a fine example here at the entrance of Abarku, coming from Esfahan or Shiraz or, if this is not convenient, there is a restored one near Azadi Square in Kerman. As with the cisterns and wind towers, these are made of fired brick and probably those that have survived are no earlier than the 19th century in date. The basic

At the heart of Sufism is the belief that within everybody is a spark of the Divine, the Creator, and that through dedicated ritual and practice, this spark may be ignited so that the individual becomes one with the Divine, perhaps for a mere split second, perhaps longer. (The word 'Sufi' is traditionally thought to come from the *suf* or woollen robe worn by devotees during their meetings.) Today there are still a number of Sufi orders or fraternities; arguably the most famous in the West are the Mevlani, known popularly as the whirling dervishes. Following the ideas of the 13th-century mystic, Jalal al-Din Rumi, buried in Konya, Turkey, the ritual practised by this Sunni Sufi order is characterised by devotees moving in a large circle around a room while spinning clockwise to music arranged in four musical movements, each representing a season of the year. There is also the Naqshbandi fraternity (which, incidentally, has a keen following in Peckham, south London), again among the Sunni community, which has no esoteric ritual but dedicates all actions and deeds to the Divine. The ritual may be just the rhythmic voicing of the name of Allah, as it is with one order in Deptford, Kent (UK). The aim is the same, the sublimation of the material self and ego, thus freeing the spirit so that the divine spark may ignite.

Historically the government and the established clergy have often expressed hostility towards the Sufi orders because the fraternities were often organised as lodges separate and dissociated from the mosques, and their *pirs* (masters) were rarely reticent in pointing out any social injustices, worldliness or sham devotions of the *ulama*. Also, women were often given greater access within these 'unofficial' circles, which could include visiting dervishes who had given up their home and family life to show others the 'way'. One of the greatest mystics was Rabi'a of Basra (d801CE) who caused an outcry among the *ulama* when she announced: 'I have ceased to exist and have passed out of self. I exist in God and am altogether His.'

plan is that of a large brick dome chamber set deep into the ground, with a single door for access. Outside, there should be the remains of a long high mud-brick wall facing south to keep the lower dome section in shade. Beneath, there may still be signs of shallow beds along the wall. In winter months, 15–25cm of water was let in to flood these beds and freeze overnight. The ice was then broken up into blocks for storage, and insulated with straw in the chamber for summer use. Simple but very effective.

After the last roundabout on the very outskirts of Abarku (in the direction of Yazd) there is a huge brick complex set back to the right (notionally south). This was the family house of a politician who served in a pre-revolutionary parliament, and nearby there is a small fort with thick corner towers. The late 19th- and early 20th-century residence, known locally as **Amidsalar**, is ruined; the ground floor has a large and high central room surrounded by small chambers, while a well-worn exterior staircase at the back gives access to the first floor. To get into the **fort**, known by the same name, it is possible to scramble around the walls but, as its entrance is on the other side, it's quicker and easier to return to the main road and continue to the next (metalled) turning, which takes one almost directly to the entry gate. It is well worth exploring; you'll find the latrines, stables, bread ovens and a mosque, as well as the corner watchtowers.

In the south of the town is **Masjed-e Birun** near the cemetery. It has a two-ivan plan with a domed sanctuary, which could be earlier in date than its (ruined) Timurid minaret and repair work. The prayer chamber area was heavily restored in the 18th century.

The road to Yazd goes through a 'desert' area with a salt lake lying to the south; there has been systematic planting of camel thorn and other desert shrubs here in an attempt to prevent the spread of the saline earth. Approaching Yazd, between the two chains of hills (especially if you are flying in during daylight hours) you will see lines of holes, like ruined giant anthills coming from the hillside across the land. These are inspection holes marking *qanat*s or **underground channels**, which brought water to irrigate the fields. The knowledge and skill needed to locate the right spot in the hills to tap into the water table, to angle and construct the tunnels to obtain the correct flow, beggar belief. Every year the *qanat*s were checked for damage, removal of debris, etc and although modern irrigation systems are fast taking over, just occasionally one still sees a windlass device resting on top of an inspection hole.

Taft, 26km southwest of Yazd, has an important Timurid building which is now Taft Anthropology Museum (*entry 50,000 rials*). This late 15th-century Mausoleum of Shah Khalilullah and the adjoining Masjed-e Shah Vali were built by the sister of Safavid shah Tahmasp. The famous Sufi mystic, Ne'matollah Vali Kermani (see page 245) was responsible directly or indirectly for persuading the Timurid provincial governor to allocate four years of tax revenue to this complex, and since then it has always been important for Sufis of the Ne'matollah order. Later embellishments were paid for by Tahmasp's sister in the 16th century.

In the 14th century the Sufi movement evidently had a great following in this area as, some 30km from Nir at **Bidakhavid**, 57km southwest of Yazd, there are two shrines facing each other. One is the mosque-shrine of a Sufi sheikh, Taj al-Din Binyaman, identified and dated (1379) by his elaborately carved tombstone and consisting of three elements: a courtyard, a mosque and the tomb. As the shrine is a little larger than the mosque, it seems likely that this was originally built as a *khanaqeh* or meeting place for his disciples, and then became his tomb after his death. The other complex is the Masjed-e Jame, which possesses the unusual upper gallery arrangement in the square domed prayer hall, as seen in Yazd (see pages 234–5). Its stone *mihrab* is decorated with Quranic verses (Q3:38–40) and dated 1437, perhaps marking the completion of the building works.

Right before the police checkpoint 20km southwest on approach to Yazd lies the small Zoroastrian village of **Cham** (signposted). Drive past the first group of houses along the tarmac road towards the hill with its *dakhmeh*, a Zoroastrian tower of silence. Its platform is nicely laid out of stone, unlike the two examples in Yazd (see pages 236–7).

YAZD *Telephone code 0351*

The town (altitude 1,215m; population 551,000; 677km southeast from Tehran) has long been associated with Zoroastrianism, and the production of textiles. It fell to the Arab invaders in 642CE but the Zoroastrian community was strong here until the late 17th century. There were still plenty of adherents left in the 19th century, when official persecution caused many to flee to India or to Tehran, where the presence of foreign diplomatic missions offered more protection. Today, Zoroastrians form less than 10% of the town's population; in 1995 there were an estimated 12,000 or fewer in the city, mainly located in the Pusht-e Khan Ali quarter. When Marco Polo visited in 1272, noting its fine textiles and its strategic location on trade routes from

India and central Asia, this 'Good and Noble city' was walled, but undoubtedly today he would get hopelessly lost in the confusion of ring roads and roundabouts.

Today Yazd is one of the most tourist-friendly cities in Iran and offers excellent souvenir-shopping opportunities. Look through the workshops selling handwoven silk cloth *termeh*, produced solely in Yazd. Traditional hotels are abundant and conveniently located in the old town centre, while many tourists and backpackers use the city as their base to explore nearby desert dunes. Yazd is also known as the Hosseiniyeh of Iran, the centre of the Imam Hossein commemorative celebrations in the country.

GETTING THERE AND AROUND There are at least two **flights** daily to Yazd from Tehran and once a week to Baghdad and Najaf in Iraq. Flying time from Tehran is only an hour. There are daily overnight **buses** and **train** connections from the Iranian capital and most major population centres to Yazd. Within the town, **walking** is possible in the historic centre. To travel to and from the airport (10km away from the city), bus terminal and railway station, as well as for excursions to the hinterland, **taxis** are available. It is not recommended, in particular for single female travellers, to walk unaccompanied in the old town quarter after dark.

TOURIST INFORMATION AND TOUR GUIDES The **tourism information office** (*opposite Alexander's Prison;* ✆ 6216542; f 6216546) can assist in hiring a taxi and has a wide range of maps and information leaflets. For personalised and guided tours, contact the very knowledgeable English-speaking guide **Mohsen Hajisaeid** from Yazd Tourism Grand Society (*34 13th Alley, Rejaei St;* ✆ 6205205; m 091 33514460; e *yazdguide@yahoo.com; www.iranpersiatour.com*) or his wife **Pegah Latifi** (m 091 33524460), also a tour guide.

 WHERE TO STAY AND EAT All hotels below, except Safaiyeh Hotel, are located in traditional houses with bedrooms generally below street level in order to remain cool in hot weather and hence have no 'view'. Each hotel, however, has a good traditional restaurant, serving excellent Yazdian sweets and tea, and budget accommodation here is easily the best in the country. The large number of tourists in Yazd and the recent renovations mean Wi-Fi is available in all the hotels below. It might not always be reliable, but generally works. A number of traditional and slightly more expensive hotels operate under the Mehr chain. For more information contact Mehr information office ✆ 6216543–5. For location of listings see map opposite unless otherwise stated.

⌂ **Dad Hotel** (61 rooms) 214 Farvardin St; ✆6229400; e info@hoteldadint.com; www. hoteldadint.com. The largest & one of the more expensive traditional hotels, it is located in a former 19th-century house & still managed by the descendants of the person who made it into a hotel 80 years ago. Has a pleasant rooftop restaurant as well as a very fancy indoor restaurant that may be booked for ceremonies or public events. **$$$**

⌂ **Safaiyeh Hotel** (192 rooms) Safaiyeh, Shahid Fallahi St; ✆8260210–20; e info@ safaiyehhotel.com; www.safaiyehhotel.com. Modern & flashy, although built in traditional style, it has a swimming pool, sauna & all kinds of facilities to impress. Self-proclaimed as a 5-star hotel, it offers solid 3-star accommodation. The interior is a mix of old & new, & much less authentic than the options below. A little too far from the centre & requires a taxi ride to get to the old town. **$$$**

⌂ **Fahadan Mehr Hotel** (16 rooms) Opposite Alexander's Prison, Fahadan St; ✆6300600–1. The inner courtyard is overflowing with traditional curios & the large parrot, who dwells at the yard welcoming guests, adds some charm. The staff are friendly & helpful, albeit a little full of importance.

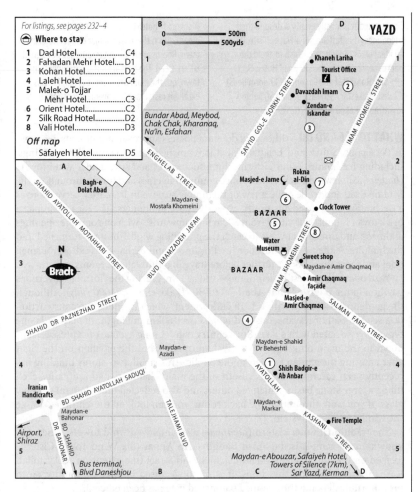

For listings, see pages 232–4

🛏 **Where to stay**

1	Dad Hotel	C4
2	Fahadan Mehr Hotel	D1
3	Kohan Hotel	D2
4	Laleh Hotel	C4
5	Malek-o Tojjar
	Mehr Hotel	C3
6	Orient Hotel	C2
7	Silk Road Hotel	D2
8	Vali Hotel	D3

Off map

Safaiyeh Hotel D5

YAZD

It is perhaps the only traditional hotel in Yazd that charges (*15,000 rials*) just to have a look inside. Others let you wander around for free. **$$**

🛏 **Laleh Hotel** (38 rooms) Next to Ab Anbar Golshan (reservoir), Taal area, Bassij Bd; 📞6225048; e info@yazdlalehhotel.com; www. yazdlalehhotel.com/en/. A traditional hotel since 2004, its design is perhaps a little excessively modern, which at times overshadows the historic Qajar residence the hotel is in. **$$**

🛏 **Malek-o Tojjar Mehr Hotel** (10 rooms) Inside the Panje Ali Bazaar; 📞6261478. Qajar-era home converted to an atmospheric traditional hotel with a small reception area & a lovely inner courtyard. The staff come across as a little uninterested & it might prove to be a challenge to locate the hotel, as you have to walk through the bazaar itself. **$$**

🛏 **Vali Hotel** (16 rooms) Imam Khomeini St, across from Shahzadeh Fazl; 📞6228050–4. Popular with locals, this hotel is somewhat neglected by foreign tourists. It has one of the nicer inner roofed courtyards you will come across in Yazd & staff are pleasant & accommodating. **$$**

🛏 **Kohan Hotel** (20 rooms) Right before Alexander's Prison; 📞6212485, 6211297. Family run, this is one of the oldest traditional hotels in Yazd offering private rooms & also dormitory-style accommodation. Located in the heart of the old town, it has a welcoming reception area & polite staff. **$**

🛏 **Orient Hotel** (16 rooms) Off Masjed-e Jame St & across the main road leading up to Silk Road Hotel; 📞6267783. Excellently located, this hotel has, however, lost some of its character.

En Route to Yazd and Kerman   YAZD

11

233

The restaurant is mostly empty & despite their friendliness the staff are not always on site. It is an ideal place though if you wish to avoid the backpacker banter in the Silk Road Hotel. **$**

🏠 **Silk Road Hotel** (9 rooms & 12 dorm beds) 5 Taleh Khakestary St, Masjed Jame St, behind Imamzadeh Rokna al-Din; ✆ 6252730;

e silkroad_hotel@yahoo.com. A backpacker's dream, this is the most popular budget hotel in town. Rooms are small but traditionally designed & very clean. The staff are not the friendliest in town, but the manager is polite & helpful. Has excellent restaurant & convenient location. **$**

WHAT TO SEE AND DO   Although it does not possess any royal monuments like those at Persepolis, Shiraz and Esfahan, Yazd is renowned for its **vernacular buildings**, including ice houses, water cisterns, domestic houses and spectacular wind towers (*badgirs*). Such wind catchers were once common in cities and towns throughout the Middle East, and while quite a few of them now survive in Iran, they serve more as a decoration since residents prefer expensive air conditioners. The idea is simple: a brick tower is built – anything from 30cm high upwards – with one or more openings at the top and directional vents to catch the prevailing wind. The air is funnelled into the building, either at ground-floor level or lower, and perhaps passed over a small pool and fountain to cool it further before travelling through the rooms.

Yazd boasts the tallest *badgir* in the world at 33m, gracing the (former) governor's pavilion in the **Bagh-e Dolat Abad** (☉ *07.30–17.00; entry 150,000 rials*). Although the garden is associated with a 1718 endowment, which included the construction of a school, bath, caravanserais and *qanats* over 60km in length, the layout is one typically associated with a late 18th-century date. A long avenue of cypresses leads down to the main building (now private property), but the pavilion on the right after entering the garden is open to the public. This small, two-storey building has recently been carefully repaired. Both of the main chambers had fountains, each filling a large stone basin, which fed others and also reflected the colourful window glass. If you walk through to the back room, you can look up the 'chimney' to see the wind ventilation system.

The traditional water cistern (*ab anbar*) also employed wind towers. One well-known Yazd example is the **Shish Badgir-e Ab Anbar** (Six Wind Tower Cistern) located on the north side of Shahid Dr Beheshti Street (the extension of Ayatollah Kashani Street) behind the shops. It is no longer used by the community, so to prevent rubbish being thrown in, a padlocked gate has been erected.

An interesting cluster of historic buildings lies further north around the **Masjed-e Jame**, which was founded by the local Seljuk commander in 1119 over a ruined Sassanid fire temple, and largely rebuilt during the 14th century. Visitors to the mosque are immediately struck by the disproportionately high minarets over the entrance, which render the (double) dome almost insignificant. These are the first indication of 14th-century work, along with the 1324–28 entrance vestibule decorated with numerous plaques recording local decrees, taxes and endowments. Most of the splendid ceramic patterning in the main prayer hall beyond was put in place 40 or so years later. The work is worth looking at, whether for the geometric strapwork in turquoise against a brick surface with intricately cut and moulded plaster infills, or the 'mosaic' jigsaw panels of the magnificent 1375 *mihrab* – although each year it seems more replacement tile pieces have been inserted. The prayer hall has an unusual gallery arrangement (for women?) occasionally seen in other late 14th-century mosques, but here the heavy piers and vaulting system disperse the weight, allowing the side walls to be pierced by windows, bringing shafts of light into the chamber. On the right is a large winter prayer hall built in the 16th century by the Safavid architect Saad Ibn Mohammed Kaduk. The bare whitewashed walls make the beautiful proportions and transverse vaulting fully apparent. In the courtyard (104 x 99m) there are steps on this side, leading down to an underground room with a disused *qanat*.

Leaving by the same entrance, take the second left in the parking area and nearby, on your immediate right, is the small entrance into the popular shrine **Imamzadeh Rokna al-Din** (🕐 *08.00–13.00 & 16.00–20.00, mornings only on Fri*), dating to 1325. Little, but enough, remains of the original complex of school and library that was once renowned for its mechanical sciences. Its minarets were surmounted with automata such as a bird, which turned to face the sun, and chroniclers described a huge circular wall calendar whose rings and sections constantly moved to show the passage of time. The exterior still retains some exquisite detail, which is easily overlooked. Inside the gloomy, single-domed chamber housing the cenotaph is a mass of low relief plasterwork carved and painted (and originally gilded) in strong 14th-century central Asian style, akin to that of the architecture in Samarkand and Shahri Sabz, Uzbekistan. The high walls are decorated with plaster moulding in blind niche forms of varying size in rows, and panels of plaited Kufic calligraphy. Huge teardrop medallions in plaster embellish the dome interior (diameter 12m) and underneath is the silver-gilt grille protecting the cenotaph. At certain (undefined) times, groups of women come to pay their respects, in which case male visitors are requested to view the interior from the doorway.

Continue along this alley, crossing the modern Hosseiniyeh space (if in doubt bear left) and eventually you will reach **Zendan-e Iskandar** (Alexander's Prison) (*Zaiee Sq;* 🕐 *08.00–17.00, till 20.00 in summer; entry 100,000 rials*) tucked back in the same open space as the **Davazdah Imam** (12 Imams). Safavid history tells that Alexander the Great built a castle in Yazd (then known as Kasah), but local tradition says he was actually imprisoned here in the extensive underground chamber beneath the courtyard. The present building is much later, finished in 1305, and is now used as a theological college. It was largely rebuilt in 1671, although the domed prayer hall to the right of the entrance retains some 14th-century decorative plaster. It is quite a trek to walk here but the additional presence of the little Davazdah Imam which has recently reopened after restoration makes the walk worthwhile. This latter building of 1038 is known for having fine-quality plasterwork in the *mihrab* and dome but, despite its name, none of the imams or their relatives was interred here. It is thought the two Shi'a brothers who paid for the construction meant it to be purely a commemorative building, for the painted inscriptions (including Q2:158, 163, 255–6; Q40:65, 67) stress belief in the Imamate and are clearly a personal selection. You could walk north from here, asking directions to the **Khaneh Lariha** (🕐 *08.00–17.00, till 20.00 in summer; entry 100,000 rials*), a conserved and repaired 19th-century merchant's house. It has a charming atmosphere with a large pool in the central courtyard over which sits a huge, gently disintegrating wooden *charpoy*. All explanations inside the house are in Farsi only.

In the central bazaar area around Maydan-e Amir Chaqmaq, you could visit the Amir Chaqmaq complex and the mosque of **Amir Chaqmaq** both named after the former ruler of Yazd. The mosque (🕐 *during prayer times only*) was constructed in 1437, along with a hostel, cistern and *qanat*, bath and caravanserai, built by a local prince and his wife, who was linked to the central Asian family of Timur Leng (d1405); only the mosque and her tomb remain. The mosque layout, with its 16m² courtyard, two *ivans* and the prayer chamber with an upper gallery like the Masjed-e Jame are original, as is the 'mosaic' tilework in the prayer chamber and on the *mihrab*. The eastern section, on the other hand, was extensively repaired in the 19th century.

Most visitors, however, are attracted by the multi-storey building at the end of the *maydan*. Like the Palace of the Winds, Jaipur (north India), it is pure **façade**, constructed in the 19th century on early 15th-century foundations to provide a viewing stand for city parades and ceremonies, especially those of Moharram. A huge wooden *nakhl*, shaped like a giant (palm) leaf, stands on the right, waiting to be draped in black cloth and carried by 70 or so young men next year. The central gateway used to lead into another bazaar, now demolished; the few remaining shops include makers of sugar-cones, who are happy for visitors to take photographs (though the atmosphere will quickly catch the throat).

Turning away from the Amir Chaqmaq complex façade, walk ahead towards the main crossroads. On the corner is Yazd's famous **sweetmeat and biscuit shop** (*Haj Khalife Ali Rabar*). Also in Amir Chaqmaq Square is the **Water Museum** (⊕ *08.00–14.00 & 15.30–19.00 daily; entry 10,000 rials*), in a traditional merchant's house of about 1890. There is good plasterwork especially in the audience platform area and the exhibition showing the system of cooling and underground living is in the basement with good information and colour pictures of *qanat* construction and repair, along with the tools; there are some English captions.

After the crossroads on the other side of the road are some high-quality nut and dried fruit shops. Walking down this side takes you past a marvellously understated pair of **wooden doors** dating from the Safavid period; the detail is superb. On the opposite side of the busy road are passageways into the fabric, furnishings and gold shops of the bazaar, but continue for another 400m or so and ask directions to **Maydan-e Khan**, the fruit and vegetable section. At the far end of this huge courtyard is a small office of a *naqqash* (traditional textile designer) with his cartoons and drawings (for carpet making) ready for sale or hire. The narrow passage to its immediate right leads to the **Hamam Khan** of 1797, a former bathhouse. It is now a traditional restaurant that you are welcome to walk around for a fee of 5,000 rials, as stated in Farsi on the plaque at the main entrance.

Before leaving Yazd, make time for the central **Zoroastrian fire temple** (Ateshkadeh) (*Kashani St; ⊕ 08.00–17.00; entry 10,000 rials*). Located in a side street off Ayatollah Kashani Street, it has the appearance of a family house set within a garden. Accommodation for pilgrims is located in the main section, which, as with the actual temple area, is off-limits to casual visitors. Nevertheless, the sight of the sacred fire burning in a huge steel vessel brings the philosophy and history of Zoroastrianism home. This fire, protected by a glass screen to prevent pollution from people's breath, has been burning since 470CE if not earlier (see page 173). In all there are some 18 fire temples operating in Yazd itself and the surrounding villages.

Two *dakhmeh* (also spelt 'dakhma', Zoroastrian 'towers of silence') are situated a little south of town, after the hotel and restaurant Safaiyeh. In accordance with Zoroastrian laws governing the sanctity of earth, fire, air and water, in Achaemenid times the dead were exposed and their bones later gathered to be placed in ossuaries or tombs in rock. But in later centuries large circular stone walls were built on rock and the bodies of Zoroastrian men, women and children were placed on their designated, paved zone on the open stone platform inside. A small central pit, filled with sand, charcoal and phosphorus to prevent pollution of the earth, acted as the drain. These towers are no longer in use (Zoroastrians are now interred in the nearby cemetery within a concrete chamber to avoid pollution of the earth), so with time and energy visitors may climb up them – the smaller, lower one on the right entailing a marginally shorter, easier clamber with access high up. Access into the other *dakhmeh* is best made from the gentle rise on the extreme left rather than the track on the extreme right. These towers were constructed according to strict observance of prayer and ritual, so please treat them accordingly, even though others clearly have not. Below, there is a collection of buildings, a water cistern with two wind towers and rooms for mourners. There is also a mortuary reception area, where the body would be cleansed and dressed in a clean but old sacred shirt (*sudreh*), before being tied to a metal bier by the sacred girdle (*kusti*) for carrying to the platform. The local authorities have turned a blind eye to vandalism of these buildings, which only serves to fuel foreigners' negative perceptions of religious tolerance in modern Iran. If you come here for the sunset, climb up the lower of the two towers as the top platform on the higher *dakhmeh* has high side walls blocking the view.

North of Yazd A day trip from Yazd can be combined to visit **Meybod**, 50km northwest, with the remains of the mud-brick **Narin Fort** (*entry 100,000 rials*) that once protected the old caravan route and the town itself. As the name suggests, this used to be a strong Zoroastrian centre (*moybed*: priest). A nicely restored caravanserai with traditional double-cloth *zilu* workshops is well worth a five-minute taxi ride from the fort. Adjacent to the caravanserai you find a welcoming **post office museum** (*entry 10,000 rials*), located in what used to be one of the 99 similar post office stations, known as *chaparkhaneh*, around Iran. This is the last remaining. Here you can also ask for the key to the *yakhchal* (ice house) right across the road. Meybod is known as a production centre for domestic pottery incorporating 'traditional' patterns and colouring. It also possesses a 15th-century Masjed-e Jame (in the mid 1970s the mosque still owned a historic *zilu* or floor-covering with a woven date corresponding to 1405).

In **Bundar Abad**, 35km northwest of Yazd, there is a 14th-century complex honouring the Sufi sheikh Taq al-Din Dada Mohammed (d1301) buried here in 1321. It has one of Iran's mere handful of tiled *minbars*, patterned with eight- and twelve-star motifs, probably made and installed at the same time as a carved marble panel, in 1473.

Some 80km northeast of Yazd is **Kharanaq** which you should consider visiting for the ruined Safavid village and its shaking minaret. The nearby caravanserai once functioned as a Silk Road guesthouse with a traditional restaurant, but has since closed.

You must find time for **Chak Chak** (Pir-e Sabz Shrine), some 50km northeast of Yazd (turning at Hossein Abad), to visit the **shrine of Banu Pars** (*entry 10,000 rials*), dedicated to the goddess Anahita. The taxi will drop you off at the parking area to let you climb the numerous flights of steps up to reach the small grotto shrine. This is no living village, rather a desolate collection of houses and communal kitchens to accommodate pilgrims. Only a few families look after the place, including a reticent shrine attendant who ensures all visitors remove their shoes. The shrine itself is understated, consisting of a grotto housing an ancient *chenar* (oriental plane) tree with the marble grotto floor covered in water dropping from the mountain (in Persian *chak chak* means water dripping). The doors and walls date only from the early 1960s but it is known that pilgrims have come here in June since 1626, if not earlier. According to Islamic chronicles, however, this was the place where a daughter of the last Sassanid shah, Yazdegerd III (d651), pursued by the invading Arabs, begged for help. Desperately thirsty, she was offered a bowl of milk, only for it to be overturned by a cow before she could drink it (Anahita was traditionally offered bull sacrifices). Terrified for her life, she prayed that the rock face would open up for her and she disappeared into it; similar stories are connected with the shrine near Rayy (see pages 86–7) and further afield in Maaloula near Damascus, Syria, at the grotto of St Tikla.

Towards Kerman On the road to Kerman, the most visible monuments are caravanserais, the first standing to the west of the main road about 55km from Yazd, the other approximately 65km further on and almost straddling the modern highway. The first is known as the **Robat-e Zayn al-Din**, built by a Safavid governor of Kerman. It consists of a circular enclosing wall with five towers and a monumental entrance. Inside, the accommodation and relaxation areas were arranged around a 12-sided court with a large hall opposite the main door. The whole building has been so extensively restored that the functions of the various rooms can no longer be distinguished, but in a caravanserai of this size there should have been a small mosque, kitchen area and perhaps a *hamam*. About 100m away is the ruined, two-storey stable block with its mangers still intact. Heavily vitrified bricks in the broken dome of the small corner chamber, with two broken fireboxes in the extreme right corner of the courtyard, suggest to us that this was the blacksmith's forge for making horseshoes and the like. The second caravanserai before Anar is thought to be earlier in date. The smaller section on one side of the building perhaps acted as the toll house, levying the dues from passing merchant trains, while the main building offered accommodation and stabling.

Around 40km southeast along the same road, but turning towards Mehriz, lies a small village of **Sar Yazd**, with the remains of what is known as the Fortress of Sar Yazd and a number of other examples of Sassanid architecture, including water cisterns, a post office and a caravanserai.

From here head on to Kerman via **Rafsanjan**, from where the former Iranian president takes his name. There are numerous groves of pistachio trees on either side of the main road. It is not a dramatic landscape but there is another large caravanserai complex about 10km the other side of Rafsanjan, and with all the *qanat* inspection holes dotted across the plain, you might spot local repair teams in action.

KERMAN   *Telephone code 0341*

Perhaps founded by the Sassanid shah Ardashir I in the early 3rd century (it was called Beh-e Ardashir until Safavid times), the town of Kerman (987km south from Tehran) quickly succumbed to the Arab armies in 642CE. Thereafter, all the major regimes in the region were eager to control this important town linking the old caravan routes from Afghanistan, India and the south coast into the Iranian heartlands. It came under Seljuk authority in 1041, but severe damage by Turkoman tribesmen in 1187 resulted in Zarand (87km northwest) becoming the provincial centre, and this opened the way for a Mongol general to establish a short-lived principality here. The town continued to pass from hand to hand – Muzaffarid authority to Timurid (until that empire fragmented) to the Qara Qoyunlu and then the Aq Qoyonlu tribal confederations – until Iran was 'united' under Safavid control. Kerman had always had a large Zoroastrian community, but in the last years of the 17th century the Safavid shah Soleyman yielded to theological demands that the community be relocated to the north of the city. By the mid 19th century, perhaps only 150 Zoroastrian families remained in Kerman itself. From 1750 until 1792 the region, including Bam, was controlled by the Ismailis with the agreement of the Zand family. With the Qajar advance and takeover of Zand authority, the Ismaili community left for Tehran and then migrated to India.

Despite such a troubled political history, the region had a long-established reputation in textile production, especially carpet weaving, even before Safavid shah Abbas I established a royal carpet workshop here. Marco Polo mentioned its leather workers and silk embroiderers in 1271. Keep an eye open for the distinctive Kerman embroidery of chain-stitch and *tambour* (referring to the embroidery patterns made on fabric stretched over a drum-shaped frame) on scarlet-red wool cloth (but reject cheaper manmade fabrics); again one pays for quality. Its rug production achieved such quality that Kerman carpets graced the imperial Mughal court of northern India as well as Safavid palaces and pavilions. Such carpets were described by Engelbert Kaempfer (d1716), doctor and secretary to the Swedish envoy, as decorated with animal motifs, so possibly the famous 16th- and 17th-century 'Animal' and 'Hunting' carpets (such as those housed in the Victoria and Albert Museum, London, and the Metropolitan Museum, New York) were actually woven here.

These days Kerman has a population of more than 621,000 and is the most important city in the region. It has a lovely old town with a vast bazaar and a good choice of jewellery shops. Kerman is also the best place to explore one of the most picturesque Persian gardens in the country, Bagh-e Shahzade in Mahan, as well as the desert areas to the northeast. It boasts a wonderful museum of modern Persian art – that alone is a worth a trip all the way here.

GETTING THERE AND AROUND IranAir operates three direct weekly **flights** from Tehran: two early morning departures and one in the evening and they take 1½ hours. There are also three daily **bus** departures from Yazd passing through Rafsanjan, with a journey time of three hours and a fare of 40,000 rials. If coming from Shiraz, you can hire a **private taxi**, leaving the city in the morning and driving through Persepolis, Pasargadae and Naqsh-e Rostam, covering a distance of around

THE HAMAM

Here is the account of an early 19th-century traveller's reaction to bathing, Persian-style:

The bather having undressed in the outer room, and retaining nothing about him but a piece of loose cloth around his waist, is conducted by the proper attendant into the hall of the bath; a large white sheet is then spread on the floor, on which the bather extends himself [and warm water is poured over him] … The attendant then takes his employer's head upon his knees, and rubs in with all his might, a sort of wet paste of henna plant, into the mustachios and beard … Again he has recourse to the little pail, and showers upon his quiescent patient another torrent of warm water. Then putting on a glove made of soft hair, yet possessing some of the scrubbing-brush qualities, he first takes the limbs, and then the body, rubbing them hard for three quarters of an hour [after which, follows pumicing] … To this succeeds the shampooing, which is done by pinching, pulling, and rubbing, with so much force and pressure as to produce a violent glow over the whole frame. Some of the natives delight in having every joint in their bodies strained till they crack … that the very vertebrae of the back are made to ring a peal in rapid succession … This over, the shampooed body, reduced again to its prostrate state, is rubbed all over with a preparation of soap confined in a bag, till he is one mass of lather. The soap is then washed off with warm water, when a complete ablution succeeds by his being led to the cistern, and plunged in.

From R Ker Porter, *Travels in Georgia, Persia, Armenia* …,1821, vol I, pp231–2

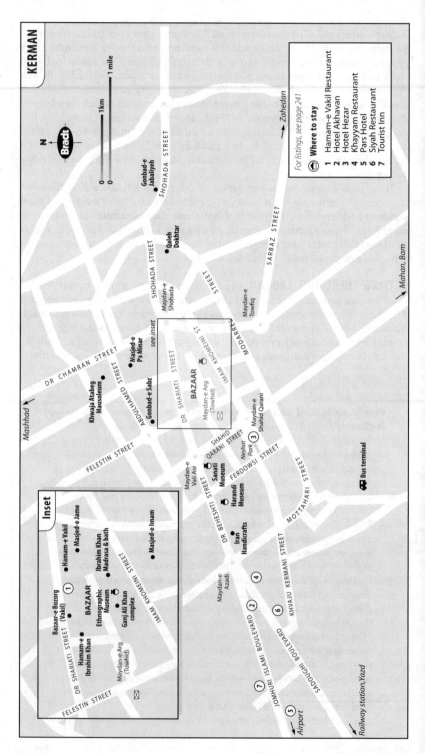

KERMAN

N

Bradt

0   1km
0   1 mile

Mashhad

Gonbad-e
Jabaliyeh

SHOHADA STREET

Qaleh
Dokhtar

SHOHADA STREET

Maydan-e
Shohada

see inset

DR CHAMRAN STREET

Masjed-e
Pa Minar

Khwaja Atabeg
Mausoleum

ABDULHAMED STREET

Gonbad-e Sabz

SHARIATI STREET

IMAM KHOMEINI ST

FELESTIN STREET

BAZAAR

DR SHARIATI STREET

Maydan-e Arg
(Towhid)

Maydan-e
Towfiq

SARBAZ STREET

STREET

MODARRES

Zahedan

Mahan, Bam

SHAHID
QARANI STREET

Maydan-e
Shahid Qarani

Neshat
Park

③

FERDOWSI STREET

Maydan-e
Vali Asr

Sanati
Museum

Harandi
Museum

DR BEHESHTI STREET

Iran
Handicrafts

Maydan-e
Azadi

④

MOTTAHARI STREET

Bus terminal

Inset

Hamam-e Vakil

Masjed-e Jame

Bazaar-e Bozorg
(Vakil)   ①

BAZAAR

Ibrahim Khan
Madrasa & bath

Ethnographic
Museum

DR SHARIATI STREET

Hamam-e
Ibrahim Khan

Ganj Ali Khan
complex

Maydan-e Arg
(Towhid)

IMAM KHOMEINI STREET

FELESTIN STREET

Masjed-e Imam

JOMHURI ISLAMI BOULEVARD

②

⑥

⑦

SADOUGHI BOULEVARD

⑤

KHAJU KERMANI STREET

Airport

Railway station, Yazd

For listings, see page 241

Where to stay
1 Hamam-e Vakil Restaurant
2 Hotel Akhavan
3 Hotel Hezar
4 Khayyam Restaurant
5 Pars Hotel
6 Siyah Restaurant
7 Tourist Inn

800km for only US$80, including driver waiting time at the above sites. Tipping in this case is recommended.

Kerman has two **bus** stations, one for southern departures, the other for northern. The two are located across the road from each other. Any of the parked taxi drivers can tell you which is which.

For **tours** in Kerman and the province, contact English-speaking guide **Hossein Vatani** (✓f *2237591;* m *091 33435265;* e *info@vatancaravan.com; www. vatancaravan.com*).

WHERE TO STAY AND EAT The choice of accommodation in Kerman is quite poor and it's recommended you stay in one of the hotels listed below. For location of listings see map opposite unless otherwise stated.

🏠 **Pars Hotel** (265 rooms) Jomhuri Islami Bd; ✎2119331; f 2119333. Popular with business tourists, this is by far the best hotel in town, but is unfortunately not good value for money. While the rooms are large & Wi-Fi is working, the staff are scatty. There is also an apparent lack of maintenance of the public areas. **$$$**

🏠 **Hotel Akhavan** (40 rooms) Ayatollah Sadoughi St; ✎2441411. Privately owned by 2 friendly & helpful brothers, with a good restaurant. Has a pleasant homely atmosphere & a large lobby. Rooms are spacious, albeit the décor a little old-fashioned. The hotel is overall well maintained & popular with both group tours & individual travellers. **$$**

🏠 **Hotel Hezar** (40 rooms) 5 Neshat Park; ✎2260040; e info@hezarhotel.com; www. hezarhotel.com. Standard hotel with simple, but clean rooms & central lobby. In the northwest outskirts of the town on the way to a restored ice house (see page 242). **$$**

🏠 **Tourist Inn** (53 rooms) Jomhuri Islami Bd; ✎2445203–5; f 2444087. Rooms have been renovated but tend to be on the small side. **$$**

✖ **Hamam-e Vakil Restaurant** Bazaar Vakil; ⏰ 12.00–14.30 for lunch only & until 20.30 for tea & *qalian;* order & pay at the entrance. Beautiful 19th-century underground tea house, easily the most atmospheric place to eat & often there is live traditional Sufi drumming at lunchtime. Try local *kolompeh,* walnut-&-date-filled baked biscuit. **$**

✖ **Khayyam Restaurant** Ayatollah Sadoughi St; ⏰ after 19.00. One of the best restaurants in Kerman. There is lovely traditional music in the evenings & a wide range of Iranian dishes on offer. **$**

✖ **Siyah Restaurant** Jomhuri Islami Bd, across the road from the Arts Engineering University; ✎2116090, 2110126; ⏰ 12.00–15.00 & 19.00–24.00. Another good restaurant, though the décor & atmosphere are very modern. Offers buffet & à la carte menu. **$**

WHAT TO SEE AND DO Comparatively few foreign tourists make it to Kerman, and those that do have mostly come to visit Bam, which necessitates a day trip (see pages 246–8). Yet Kerman itself has a relaxed atmosphere and its bazaars hold great attractions, and not only for buying. Inside the **Bazaar Bozorg** (also called Bazaar Vakil) is the Safavid **Ganj Ali Khan** complex, essentially 17th century in date, which includes a mint, a caravanserai and *hamam.* The last is now an **Ethnographic Museum** (⏰ *09.00–17.00 Tue–Sun; entry 50,000 rials*) displaying all the accoutrements one needed to visit the bathhouse in Safavid times; the exterior painted decoration is some two centuries later in date. There is an opportunity for men to go to an operating bath nearby, the 1817 **Hamam-e Ibrahim Khan**, whose rents, with those of the neighbouring *khan* (warehouse), went to endow the *madrasa* next door, both built and colourfully decorated by a local governor (and son-in-law) of the Qajar shah, Fath Ali Shah. Much of the bazaar was constructed in Safavid times but as its other name, Bazaar Vakil, suggests, many of the *khans* off the main passages were part of extensive rebuilding by another energetic Qajar governor (*vakil*), Mohammed Ismail Khan, 1859–66. A caravanserai bearing the name Vakil is still in use as offices for local merchants. Drop in for a cup of tea to the nearby **Hamam Vakil restaurant** and further down the main avenue from here, on the other side, look out for a richly ornamented doorway in Qajar style. Its blue-tiled panel identifies it as the 19th-century office, which dealt with locals wishing to make the hajj pilgrimage to Mecca.

The **Masjed-e Jame** is located just off the main Maydan-e Shohada. The basic four-*ivan* plan dates from its construction in 1349 by Mubariz al-Din (r1314–58), the founder of the Muzaffarid regime (1314–93), but there have been extensive repairs since the 16th century. The modern additions (glazing in the courtyard, etc) are cheap and nasty, but some splendid tilework in both 'mosaic' and *cuerda seca* techniques remains in the prayer chamber. Visitors are usually riveted by the intriguing notices written in English, and the Farsi notices are just as confusing. Some 200m northwest is the **Masjed-e Pa Minar**, which is heavily restored. Its 1390 entrance portal did have (note the past tense) splendid 14th-century tile decorations which were still *in situ* in the late 1970s; visit, if only to mourn the substitution of such bad-quality work.

But the **Masjed-e Imam** (formerly the Masjed-e Malik), with just a stub (7.5m) of its original Seljuk minaret standing, is worth some time. The main domed prayer chamber dates from the late 11th century, perhaps slightly post-dating the essential four-*ivan* plan, but the prayer *ivan* and portal, with its geometrical brick patterns and fragmentary inscription in deep relief, date from about a hundred years later. Even a cursory glance at the tilework reveals wide-ranging repairs in the Safavid period, and the essentially black and pink tiling with yellow inscription in the prayer hall can only be 19th-century Qajar work. Publications of the 1970s mention 12th-century stucco *mihrabs* in the prayer hall, but these have now been relocated to the roof. To see them, first pay the custodian 10,000 rials, then find the narrow staircase to the extreme left (facing the prayer *ivan*) and, emerging at roof level, look for a metal canopy to the left. The three carved *mihrabs* are there, damaged and dusty but lovely. Another interesting – and obviously early – *mihrab* is now kept behind locked doors downstairs, so you need to find the knowledgeable building supervisor, who clearly loves the place. He thinks this fourth *mihrab* is pre-Seljuk and describes how local tradition says it was visited by Hassan, Ali's son (the second imam). The whole complex is undoubtedly Seljuk but now so heavily restored that little of its original glory is visible.

In the first edition of this guide, we wondered if anyone knew the location of the 12th-century Seljuk tomb tower of **Khwaja Atabeg Barghush**, and a reader made contact in September 2003. It lies on recently cleared ground not far from Abdulhamed Street, behind the bazaar. It has been renovated after collapsing in a 1897 earthquake and the dome was eventually rebuilt. As a result of the years of neglect the octagonal exterior has been shorn of its decorative patterned brickwork highlighted with coloured ceramic tile elements. The tomb itself is closed, but you can see inside through the fenced door.

Kerman postcards often show a simple octagonal mausoleum, the **Gonbad-e Jabaliyeh** (⊕ *09.00–19.00 Tue–Sun; entry 100,000 rials*) located in a cemetery, east of the Maydan-e Arg on the outskirts of town. Some scholars consider it to be one of the earliest surviving tombs with a double dome in Iran, but it is debatable if anything of the original fabric now remains; it is located in a park and serves as a museum of grave markers. There is a Safavid-period **ice house**, somewhat heavily resored, close to a restored section of city wall with views of the citadel. But another reason for making this short journey is to see the extensive remains of the old Sassanid fortifications, the **Qaleh Dokhtar**, built by Ardashir I, whose castle is situated on the other side of the road, up on the hill behind the houses before the mausoleum. There is aslo a well-preserved *yakhchal* on the way here.

Kerman boasts an excellent museum of contemporary art, which you should consider visiting. The **Sanati Museum** (*Shahid Beheshti St;* ⊕ *09.00–12.00 & 17.00–19.00; entry 20,000 rials*) used to be an orphanage established by a Kermani philanthropist Hajj Akbar Sanatizadeh and is now home to numerous works by renowned Iranian artists such as Ali Akbar Sanati (d2006), Sohrab Sepehri (d1980) and Kamal al-Molk (d1940). Most labels are in Persian only. In this part of the city there also used to be an Anglican Church of St Andrew (Kelisa Moqaddasi), as in the 19th century Kerman was an important centre for Western Christian missionary work. Coming up towards the museum you will pass by a well-preserved *yakhchal*.

Another fine museum here is **Harandi Museum** (Bagh-e Muzeh Harandi) (*Ferdowsi St;* ⊕ *09.00–19.00 Tue–Sun; entry 150,000 rials*) located in a formerly private Qajar home of the Harandi family. Reza Shah Pahlavi himself stayed here whenever he visited Kerman. The ground-floor displays are dedicated to music and traditional musical instruments such as *tar, barbat* and *tombak*, but the first floor is the main reason to visit, with objects ranging from metalwork to sculpture from Jiroft (see page 6) and Shahdad.

East of Kerman There are a few interesting historical and natural sites east of Kerman, which can all be visited in a one-day trip. The first stop along the desert road to Mashhad is the village of **Sirch**, which lies on the earthquake fault line of the province. Driving in the direction of **Shahdad**, 95km from Kerman, past the small village of **Shafi Abad** with the remains of a Qajari caravanserai and its unusual towers, you finally arrive at the spectacular desert **Kalut**, which often features on posters around Kerman.

South of Kerman To the southwest, past Kerman Airport on the road to Sirjan, is **Bardsir** with **Tel-e Iblis** (Devil's Mound); American-funded archaeological work here in the mid 1960s found evidence of continuous settlement from c4400BCE to 400BCE, and proof that both copper smelting and ceramic production were in operation. And in Bardsir itself there is a 13th-century tomb of **Sayyid Mohammed**, with later buildings around. It has a double dome, good plasterwork and fine *muqarnas* along with three historic cenotaphs.

Returning to the Sirjan road, continue for another 20km to **Negar**, off a side road. Here there are the remains of a Seljuk citadel and a minaret probably from 1216 with a brick inscription from the Quran (Q97); glazed infills provide colour to the patterning. Both the mosque and the old *hamam* nearby could be Seljuk in plan. This village is on the centuries-old migration route, so there is a possibility of seeing families and flocks on the move in the spring and autumn. About 23km east of here is **Ghubeyra**, an Islamic site probably destroyed by Timur Leng's armies in 1393. It was excavated in the early 1970s by a British team of archaeologists.

Sirjan is another 100km on the main road. Some 5km before it and to the east, you should catch sight of **Qaleh Sang** (Stone Castle), a huge medieval fortress which managed to resist Timur Leng for two years. The town itself was a regional capital from Sassanid times until the 10th century, and before the revolution the British Institute of Persian Studies undertook preliminary excavations that revealed an important medieval complex which, judging by the richness of its decorative plasterwork, could have housed the governor.

About 10km from Qaleh Sang you can stay at the clean and comfortable **Tourist Inn** (*50 rooms; Khayyam St, Jahangardi;* ☏ *0345 3227878;* e *sirjan@ittic.com;* **$**).

Continuing down this road towards Bandar-e Abbas, and before reaching Haji Abad (approximately 300km from Kerman), turn left at Aliabad on the road leading to Dolat Abad; 30km further on is the site **Tappeh Yahya**, first systematically excavated by the Peabody Museum of Harvard University (US) in the late 1960s. Some seven distinct layers were identified, the earliest dating from c4500–3800BCE, when the inhabitants were evidently growing cereals and raising domesticated animals. By 3500BCE the settlement was prosperous enough to import turquoise, alabaster and ingots of copper. Occupation of the site continued without a break until the late Parthian or Sassanid period. The latest level and Period 2 (second level down) is clearly Achaemenid in date, leading scholars to believe this was Carmania, where Alexander the Great stationed his men returning from the India campaign. About another 100km further east near to the town of Sorkhan, is the gorge, **Tang-e Mordan**, again associated with the Macedonian warrior, with rock reliefs and a 'fantastic number of cairn burials' according to Sylvia Matheson. A handful of similar cairn tombs at Sar-e Asiab, 40km north of Kerman, were also excavated by the Peabody Museum. The finds ranged widely in date, even up to the 7th century CE, although it is generally considered the cairns, originally standing perhaps 2.5m high, were erected in prehistoric times.

If you have had the time and the inclination to view the archaeological finds in the Sanati and Harandi Garden museums in Kerman (see page 243), you will probably be drawn to visiting **Jiroft** itself, a site that was largely a chance discovery occasioned by flash floods in 2000. It may prove, according to at least one archaeologist, to be the lost Bronze Age city of Aratta mentioned in Sumerian records from c2100BCE. The visit can be undertaken from Kerman by travelling down the road towards Bam and then turning right at Abarek. A further 100km on a metalled road crossing a stony desert and you will arrive. There is a good **museum** (☉ *closed lunchtimes; entry free*) displaying some of the objects, largely in a greenish soft stone called chlorite, excavated from the principal site, Konar Sandal, some 45 minutes away. The artefacts are extremely lively with vegetal, zoomorphic and anthropological representations. There are some English labels and an informed guide who speaks French is often available. Perhaps you can persuade him to accompany you to the site. **Konar Sandal** has two ancient hills, north and south. The northern hill has been dated to c3rd millennium BCE and appears to have consisted of a multi-storey, ziggurat-type religious building of mud brick, clay and straw plaster. The southern mound, some 1,300m from the other hill, revealed the remains of a large structure, possibly a local ruler's residence, on older remains. Artefacts such as bowls appear to have been exported to all regions of Mesopotamia. Large parts of the site are still untouched with many shards littering the surface. There are good views from the tops of the mounds.

The fact that the early years of the 21st century saw the arrival on the European market of many artefacts extracted or trafficked illegally from this site, prompted the Dutch in particular to take an active part in convincing the authorities to protect the site and display the finds. This Bronze Age culture, now dubbed 'Jiroft Culture', is agreed to be widespread in the Halil river basin. Some evidence of writing has also been found although the script has not yet been deciphered.

You can stay and eat here at the simple **Hotel Jam-e Jam** (*8 rooms; Dowlat St;* ☏ *0348 2210340;* **$$**). Alternatively, you could stay in Mahan (see opposite).

West of Kerman Some 27km from Shahr-e Babak is the ancient rock village of **Meymand** (*entry 100,000 rials*), which in 2005 was awarded a Melina Mercouri Unesco Prize for the Safeguarding and Management of Cultural Landscapes.

It numbers around 140 residents who continue the semi-nomadic lifestyle maintained by their ancestors over the past few thousand years. Their cave houses were built on the mountain, 2,200m above the sea level, without the use of any modern housebuilding tools and are similar to those in the Kandovan village near Tabriz (see page 165). The Meymand mosque, albeit more than 150 years old, is nonetheless the most recently built structure here and it is the only building in the village with white inner walls, as there has never been a fire lit inside it.

Northwest of Kerman The road to the northwest of Kerman leads to **Zarand** (87km), which at the end of the 12th century superseded Kerman as the provincial centre, and was also famous for its textile manufacture. Its **Masjed-e Jame** was founded in the 10th century but, other than the remains of a minaret constructed sometime before 1074, the present building is 18th century. Just a little backtracking on the main road, brings you on to a main highway to Mashhad.

MAHAN

From Kerman, most foreign visitors head southeast for **Bam**, stopping *en route* to see the shrine and gardens at **Mahan**, which takes a full day. Arguably Mahan, 40km from Kerman, is best visited in the evening, perhaps on a return journey from Bam, for during the summer the **Qajar Garden** and pavilion, the **Bagh-e Shahzade** (⏰ *09.00–21.00, until 23.00 in summer; entry 150,000 rials*), are open and illuminated at night. Set back about 2km from the main road, the layout of this restored garden is one of the few in Iran that retains its original plan. A series of terraces descends down the hillside with main and side water channels. On occasions the fountains are switched on, to the enjoyment of both ducks and visitors. The 19th-century pavilion offers a splendid place to take and enjoy both a *qalian* (see page 42) and the lovely view over the garden.

Mahan itself is known for the famous shrine complex of (Shah) **Ne'matullah Vali Kermani** (d1430), the Sufi mystic poet-saint who spent his last 25 years here after residing in Mecca, Karbala and Samarkand, where he had incurred the wrath of Timur Leng. Called the Iranian Nostradamus, he is said to have foretold the rise of the Safavid regime, the separation of Bangladesh from Pakistan and the Islamic Revolution in Iran.

The main entrance has bright yellow and blue tiles from Qajar restoration work in 1871, as recorded on the floral tiles in the shrine doorway. A courtyard with reflecting pool and trees leads to the main shrine complex. The original silver grilles of the cenotaph and an enormous gold-inlaid steel *kash-kul* (dervish begging-bowl) presented to the shrine by a Safavid shah are kept in the centre. Apart from a large gift- and bookshop, all other rooms in this courtyard offer basic accommodation for pilgrims.

The actual shrine building itself is an engaging mixture of architectural and decorative styles. If it is not crowded, do enlist the help of the kind and very knowledgeable guardian (Farsi-speaking only), who will also willingly (for a small fee at your discretion) let you go up to the roof to enjoy wonderful views (a good-will gesture reserved for foreigners only). The inner square chamber dates from 1436 and its inner walls are still decorated with high-quality Timurid 'mosaic' tilework, while a new steel and glass screen protects the Sufi's cenotaph. Off the upper left-hand corner of this central space is the tomb of the original patron, a student of the Sufi. The room is painted, has relief plasterwork and the dome is in the shape of the Sufi's hat. There are signs of flood damage on the lower part of these walls. The doorway into this area opposite the main door has a 19th-century three-images-in-one glass picture on each wall, one with different verses of the Quran, and the other showing Hossein's head, his tent at Karbala and his desecrated body. The carpets to the left are of Mahan production, incorporating the saint's poetry in the long cartouches. Walking anticlockwise – so the cenotaph chamber is on the left – look at the vaulting. The superbly proportioned fan of intersecting ribs was constructed in 1436 on the order of Ahmed I Bahmani, ruler of Bidar, a state in the Indian Deccan and a devotee of this Sufi master. Halfway round, the Safavid alterations are visible to the right of the cenotaph chamber, where the Timurid tiling disappears under a later Safavid wall constructed to support the vaulting system. On the outer wall are double wooden doors, which the guardian will proudly open to allow you to inspect them and see how the complex was enlarged in the 19th century to make it symmetrical. Returning to the central area, the room in the next corner is richly decorated with magnificent early 17th-century calligraphy arranged in a giant sun whirl around the vault; this was the *chehelkhaneh* where, as the name suggests, Sufis spent 40 nights in spiritual devotions.

The next door leads outside the shrine complex to a photogenic view of the shrine's exterior. Back within the building, look for a wooden door further along. Small figures along the top depict Sufi sheikh Abu'l Hassan Kharaghani (d1033, see page 151), known for his miraculous abilities to tame wild animals, riding a lion and using a snake as a whip. A simple, small chamber in this final section is the resting place of the master who died recently. Currently behind the complex is a large caravanserai, which was originally at the front of the building; it is currently being restored.

A detour to 'mini-Bam' in **Rayen** just southwest of the main road about 50km beyond Mahan, will enable you to explore a similar fort city, the **Arg-e Rayen** (⊕ *09.00–18.00; entry 100,000 rials*), though it is unlikely to be as ancient. It too consists of a vast walled complex of linked buildings constructed of sun-dried brick with the usual *qanat* and cooling systems characteristic of this desert region. As in Bam, a small *zurkhaneh* survives (see box, page 120). If you have time to spare, 13km east from Arg-e Rayen there is a picturesque waterfall with a picnic area.

BAM

From Mahan it is about 170km to Bam (*vahma*: glorification, prayer; population: 126,000), which was struck by a severe earthquake on 26 December 2003. It is thought to be the city of Haftvad mentioned in the Iranian epic, *Shahnameh*. The story goes that Haftvad's daughter was spinning cotton with friends when she spotted a worm in her apple. Refusing to kill it, she found her output magically increased as the worm munched and grew in size. As it brought great wealth to her family and town, a citadel was built to protect it, but this only aroused the interest of the Sassanid shah, Shapur. Eventually killing the giant worm by forcing hot metal down its throat, he took the city and its riches. This sounds purely the stuff of legend, but we know that, according to Iranian tradition, it was Shapur I (or perhaps Shapur II) who destroyed the Chinese silk monopoly, by actively promoting silkworm cultivation and silk production in Iran and promoting Bam as a trading station for eastern caravan routes. Furthermore in silk processing, to avoid the pupa damaging its silk cocoon, it is killed by heat of which there is plenty in the sunshine of the area (see box, page 146).

Aerial photographs taken shortly after the devastating earthquake have revealed the complexity of the medieval *qanat* system, and evidence that the site was occupied as early as 2600BCE. The town was an important frontier and commercial post, trading in dates, cotton and other textiles until it fell to rebel Afghan forces in 1719. Its economy never fully recovered. Then the citadel's defences were partially dismantled in the 19th century, following Agha Mohammed Qajar's capture of the Zand ruler, Lotf Ali Khan (see page 13) in 1794. More local trouble in 1838 caused the Qajar shah to take direct control, and many of the townspeople were moved to a new residential area to the south. By 1958 most families had left the old walled town, and the site was declared an open-air museum. It was the new town that suffered most in the 2003 earthquake but the historic walled city was also gravely damaged. Since 2004, Bam has been included on the UNESCO World Heritage List.

Bam city has been rebuilt in a rather unsympathetic style though a few families are still inhabiting containers placed after the earthquake of December 2003. The citadel at Bam is being worked on by hundreds of workmen but is still a wreck and propped up by scaffolding and rather grotesque newly installed benches all across the open-for-tourists perimeter. Repair work aims, with the aid of photos, to restore it to its earlier form, as has happened with mud-brick structures through the ages.

Similarly to Kerman, Bam used to have a Zoroastrian community and the remains of the Qajar-period Zoroastrian bazaar and official quarter, all destroyed in the 2003 earthquake, attested to that.

GETTING THERE There is an airport to the east of the town, now repaired and with a one weekly **flight** operated by Iran Aseman Airlines to and from Tehran Mehrabad Airport. A one-way fare is around 2,000,000 rials. In common with other Iranian cities, there are hourly (up until 19.00) **buses** from Kerman (40,000 rials each way) that take just under three hours, but may be longer depending on the time spent at security checkpoints along the way. For location of Bam see map, page 228.

WHERE TO STAY
Bam Tourist Inn (8 rooms) Imam Khomeini St; \ 0344 2313321; f 0344 2313005. A reliable ITTIC hotel with a good restaurant & pleasant staff. **$**

WHAT TO SEE AND DO A walk in the **walled town**, the citadel, known as **Arg-e Bam** (⊕ *07.15–18.00; entry 150,000 rials*) before the earthquake was unforgettable. Surrounding an area of approximately 3km diameter, the main defence wall was over 12m high, with ramparts 3m wide, four gates and an external moat. It housed the bazaar, various noble houses and mosques, of which there is little left. Enough remained for the visitor to see the main housing, shops, work units (including a bakery and police station), caravanserai and the main mosque, all located just inside this wall. Above, defended by a further wall, were the barracks, stabling and housing for the bureaucrats and soldiers, while a third enclosing wall protected the inner citadel and the governor's apartments. Right at the top were a **watchtower** and **pavilion** of the four seasons, both offering marvellous panoramic views over the plain, but it was these upper sections that were most severely damaged in 2003. Originally the tower was seven-storeyed but in the 1810 Qajar dismantling, three floors were demolished. Below, on the second level, a massive repair and rebuilding programme had just been completed before the earthquake and, perhaps because of this strengthening work, this area has suffered less. It contains the **officers' quarters**, a series of rooms around courtyards set behind the main street. On the way down to the next gate there are more **barracks** and also a huge water **cistern** (not in evidence in 1994) to the right. The walkway led down to the second gate, which is now no longer extant. At ground level, the avenue to the left led to a small caravanserai, which had been converted into a restaurant, its two main chambers cooled by multi-vent *badgirs*. This area and beyond containing a *hosseiniyeh* (with a characteristic 'theatre' stage and 'boxes' for the audience), a school, and a large mosque perhaps founded in the 7th century were largely levelled in the 2003 earthquake. It is unclear whether a large domed building to the left, in the distance, still stands. This was a *zurkhaneh*, possibly the earliest surviving Iranian example, complete with its octagonal wrestling pit (see box, page 120). Walking around the main wall past the ticket kiosk you will eventually arrive at the cupola-shaped **Mirza Ebrahim Tomb**, built for this member of the Bam nobility during the Qajar period. Outside the structure is not that impressive, but it certainly is inside, despite the scaffolding.

The road from Bam towards Zahedan is marked with remains of a number of historic signal towers, the most important being at **Fahraj**, 100km from Bam. Its signal tower, **Mil-e Naderi**, stands 19m high with a diameter of 13m, was perhaps built on 10th-century foundations, but the brickwork pattern dates from the reign of Nader Shah Afshar (d1747). Beacons would be lit for signalling communication to Kerman and beyond, and they served to guide the trade caravans making their way into and from central Iran; another beacon lies some 15km away to the north near Shur Gaz. Do note, however, that travelling further south beyond Bam may be considered hazardous and inadvisable, and unless you are travelling in a specially organised group or with an Iranian friend, single travellers (especially women) should reconsider their journey plans.

ZAHEDAN AND AROUND

Zahedan (population 580,000) is the capital of the Sistan and Baluchistan province, which is the only Iranian province bordering Pakistan. The city itself is located just a few kilometres away from the border and is surrounded by mountains. Zahedan is only around 90 years old and does not have any historic sites. It is, however, an important transfer point between Iran and Pakistan.

GETTING THERE From Bam, a road south leads to Minab and Bandar-e Abbas, but the main Kerman–Bam road continues to the Irano–Pakistani frontier beyond Zahedan; petrol stations are few and far between.

Aside from road transport from Bam, there are daily **flights** from Tehran; other cities, namely Esfahan, Kerman, Mashhad and Chabahar (on the coast) are served less frequently. Long-distance **bus** services link Zahedan to all the major centres of Iran, and the **railway** has now been extended from Bam to Zahedan, which already has a railway station linked to the network in Pakistan. The service is very unreliable but a train should, in theory, run between this city and Quetta (Pakistan) twice a month. It is also possible to reach the frontier by scheduled bus or by shared or private **taxi**. Zahedan and Quetta used to be on the hippy trail in the early 1970s, but since then services have deteriorated badly.

The whole region has a reputation for drug trafficking, so expect a stringent searching of vehicles and lengthy document checking, both in town and on the road. Also there is large-scale smuggling into Afghanistan and Pakistan of cheap Iranian petrol contained in secret compartments underneath the intercity/frontier buses. There is, however, no official crossing point into Afghanistan here.

So few Westerners now come this way that their presence attracts much interest. Be careful, *very* careful. Think before travelling in this region. Although consulates for Pakistan and India exist in this town, neither is likely to issue you a visa and you should arrive with your papers in order if you hope to cross into Pakistan.

WHERE TO STAY AND EAT The cheaper hotels in Zahedan are not licensed to accept foreigners. For location of Zahedan see map, page 228.

Esteghlal Hotel (75 rooms) Azadi Sq; \0541 3238068; f 0541 3222239. Currently the best in town. **$$$**

Tourist Inn (70 rooms) Montazeri St; \0541 3224898; f 0541 3224440. No sgl-bed rooms available. **$$$**

WHAT TO SEE AND DO Zahedan has little to offer other than its **bazaars**, but the surrounding landscape is strewn with the crumbling remains of caravanserais and signal towers.

To the north of Zahedan lies Tasuki, about 35km after the turn-off for Zabol. The ruins of **Qaleh Gird**, about 20km from the Gird-e Gahr police checkpoint, are visible with its well-preserved towers and walls. Further on there are some 14th-century buildings, but the proximity to the Afghan border means the authorities may wish foreigners to avoid the area; which you will do if following British government advice (see page 279). Northwards is the excavated *tappeh* of **Rod-e Biyaban**, where the remains of some 50 large kilns were found, dating from the 3rd millennium BCE. About 25km further on (56km south of Zabol) is the similarly dated site of **Shahr-e Sukhteh** (Burnt City – now also UNESCO-listed) which an Italian archaeological team excavated from the mid 1960s until 1978, and which the Iranian authorities have continued to explore since 1997. A series of rectangular buildings was uncovered, some with walls still 3m high, with doorways, windows, staircases and roofing timbers in a fine state of preservation, 'as if kept in a pot of pickles', covered in a thick layer of saline earth. It turned out that what were first identified as floor levels were in fact the roofs of buildings. Four main periods of settlement were identified: Level I (c3100–2900BCE), then Levels II and III, with pottery similar to that found at Bampur from c2500–1900BCE, and Level IV, about 500 years later and characterised by pottery animal figurines. A huge burial site over 42ha, containing about 40,000 graves of nine types, was found with 'literally tens of thousands' of skeletons laid in a horizontal 'kneeling' position facing east, the largest known Bronze Age cemetery in the Middle East. The rich pottery (often decorated with stylised scorpion motifs), over 40,000 clay figurines, flint tools and beads point to a prosperous community dating back over 5,000 years, but the whole settlement seems to have been destroyed in an intense fire in c1250BCE, and abandoned after the river changed course. The finds again prove a strong trading connection both with the northern Indian subcontinent and with Oman.

Some 6km away from here and about 70km southwest of Zabol, is **Qaleh Rostam**, locally associated with the Persian warrior-hero in the *Shahnameh* epic (the *Sohrab and Rostam* of Matthew Arnold). Noted as an attractive town in its own right during the mid-1970s, Qaleh Rostam has clearly had a long history of settlement, as over eight prehistoric mounds have been identified and there are signs of an important Sassanid fort. The road leads on to **Zabol**, about 55km away, where for many years the Italian archaeological team of Shahri Sokhta had its headquarters. The proximity of the Afghan border means a heavy military and police presence in Zabol and the surrounding region.

The site of **Kuh-e Khwaja**, some 30km southwest of Zabol, on Lake Hamun, and is visible from a distance but reachable only by boat during the spring and autumn. This mound has been revered by both Zoroastrians and Muslims for centuries, and every Nou Rouz pilgrims still come to pay their respects. **Lake Hamun** (originally known as Kasaoya, and mentioned in the *Avesta*) is the location where Zoroastrians believe their messiah, Saoshyants, will be conceived. The lake is seasonal with

11

varying water levels, depending on the amount of rainfall and melting snow from the surrounding mountains. On the site, a small fire temple complex could perhaps date from the Achaemenid period but many believe it to be later, pointing out similarities in layout with the Adur Gushnasp fire sanctuary at Takht-e Soleyman in the Zagros Mountains (see page 170). Extensive Parthian and Sassanid remains were uncovered, with plaster wall frescoes of a king and queen, attendants and a line of deities, which formerly decorated a Parthian palace compound. Unfortunately they are no longer *in situ*, but two pieces are in the Metropolitan Museum of Art, New York. Archaeological work has been carried out since the mid 1990s and remains of a citadel with a religious precinct including a fire temple have been found, probably dating from early Sassanid times, 3rd–4th century CE. **Bibi Dost** is situated about 35km from here, where again there are clear signs of historic occupation. Just to the southeast are the ruins of **Deh Zahedan** (also known as Deh Reza), perhaps once the old city of Zaranj, with a citadel, forts and mosque.

A series of old forts and caravanserais mark the landscape, but few have been securely identified or dated. One of the sites much further south, excavated in the mid 1960s, is **Bampur**, close to **Iranshahr**. The dig focused on a site west and northwest of the post-medieval citadel mound; six stratified levels were found, with interesting pottery and other finds proving that as early as c2500–1900BCE there were strong trade links with Afghanistan and Oman. Much of this region was destroyed during Timurid times in revenge attacks by Timur Leng and his son, and it has never recovered. We know that Alexander the Great passed through on his campaigns to India and, as the Persepolis reliefs suggest, earlier there had been close military co-operation between the people of Sistan (or Drangiana as it was then known) and the Achaemenid emperor. The region was considered strategically important during Parthian times, some saying that a local ruler Gondophernes (r20–48CE) was none other than Caspar, one of the Three Wise Men.

To Mashhad and Beyond

The city of Mashhad is considered the holiest city in Iran, renowned as the burial place of the eighth imam, Reza. This region of Iranian Khorasan once formed an enormous province encompassing sections of today's Turkmenistan, Uzbekistan and Afghanistan. This province (in 2004 it was split into North Khorasan, South Khorasan and Razavi Khorasan provinces) was not always under Iranian authority, so its historic monuments record the patronage of such regimes as the Khwarizm shahs, the Mongol Ilkhanids and the Timurids as well as the Safavids, the short-lived Afsharid dynasty and the Qajars. This section looks at the region east of Gonbad-e Qabus and Shahrud (see page 151), Mashhad and sites close to the Afghan border. The security situation near the Afghan border is presently good but the gendarmerie advises that road journeys should be completed before sunset, as there have been isolated incidents of cross-border robbery and kidnapping. Additionally, the border crossing is only open from 07.30–16.30.

MASHHAD   *Telephone code 0511*

It was here, when the town was known as Sanabad, that the famous Abbasid caliph, Harun al-Rashid, died in 809CE; 19th-century Western literature always associated him with the anthology *Tales of 1,001 Nights*, written centuries later. His son, al-Ma'mun, ordered a tomb for his father, and another to commemorate his son-in-law, Reza, in whose death in 817CE he was strongly implicated. This is the Imam Reza, honoured in Shi'a Islam as the eighth in the line of 12 Imams and to whom today's **huge shrine complex** is dedicated. Almost two hundred years later this tomb to Imam Reza was destroyed by the local Sunni ruler, who forbade any rebuilding, but Sultan Mahmud of Ghazni (r998–1030), inspired by a dream – or perhaps the need to win the loyalty of his Shi'a subjects – ordered its reconstruction in 1009. From then on, the town's fortunes were inextricably linked to the shrine.

But the city's vulnerable location offered rich pickings for any marauding force, such as the Turkoman in 1153, or the Mongols in 1221, and the shrine was always hit during such attacks. Piecemeal repairs were undertaken by local Sunni rulers, but major rebuilding was undertaken only by the son of Timur Leng, Shah Rukh (r1405–47; see box, page 254), from 1418 along with the construction of gardens and a royal pavilion to enhance the shrine. His queen, Ghawhar Shad, 'Jewel of Happiness', an active architectural patron in their capital, Herat, Afghanistan, was already having a new *madrasa* built. A century later it was the Shi'a Safavid regime that promoted the city as a major Iranian pilgrimage centre. The shrine's main dome and minarets were gilded and much of the Timurid eastern section was demolished to cater for the thousands of Iranian pilgrims flocking here, rather than undertaking the long, hazardous hajj to Mecca and Medina, then in Ottoman control. The city's

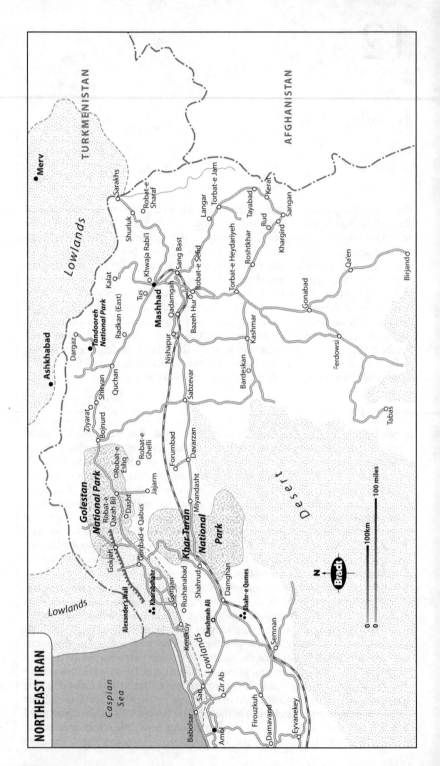

NORTHEAST IRAN

Caspian Sea

TURKMENISTAN

AFGHANISTAN

Merv

Ashkabad

Lowlands

Tandooreh National Park

Dargaz

Radkan (East)

Sarakhs

Robat-e Sharaf

Shurluk

Khwaja Rabi'i

Sang Bast

Langar

Torbat-e Jam

Tayabad

Kerat

Sangan

Rud

Kalat

Tus

Mashhad

Qadamgah

Robat-e Sefid

Torbat-e Heydariyeh

Roshtkhar

Khargird

Ziyarat

Bojnurd

Shirvan

Quchan

Robat-e Ghelli

Nishapur

Bazeh Hur

Kashmar

Qa'en

Birjand

Gonabad

Robat-e Eshq

Forumbad

Sabzevar

Bardeskan

Ferdowsi

Golestan National Park

Robat-e Qarah Bil

Dasht

Jajarm

Davarzan

Tabas

Gonbad-e Qabus

Khar-Turan National Park

Miyandasht

Desert

Gokleh

Kharabshahr

Gorgan

Rushanabad

Shahrud

Damghan

Shahr-e Qomes

Alexander's Wall

Korduy

Cheshmeh Ali

Semnan

Lowlands

Sari

Zir Ab

100km

100 miles

N

Bradt

Babolsar

Amol

Firouzkuh

Damavand

Eyvanekey

0   100km
0   100 miles

royal association continued into the 18th century. Sweeping away the remnants of Safavid power, Nader Shah Afshar (d1747), though a Sunni, had his son marry the daughter of the Safavid shah Tahmasp II here, established his capital in Mashhad, ordered costly and highly visible repairs to the shrine after his successful Indian campaigns, and was buried here. Re-establishing the Ithna 'Ashari Shi'a faith as the state religion, the Qajar shahs then undertook a massive restoration programme in the shrine, extensively covering surfaces with tiles and mirror work and regilding the dome. Official pressure in the 19th and early 20th centuries caused many in the Jewish and Christian communities in Mashhad to move to Afghanistan or central Asia, where their expertise in both manufacture and commerce were fully utilised; but at least one church still survives in Mashhad, close to the hotels Asia and Jam.

Although Qom is now acknowledged as Iran's leading theological training centre, Mashhad (altitude 985m) has grown significantly since 1979, now having more than 2.7 million residents. It is the second-largest Iranian city after Tehran. Numerous houses and bazaars have been demolished to improve access to the shrine area.

GETTING THERE Be aware that all means of transport, especially trains, are heavily booked at holiday time and peak pilgrimage seasons.

By air Mashhad has an international airport and is served by Aseman Airlines, IranAir, Mahan Airlines and Zagros Airlines from Dammam in Saudi Arabia, Najaf and Baghdad in Iraq, Kuwait and Dubai, though none has a daily service. In 2013 Turkish Airlines started operating five **flights** each week to Mashhad from Istanbul, although fewer will operate out of season. A return flight from London to Mashhad with Turkish Airlines costs around £500. It will be cheaper to fly via Istanbul from other European cities. Some routes are seasonal and subject to availability. Within Iran there are three daily flights to Tehran – a one-way air ticket costs around 1,300,000 rials (US$40) – as well as direct flights from most of the important cities in the country, including from Kish and Qeshm islands.

By train Mashhad is well connected to the rest of the country by the intercity rail network. An overnight train service links Tehran to Mashhad in seven hours (350,000–400,000 rials, depending on service and class). There is also a direct train from Esfahan with a stopover in Tehran, but the journey of up to 18 hours is tedious.

By bus There are numerous bus services from all over the country to this popular pilgrimage centre. From the Tehran direction there are two main roads eastwards: a northern one skirting the Caspian Sea to Gorgan, Shirvan and Quchan to Mashhad (it is this one that the *By car/taxi* section details below); and the more southerly route following the old caravan trade road from Shahrud via Sabzevar and Nishapur. An overnight VIP bus Mashhad–Tehran costs 290,000 rials.

The best time for travelling in Iran's eastern provinces is in the late spring (April and May) and early autumn (late September and October), as the winters in the Khorasan province are long and bitter, with heavy snowfalls – as one 11th-century ruler, Amir Qabus Ibn Wushmgir, found to his cost (see page 150).

By car/taxi
The northern road to Mashhad Note that on this route there is limited but adequate accommodation at Gorgan (see page 149), and south of Mashhad at Tayabad and Sabzehvar (see page 270), but elsewhere the situation is much more difficult. However, Mashhad itself is awash with hotels, so it is perhaps best to

reach and stay in Mashhad and make day visits from there to the places mentioned below by local taxi or bus. Such excursions make the long journey to Mashhad and Khorasan worth the time, expense and effort.

The road east runs for 98km from Gorgan to Gonbad-e Qabus and then for another 485km towards Mashhad, quickly leaving rice fields and sloping farm roofs behind, winding up into wooded hills populated by wild boar and deer, passing **Golestan National Park**, Iran's oldest national park that has been protected since 1956, at least in theory. At present the motorway is effectively running through the park and human presence has further damaged the area's flora and fauna. In 2007 the Iranian government applied to UNESCO to add the park to the World Heritage List, but to date it remains on the tentative list. Continue on by cutting through shrubby hillsides that are ideal trekking or riding territory. Close to the road are three known Timurid caravanserais dating from c1487, and probably many more are still to be identified, as the then governor of Astarabad, Mir Ali Shir, is known to have built 49 altogether in his lifetime to serve this important trade and pilgrimage route. The **Robat-e Qarah Bil** is situated 25km east of **Dasht** in the village under the same name, behind the roadside gendarmerie. (If a ruined caravanserai isn't appealing, the numerous inquisitive *pika* 'gerbils' that inhabit the site are.) Its

SHAH RUKH

The fourth son of Timur Leng (Tamerlaine, as he is known in the West), Shah Rukh owed his name to the moment of his birth, which coincided with his father taking his opponent's castle (*rukh*) at chess. As Mongol tradition laid down that territorial possessions should be split between the ruler's sons, he was appointed governor of Mazandaran, Khorasan and Sistan in 1397 at the age of 22, but arguments between the brothers continued. He had two wives: Ghawhar Shad and, to keep the bloodline of Genghis Khan in the Timurid house, he married the young Malikat Agha, widow of one of his brothers. On Timur's death in 1405 he made no move to take the throne but bided his time until Timur's successor died two years later. Shah Rukh immediately went into action, installing his son, Ulugh Beg (who gave the mathematical world sine tables) as governor of Samarkand while he remained in Herat. Through his generals, he restored Timurid authority in the steppes of today's Turkmenistan, crushed local warlords and difficult nephews attempting to seize control of the Isfahan region in 1417, and then successfully moved against the Qara Qoyunlu in Azerbaijan.

A ruler who preferred to hunt around Sarakhs and to visit Mashhad than lead his troops on the battlefield, Shah Rukh ordered many gardens to be built in his capital of Herat, but he was also known for his piety, personally accompanying Muslim officials to remove the secret wine stores of his son and grandson. He was heartbroken when his favourite son died, and powerful factions centred around both queens broke out at court. The target of at least one assassination attempt, he was stabbed in the stomach when leaving Friday prayer in 1427 but made a full recovery. The intrigue continued, especially when he fell seriously ill during 1444, and Ghawhar promoted her own candidate as the rightful heir apparent. Many court officials were banished from the Herat palace when Shah Rukh's health improved. He died in 1447 (Ghawhar survived for another ten years) and, within 15 years, the house of Timur Leng had fallen and the empire was in fragments.

south entrance once led immediately into the stables along this façade and on both sides. Despite the caravanserai's present state, even a casual inspection will reveal the different phases of construction, with certain chambers built in the late 16th century to provide more stabling. The vestibule led into a four-*ivan* courtyard, 16m², with living quarters on all sides. This essential plan was followed in two other caravanserais, both a day's journey away in pre-motoring times: **Robat-e Eshq**, 23km east off the main road at Chaman Bid, which also included a small mosque on site, and the **Robat-e Ghelli**, 30km southeast. From Robat-e Qarah Bil or Robat-e Eshq, **Jajarm** is about 55km due south. Its position on the former main caravan route from Nishapur to Bastam presumably accounted for the need for a protective fortress, whose remains are still visible. Its Masjed-e Jame, surprisingly small in size, probably dates from the late 15th century.

The good road skirts the mountainous barrier between Iran and today's Turkmenistan Republic through **Bojnurd** and **Shirvan**, passing petrochemical and cement works. Some 6km west from Shirvan (market day Monday) is **Ziyarat**, so called after its Ziyarat-e Timur Leng located in a modern cemetery. It is not the main, centrally placed building with a brick-patterned dome, the interior of which is decorated with a beautiful star-burst ceiling of plaster *muqarnas*, that has interested scholars, but the octagonal tomb behind it. Some think this dates from the 1330s but others, looking at its kite-shaped squinches in the zone of transition and other architectural details, argue that, as its name suggests, it is Timurid, c1430. Local children will happily show you the internal staircase up to the roof. Hardly anything now remains of the painted internal drum inscription and medallions recorded in the mid 1970s.

North of **Quchan** and close to the Turkmenistan border, 3km northwest of Dargaz (also spelt Darreh Gaz), the Iranian Archaeological Service has been carrying out excavations at **Bondiyan** (also spelt Bandian), since 1994. From the brief reports published so far, a Sassanid columned hall with a corridor and room with remains of rich plaster decoration to a height of 70cm have been unearthed. These depict scenes of hunting, battle and feasting, resembling both in content and composition the (later) painted walls at Perijikent, Tajikistan, south of Samarkand in central Asia. Fragmentary Pahlavi inscriptions carved into the plaster refer obliquely to two military commanders controlling this region, one of whom is recorded as serving under the Sassanid shah Bahram V (r429–37). The work is lively but atypical and, according to the usual Sassanid scale of proportions, the figures have overlong arms. The archaeologists now think this was a Zoroastrian fire temple complex including a tower of silence.

Well worth a short detour for its early 13th-century tomb tower is **Radkan**, known in certain publications as Radkan East (Radkan West tower is south of Kordkuy; see page 149). Some 75km before Mashhad, after Quchan and the village of Seid Abad, there is a turn-off for the village. The village roundabout, boasting a modern replica of the tower, soon comes into view, but there is no signpost to the actual monument, which is on a rough but serviceable road across agricultural land. The tower's octagonal brick base is quickly transformed into a 12-sided exterior, presumably symbolising belief in the 12 Imams, decorated with 36 semicircular engaged columns terminating in trilobed forms. Here and there are fragments of turquoise-glazed inserts, also used for the Kufic inscription. Only the exterior tent roof survives but inside the octagonal chamber, the brick supports for the internal dome are still visible. Take care where you tread inside as local shepherds keep a few sheep and donkeys in the tower. Looking around, one sees the ruins of a huge four-towered caravanserai, also used for local flocks, and in the village there's an ice house.

Back on the main road, just before hitting the outskirts of Mashhad, is **Tus** (also called **Ferdowsi**), the birthplace of the famous medieval poet, Ferdowsi (d1020). The confusing road directions indicate only Ferdowsi, but local bus companies still refer to 'Tus'. Given the continuing construction of ring roads and the inadequate road signs on the motorway, it is probably easier and quicker to continue into Mashhad and then come here by local taxi or bus.

GETTING AROUND The quickest and easiest way to sites in and around Mashhad is undoubtedly by local **taxi**: half a day (eg: 3½ hrs from the city) should cost about US$30, which if divided between three or four passengers, is good value. For the more intrepid, there is a fairly efficient local **bus** network within the city and a new Chinese built two-line **metro** system. Most local bus fares are around 2,000 rials, payable to the driver, and metro tickets cost 2,500 rials and can be purchased from one of the kiosks or the ticket office at each of the stations.

There are good road maps (Persian with some English) on sale from most bookshops in town, in particular around Saadi Square. Shrine maps in English are available from the small information kiosk opposite the Bab ol-Reza entrance to the shrine.

 WHERE TO STAY As the hotels cater for tens of thousands of pilgrims visiting during Ramadan, Moharram and the following Muslim month of Safar, accommodation is much easier to find outside these times. **Budget** hotels as such have almost disappeared and the quality of rooms and service in **mid-range** hotels is usually quite good. Rooms on average are reasonably large, to accommodate visiting pilgrims and their families and most mid-range hotels have a choice of rooms with squat-style or Western-style toilet facilities. Enquire at reception in case of preference. For location of listings see map opposite unless otherwise stated.

Above average

Ghasr Hotel (304 rooms) Imam Reza St; 8512000; f 8596914. Ideally located for the shrine, the hotel has a blindingly shiny lobby with perfectly polished floor tiles. The rooms are a little small & poorly lit, but technically well equipped. The furniture is new, albeit some appliances are in need of repair. The service overall is excellent & there is a good crowd of people to take care of all your needs. Wi-Fi is bad, but this seems to be across the spectrum in this part of Iran. **$$$**

Homa 2 Hotel (210 rooms) Khayyam St; 7611001; www.homahotels.com. Swimming pool with separate gender timings & a variety of restaurants. In own grounds, far from the shrine, but with a lovely garden for a stroll or a cup of tea. Homa 1 Hotel is still under construction, but promises to surpass the original in its grandeur. Furniture & room décor are a little old-fashioned, but well maintained & some rooms are equipped with a kitchenette. **$$$**

Hotel Pars Mashhad (228 rooms) Vakilabad St; 8689201; www.pars-hotels.com. Recently completed, the hotel has a wide range of facilities, shopping, tennis courts & a swimming pool with separate gender timings. Some way west of the centre & you would have to get a taxi or a metro ride to the shrine. Has lovely grounds with an outdoor garden & some rooms come with a view of a small lake. **$$$**

Mid-range

Arya Hotel (47 rooms) Imam Reza St, Danesh Crossroads; f 8545571–9919, 8598627. Very central with simple décor, but clean rooms & good service. Rooms to the back are quiet, while the main façade is facing the busy Imam Reza Street. The staff are accommodating & helpful. **$$**

Atlas Hotel (188 rooms) Falkeh Ab Sq, look up for the large hotel sign; 854506–3, 8547799, 8542560; e manager@altasgrandhotel.com. Very central with the façade overlooking the Bab ol-Reza of the shrine. If you are lucky, you might even get a room with a view of the shrine; it is wonderfully lit at night. **$$**

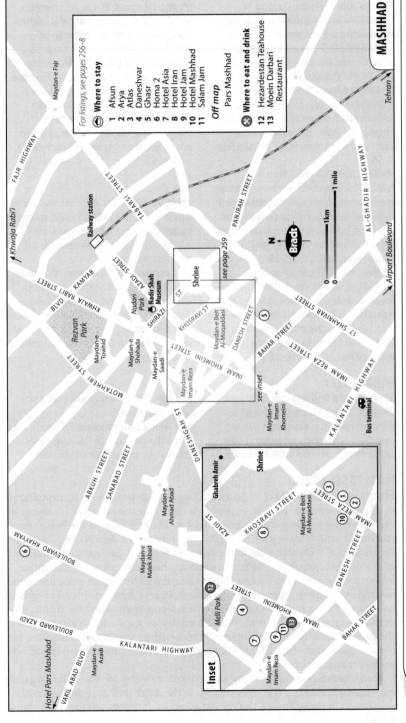

MASHHAD

For listings, see pages 256–8

⏿ Where to stay
1 Afsun
2 Arya
3 Atlas
4 Daneshvar
5 Ghasr
6 Homa 2
7 Hotel Asia
8 Hotel Iran
9 Hotel Jam
10 Hotel Mashhad
11 Salam Jam

Off map
Pars Mashhad

✗ Where to eat and drink
12 Hezardestan Teahouse
13 Moein Darbari Restaurant

🏠 **Hotel Asia** (154 rooms) Pasdaran St; ☏2220071–4; e info@asiahotel.ir. Good value for money with large & well-lit rooms. The staff are helpful & obliging. This hotel administers a number of hotels around Mashhad; enquire about other locations if fully booked. **$$**

🏠 **Hotel Bakhtar** (38 rooms), Pasdaran St; ☏2253011–3. Located in a 5-storey building, Bakhtar was built just over 30 years ago & offers Iranian 3-star quality accommodation, & simple, clean rooms away from the buzz of the Imam Reza St. **$$**

🏠 **Hotel Iran** (164 rooms) Khosravi St; ☏2228010; e info@irhotel.com; www.irhotel.com. In operation for over 40 years, it is comfortable & conveniently located away from the hectic Imam Reza Street, but still only walking distance to the shrine. Rooms are clean & cosy & there is a 20% discount when booking online. **$$**

🏠 **Hotel Jam** (153 rooms) Pasdaran St; ☏8590041–5; e info@jam-hotel.com; www.jam-hotel.com. The best in the lower mid-range price scale & identical to the hotels above in service. Rooms are large & come with small balconies. Close to Hotel Asia, with a good, helpful travel agent next door. Recommended. **$$**

🏠 **Hotel Mashhad** (137 rooms) Imam Reza St; ☏2222701; e contact@mashhad-hotel.com; www.mashhad-hotel.com. Built in 1975 this central hotel is very popular with travellers & often fully booked. Over the past few years has gone up in price from budget to upper mid-range. Rooms, in particular fitted apts, are spacious & comfortable. Wi-Fi is in the lobby only. **$$**

🏠 **Salam Jam** (68 rooms) 6 Pasdaran St; ☏8518950–58; f 8518959. Another good lower mid-range option with standard 3-star hotel facilities. **$$**

Basic

🏠 **Afsun Hotel** (16 rooms) In the small lane off 6 Imam Reza St; ☏8539006. Very basic, but central budget option with squat-style toilet facilities. B/fast is simple & so is the service, but the staff are polite. Your last resort. **$**

🏠 **Daneshvar Hotel** (32 rooms) 8th Chamran St; ☏2282900–5; f 2282908. Offers very clean standard accommodation. Single rooms are small & windowless with toilet facilities in the hall. Ideal for budget travellers, spending most of their time outdoors. Couples or groups should consider one of the mid-range hotels above. **$**

✖ WHERE TO EAT

✖ **Hezardestan Teahouse** Jannat St, Jannat Bazaar; ☏2222943. A beautiful traditional tea house that functions as a museum as well, but photography is regrettably not permitted. Offers excellent traditional Iranian *sofreh* & good *dizzi*. On arrival you will be welcomed with a rose & bitter orange flower drink. **$**

✖ **Moein Darbari Restaurant** Pasdaran St, across the road from Hotel Bakhtar; ☏8598898. Serves delicious local skewered meat called *shashlik*. **$**

WHAT TO SEE AND DO

Shrine of Imam Reza (⏰ *24hrs; no bags or cameras allowed, depositories available at entrance; women must wear a* chador, *available to rent in theory at every entrance but definitely at the Wheelchair Delivery office at the Bab ol-Reza, you would need to leave your ID (better just a copy) as a deposit)* You can't miss the shrine – it is situated right in the centre of Mashhad. Since the establishment of the Islamic Republic, much more money has been spent on the shrine – known locally as Haram-e Rezavi – including the gilding of the main dome and minarets using four times more gold than before, retiling, construction of new courtyards and so on. The main road, which formerly encircled the shrine, now runs underground. The former walled complex of some 30 historic structures, the oldest dating to the 14th century, connected by four huge courtyards, has been transformed with additional courtyards. The result is bewildering and aesthetically unsatisfactory.

Non-Muslims were previously not allowed to enter by the main pilgrim's entrance and could not visit most sections of the shrine, but there are currently no restrictions in place. To avoid being told *mamnua'* (not allowed) too many times,

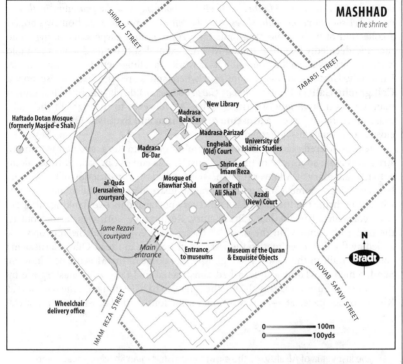

Map labels:
SHIRAZI STREET
TABARSI STREET
New Library
Madrasa Bala Sar
Madrasa Parizad
Haftado Dotan Mosque (formerly Masjed-e Shah)
Enghelab (Old) Court
University of Islamic Studies
Madrasa Do-Dar
Shrine of Imam Reza
al-Quds (Jerusalem) courtyard
Mosque of Ghawhar Shad
Ivan of Fath Ali Shah
Azadi (New) Court
Jame Rezavi courtyard
Main entrance
Entrance to museums
Museum of the Quran & Exquisite Objects
N
Bradt
NOVAB SAFAVI STREET
Wheelchair delivery office
IMAM REZA STREET
0 — 100m
0 — 100yds

do leave at the hotel or depositories everything except your camera-phone and some cash for the museums. Following a bomb explosion here in the mid 1990s, all bags, cameras, etc must be surrendered with proof of identity (ie: passport) to the depositories (gender separated) at each entry point. All female visitors have to don the *chador* to enter the complex and must also ensure their hair is fully covered at all times, otherwise the guardians won't miss an opportunity to point at your hair with their long dust brushes.

'Fluvius' (see box, pages 64–5) has been fortunate in witnessing the blowing of long alpine-like horns, some 2.5m in length, at the shrine's roof levels. This means a miracle has occurred to a supplicant within the complex but, as he warns, 'this cannot be organised to fit into a tourist schedule'. You can, nonetheless walk around the shrine and its museums whilst observing the faithful perform their religious duties. It is an active shrine always buzzing with locals and visitors from abroad, in particular from Saudi Arabia and Iraq.

The main **museum** (⏰ *08.00-17.30, holidays 08.00–12.00 daily; entry 5,000 rials*) with its numerous sections displays selected treasures of the shrine on three floors; some are outstanding, such as two 14th-century *mihrabs* of Kashan lustre tiles, while others, like the extensive seashell display on the top floor, look decidedly out of place. A number of 19th- and 20th-century paintings are shown, indirectly revealing which styles have 'official approval'. (A small collection of framed photographs on the ground floor record the totally ruinous state of the other Mashhad monuments before 1960; for this reason, no detailed description of the heavily reconstructed buildings has been included in these pages.) Labels are mainly in Farsi but there is also some information in English, and the exhibits are well displayed. A little further on is the **Carpet Museum** (⏰ *08.00–12.30 Sat–Wed,*

08.00–11.30 *Thu; entry 5,000 rials; if visiting both parts of the museum, in theory one ticket should cover both; shoes must be left at entry)*, arranged on two floors, a collection of mainly late 19th- and early 20th-century carpets, including some rare and decidedly beautiful Indian Moghul examples, two fine double-sided pile 'curtain' carpets as well as bucolic Qajar work. Labelling here is minimal and in Farsi only. Upstairs, accessed from near where shoes are left, there is also now a **Calligraphy Gallery** (☉ *same hrs as Carpet Museum*) displaying historical Quran manuscripts in a variety of writing styles. As you exit, to the right of the main museum entrance there is a **Museum of the Quran and Exquisite Objects**, but it is closed at present with no reopening date.

The most sacred place is the **tomb chamber** of Imam Reza, situated within the structures lying southwest of the Old Court. It was laid out in Safavid times along with the sanctuary of Allahverdi Khan, who ordered the construction of the famous Isfahan Bridge. Some 13th-century ceramic lustre tiles may still remain *in situ* within the shrine but the tall golden sanctuary portal and its two flanking minarets were constructed in the late 15th century. Restoration work was carried out in the mid 18th century on the order of Nader Shah Afshar, and the mirror work added by the Qajar regime. To the west when walking to the al-Quds (Jerusalem) courtyard built in the 1980s, you'll glimpse the dome of the **Mosque of Ghawhar Shad**, which the Timurid queen had constructed in 1416–18. A masterpiece by the Shirazi architect, Qavam al-Din, thought also to have designed the *madrasa* at Khargerd (see pages 266–7), it was built on the four-*ivan* plan with two minarets,

IMAM REZA

The last years of Ali al-Reza, the eighth imam in Iranian Shi'ism, encapsulates the tensions at the Baghdad court and throughout the Abbasid Empire in the early 9th century. Exploiting the Shi'a cause, the Abbasid family had overthrown the Umayyad regime in 749ce, but quickly proclaimed its allegiance to Sunni Islam. Before his death in 809ce the Abbasid ruler, Harun al-Rashid, tried to ensure a smooth succession by securing the agreement of all concerned to his two named heirs: al-Amin, and his brother al-Ma'mun, then governor of Khorasan. But within two years al-Amin had reneged on the agreement, and al-Ma'mun in Merv (Turkmenistan) retaliated by proclaiming himself caliph. Al-Amin's action won few friends and he was killed in 813ce. Chaos ensued in the heartlands of Abbasid authority with Shi'a uprisings throughout Iraq, threatening the capital Baghdad. Court officials raced to Merv hoping to persuade al-Ma'mun to leave his stronghold and take charge; they also advised he join forces with the young Ali al-Reza (765ce), living in Medina near Mecca, who was recognised among Ithna 'Ashari Shi'a as the eighth imam. Imam Reza (his title within his community) agreed to go to Merv in 816ce and within a year al-Ma'mun named him as his heir, and marriages between the two families were arranged. Finally yielding to pressure, al-Ma'mun left Merv for Baghdad, but one of the court advisors who had stressed the importance of Imam Reza's support was assassinated. Imam Reza too died unexpectedly on the journey (September 818ce), supposedly after eating grapes sent by al-Ma'mun. Al-Ma'mun continued on to Baghdad and seized control, eventually dying in 833ce, knowing that the Ithna 'Ashari community held him directly responsible for Imam Reza's death.

with beautiful proportions and an emphatic rhythm of arcading and galleries. The mirror work was installed in the late 19th century. How much of the original extensive tilework, 'the most beautiful example of colour in architecture ever devised' (Robert Byron), still survives is questionable as the north and south *ivans* were demolished in 1977 and then rebuilt; the southeastern façade is clearly new work. The high portal, taller than usual, necessitated a very tall drum and dome, the latter replaced by a concrete one in the 1960s.

Close to that mosque was built the four-*ivan* college, **Madrasa Parizad**, possibly paid for by Ghawhar Shad or one of her attendants. Both this and another, **Madrasa Bala Sar** to the east, were extensively repaired in 1680 and restored in the 1970s, as was the adjoining 1439 **Madrasa Do-Dar**, used as a college until 1975. Then it was still possible to see wonderful 15th-century decorative plasterwork, 'more surviving than any other Timurid monument', in the barrel vault of the latter's mosque entrance. The college was donated by a governor of Qom, Yusuf Khvafa (d1443), who's interred in the southern dome chamber, where the drum inscription reminded visitors that the only access to paradise is through love of the Prophet.

Many of the great and good have been laid to rest in the shrine and city: Allahverdi Khan, the Safavid kingmaker (see page 130), whose tomb was constructed with a soaring 21m-high dome and superb tilework, and another important Safavid vizier commemorated in the Gonbad-e Khatemkhaneh of 1609. Then, of course, Nader Shah, whose tomb was rebuilt in the 1960s complete with a huge sculpture in the 'Soviet realism' style; the tomb now operates as a small museum.

Haftado Dotan Mosque or Mosque of 72 Martyrs (*Exterior visible only; now offices & closed to the public*) Leaving the shrine of Imam Reza by the same entrance you entered through, walk a short distance (east), keeping the shrine's new perimeter fence on your right, to see at comparatively close quarters a lovely 1451 building, the former Masjed-e Shah repaired in 1708. To Professor Pope, doyen of Iranian architectural history, its Timurid dome was the perfect form, but his contemporary Robert Byron felt it had 'an uncouthness which has no parallel' in other similarly dated buildings in the region. It was built as a double-domed structure, the exterior shell resting on eight internal brick buttresses. The tilework is still good on the exterior, especially the fine-quality 'mosaic' work by a Tabrizi tile cutter, with a green hexagonal tile dado, once embellished with gold stencilled decoration and a tiled inscription in the portal with a Hafez couplet: 'Written in gold on this emerald arcade /Nothing will remain except the good of the generous'.

Presently, the exterior, with its two corner minarets, retains most of its original tilework and its deep jewel-like colouring, despite a restoration programme completed in 1977.

The shops around here form one of Mashhad's many **bazaars**, selling tourist mementos such as posters and 'instant' prayer sets consisting of a rosary, *mohr* (clay tablet) and cloth, perfume, etc, and green fabric swatches for touching the grilles in the holy sanctuaries. On their return home, pilgrims will cut the swatch up and distribute the pieces among family and friends to share its *baraka* (blessings). Mashhad is also (perhaps justly) famous for its saffron, as well as for turquoise sold in great chunks (see box, page 269), set in 21-carat gold, and sheepskin waistcoats. There is a noticeable use of the Cyrillic alphabet on shop signs, as in the early 1990s President Rafsanjani worked at revitalising the historic Silk Road routes with the new republics of Tajikstan, Uzbekistan and Turkmenistan, even extending the railway to the Turkmenistan border.

AROUND MASHHAD

Several half-day and day excursions may be made from Mashhad. One is northwest to **Ferdowsi** (also called **Tus**), the birthplace of the medieval Persian poet, Ferdowsi (d1020), author of the renowned epic poem, the *Shahnameh*, narrating the exploits and adventures of the legendary kings of Iran (see box below). Once again, after some 20 years' silence, it is now sometimes possible to hear verses recited in *chaykhanah*s and restaurants. Tus was sacked in 1389 by Timur Leng and then largely abandoned a century later as Mashhad assumed growing importance, but remnants of its citadel walls are still visible from the modern **gardens and tomb** (⊕ *08.30–18.00; entry 100,000 rials, plus 50,000 rials for the separate museum*) commemorating the poet. His memorial is a ponderous stone structure (not at all like his poetry) with architectural details loosely based on Achaemenid work. Contemporary plaster panels depicting various characters or episodes linked to the *Shahnameh* decorate the steps down into the cavernous basement, where a similar theme forms the decorative friezes.

About 1km before the Ferdowsi gardens is a much earlier but heavily restored mausoleum, **Haruniyeh**, said to be that of the Abbasid caliph, Harun al-Rashid (d809CE). The mud-brick ruins in the fields behind the tomb are locally known as Harun's Palace, but most scholars think this mausoleum in fact marks the burial place of the Muslim philosopher, al-Ghazali (d1111). Is a taxi drive worth the expense?

FERDOWSI AND THE *SHAHNAMEH*

As England's national poet is William Shakespeare, so Ferdowsi is seen to embody Iranian history and culture, saving from oblivion the Persian language, legends and history He started work on composing the 60,000 couplets that were to form his *Shahnameh* ('Book of Kings') when he was 40 years old, c980CE, working from at least three versions. Despite being the son of a prosperous landowner in Tus, he soon needed to look for financial support and approached Mahmud of Ghazni (d1030) who, it is said, promised him a gold coin for every couplet written but paid only a silver pittance. Ferdowsi was practically destitute when his great work was completed.

The opening chapters concern the creation of the world and the first rulers who brought civilisation and culture to the people of Iran, whether it was the skill of weaving or the invention of fire. Ferdowsi then saw later developments as a series of cyclic events, in which just rule descended into periods of anarchy and despair redeemed only by the superhuman strength of spirit, courage and family loyalty of the individual. Progress was marked by a constant battle between good and evil, vividly portrayed throughout this epic poem, concluding with the reign of the last Sassanid king and the Arab invasion, c640CE. The couplets relate court intrigue and sibling rivalry, military triumphs and disasters, and immense strength and heroism pitted against supernatural demons and wicked rulers. The imagery remains powerful even after a millennium; no-one in the late 1970s could fail to understand political posters depicting the late shah as Ferdowsi's despotic ruler Zahhak, whose wickedness was manifested by two snakes growing from his shoulders; indeed, this same imagery, with the faces of Hitler, Himmler and Goebbels, was used in World War II British propaganda distributed in the Middle East.

Yes, if you combine your visit with one to the spectacular tomb tower at Akhangan, nearby off the branch road to Sarakhs, or with a drive to Kalat (see below).

Mil-e Akhangan is an early 15th-century Timurid mausoleum in good condition with an unusual prismatic 'pleated' roof, now banded in turquoise and cobalt blue tiles. The cylindrical brick exterior is broken by eight rounded, engaged columns forming frames for (one-time) tiled stars and crosses; those have long since gone but their imprint remains. With such detail it's easy to believe the local tradition that it was constructed to honour the sister of Queen Ghawhar Shad. It is located 22km north of Mashhad in agricultural land some 4km off the main road between Dorqi and Faimad on the road to Kalat.

KALAT (also known as Kalat-e Naderi) The 140km drive north on the signposted Kalat and Kavud Gonbad roads will take a full day but the light industrial buildings on the Mashhad outskirts are quickly left behind for dramatic but gaunt scenery, with hairpin bends and long curves climbing up into the hills that mark the frontier with today's Turkmenistan. Signposts are few and far between once you reach this region; just a few distance markers. At the bridge over Qara Su (Black Water), the road tunnel will take you directly into the village of Kalat, which occupies a long fertile east–west valley (altitude 765m) between two hill chains – a superb natural defence. As Lord Curzon wrote in the late 19th century: 'If in their war with Olympian Zeus the Titans had ever occasion to build for themselves an unassailable retreat, such might well have been the mountain fortress that they would have reared.' This was the place where Nader Shah Afshar (d1747) returned after his victories in India, with so much booty that his army could stagger back at only four miles a day. He ordered the building of a large octagonal pavilion, the **Khorshidi Palace** (☉ *07.30–17.00; entry 150,000 rials*) set in a garden, perhaps as his mausoleum, but early 20th-century writers said that the vault was never intended to be a crypt but a secure place for his treasures. Its rose-pink sandstone, the fluted drum-tower and the carved exterior panels depicting flowering plants all speak of Moghul Delhi, but the painted interior recalls Safavid Esfahan. Originally, marble slabs brought from Orumiyeh 1,900km away, embellished the lower internal walls.

The garden kiosk has a good pack of postcards, and the manager will direct you to the 18th-century **mosque** at the far end of town and the **dam** (approximately 6km in same southeast direction) constructed by Nader Shah to ensure a good water supply to the village. The mosque is built on the four-*ivan* plan with enough of the original tiling remaining to show the decorative scheme, but the actual chambers – including the large domed chamber – have been completely replastered and/or painted.

SARAKHS AND ROBAT-E SHARAF Another day trip (or a long half-day if only the nearer Robat-e Sharaf is visited) lies to the east of Mashhad, leaving by the Hemmat Highway; Sarakhs, some 175km away, is also one of the border crossings with Turkmenistan. Frontier formalities here crossing to and from Ashkhabad involve much time and patience and Sarakhs has little else to offer than a 1356 **Mausoleum of Sheikh Baba Loqman**, a famous 10th-century storyteller. Located on its far western outskirts on agricultural land, the mausoleum has a similar plan to the Haruniyeh near the Ferdowsi tomb, but both have been heavily restored. Something remains of a surprisingly shallow plaster inscription set with a tight arabesque scroll over the door, and of the blue glazed inserts in the ruined soffit arch of the entry portal. Inside, two internal staircases (now blocked) led to the upper gallery running between the four deep *muqarnas* alcoves.

Some 58km from Sarakhs (or 125km from Mashhad) is the Seljuk caravanserai, **Robat-e Sharaf**; take the minor road (southeast) at the roadside village of **Shurluk**, and then almost immediately the dirt track straight ahead for 7km. Don't despair: this caravanserai on what was the old Merv–Nishapur desert trade route is wonderful; you may just be fortunate enough to encounter the enthusiastic architect in charge of restoration, Mr Kandarhari, who may agree to take you round; after years studying in Hamburg, his spoken German is very good. Probably constructed in 1115 with changes made to its layout some 40 years later, it is called a caravanserai but the patterned brickwork and plaster decoration have led scholars to wonder whether at sometime it served as a royal lodge. The exterior looks like a fortress with one main entrance, but inside it is fit for a king. There are two main sections, both with courtyards displaying amazing brick patterns, dome supports, carved plaster, decorative brick end-plugs and intricately plaited Kufic inscriptions. Inside the caravanserai there is the usual arrangement of stabling and rooms, with at least one small mosque, complete with plaster *mihrabs*, off both courts, and at the far end there are rooms with underground cisterns. As yet a kitchen area or 'refectory' have not been identified, nor is there sign of a bathhouse, but a number of rooms and chambers were blocked off or altered during the mid 12th century. This work is recorded in the beautiful plaster and brick inscription of the portal leading into the second courtyard, giving the date 1154 and mentioning Sultan Sanjar (whose father is commemorated in Esfahan's Masjed-e Jame). As Sanjar was then a prisoner of the Turkomens in Merv, it is thought his wife ordered this work, possibly to repair damage inflicted by these marauding tribesmen after their sacking of Nishapur.

KHWAJA RABI'A Returning to Mashhad from Robat-e Sharaf or indeed from Ferdowsi, look for road signs on the ring road for this shrine 6km northwest of the centre, now within the city confines. It commemorates Rabi'a Ibn Khothaym, who led 4,000 men to help Ali, the son-in-law of the Prophet Mohammed, and as such was visited by the eighth imam, Reza. However, the structure today dates from the first quarter of the 17th century, financed by Shah Abbas I in 1618, and its design is said to have influenced the form of the world-famous Taj Mahal in Agra, India. Immediately to the right of the entrance, a small chamber has been made into a memorial to a local theologian, and his two sons killed in 1974. Much of the exterior tilework and painting has been recently restored and further messed up by air conditioning units and scaffolding, but look for two small dragon heads worked in Safavid 'mosaic' tiles around to the far left of the entrance. Inside, a great deal of the Safavid gilded plaster ornament remains, but in dire need of cleaning.

SOUTH OF MASHHAD

The road south also offers some interesting sites, especially if you like Timurid buildings (some interiors are very dark so a torch is useful). Just as one leaves the city, after the bus terminal and following signs for Torbat-e Heydariyeh, are two popular shrines. The first commemorates **Khwaja Abbasalt** (*sic*) **Haravi** (dc851CE) who, it was said, witnessed the death of Imam Reza, who died after eating poisoned grapes from his father-in-law, the Abbasid caliph al-Ma'mun. In the 1970s the shrine still retained elements of its Safavid construction. Not today. Words fail us. Less than 5km further south along this main road – look for an avenue of trees from the roadside leading into the hillside – is **Khwaja Murad,** commemorating a famous orator of the Karbala story (d832CE). The gift of such narrators is difficult to communicate, but perhaps you too have stood entranced with other non-Farsi speakers listening as a storyteller speaks to Iranian Shi'a pilgrims in the Great Mosque of Damascus. The shrine building itself is small and unremarkable but it is a pleasant family picnic spot with stalls, an airy cafeteria and even a small photographic studio offering the sitter a backdrop of the Mashhad shrine, Caliph al-Ma'mun handing Imam Reza the lethal grapes, or even Bruce Lee fighting a dragon.

There are richer treasures further south along this road in both the southeast and southwest directions. Branching off the Torbat-e Heydariyeh road, southeast to Torbat-e Jam brings one quickly to the Sang Bast junction.

SANG BAST A white building, formerly the caravanserai **Robat-e Sang Bast**, marks the turning leading to the (possibly) 11th-century tomb (locally known as Mil-e Ayaz) built for Arslan Jadhib, former governor of this region for the Ghaznavid dynasty of Afghanistan. The caravanserai's internal location of stabling, staircases in the vestibule area, raised platforms, etc, has suggested to scholars that it was built around 1400, with further stabling facilities added before its use in 1856 as barracks during the Qajar campaigns against Herat. It then served as a gendarmerie and is now a prison, so access is not permitted.

The **Mil-e Ayaz tomb**, important for architectural historians as the only surviving Ghaznavid monument on the Iranian side of the Afghan border, stands now in a deserted area pockmarked with small craters, not the result of mortar shelling but of illicit digging for medieval ceramics and other artefacts. It was Arslan (Lion) who advised Sultan Mahmud of Ghazni (d1030) to cut off the left thumb of every man taken captive in his military campaigns, thus preventing them using a bow in battle again. Sultan Mahmud may have concurred but it didn't stop Seljuk tribesmen from later controlling most of Iran and present-day Turkey, following their victories over Mahmud's successors. Essentially, this tomb follows the Sassanid fire temple plan of a cube broken by four arches (now blocked) surmounted by a dome. Very little of its decoration survives, but in the mid 1970s the external dome inscription consisted of Quranic verses (Q21:35–6 and Q12:101), while on the inside a painted band (Q10:25–6) could be seen alongside a quatrain asking for heavenly rain and decorative brickwork. Close by is a 20m brick minaret, c1028, with a Kufic inscription (Q41:33) naming the builder as coming from Sarakhs, but there is no sign of the mosque it once served.

LANGAR If Timurid history or Persian poetry is a passion, you'll want to make a short detour to see a small building at Langar, 25km northwest before Torbat-e Jam, just off the asphalt road. This village was the birthplace of the Persian poet al-Jame, but the late 15th-century square building (restored in 1966) with two deep alcoves inside is not a memorial to him. It was dedicated to the mystical poet Qasem-e Anvar, who worked with the great Timurid ruler and scientist Ulugh Beg (d1449) in Samarkand, and it probably functioned as a *khanaqeh* or hostel with a kitchen (or *langar*; thus the village name) to accommodate eager disciples. A short distance away is the water cistern with stepped dome, of the same date.

TORBAT-E (SHEIKH) JAM Some 160km southeast from Mashhad, Torbat-e Jam is known for its complex honouring the memory of the mystic, noted author and teacher, Sheikh Ahmad Ibn Abdul Hassan (d1141). The guardians may ask for a permit, directing visitors to the large domed chamber opposite the main (north) gate and then to the local archaeological office just around the corner; the procedure is very quick and everyone is very helpful. We recently visited on the afternoon of the Prophet Mohammed's birthday; that is 'ladies' day' so no men were permitted entry and the main chambers were firmly padlocked. Hordes of bored, hyperactive children and masses of very inquisitive, friendly women meant decibels soared, a surge of bodies swept every which way and we had to retire gracefully without seeing the central domed chamber of 1236, as well as the five-bay chamber to the east, with its rich plaster decoration, *muqarnas* vaulting and rib-network of the mid 14th century. The work in the west chamber of Gonbad-e Safid is similarly dated, but not as elaborate or exquisite. Nothing remains of a mosque built around 1320 behind the five-bayed hall, nor much from the so-called 'new' mosque erected in 1440–43; only a mass of new brickwork and white plaster is visible. The small high-domed 1441 building to the west was probably conceived as a *madrasa* and mauseolum for Amir Jalal al-Din Firuzshah, chief commander to Shah Rukh, but never finished before his fall from grace. His 35-year service and status should have ensured him burial in Herat, then the Timurid capital but, inadvisedly, when Shah Rukh (see box, page 254) was taken seriously ill, he openly supported the favourite son of Ghawhar Shad instead of the official heir apparent. Shah Rukh recovered and exacted revenge.

TAYABAD AND AROUND From Torbat-e Jam it is 60km to Tayabad (or Taybad), close to the Afghan border (225km southeast of Mashhad), passing villages with small barrel-vaulted houses topped with small windcatchers that resemble miniature periscopes.

Where to stay and eat There is a small **Tourist Inn** (*7 rooms; $$*) in Tayabad which can offer accommodation and has a simple but adequate restaurant, so visitors could stay overnight, continue via Khargerd to Torbat-e Heydariyeh and then return to Mashhad on the southwest route. For location of Tayabad see map, page 252.

What to see and do The reason for coming here is the 14th-century **Masjed-e Mawlana** (⊕ *07.00–17.00; entry free*) honouring an influential Sufi mystic Sheikh Zayn al-Din (d1389), whose grave lies in front of the main *ivan* portal. Timur Leng visited him in 1381 before attacking Herat, and was well pleased to hear that only the Angel of Death would prove his better. Built by a vizier for Shah Rukh, and completed in 1444–45, it is an intimate building although at first the portal looks disproportionately tall. The tile decoration here (including Q18:1–11, the story of the Seven Sleepers) is exquisitely elegant, especially the lyrically flowing calligraphy in clay set on a turquoise tiled ground, and scholars have linked both the building and decoration to Mashhad (Ghawhar Shad's *madrasa*) and Khargerd (see below), suggesting it is the work of the same architect. The guardian will proudly open the actual prayer chamber and, despite continuing problems with dust and damp, the visual impact of the 'virtuoso complexity' of the *muqarnas* vaults and rib-network is stunningly beautiful. On the floor, double-sided blue and white *zilus* (flat-weave floor coverings) from Torbat-e Jam date from the late 1980s.

Having come all this way, don't turn back just yet but continue south. About 30km further on at **Kerat** there is a beautiful Seljuk minaret (c1106) by the side of the road. Its very location on a slope suggests it served more as a lighthouse for travelling caravans than for a mosque. Here and there a few glazed inserts survive among the complex brick patterns.

KHARGERD At Sangan, some 40km on, turn northwest for Khargerd and the mid 15th-century Timurid **Madrasa Ghiyathiyeh** (also spelt Ghiassieh). Over 25 years of restoration work remains unfinished, but at least it hasn't been as heavy-handed as elsewhere. It has the typical four-*ivan* ground plan, with a very symmetrical arrangement of arcades and galleries working to a strict set of proportions. For at least one scholar, the careful arrangement and proportions of windows, niches and arches create a 'visual crescendo' where everything works in harmony. Just enough remains of the original tiling to show the various pattern schemes and, despite the grime, pigeon droppings and repairs, the *muqarnas* decoration of both chambers either side of the entry portal – the small mosque on the right, the main lecture hall on the left – is fine work. But virtually nothing now survives of the painted wall decoration, recorded in the mid 1970s. In the court, staircases in each corner lead to the upper accommodation. Each room comes with a niche for books and belongings, and a chimney. Behind the far *ivan* a *badgir* (wind tower) has been constructed.

If you can't get here, you can see an example of the original superb workmanship by visiting the British Museum and the Victoria and Albert Museum in London or indeed New York's Metropolitan Museum, all of which managed to 'acquire' samples of the tilework, especially the star tiles. The inscriptions record that the patron of this beautiful college, far away from any centre, was not a member of the Timurid house but one of their long-serving viziers, Pir Ahmad Khvafi, born in the area and linked with this monument. Whether it was an act of piety or a guarantee against royal confiscation if he fell from power (by consigning his property and land as an endowment) is unclear.

Also in the village is the Seljuk **Madrasa Nizamiyeh**, c1154, named after its patron, another famous vizier, Nizam al-Molk, linked with the superb domed chamber in the Masjed-e Jame in Esfahan. Hardly anything remains except fragments of its plaited, floriated Kufic inscription but it must have been a superb building. About 3km northwest is (Khvaf) **Rud** with a Masjed-e Jame. It was built about 1503, a date given on the seven-stepped *minbar* (a section is now in the Mashhad Imam Reza Shrine Museum, pages 258–9), but has been much repaired since. It is probable that the domed prayer chamber and its *ivan* are Timurid, if not earlier, but the two winter prayer rooms could well be a product of the extensive repair programme of 1971. **Roshtkhar** (or Rushkhvan) is about 55km from Torbat-e Heydariyeh; in the mid 1970s its Masjed-e Jame was collapsing, but something of the Seljuk vaulting remained, with a domed prayer chamber and splendid herringbone brickwork. The painted inscription around the zone of transition consists of Quranic verses (Q48:1–14) with a date of 1455.

If you are returning to Mashhad from here via Torbat-e Heydariyeh, look out for the village of **Bazeh Hur**, some 65km before Mashhad. Its late 15th-century caravanserai **Robat-e Safid** behind the roadside shops is unloved and rapidly collapsing (there are much better, restored ones, on the road to Mashhad) but it's worth stopping at the lime kilns just before the shops to take a photograph of the restored 3rd-century CE Zoroastrian fire temple set high before the hills.

TO KASHMAR

You could extend your journey west from Torbat-e Heydariyeh to Kashmar, which possesses two *imamzadehs*, one dedicated to Hamza and totally renovated in modern times, and the other at the end of a long avenue of trees, the **Imamzadeh Sayyid Murtadeh**, essentially a Safavid construction but restored in 1975. The road west goes through a lovely landscape of vineyards behind mud walls, each with one or more drying sheds. About 10km before Bardeskan is a minor road north to **Ali Abad Kashmar**, leading to the village *hamam* and then the magnificent **tomb**

tower, standing among the houses. Its exterior is basically 12-sided, presumably to remind visitors of the 12 Imams, but with alternate flanged and rounded engaged columns with moulded turquoise tile inserts highlighting aspects of the brick decoration. It is a masterpiece of 13th-century architecture but very dark inside, so a torch is useful. Local children will readily fetch the guardian to unlock the door to the octagonal interior and then race up the internal staircases to the upper gallery, to the space between the inner and upper domes, to peer down on you.

The region south of Kashmar and Torbat-e Heydariyeh was Assassin country in the 12th century. One of their strongholds, very effectively dismantled by the Mongols, is at **Qaleh Dokhtar**, about 30km south of Kashmar. Further south, Gonabad and Ferdows also lived in the shadow of Assassin castles, but earthquakes in 1968 and more recently, which destroyed most of Tabas, caused much damage. **Tabas** is a historic town devastated by an earthquake in 1978 and uniformly rebuilt in dreary yellow brick; historic it may once have been but all is now obscured. The famous gardens unfortunately contain three pelicans that the local children like to chase and an owl and an eagle improbably sharing a cage. There is an enormous modern *imamzadeh* on a roundabout on the edge of the town, white marble and with overly bright tiles and arguably the very worst hotel in Iran. The so-called Tourist Inn houses the homeless so is closed to foreigners; we were obliged to stay at the grizzly **Hotel Bahman** (✆ *0353 4225951–4; $$*) near the modern *imamzadeh*, There is nothing to detain you in Tabas.

NISHAPUR AND AROUND

According to the locals, the road north to Nishapur from Kashmar is good but not first class, and if you wish to visit Qadamgah, 20km east of Nishapur, you may wish to backtrack to Mashhad. Alternatively, if you are coming to Mashhad by train, you can get off at the Nishapur station and then continue on to Mashhad by bus. **Qadamgah** (Place of the Foot), has a small 17th-century octagonal shrine erected by the Safavid shah Soleyman in 1642 and restored by the Qajars, in honour of a large black stone bearing the imprint of two highly arched feet, those, it is believed, of Imam Reza. A conservation team has been working on the painted ceiling and vaults so scaffolding may yet again mar the view. Nearby is a well-preserved Safavid caravanserai called Fakhri-e Da'ud, and another as you near Nishapur.

Just the name 'Nishapur' – like that of Tashkent – conjures up images of medieval buildings, busy bazaars, camel trains and dramatic landscape. Unfortunately, like today's Uzbek capital, virtually nothing historical is left in **Nishapur** despite its well-chronicled past. The original settlement was destroyed by an earthquake, so the Sassanid shah Shapur II (r309–379CE) rebuilt the city, recorded in its new name Niv Shapur (Shapur's good deed), and if it was true that one of the four sacred fires of Zoroastrianism, the Adur Burzin Mihr of the agricultural class, was located nearby, this would have had added importance for the Sassanid court. Finally taken by the Arabs in 661CE, it became the administrative centre of Khorasan province (then including Afghanistan) and later of the Seljuk sultan Toghrol Beg (d1063), who established well-stocked libraries and two universities here. However, if Westerners recognise the city's name today, they associate it either with the splendidly decorated slip-painted earthenware ceramics, made in the region during the 10th–11th century, or with the poet and mathematician, Omar Khayyam (d1131). A catalogue of disasters – serious earthquakes in 1115 and 1145, followed by Turkoman incursions, then the Mongol conquests of the 1220s and Timur Leng's destructive campaigns c1390 – meant few historic buildings survived. In later centuries, Mashhad's growing importance as a pilgrimage centre and then as Nader Shah Afshar's capital meant Nishapur received little investment. It is now a city with around 270,000 residents and is worth a detour essentially for its historical glory and Omar Khayyam's tomb.

The two-*ivan* **Masjed-e Jame** was largely rebuilt in 1494 by Ali Kurukhi, a local notable, whose tomb is to the left of the entrance through an office. The foundation inscription in the *qibla ivan* gives him the title of *pahlavan*, which suggests he was a champion warrior or indeed wrestler (see page 120). His wish that 'this building remain as a memorial for the town of Nishapur' has been honoured, but only at the expense of extensive reconstruction. The *mihrab* records many early 18th-century repairs to the building, but because its Quranic verses (Q36:55; Q89:27–30) relate more to a mausoleum than a mosque, there is some debate whether this *mihrab* was moved here as part of those repairs. An inscription on the entrance portal tiles speaks of further work undertaken in 1869, and in the courtyard there is much new tiling.

In the southeastern outskirts, across the railway line, are the **gardens** (⊕ *08.00–20.00; entry 100,000 rials*) including the modern **tomb** canopy to honour Omar Khayyam, much liked in the West, but somewhat neglected in modern Iran due to his rather frequent poetic references to life's pleasures, such as wine. Another poet-scientist, Farid al-Din Attar, is commemorated with a small garden about 1km further along the tarmac road. Farid al-Din was the writer of *The Assembly of Birds*, a deeply mystical work. Local tradition has it that his tomb was built by a penitent Hulagu, grandson of Genghis Khan, who had ordered the execution of this renowned mystic in 1221 but, as Farid al-Din died around 1194, this is unlikely. Today's double-domed tomb probably dates from the late Qajar period, as an earlier Safavid building was seen in ruins in 1909. A majestically tall pillar gravestone of 1486, now encased in filthy glass, recalls this saintly man: 'Who was such a fine perfumer (*attar*) that from his breath /The world from one end to another was fragrant.'

In the gardens under a modern tiled canopy is the grave of the famous Qajar painter Kamal al-Molk. To the south in the fields beyond were the remains of old

TURQUOISE MINES OF NISHAPUR

To my unpractised eye there was nothing different in that one hill from any of the others around. It was apparently composed of the same dark-coloured rock that is so common throughout the country ... The only implements used by the miners are short iron jumpers about eighteen inches in length, and a small hammer with which they drive holes into the rock, which is then blasted out with common country gun-powder ... outside a lot of small boys break the rock into little pieces with small hammers and pick out any bits of green or blue they see ...

Turquoises at the mines are divided into three kinds – first, the *Angushtari*, or stones fit for rings; second, the *Barkhana*, or stones fit for trappings, and third, the *Arabi*, or stones fit for Arabia. The first are all carefully cut and polished at Mashhad, and are always sold separately ... The first two [grades of the second category] ... are largely exported to Europe, while the third is sold in Persia for the ornamentation of *qalian* ['hubble-bubble'] pipe-heads, horses' trappings, and small-arms, etc. The third kind are as a rule bad and light-coloured stones, for which there is no sale in Persia. The name arose owing to some of the miners going on pilgrimage to Mecca ... and found a good sale for them in Arabia, which is now the market for them and the origin of the name.

C E Yate, *Khurasan and Sistan*, 1900, pp 400–1, 406

Nishapur, excavated in the 1930s by the Metropolitan Museum, New York, which yielded numerous finds of decorated plaster, glass and slip-painted ceramics, produced before Hulagu's devastation of the region in 1220.

In the nearby village of Chubin, around 10km southeast from Nishapur, lies a unique example of wooden architecture, the famous **wooden mosque** (Masjed-e Chupi) (*entry 10,000 rials*). Part of a large complex comprising library and museum, it was built from the resistant wood that can withstand earthquakes of 8 magnitude on the Richter scale.

The mountains to the northeast are rich in turquoise mines. Here lies **Sabzevar**, some 115km further west from Nishapur, once a small town in the shadow of nearby prosperous **Khosrowgerd**, less than 10km west. Both towns suffered severely from the Mongol invasions and then from the Timurid armies in 1381 but miraculously their **Seljuk minarets** survived. The one at Khosrowgerd was constructed in 1111 and today stands with glorious brick patterning about 18.5m high, whereas the Sabzevar minaret is not quite as tall. To see the latter, ask in Sabzevar for Masjed-e Pa Menar off Maydan 22 Behman, situated near the gendarmerie. A nasty group of thuggish teenagers roam the streets around the *masjed*, so take care of your bags, cameras, etc.

Head some 75km further west to Darvazan, then north up into the hills to the village of **Forumbad** (also spelt Farumbad), charming in the 1970s and now rapidly being swamped with new buildings. Dating from Seljuk times, its two-*ivan* Masjed-e Jame was revamped around 1320 when the small town became important to the local Ilkhanid rulers, who built a good hospital and library. The building may have seen better days, but the interlaced terracotta square tiles, the plasterwork and glazed brick inserts are high quality and it is worth a short detour; the guardian lives nearby.

Returning to the main road, another 70km or so brings one to **Miyandasht**. Boasting no fewer than three caravanserais linked together, it gives some indication of the huge numbers of travellers and pilgrims along this road in the 19th century. The smallest, about 50m² and situated to the left of the main entrance, was constructed in the early 17th century. Following the typical Safavid plan, it is octagonal in layout with the main chambers located in the eight corners, and stabling behind protected by the outer wall. It was repaired in Qajar times when two large additions were made to cater for increased traffic: the caravanserai that is now the main central courtyard with accommodation, and another one adjoining immediately to the right. The guardian is delighted to show the various staircases to the roof areas. Two *ab anbar*, or water cisterns, are located in the central court and at least one other is outside. Another 110km brings you to Shahrud (see page 151).

Appendix 1

LANGUAGE

FARSI For background information see pages 24–6. A surprising number of French words have found their way into Farsi. Pronunciation is fairly straightforward except for the letters 'kh', which have a guttural sound, similar to the 'ch' in the Scottish 'loch'.

Greetings

Hello	*Salaam*	سلام
Goodbye	*Khodaa-haafez*	خداحافظ
	(pronounced 'ho-da fiz')	
Good morning	*Sobh-bekheyr*	صبح بخیر
Good evening	*Shab-bekheyr*	شب بخیر
How are you?	*Hal-e shomaa chetoreh?* (formal)	حال شما چطوره ؟
	Khoobeed? (informal)	خوبید ؟
Fine, thank you	*Khoobam, mersee/*	خوبم مرسی /
	Khubam motshakeram	خوبم متشکرم

Useful words and phrases

closed	*basteh*	بسته
excuse me	*ma'zerat meekhaaham/bebakhsheed*	معذرت میخواهم / ببخشید
	(to get attention/apologise)	
help	*komak*	
I	*man*	من
I am ill	*mareezam*	مریضم
no	*nakheyr/na*	نخیر / نه
open	*baaz*	باز
please	*khaahesh meekonam*	خواهش میکنم
thank you	*mersee/motshakeram*	مرسی / متشکرم
yes	*baleh*	بله
you (polite)	*shomaa*	شما
I am English	*man engelisi hastam*	من انگلیسی هستم /
(American/Canadian)	*(amrikaa'i/kaanaadaa'i)*	آمریکائی / کانادائی
I don't speak Farsi	*man faarsee nemeedaanam*	من فارسی نمیدانم
I don't understand	*memeefahmam*	نمیفهم
How much is it?	*chand ast?*	چند است ؟
Please help me	*khaahesh meekonam beman/*	
	bema komak koneed	

271

Where is … ?	… kojaast?	...... کجاست ؟
	(eg: Toilet, kojaast?)	
Please show me the way to	… raah raa beman neshaan daheed …	راه را بمن نشان دهید
airport	foroodgaah	فرودگاه
bank	baank	بانك
bus station	eestgaah-e otobus	ایستگاه اتوبوس
church	keleesaa	کلیسا
embassy	sefaaratkhaaneh	سفارتخانه
hospital	beemaarestaan	بیمارستان
hotel	hotel/mehmankhaaneh/mehmaansaraa	هتل / مهمانخانه / مهمانسرا
mosque	masjed	مسجد
museum	mooseh	موزه
police station	edareh-e polees	اداره پلیس
police	polees	پاسبان / پلیس
post office	post khaneh	پست خانه
railway station	eestgaah-e raah aahan	ایستگاه راه آهن
restaurant	restooraan	رستوران
station	eestgaah	ایستگاه
toilet	tualet	توالت
tourist inn	mehmaankhaaneh/mehmaansaraa	مهمانخانه / مهمانسرا
I need a …	Man ehtiyaj be … daaram	من احتیاج به .... دارم
ticket/seat 1st (2nd/3rd)	beleet-e darajeh yek	بلیط درجه یك / درجه دو /
class for …	(dou/se) baraayeh …	درجه سه / برای ..
doctor	doktor	دکتر
dentist	dandaan pezeshk	دندان پزشک
room for one/	otaaq baraayeh yek shab/	اطاق برای یك شب /
two/three nights	dou shab/se shab	/ دو شب / سه شب
taxi	taaksee	تاکسی

Numbers

1	yek	یك	8	hasht	هشت
2	dou	دو	9	noh	نه
3	se	سه	10	dah	ده
4	chahaar	چهار	11	yaazdah	یازده
5	panj	پنج	12	davaazdah	دوازده
6	shesh	شش	100	sad	صد
7	haft	هفت			

Days of the week

Saturday	shanbeh		Wednesday	chahaar shanbeh
Sunday	yek shanbeh		Thursday	panj shanbeh
Monday	dou shanbeh		Friday	jom'eh
Tuesday	se shanbeh			

Appendix 2

GLOSSARY

'alam	Standard, of the type carried in Muharram ceremonies.
ab anbar	'Water storage/reservoir' in Persian, is a traditional underground drinking water reservoir usually with cone-shaped dome and *badgir* towers (see below).
ayatollah	Literally 'sign of God' (Q41:53); an honorific title for theologians used much more frequently since the 1950s; in the past it was rarely bestowed by public acclaim on any notable, fully qualified Muslim jurist of superior learning.
badgir	Literally 'wind catcher' towers used for ventilation and air conditioning purposes in traditional Iranian houses.
bagh	The 'Persian' garden. The original Persian word *pairidaza* (later *firdaws*) passed into Greek, and later into Middle English as 'paradise'.
barsom	Broom of twigs for tending the sacred fire in the Zoroastrian context.
chador	A full-length fabric wrap, roughly semicircular in form and often black in colour, worn by Iranian women. As Ayatollah Khomeini announced that the (black) *chador* was the 'flag of the Islamic Revolution', it is required dress for women in government service.
chaparkhaneh	From Persian 'house of courier' and refers to Achaemenid era postal service station located at various stops along the main road. In modern Persian *'edareh-e post'* stands for post office.
cuerda seca	A ceramic glaze technique whereby different opaque coloured glazes (eg: on a tile) are kept separate from each other by manganese oxide. (Confusingly, several art historians use this specific technical term when referring to both under- and over-glaze painted decoration on clay.)
caravanserai	A pre-car 'motel', often built by rulers and governors to provide accommodation for travellers and their pack animals on the caravan routes, generally sited one day's journey (approximately 35 km) apart.
chehelkhaneh	Room or building where Sufis pass 40 nights in devotions.
dervish	Literally 'door', 'path'. A mendicant Sufi who has removed himself from his family in search of the ultimate truth, largely dependent on the charity of others.
ghelim	Traditional tapestry-woven carpet or rug usually of bright colours and geometric designs. In English often referred to as 'Kelim'.

gonbad	Tomb tower constructed to commemorate a deceased individual.
hamam	'Turkish bath' developed in the Islamic world from the Roman bathhouse. There were three main chambers: the first room, *frigidarium*, was where one undressed and later relaxed with friends; the *tepidarium*; and finally the hot room, *caldarium*. Like the 17th-century European coffee house, it was and is a place for gossip, business and meeting friends.
hosseiniyeh	A congregation hall for Shi'a mourning ceremonies during the month of Moharram.
imamzadeh	Strictly speaking, a tomb or shrine honouring one of the 12 Imams of Ithna 'Ashari Shi'ism in Iran, or their immediate relatives; over time, local shrines without such a proven family association have been given this title.
ivan	A tall, vaulted portal or doorway, fully developed in Seljuk architecture from the 11th century.
khan	The historic equivalent of a bonded warehouse for the storage and transit of a specific kind of goods from wholesalers to retailers.
khanaqeh	A meeting place/hostel for Sufis.
Kufic	An Islamic calligraphic script, characterised by a definite horizontal base line and vertical letter strokes, often with angular letter forms.
Masjed-e Jame	Literally 'congregational mosque', often called a Friday mosque. In past centuries only one mosque in any given town or city was 'licensed' to have the imam give a homily at the main prayer time on Fridays
mihrab	A niche or panel, often very decorative, showing the correct direction to align oneself for prayer prostrations (see *qibla* below).
minbar	A stepped construction, often made of wood or stone, situated near the main *mihrab* within a mosque, from which the Friday homily was given.
mohr	Clay tablet used by the devout Shi'a Muslim between his forehead and the prayer mat or other surface during prayer. (Also known as *turbah*.)
muezzin	The mosque official who called the faithful to prayer three times a day in some Shi'a communities (five times in the Sunni world and some Shi'a groups)
muqarnas	Architectural detail usually found decorating vaults, domes and door lintels, formed of separate 3D units composed into a 'honeycomb' layout.
nakhl	Literally date palm; palm-shaped wooden structure representing the bier of Hossein which, draped in black cloth, is carried in Moharram processions.
naqqash	Painter, particularly of designs for carpets.
Pahlavi	The Persian script largely abandoned after the 7th-century Arab conquests; also the dynastic name adopted by Reza Khan (d1941).
pahlavan	A champion athlete, especially a wrestler.
qibla	The direction for prayer, ie: towards Mecca, usually marked in a Muslim religious building by a *mihrab* niche.
Shi'a	From Arabic 'followers of Ali' and refers to those who favoured the rule of Ali, Prophet Mohammed's cousin, after the Prophet's death in 632CE. Shi'a Muslims constitute the largest Muslim group after Sunni (see page opposite).

Sufi	A Muslim, Shi'a or Sunni, seeking an individual spiritual path to achieve mystic union with the Divine, often through initiation and ritual practices. Traditionally associated with wearing a woollen garment (*suf* = wool).
Sunni	From Arabic 'of the tradition'/practice of Prophet Mohammed and refers to the largest branch in Islam, whose followers believed that Mohammed's companions were to succeed the Prophet after his death in 632CE. This contradicts the bloodline approach adopted by the Shi'a branch (see page opposite).
talar	Veranda or terrace; in royal pavilions, often used for public audiences.
tappeh	Archaeological mound.
timcheh	A small caravanserai or inn, but essentially space for storing goods of high quality, eg: carpets.
yakhchal	Literally 'ice pit' in Persian. A cone-shaped ice cooler used to store ice, water and even food during hot summer months.
ziggurat	Terraced-pyramid-shaped structure originating in Mesopotamia; part of a larger temple complex.
zurkhaneh	Gymnasium where wrestlers practise.

OTHER ARCHITECTURAL TERMS

arch-soffit	The underside of an arch, often decorated.
cartouche	Oval-shaped frame taken from French word for cartridge.
ground plan	The disposition of the parts of a building at ground level in diagrammatic form.
Level I, II, etc	Refers to the strata seen in archaeological excavations and dated usually by means of finds within them.
'mosaic' tilework	Predetermined shapes cut from monochrome glazed tiles, and reassembled as a jigsaw, held in place on a plaster bed.
squinch	An architectural load-bearing structure essentially in the form of a hollow half of a hemisphere placed over a corner to support the weight of the dome.
strapwork	Ornament consisting of interlaced bands.
trilobed	Three lobes or compartments within a squinch.

Appendix 3

FURTHER INFORMATION

Following the Islamic Revolution in Iran and the broadly hostile media reaction in the West, few publishers could be persuaded to commission or publish any work on Iran unless it concerned contemporary political figures and issues. Therefore, many of the titles suggested below are now out of print, but a good library should be able to help, and of course searches in secondhand bookshops might bear fruit. Also, most publications are weighty in more senses than one, written primarily for the specialist academic market and priced accordingly. As public demand grows, surely publishers will re-evaluate their lists.

BOOKSHOPS In London, there are three 'specialist' bookshops, two known particularly for their selection of books on (Islamic) art, architecture and history, and the third for its travel selection:

Al-Saqi Bookshop 26 Westbourne Grove, London W2 5RH; 020 7229 8543; www.alsaqibookshop.com/default.asp
Arthur Probsthain 41 Great Russell St, London WC1B 3PE; 020 7636 1096; www.apandtea.co.uk/index.html

Daunt (Travel) Books 83 Marylebone High St, London W1U 4QW; 020 7224 2295; www.dauntbooks.co.uk

Do also investigate the British Museum bookshop, which stocks not only its own publications and those of the British Library, but also others in the same field.

FURTHER READING An invaluable publication for those new to Iran and travelling on business is Maria O'Shea's *Culture Shock – Iran: A Guide to Customs and Etiquette* (Graphics Arts Center Publishing Company, London 2003). For those with access to a university or major library with a Middle Eastern collection, the ongoing publications forming the multi-volumed *Encyclopaedia of Islam*, and especially *Encyclopaedia Iranica*, are invaluable reference works. Highly recommended are Michael Axworthy's books on Iran – *Iran: Empire of the Mind* (Penguin, 2008), well and beautifully written, and the more recent *Revolutionary Iran: A History of the Islamic Republic* (Allen Lane, 2013).

Religion, history and literature One of the foremost writers on Zoroastrianism was Mary Boyce; her paperback *Zoroastrians: Their Religious Beliefs and Practices* (RKP, London 1986) is clearly written, exploring the development of ritual and practice. Malise Ruthven's *Islam in the World* (Penguin, London 1991) discusses Islam in the modern world in an interesting and readable account, while N Keddie's *Iran: Religion, Politics and Society* (Cass, 1980) examines this in the context of Iran. For Safavid history, search out any publication by Roger Savory (Canada). *Persian Literature* edited by Ehsan

Yarshater (Columbia University Press, 1988) is a useful academic survey of classical and contemporary literature. These should be obtainable through inter-library loan.

Travellers' accounts No-one can argue that most contemporary travel accounts pale in comparison with those of 19th-century Western writers, who indefatigably asked all the right questions, checked the responses and recorded everything in detail. A particular favourite is Isabella L Bird, author of *Journeys in Persia and Kurdistan*, vols I & II (originally printed 1891; reprinted Virago Press, London 1989), and the abridged account of an earlier traveller, Sir John (Jean) Chardin, *Travels in Persia, 1673–77* (Dover, New York 1988) is still available and very, very entertaining. If you can't get hold of it, R W Ferrier produced a commentary of those travels: *A Journey to Persia ... Jean Chardin* (I B Tauris, 1996). Robert Byron's waspish wit comes through in his *The Road to Oxiana* (Picador, London, reprinted 2000); his comments on architecture force you to look again.

Archaeology John Curtis of the British Museum has written an informative introduction to pre-Islamic archaeology in Iran, *Ancient Persia* (British Museum Press, London reprinted 2000), while D T Potts examines in detail the Elamite region and civilisation up to the 4th century CE in *The Archaeology of Elam* (Cambridge University Press, 1999). Time-Life's publication *The Persians: Masters of Empire* (Lost Civilizations series, 1995) is a clear, readable account aimed at the general reader with good maps and an interesting selection of images. It is both entertaining and intriguing to read Herodotus (490–80BCE) for his views on Achaemenid history, the court intrigues and the military campaigns (*The Histories*, Penguin Classics). Josef Wiesehöfer's book *Ancient Persia from 550BC to AD650* (I B Tauris, London, reprinted 2004) has a strong academic flavour but does provide interesting information. For Dutch readers, the 1993 Brussels exhibition catalogue *Hofkunst van de Sassanieden* (KMvKG) has both an informative text and superb photographs of Sasanid pieces; available in the UK on inter-library loan. *Forgotten Empire: The World of Ancient Persia*, edited by John Curtis and Nigel Tallis (British Museum Press, 2005) is a catalogue to accompany a major exhibition of the same name at the British Museum.

Islamic art and architecture One of the best introductions to Islamic art and architecture is Barbara Brend's *Islamic Art* (British Museum Press, London 1991), while Patricia L Baker's book *Islam and the Religious Arts* (Continuum, 2004) approaches the subject from a different angle. The *Arts of Persia* (Yale University Press, 1989) under the editorship of R W Ferrier examines certain art forms in more detail. Lisa Golombek and Donald Wilber's *Timurid Architecture in Iran and Turan* (1988) has already been mentioned in the introduction to this guide, along with the work of Bernard O'Kane on 14th–15th-century Timurid architecture, essential for any serious in-depth research: *Timurid Architecture in Khurasan* (1987). Similarly the studies of Sheila Blair on historic inscriptions are seminal; see, for example, *Islamic Inscriptions* (Edinburgh University Press, 1998). Any keen student of Islamic architecture should aim to acquire Robert Hillenbrand's *Islamic Architecture: Form and Function* (Edinburgh University Press, 1994), which contains a wealth of material.

Sheila Canby's book *The Golden Age of Persian Art, 1501–1722* (British Museum Press, 1999), which gives a good overview of the arts in the Safavid period, is still available. On contemporary Iranian art with a strong political content, the paperback *Picturing Iran: Art, Society and Revolution* edited by Shiya Balaghi and Lynn Gumpert (I B Tauris, 2002) is highly recommended. To these may be added *Peerless Images: Persian Painting and its Sources*, Eleanor Sims (Yale University Press, 2002) and Sheila Canby, *Shah 'Abbas: The Remaking of Iran* (British Museum Press, 2009) to accompany the first major exhibition dedicated to Shah Abbas.

Islamic history For those interested in the role of the Ismailis and the Assassins during the Crusades, Bernard Lewis's small book on *The Assassins: A Radical Sect of Islam* (Phoenix, reprinted 2004) has not yet been bettered. The well-acclaimed *Alamut* (North Atlantic Books, 2012) novel by Slovenian writer Vladimir Bartol, translated into English in 2004, would also be of interest.

A collection of articles examining various and varied aspects of Safavid history was published in 1996 under the editorship of Charles Melville, *Safavid Persia*, published by I B Tauris, London.

Crafts Although Hans E Wulff published his *Traditional Crafts of Persia* (MIT) in the 1960s, it has not been bettered. He traces the history and technology of the major crafts including agricultural implements and building skills, as well as ceramics and breadmaking. There are numerous publications about carpets, often not worth the paper they are printed on, but if you can find a copy of A C Edwards's *The Persian Carpet* (Duckworth, 1953, reprinted 1983), it records the state of carpet weaving in Iran in the 1950s; his concept of a 'carpet aesthetic' and regional identification has, rightly or wrongly, proved to be very influential. See also Patricia L Baker's *Islamic Textiles* (British Museum Press, London 1995).

Literature, biography and fiction *Shahnameh: The Persion Book of Kings* by Abolqasem Ferdowsi, translated by Dick Davis (2006) and *Persian Love Poetry*, edited by Vesta Curtis and Sheila Canby (2005). We simply could not put down Sattareh Farman Farmaian's *Daughter of Persia* (Bantam, London/New York, reprinted 2000), a critical but affectionate account of her family and Iranian society from the 1920s until the first years of the revolution. A tender and often humorous book in strip-cartoon format is Marjane Satrapi's *Persepolis: A Story of a Childhood* (Jonathan Cape, London 2003), first published in France; the title and format do not prepare the reader for its political content. This has since been made into an animated film, *Persepolis* (2007). *In the Rose Garden of the Martyrs* by Christopher de Bellaigue (HarperCollins, 2004) compares and contrasts his memories of Iran in the late 1970s with today's actualities, and has been critically acclaimed. *The Safron Kitchen*, by Yasmin Crowther (Little, Brown, 2006) is a haunting story taking place both in the UK and in eastern Iran. Not perhaps so well received in Iran as it was in the West was Azar Nafisi's *Reading 'Lolita' in Tehran*, originally published by I B Tauris, now widely available in paperback.

The satirical and political novel, *My Uncle Napoleon*, by Iraj Pezeshkzad, translated by Dick Davis, offers insight into Iranian perceptions of the West.

ASSOCIATIONS AND INSTITUTES
The British Institute of Persian Studies (*c/o British Academy, 10 Carlton Hse Terrace, London SW1Y 5AH;* ✆ *020 7969 5203;* e *bips@britac.ac.uk; www.bips.ac.uk*) Annually publish an academic journal, *Iran*, which contains recent research on the art, archaeology and history of pre-Islamic and Islamic Iran, and organise a number of public lectures. The Tehran office is again open after 30 years of closure and there is a hostel in Iran for members undertaking research. For details contact the secretary.

The Institute of Ismaili Studies (*210 Euston Rd, London NW1 2DA;* ✆ *020 7881 6000;* e *info@iis.ac.uk; www.iis.ac.uk*) Publishes teaching materials and organises a graduate teaching programme.

The Iran Society (*2 Belgrave Sq, London SW1X 8PJ;* ✆ *020 7235 5122;* e *info@iransociety. org; www.iransociety.org*) Has a programme of lectures and meetings; membership subscription. For details contact the secretary.

The Iran Heritage Foundation (*5 Stanhope Gate, London W1K 1AH;* e *info@ iranheritage.org; www.iranheritage.org*) A non-governmental organisation, sponsors various activities in the UK, including exhibitions, occasional lectures, conferences, concerts, poetry readings, and film showings concerning the cultural heritage of Iran, past and present. For details contact the secretary.

Zoroastrian Centre (*440 Alexandra Av, Harrow, Middx HA2 9TL;* ☏ *020 8866 0765;* e *secretary@ztfe.com; www@ztfe.com*) A friendly organisation running a series of classes and lectures examining the beliefs, civilisation and history of Iranian Zoroastrians and the Parsi communities. Part of the world Zoroastrian organisation.

Baha'i Faith National Centre (*27 Rutland Gate, London SW7;* ☏ *020 7584 2566*) For information about the Baha'i community.

WEBSITES There are thousands of websites on Iran: some are markedly partisan, others less so; some informative but most with outdated telephone/fax regional codes and numbers for hotels, etc. More and more Iranian companies involved in tourism operate websites but these can vary greatly in quality, from the informative to the 'useless'.

www.bbc.co.uk/news/world-middle-east-14541327 The BBC has a reliable country profile and timeline.
www.cais-soas.com Excellent for information on ancient Iranian sites is CAIS, the Circle of Ancient Iranian Studies at SOAS, the School of Oriental and African Studies, University of London.
www.gov.uk/foreign-travel-advice/iran To check the latest advice on visiting conditions and requirements.
www.iran-daily.com and **www.tehrantimes.com** If you wish to keep up with the news as published in Iran, two of the Tehran English-language papers are available on the internet: *Iran Daily* and *Tehran Times*.
www.iranianvisa.com For Iranian embassy and visa information.
www.iycs.ir Iranian Youth Cinema Society information portal for those interested in Iranian cinema.

Index

Page numbers in **bold** indicate major entries; those in *italics* indicate maps

INDEX OF ADVERTISERS

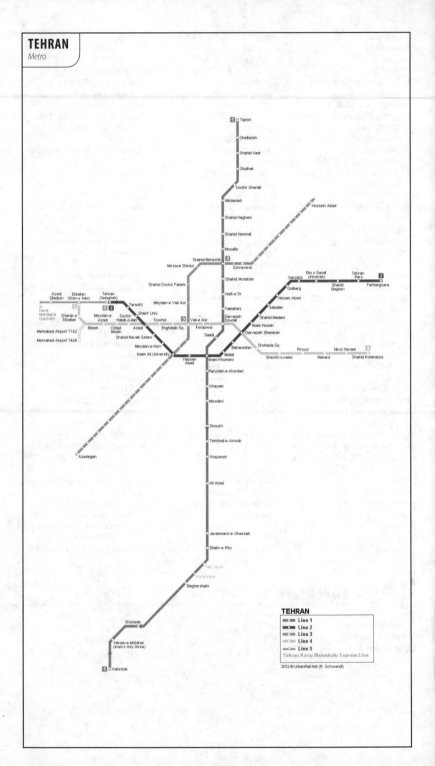

TEHRAN
Metro

TEHRAN
- Line 1
- Line 2
- Line 3
- Line 4
- Line 5
- Tehran-Karaj-Mehrshahr Express-Line

2012 © UrbanRail.Net (R. Schwandl)